TREES OF NORTH TEXAS

Number Fourteen

The Elma Dill Russell Spencer Foundation Series

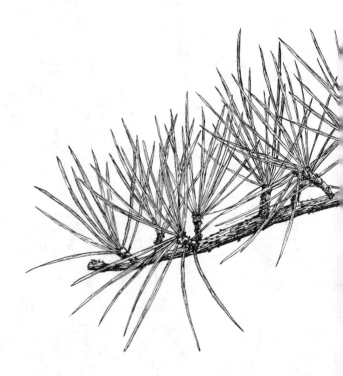

Trees of North Texas

BY ROBERT A. VINES

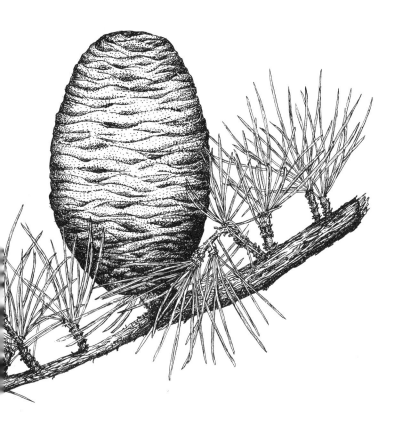

 UNIVERSITY OF TEXAS PRESS, AUSTIN

Requests for permission to reproduce material from this work should be
sent to Permissions, University of Texas Press, Box 7819, Austin, Texas
78712.

Library of Congress Cataloging in Publication Data

Vines, Robert A., 1907–
  Trees of north Texas.

  (Elma Dill Russell Spencer Foundation series; no. 13)
  Includes index.
  1. Trees—Texas—Identification. I. Title. II. Title: North Texas. III.
Series.
QK484.T4V53   582.1609764   81-1644
ISBN 0-292-78018-4   AACR2
ISBN 0-292-78020-6 (pbk.)

This book is dedicated to my wife,
RUBY VALRIE VINES,
who has shared thirty-nine years
of wonderful botanical adventures
with me

CONTENTS

PUBLISHER'S NOTE

Trees of North Texas is the second volume in a series of field manuals extracted from *Trees, Shrubs, and Woody Vines of the Southwest*, written by Robert A. Vines and published by the University of Texas Press in 1960. *Trees of East Texas*, the first in the series, was published in 1977. Prior to his death in 1978, Mr. Vines had prepared the outline for the content of this volume and the volume devoted to central and west Texas and had begun an outline for south Texas. The Press' managing editor, Barbara N. Spielman, worked closely with Mr. Vines on both the books and the outlines and will continue to oversee the remaining volumes in the field-guide series.

ACKNOWLEDGMENTS

Special thanks are acknowledged herewith to the staffs of various herbaria for the loan of plant materials for study. Without such assistance this work would have been impossible. These include the United States National Herbarium, United States National Arboretum, New York Botanical Garden, Missouri Botanical Garden Herbarium, Harvard University Gray Herbarium, Southern Methodist University Herbarium, Chicago Museum of Natural History Herbarium, and University of Texas Herbarium.

Marshall Conring Johnston of the University of Texas Botany Department has been very helpful in providing plant material, but most helpful of all has been the book he coauthored with Donovan Stewart Correll, *Manual of the Vascular Plants of Texas*. This excellent work substantiated and clarified many things for me.

Also, I wish to give special thanks to Cornelius H. Muller for his advice on the revision of the oaks of Texas. George Avery of Miami, Florida, has been very helpful in providing information on the subtropical plants.

My thanks should also go to the various artists who prepared the illustrations, namely Sara Kahlden Arendale, Margaret Beggins, Pat Beggins, Jan Milstead, Felicia Bond, and Michele Cox.

INTRODUCTION

The purpose of this field guide is to identify by full descriptions and illustrations all the native and naturalized trees of the north Texas zone. The very nature of a field guide, however, limits the amount of material it can contain and still be easily carried and used in the field. Because of this limitation, detailed data on the varieties, horticultural forms, propagation, and medicinal uses of the trees have been omitted. The reader who seeks a more in-depth discussion is referred to the author's *Trees, Shrubs, and Woody Vines of the Southwest*, upon which this guide is based.

North Texas refers to that large portion of Texas west of the Pineywoods and Post Oak Savannah and north of the limestone Edwards Plateau of central Texas. Due to the decreasing rainfall, colder temperatures, and higher altitudes, the vegetation becomes much sparser westward. Since good tree growth requires sufficient water, the dry western parts of north Texas cannot sustain large forest tracts and are principally grasslands.

What Is a Tree?

A native tree is one which grows without cultivation. A naturalized tree is one which is introduced from other regions but escapes cultivation and grows freely. A somewhat general definition of a tree has been suggested by some authorities but is not accepted by all. The definition often given is that a tree is a plant with a single woody trunk at least four inches in diameter four feet above the ground, with a definite branched crown, and with a height not less than twelve feet.

This rule may have some exceptions because some trees may have several trunks growing from the base, and some are tall enough but fail to attain the stipulated trunk diameter. Also, some shrubs are treelike but have a number of stems rising from the base. Under unfavorable conditions of soil or climate a true tree may become shrublike, or in favorable circumstances a shrub may become treelike. Also, some species are fast growing and reach maximum tree size much quicker than other species. Individual trees vary within the same species as to size.

Conservation Importance

Most of the trees in north Texas are found along streams or on sandy or clay ridges known as the Western and Eastern Cross Timbers. The economy of the greater part of north Texas is based primarily on ranching and agriculture, with irrigation sometimes being necessary. The principal farming area is the Blackland Prairies, where the city of Dallas is located. Fort Worth justifiably calls itself the gateway to the West, because great ranches are found over the millions of acres of the Rolling and High Plains of the Panhandle.

In the cities and towns many kinds of beautiful trees and shrubs are grown for ornament and some have become naturalized. However, in the Panhandle area, trees and shrubs which can stand droughty conditions are grown. Because of the scarcity of surface water and the declining availability of underground water on the High Plains, shelter-belt planting has become increasingly important for prevention of soil erosion. Among the trees used for this purpose are Tamarisk, mulberries, junipers, cottonwoods, dwarf scrub oaks, hackberries, elms, mesquites, sumacs, Russian-olive, Mexican Elder, Desert-willow, and various arborescent cacti and yuccas.

Many organizations have contributed to the over-all land-use program of forest conservation: federal bureaus, state agencies, district and county governments, timber producers, processors, and wood products manufacturers. The Texas Parks and Wildlife Department has coordinated the wildlife and park management. It should certainly be fully recognized that trees are of great value for purposes other than providing wood products. Humans, animals, and birds eat the seeds, fruit, and sap. Trees furnish drugs, dyes, and resins, prevent erosion, are good sound barriers, reinstitute the oxygen content in the air, and are much used for street, park, and home beautification and shade. All these uses are justifiable reasons for forest conservation.

North Texas Tree Zone Defined

For the purposes of this publication the north Texas tree zone has been divided into four sections (see map 1): Blackland Prairies section (D), Cross Timbers and Prairies section (E), Rolling Plains section (F), and High Plains section (G).

Blackland Prairies Section (D)
The Blackland Prairies are on the western edge of the Post Oak Savannah, comprising a long wedgelike section of land of 11.5 million acres from near the Red River on the north to Bexar, Gonzales, and Lavaca counties on the south. They also include the smaller Fayette County and San Antonio prairie areas on the southeast. The rainfall varies from 30 to 40 inches. The soils are clays, which are usually dark and calcareous, with sandy loams, which are grayish acid. Elevations are from 300 to 800 feet.

Although the prairies are predominantly open agricultural land, they are intermittently broken along water courses on the eastern flank by trees from the Post Oak Savannah, and on the west by trees from the Cross Timbers. Many species are cultivated in the Dallas area and in other cities. On the south end of the blacklands a contact is made with the limestone Edwards Plateau region, bringing in species not generally found on the prairies.

Cross Timbers and Prairies Section (E)
There are about 17 million acres in the Cross Timbers and Prairies. Two timbered areas are within this section: the Western Cross Timbers with about 3 million acres and the Eastern Cross Timbers with about 1 million acres. About 6.5 million acres comprise the Grand Prairie. The remain-

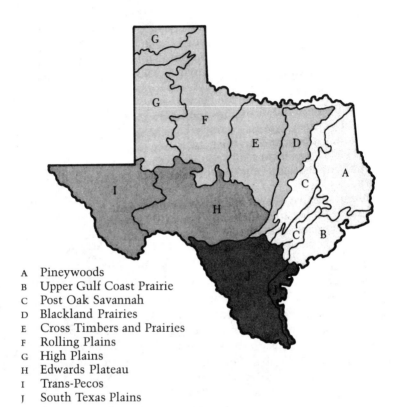

A Pineywoods
B Upper Gulf Coast Prairie
C Post Oak Savannah
D Blackland Prairies
E Cross Timbers and Prairies
F Rolling Plains
G High Plains
H Edwards Plateau
I Trans-Pecos
J South Texas Plains

MAP 1. Texas tree zones

MAP 2 (*opposite*). Mean annual temperatures by climatic divisions (1941–1970) and mean annual precipitation by climatic divisions (1941–1970)

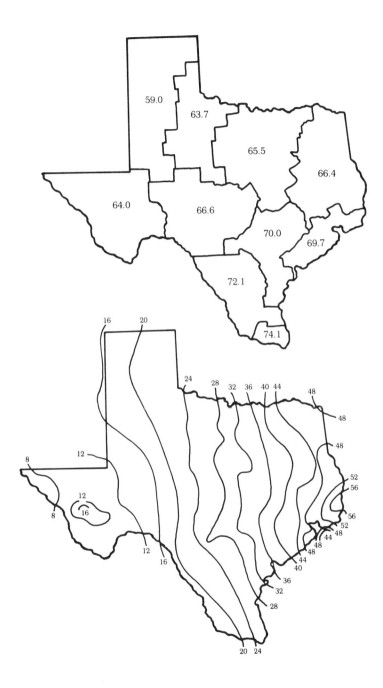

der of this section is known as the North Central Prairies, an area of patches of trees or shrubs but mostly grasslands.

The area is rolling to hilly, and Post Oak and Blackjack Oak trees are common, with a lesser scattering of eastern and northern species and some western species intruding from the west and south. The average annual rainfall is from 25 to 40 inches, the highest amounts coming in May and June. Cold temperatures increase across the area northwestward. The elevation of the Eastern Cross Timbers is from 500 to 600 feet, and that of the Western Cross Timbers is from 700 to 1,600 feet. The Grand Prairie separates the two.

Soils are characteristically sandy, with some strips and small bodies of black-colored clay. The sandy soils are usually dull red, light brown, or tan in color and have red or yellow subsoils. Some of the soil is so loose that it drifts with the wind, especially on dry plowed fields. These sandy soils mantle the sandstone bedrock.

Rolling Plains Section (F)
The Rolling Plains cover about 24 million acres in northwest Texas and the Panhandle and are part of the Great Plains. The altitude is from 800 to 3,000 feet, with rainfall varying from 22 to 30 inches. The surface is rolling or broken by small stream valleys and breaks toward the southeast. The soils are clays, which are reddish toward the east (red beds), or shales, with some sands along the streams.

Most of the land is prairie grassland with large ranches, but some trees are found along the streams. Some of these trees are western species, and some eastern ones intrude from the Cross Timbers on the east. On the south, where contact is made with the limestone Edwards Plateau, species from the southwest appear.

High Plains Section (G)
The High Plains comprise the westernmost part of the Texas Panhandle with about 20 million acres and are part of the Great Plains. Their eastern boundary is the Cap

Rock escarpment, which forms a high plateau of 3,000 to 4,500 feet, broken by the Canadian River valley. The rainfall varies but averages from 15 to 21 inches. Most of the area is grassland, and there are large ranches. Large trees are scarce, but some cottonwoods, willows, and junipers are found along the small playa lakes or narrow breaks on sandy sites. The clay or hardland sites overlay caliche strata and support the native grasses, mesquites, yuccas, shinnery oaks, and various sagebrush species.

TREES OF NORTH TEXAS

PODOCARPUS FAMILY (Podocarpaceae)

Japanese Yew

Podocarpus macrophylla D. Don [D, E]

Field Identification. A cultivated, evergreen resinous tree to 50 ft tall or more. The branches are spreading, and the bark is brownish or gray and shreddy. The dense narrow leaves are glossy, and the staminate and pistillate flowers are usually on separate trees. The fruit is an oblong, fleshy, purplish drupe.

Flowers. Dioecious, or rarely monoecious. Staminate catkins sessile, fascicled or solitary, 1–1½ in. long, composed of spirally disposed 2-celled anthers; pistillate on leafy shoots, axillary, solitary, scalelike, inclosing the ovule with several bracts at its base, with 1 or more carpels and 1 ovule.

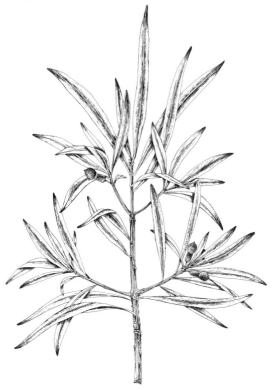

Fruit. Drupelike, ovoid or oblong, ⅓–½ in. long, the fleshy aril greenish or purplish; seed nutlike.

Leaves. Dense, alternate or opposite, somewhat whorled; shape linear-lanceolate, 3–4 in. long, ⅓ in. wide; apices acute or obtuse; upper surface dark glossy green; lower surface paler, greenish yellow or somewhat glaucescent; midrib distinct, other veins obscure; petioles very short or leaf base narrowly winged and sessile.

Twigs. Stout, when young green, glabrous and somewhat sulcate; when older light to dark brown, tending to break into shreddy thin scales.

Range. A native of Japan. Often cultivated for ornament in the southern United States.

Remarks. The genus name, *Podocarpus,* is from the Greek for "foot" and "fruit," referring to the fleshy fruit stalk. The species name, *macrophylla,* is for the large leaves. It is also listed under the names of *P. longifolia* Hort. and *Taxus macrophylla* Thunb. It was introduced into cultivation in 1804.

TAXODIIUM FAMILY (Taxodiaceae)

Common Bald Cypress

Taxodium distichum Rich. [D, E]

Field Identification. Deciduous conifer growing in swampy grounds, attaining a height of 130 ft and a diameter of 8 ft. It is reported that some trees have reached an age of 800–1,200 years. The trunk is swollen at the base and separated into narrow ridges. Curious cone-shaped, erect structures called "knees" grow upward from roots of trees growing in particularly wet situations. Branches horizontal or drooping.

Flowers. March–April, staminate cones brownish, 3–5 in. long; stamens 6–8, with filaments enlarged and anthers opening lengthwise; pistillate cones solitary, or 2–3 together, clustered in the leaf axils, scaly and subglobose; scales shield-shaped, with 2 ovules at the base of each.

Fruit. Ripening October–December, cone globose, closed, rugose, ¾–1 in. in diameter, formed by the enlargement of the spirally

arranged pistillate flower scales; scales yellowish brown, angular, rugose, horny, thick; seeds 2-winged, erect, borne under each scale, dispersed by water or wind; large crops occur every 3 to 5 years with lighter crops between.

Leaves. Deciduous, alternate, 2-ranked, ½–¾ in. long, flat, sessile, entire, linear, acute, apiculate, light green, lustrous, flowering branches sometimes bear awl-shaped leaves, deciduous habit unusual for a conifer.

Twigs. Green to brown, glabrous, slender, flexible, often deciduous.

Bark. Gray to cinnamon-brown, thin, closely appressed, fairly smooth, finely divided by longitudinal shallow fissures.

Wood. Light or dark brown, sapwood whitish, straight-grained, moderately hard, not strong, very durable, weighing 28 lb per cu ft, not given to excessive warping or shrinking, easily worked; heart often attacked by a fungus, the disease being known as "peck."

Range. Texas, Oklahoma, Arkansas, and Louisiana; eastward to Florida, northward to Massachusetts, and west to Missouri.

Remarks. The genus name, *Taxodium*, is from the Greek and means "yewlike," in reference to the leaves, and the species name, *distichum*, means "two-ranked" and also refers to the leaves. Other vernacular names are White Cypress, Gulf Cypress, Southern Cypress, Tidewater Red Cypress, Yellow Cypress, Red Cypress, Black Cypress, Swamp Cypress, and Sabino-tree. Cypress wood is used for boatbuilding, ties, docks, bridges, tanks, silos, cooperage, posts, shingles, interior finishing, car construction, patterns, flasks, greenhouses, cooling towers, stadium seats, etc. It is very durable in contact with soil and water. It is easily worked and takes a good polish. The knees are sometimes made into souvenirs, and the cone resin used as an analgesic for wounds. The conical erect knees serve as a mechanical device for anchoring the tree in soft mud, and some authorities believe that the knees also aerate the roots. The seeds are eaten by a number of species of birds, including wild ducks. Common Bald Cypress is often planted for ornament and has been in cultivation in Europe since about 1640. Fossil ancestors of Bald Cypress, at one time, covered the greater part of North America in company with the ginkgoes, sequoias, and incense-cedars. At present it is concentrated in the swamps of the southern states and middle to lower Mississippi Valley. Florida has about one-third of the total amount of acreage of Common Bald Cypress.

PINE FAMILY (Pinaceae)

Mexican Pinyon Pine

Pinus cembroides Zucc. [E, F, G]

Field Identification. Conifer to 50 ft, with a rounded or pyramidal shape. The trunk is short and the lower branches often wide-spreading.

Flowers. In unisexual cones, perianth absent; staminate clusters short, dense, stamens spirally disposed; pistillate clusters red, scales spirally disposed with 1–2 ovules at base.

Leaves. Thickly covering the twigs, persistent, bluish green, glaucous, somewhat curved, ¾–1¾ in. long, slender, in clusters of 2–3, mostly threes.

Fruit. Cones mature August–September, soon falling, ovoid to globose, 1–1¾ in. long; scales large, thick and fleshy when green, reddish brown later, irregularly pyramidal, strongly keeled and resinous; seed borne in cavities usually at the base of the middle scales which spread widely at maturity, diversely shaped, triangular to rounded, somewhat flattened or rounded at the base, ½–¾ in. long, oily, brown to black, wing rudimentary, edible.

Twigs. Branches rough and scaly, young twigs very smooth, gray, leaf scars and lenticels numerous.

Bark. Reddish brown to almost black on old trunks, broken into thick broad plates with smaller thin scales and deep fissures.

Wood. Yellow, soft, light, close-grained, somewhat fragrant when burned, specific gravity 0.65.

Range. Mexican Pinyon Pine is found usually at higher elevations of 4,000–7,000 ft in west Texas, New Mexico, and Arizona to California. South into Mexico in Chihuahua to Baja California and Hidalgo.

Remarks. The genus name, *Pinus*, is the classical name, and the species name, *cembroides*, denotes its superficial resemblance to *P. cembra*, Swiss Stone Pine. Other vernacular names are Nut Pine, Rocky Mountain Piñon, Pino, and Ocote. The wood is used for fuel and posts but rarely for lumber. The tree is valued for its edible seeds which are gathered and sold in great quantities by the Mexican and Indian people. The seeds are eaten raw or roasted and have an excellent flavor. The seeds are also consumed by many species of ground squirrels, chipmunks, porcupine, black bear, Mearns's quail, Merriam's turkey, and thick-billed parrot. Goats and mule deer browse the foliage. A resin obtained from the tree is used as a waterproofing material and cement for pots and baskets and for mending articles of jewelry. The tree is usually of slow growth.

Loblolly Pine

Pinus taeda L. [D]

Field Identification. Handsome conifer attaining a height of 170 ft and a diameter of 6 ft.

Flowers. Staminate flowers yellowish green or violet, spirally arranged in slender inflorescences about 2 in. long; involucral scales 10–13, overlapping; stamens almost sessile, anthers 2, opening lengthwise; pistillate cone ovate, about ½ in. long, yellowish green, also spirally arranged in scaly catkins, each scale with 2 ovules at the base.

Fruit. Ripening September–November, the spirally arranged imbricate scales of the pistillate inflorescences harden to form a cone; cone persistent, ripening in 2 years, 3–5 in. long, elongate-oblong or ovoid, reddish brown, sessile, scales thickened at the apex and bearing short incurved or straight spines; seeds 2 on each scale, rhomboid, mottled brown, about ½ in. long, attached to a thin wing about ¾ in. long.

Leaves. Persistent, in clusters of 3, rarely a few in pairs, glaucous, light to dark green, rigid, slender, 3-sided, 5–10 in. long, sheath about ½ in. long.

Twigs. Stout, reddish brown, scaly.

Bark. Reddish brown, rough, thick, deeply furrowed, scaling into coarse, large segments with large, appressed, papery scales.

Wood. Streaky yellow and brown, coarse-grained, resinous, soft, brittle, weighing 34 lb per cu ft.

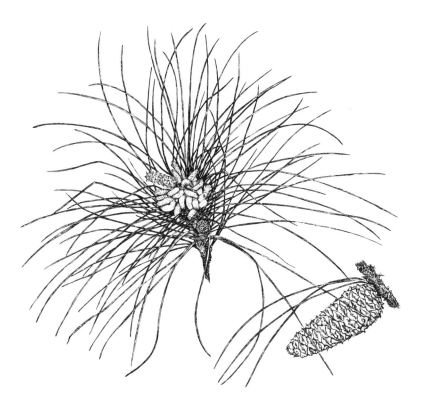

Range. Over wide areas on low grounds. East Texas and Louisiana; eastward to Florida and north into southeastern Oklahoma, southern half of Arkansas, southern Tennessee, Georgia, South Carolina, North Carolina, Virginia, Maryland, and Delaware.

Remarks. The genus name, *Pinus*, is the old Latin name. The species name, *taeda*, is for the resinous wood. Other vernacular names are Frankincense Pine, Black Pine, Lowland Shortleaf Pine, Torch Pine, Slack Pine, Sap Pine, Swamp Pine, Bastard Pine, Long-straw Pine, Indian Pine, Long-shucks Pine, Fox-tail Pine, Shortleaf Pine, Rosemary Pine, and Old-field Pine. The date of earliest cultivation is 1713. The wood is used for lumber, cooperage, pulp, boxes, crossties, posts, and fuel. Loblolly Pine is not usually worked for turpentine, because the flow of gum is checked quickly and labor costs are too high. Razorbacks do not injure the saplings of Loblolly Pine as much as those of Longleaf Pine.

Shortleaf Pine

Pinus echinata Mill. [D]

Field Identification. Valuable coniferous tree to 110 ft, and 2 ft in diameter. The branches are whorled and the crown is rather short and pyramidal to oblong.

Flowers. March–April, staminate inflorescences borne in larger clusters, sessile, about ¾ in. long, yellowish brown to purple; pistillate in small clusters of 2–3 cones with stout peduncles, about ¼ in. long, rosy pink, with scaly bracts and inverted ovules.

Fruit. Maturing the second year October–November, persistent on the branches, cone solitary or a few together, sessile or short-stalked, borne laterally, reddish brown, 1½–2½ in. long, ovoid to oblong-conic; scales separating at maturity, woody, thickened at apex, armed with sharp but weak spines which are often deciduous; seeds 2 on each scale, brown marked with black, triangular, about ¾ in. long, bearing an oblique wing about ½ in. long.

Leaves. Needlelike, from persistent sheaths, usually 2 in a cluster, sometimes 3, 3–6 in. long, slender, flexible, dark bluish green, persistent. A ton of straw contains about 14.2 lb of nitrogen and 5.4 lb of phosphoric acid. Pine straw protects the soil and increases the moisture-holding capacity.

Twigs. Stiff, rough, stout, brittle, glaucous, brownish to greenish purple at first, later dark reddish brown to purple.

Bark. Thick, brownish red, broken into large, angular, scaly plates with small appressed scales and coarse fissures.

Wood. Variable in color and quality, yellow, orange, or yellowish brown, sapwood lighter, coarse-grained, fairly heavy, medium-hard, not as resinous as other yellow pines, weighing 38 lb per cu ft.

Range. Forming dense stands, doing best on uplands or foothills. East Texas, Oklahoma, Arkansas, and Louisiana; eastward to Florida, northward to New York, and west to Illinois.

Remarks. The genus name, *Pinus*, is the ancient Latin name, and the species name, *echinata*, refers to the hedgehoglike, or echinate, bristly needles. Vernacular names are Yellow Pine, Rosemary Pine, Forest Pine, Old-Field Pine, Bull Pine, Pitch Pine, Slash Pine, and Carolina Pine. The wood is valuable because of its softer and less resinous character. It is used for general construction, exterior and interior finishing, planing-mill products, veneer, cooperage, excelsior, boxes, crates, agricultural instruments, low-grade furniture, posts, poles, woodenware, toys, etc. A number of species of birds and rodents feed on the seeds.

CYPRESS FAMILY (Cupressaceae)

Eastern Red-cedar

Juniperus virginiana L. [D, E, F, G]

Field Identification. Evergreen tree of variable shape, attaining a height of 50 ft or rarely more. Leaves of two kinds, either scale-like and appressed, or awl-shaped and spreading.

Flowers. March–May, dioecious, catkins small and terminal; staminate catkins oblong or ovoid; stamens 10–12, golden brown, pollen sacs 4; female cones globular; scales spreading, fleshy, purplish, bearing 1–2 basal ovules.

Fruit. Ripening September–December, cone berrylike, on straight peduncles, pale blue, glaucous, subglobose, ¼–⅓ in. in diameter, sweet, resinous; seeds 1–2, ovoid, acute, ⅙–⅛ in. long, smooth, shining.

Leaves. Of two kinds; one kind scalelike, appressed, glandular, dark green, acute or obtuse, about ¹⁄₁₆ in. long, 4-ranked; the other awl-shaped, sharp-pointed, glandless, glaucous, ½–¾ in. long; some of the leaves are intermediate between the two forms.

Twigs. Reddish brown, round or angled.

Bark. Light reddish brown, separating into long fibrous strips; trunk more or less fluted and basally buttressed.

Wood. Red, sapwood white, knotty, light, brittle, soft, even-textured, compact, weighing about 30 lb per cu ft, shrinks little, very resistant to decay.

Range. Growing in all types of soil, on hilltops or in swamps. Almost throughout the eastern United States. West into Texas, Oklahoma, Arkansas, Kansas, Nebraska, and North and South Dakota.

Remarks. *Juniperus* is the classical name, and the species name, *virginiana*, refers to the state of Virginia. Other names are Red Savin, Carolina Cedar, Juniper-bush, Pencil-wood, and Red Juniper. The capital of the state of Louisiana, Baton Rouge (Red Stick), gets its name from the red wood. The wood is used for novelties, posts, poles, woodenware, millwork, paneling, closets, chests, and pencils. The aromatic character of the wood is considered to be a good insect repellent. The extract of cedar oil has various commercial uses. The tree is host to a gall-like rust which in certain stages attacks the leaves of apple trees. Twig-laden bagworm cocoons are also frequent on the branches. A few borers attack the tree, and it suffers greatly from fire damage. It is sometimes used in shelter-belt planting, and has been cultivated since 1664. The fruit is eaten by at least 20 species of birds and the opossum.

Rocky Mountain Juniper

Juniperus virginiana var. *scopulorum* (Sarg.) Lemmon [G]

Field Identification. Shrub on high, dry slopes, or a tree to 50 ft and 15–30 in. in diameter. Trunk usually short and dividing into stout branches to form an irregular round-topped crown.

Flowers. In spring, cones small, inconspicuous, yellowish, staminate and pistillate borne separately; staminate with about 6 stamens, connectives entire, anther sacs 4–5; pistillate scales spreading, acute or acuminate, obscure on the mature fruit.

Fruit. Scales of pistillate cones gradually becoming fleshy and uniting into a berrylike, indehiscent conelet, November–December, ripening at the end of the second season, subglobose, ¼–⅓ in. in diameter, bright blue and very glaucous, flesh resinous and sweet; seeds 1–2, about ³⁄₁₆ in. long, grooved and angled, acute; outer coat thick and bony, inner coat thin and membranous, hilum 2-lobed, endosperm fleshy, embryo straight.

Leaves. Scalelike, ¹⁄₂₅–⅙ in. long, closely appressed, opposite or in threes, rhombic-ovate, acute or acuminate, entire, obscurely glandular dorsally, dark green to yellowish green, often pale or very glaucous, leaves of young shoots often awl-shaped and sharply pointed.

Twigs. Slender, angular and flattened at first, rounded later, brown or gray, scaly with age.

Bark. Reddish brown to gray, fibrous, thin, fissures shallow, ridges flat and interlacing, breaking into shreddy scales.

Wood. Generally the same as that of Eastern Red-cedar, knotty, heartwood in varying shades of brown to red, or streaked lighter, sapwood thin and nearly white, texture rather fine and even (except at knots), specific gravity about 0.49, moderately weak in bending, fairly strong in endwise compression, works rather easily, shock resistance high, shrinks very little in drying, resistant to decay.

Range. Gravelly or rocky soils, dry ridges or bluffs. At altitudes from sea level to 9,000 ft. The most widely distributed juniper of the West. Western Texas, New Mexico, Arizona, Colorado, Nebraska, Nevada, South Dakota, Oregon, Washington, British Columbia, and Alberta.

Remarks. *Juniperus* is the classical Latin name; the species name, *virginiana*, is for the state of Virginia; and the varietal name, *scopulorum*, refers to its habitat of rocky cliffs and crags. Also known under the vernacular names of Western Juniper, River Juniper, Western Red-cedar, Red-cedar, Mountain Red-cedar, Colorado Red-cedar, and Cedro Rojo. The tree is slow growing and long-lived. It is used for reforestation to some extent and for shelter-belt planting on prairies and plains. It also has value in ornamental planting and has been cultivated since 1836. The wood is used for chests, closets, millwork, interior finish, posts, poles, pencils, water buckets, woodenware, novelties, and fuel and is reputed to have insect-repellent properties. The fruit is eaten by a number of species of birds and grazed by bighorn sheep.

Red-berry Juniper

Juniperus pinchotii Sudw. [F, G]

Field Identification. Scraggly shrub or evergreen tree rarely over 25 ft. The numerous branches wide-spreading and the lower ones often close to the ground, irregular or pyramidal and clump-forming.

Flowers. Cones small, dioecious, terminal or axillary on short branchlets; stamens numerous with filaments enlarged into scale-like connections with 2–6 pollen sacs at the base; pistillate cones oblong-ovoid, solitary, with small persistent bracts, minute scales

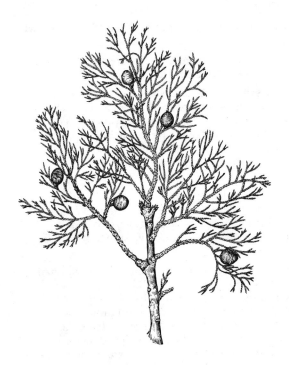

at the base with 1–2 ovules attached to the inner face, scales later enclosed by the fleshy, berrylike cone.

Fruit. Maturing within the year, a berrylike cone ¼–⅜ in. long, sessile or short-peduncled, subglobose, roughened by the scale remnants, red, somewhat glaucous, thin-skinned, mealy, resinous; seeds solitary, ⅛–³⁄₁₆ in. long, ovoid, obtuse at one end and rounded at the other, somewhat grooved, brown, lustrous; hilum large, bilobed.

Leaves. Aromatic, scalelike, yellowish green, appressed, imbricate, disposed in ranks of twos or threes, broad-ovate, obtuse or acute, keeled, dorsally glandular-pitted, ¹⁄₁₆–⅛ in. long, those on young shoots ¼–½ in. long, linear to lanceolate, acuminate, sharp-pointed, buds with a conspicuous resinous gland.

Twigs. Young twigs rather rigid, greenish, older twigs red.

Bark. Gray to reddish brown, peeling off in shaggy longitudinal strips.

Wood. Reddish brown to white, soft, moderately durable in contact with the soil, used locally for fuel and fence posts.

Range. Dry hillsides and canyons of western Texas and the Texas Panhandle area. Recorded in the following Texas counties: Kimble, Val Verde, Menard, Hood, Briscoe, Tom Green, Randall, Armstrong, Potter, and Hartley. Abundant in the vicinity of Sanderson, Texas. The type specimen is from the Palo Duro Canyon in the Texas Panhandle.

Remarks. *Juniperus* is the classical name of the Red-berry Juniper, and the species name, *pinchotii*, is for the botanist Gifford Pinchot (b. 1865). Red-berry Juniper seems to be rather hardy, especially as to fire damage, and will sprout from the stump. This trait should make the tree valuable for reforestation of burned-over areas.

Ashe Juniper

Juniperus ashei Buchholz [D, E, F, G]

Field Identification. Shrub or evergreen tree rarely over 30 ft. Usually irregular, leaning, low-branched, with a fluted and twisted trunk.

Flowers. Minute, dioecious, terminal; staminate oblong-ovoid, about ⅙ in. long, stamens 12–18; filaments enlarged into connectives which are ovoid, obtuse, or somewhat cuspidate, pollen sacs near the base; pistillate 1/12–⅛ in. long with ovate, acute spreading scales which are 1–2-ovuled at the base. The fruit is formed by the cohesion of the enlarged fleshy scales.

Fruit. August–September, sessile or short-peduncled, a fleshy, berrylike cone about ¼ in. long, bluish green, glaucous, ovoid to subglobose, skin thin and roughened somewhat by the scale remnants, flesh sweetish but resinous; seed solitary (rarely 2), ovoid, acute or obtuse at apex, rounded at base, somewhat grooved on 2 sides, lustrous, light to dark brown, about 3/16 in. long.

Leaves. Usually at the ends of the twigs, 1/25–1/16 in. long, scale-like, opposite in 2–4 ranks, appressed, imbricate, ovate, acute, keeled, minutely denticulate or fringed on the margin, usually nonglandular but resinous and aromatic; on young shoots the awllike or acicular leaves are ¼–½ in. long, lanceolate, rigid, apex long and sharp-pointed.

Twigs. Gray to reddish, scaly, aromatic, rather stiff.

Bark. Gray to reddish brown, reddish brown beneath, shredding into shaggy, longitudinal strips.

Wood. Streaked reddish brown, sapwood lighter colored, close-grained, hard, light, not strong, but durable in contact with the earth, specific gravity 0.59, somewhat aromatic.

Range. Mostly on limestone hills. In Texas, Arkansas, Oklahoma, and Missouri. The common juniper of central Texas. Southward and westward into Mexico and Guatemala.

Remarks. The genus name, *Juniperus,* is the classical name, and the species name, *ashei,* is in honor of William Willard Ashe (1872–1932), American botanist. Names used are Mountain Cedar, Cedar Brake, Texas Cedar, Sabino, Enebro, Tascate, Taxate, and Cedro. The wood is used for fuel, poles, posts, crossties, and small woodenware articles. The foliage is occasionally browsed by goats and deer, and the sweet fruit eaten by a number of species of birds and mammals, including the bobwhite quail, robin, Gambel's quail, cedar waxwing, curved-bill thrasher, gray fox, raccoon, and thirteen-lined ground squirrel. The tree is occasionally cultivated for ornament and is apparently resistant to the cedar-apple rust.

One-seed Juniper

Juniperus monosperma (Engelm.) Sarg. [G]

Field Identification. Evergreen tree sometimes attaining a height of 50 ft, with a trunk to 3 ft in diameter, often with several trunks. The branches are stout and form a rather irregular crown. Often reduced to a low much-branched shrub when at high altitudes or on sterile soils.

Flowers. March–April, dioecious, terminal or axillary, borne on branches of the previous year; staminate solitary, oblong-ovoid; stamens 8–10, filaments enlarged into entire or erose, ovate, rounded, pointed, scalelike connectives, anther sacs near the base; pistillate flowers ovoid, bearing many very small, pointed scales, some scales bearing 1–2 ovules inwardly at the base.

Fruit. In September, fleshy, dark blue to brownish, often somewhat glaucous, subglobose, ⅛–¼ in. long, flesh thin; seeds usually 1–2, sometimes extruded from the fruit apex, ovoid, apex obtuse, often angled.

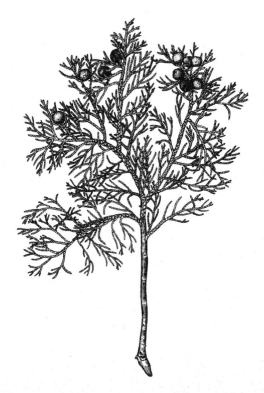

Leaves. Minute, grayish green, 1/16–1/8 in. long, opposite or in threes, apex acute or acuminate, fleshy-thickened, dorsally rounded, often glandular, margin minutely and denticulately fringed; leaves on young shoots often ovate, acutely and rigidly pointed, glandular, 1/4–1/2 in. long.

Twigs. Slender, old leaves reddish brown, the thin reddish brown bark loosely spreading.

Bark. On trunks gray, ridges rather flattened and irregular to separate into elongate, loose shreddy scales.

Wood. Heartwood light reddish brown, sapwood yellowish or white, heavy, slightly fragrant.

Range. Usually on lower hills approaching taller mountains at altitudes of 3,000–7,000 ft. New Mexico, western Texas, and western Oklahoma; northward into Colorado, Utah, Wyoming, and Nevada, westward into northern Arizona, where it is reported to reach its maximum size, and southward into Mexico.

Remarks. The genus name, *Juniperus*, is the classical Latin name. The species name, *monosperma*, refers to the solitary seed. Other vernacular names are Cherry-stone Juniper, Red-berry Juniper, West Texas Juniper, and Sabina. The fruit is sometimes ground into flour and made into bread by the Indians. The fibrous bark is used for mats, saddles, and breechcloths. The tree grows rapidly for a juniper and is long-lived. It has been cultivated since 1900. The wood is used locally for posts and fuel. The fruit is known to be eaten by at least four species of songbirds and by Gambel's quail. It is also eaten by coyote, fox, raccoon, rock squirrel, and Hopi chipmunk. It is occasionally browsed by goats.

Italian Cypress

Cupressus sempervirens L. [D, E]

Field Identification. A cultivated evergreen, resinous tree up to 70 or 80 ft high with erect or ascending branches. The bark is thin, gray, and nonexfoliating.

Flowers. Terminal or axillary, monoecious-diclinous or dioecious, solitary, small; staminate flowers oblong-cylindric, 1/6–1/5 in. long, of 6–12 decussate stamens, yellow, with short filaments and 4–6 pollen sacs; pistillate subglobose, the scales with numerous erect ovules.

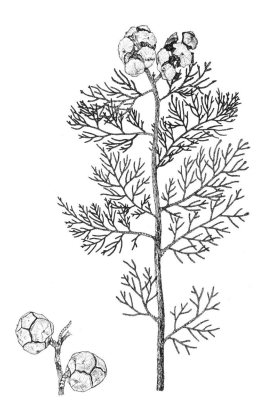

Fruit. A woody dehiscent cone, subglobose to ellipsoid, ¾–1½ in. in diameter; maturing the second year, with 8–14 peltate scales, and a short thin boss on back, and winged seeds numerous under each scale.

Leaves. Scalelike minute, closely-appressed, dark green, rhombic, obtuse at apex, glandular on back, minutely denticulate.

Twigs. Stiff, slender, cylindrical or 4-winged, brown or gray.

Range. A native of southern Europe and western Asia, often culti-vated in the United States for ornament. Cultivated for many centuries in Europe. It is the classical slender cypress of the Greek and Roman writers.

Remarks. The genus name, *Cupressus*, is the classical name. The species name, *sempervirens*, refers to its evergreen habit. Among the varieties often planted for ornament is the Columnar Italian Cypress, *C. s.* var. *fastigiata* Hansen (*C. s.* var. *stricta* Ait.), which has erect branches forming a very slender columnar upright head. Spreading Italian Cypress, *C. s.* var. *horizontalis* Gord (*C. horizontalis* Mill) has branches spreading horizontally to form a broad-pyramidal head.

Oriental Arbor-vitae

Thuja orientalis L. [D, E]

Field Identification. A cultivated evergreen, resinous shrub or small pyramidal or bushy tree to 25 ft. The branches are spreading and ascending, with very flat frondlike leafy branchlets. Bark thin, reddish brown, and scaly. Trunk usually branching near the base. Very variable and known under many horticultural form names.

Flowers. Terminal, minute, solitary, monoecious-diclinous. Staminate flowers yellow, of 6–12 decussate stamens. Pistillate flowers subglobose, with 8–12 scales in opposite pairs, with 2 erect ovules at base inside.

Fruit. Cones ovoid-oblong, erect, ½–1 in. long, fleshy and bluish before maturity. Scales usually 6, ovate, obtuse, with thickened ridge or hooked umbro at apex, the upper pair sterile. Seeds 2 to each scale, ovoid, brown, thick and wingless.

Leaves. Bright green, nearly alike on both sides; scalelike, opposite in pairs, appressed; those of main axes glandular with free-spreading apex; of lateral branches closely appressed and glandular, juvenile leaves needlelike.

Twigs. Very slender, leafy branchlets flattened in one plane.

Range. Native to northern and western China and Korea. Cultivated in many horticultural variations of size, leaf color, and shape, especially grown in the United States and Japan.

Remarks. The genus name, *Thuja*, is the classical name. The species name, *orientalis*, refers to its eastern origin. Many other horticultural forms have been developed and are sold but have not been officially recorded in botanical literature. Some of these may well be duplicates of already known forms under other names.

The wood is light, soft, brittle, rather coarse-grained, and durable in contact with the soil. It is used for construction, cabinet-making, and cooperage.

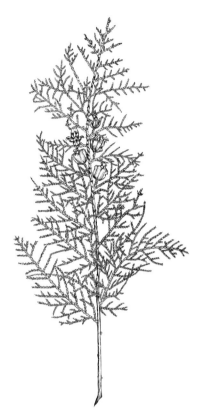

It is useful for dense hedges or as a specimen planting in the open. It does well in moist loamy soil and is easily transplanted. For propagation, seeds are sown in spring, or cuttings obtained in late summer and wintered in a cool greenhouse. Also by grafting on seedling stock in spring or early summer.

Deodar Cedar

Cedrus deodara (Roxb.) Loud. [D, E]

Field Identification. A cultivated, ornamental, cone-bearing large tree. Attaining a height of 150 ft or more in its native habitat, but usually considerably smaller in cultivation. Branches wide-spreading but drooping at the ends, more or less forming a conical

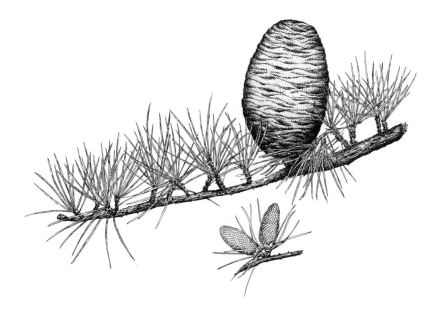

crown. Said to attain an age of 600 years. Bark light to dark gray or brownish, smooth when young, but with age thick, furrowed vertically, and cracked transversely.

Flowers. Borne September–October, monoecious or dioecious. Catkins at the ends of arrested branchlets, or spurs. Petals and sepals absent. Staminate catkins erect, cylindric, about 1–2 in. long, consisting of more or less antheriferous scales (stamens), bearing 2 or more anther cells on the back (underside). Pistillate flowers ovoid, purplish, about ½ in. long, consisting of numerous 2-ovuled scales subtended by small bracts.

Fruit. Cones usually ripen in autumn of the second year, about 13 months after flowering; barrel-shaped to ovoid or ovoid-oblong. Cones reddish brown, erect, 3½–5 in. long and 2–3½ in. in diameter; apices rounded or obtuse. Consisting of ovuliferous scales (open carpels); these closely imbricate, broadly cuneate, upper edge thin and rounded, broader than long, deciduous. The columnar axis of the cones erect and persistent when the scales have fallen. Seeds concealed by the cone scales, about ¼ in. long, with a triangular wing and rounded sides, to ⅔ in. long. Cotyledons usually 10.

Leaves. Persistent 3–5 years with very short sheaths. Alternate and single on elongated shoots and on seedlings, otherwise in dense fascicles on arrested, spurlike branchlets. Color dark green to bluish or glaucous-green; acicular with acute apices, not very rigid; triquetrous, about as thick as broad; ¾–1½ in. long. Resin canals lined with small, thin-walled secreting cells.

Twigs. Leading shoot and branchlets pendulous; young pubescent, greenish to light brown, when older glabrous and dark brown to black or gray, roughened by the bases of the old deciduous leaves.

Range. Native to Afghanistan and India. Cultivated in Kumaon and Nepal. Generally cultivated from the northern sections of the Gulf Coast states and southward. Occasionally grown as a yard tree in Houston, Texas. Its close relatives Lebanon Cedar (*C. libani*) and Atlas Cedar (*C. atlantica*) can be grown somewhat more northward than the Deodar Cedar.

Remarks. The genus name, *Cedrus*, is from *Kedrus*, the ancient Greek name. The species name, *deodara*, is a native Himalayan name. It is closely related to, and at one time was considered to be a variety of, *C. libani* (*C. libani* var. *deodara* Hook. f.).

The Deodar Weevil chews on the bark and twigs, and the larva girdles the twig and frequently kills the leader. It is also subject to damage by the Atlas Cedar aphid, which may be controlled by Malathion in an aerosol spray on the plant.

The heartwood is yellowish brown, strongly scented, very durable, with the vessels on a transverse section without pores. It consists of medullary rays, and of long, thick-walled tracheides, arranged in radial lines, with large bordered pits, usually on their radial walls only. In the earliest formed wood, contiguous to the pith, the tracheides have a spiral, or annual, thickening of their walls. The annual rings are distinctly marked by belts of very thick-walled tracheides in the outer (autumn) wood and of thinner walled tracheides in the spring wood of the succeeding year. Resin glands are found in the bark and the wood. In the wood they are vertical among the tracheides and horizontal in the medullary rays. The wood is used for building and many purposes in India. Also, an aromatic oil is distilled from it.

Young trees require shelter and a great deal of shade. In the United States, Deodar Cedar is grown only as an ornamental tree for parks, streets, or larger yards. It is sometimes almost as wide as tall and needs plenty of room. It is very attractive and the lower branches often sweep the ground.

LILY FAMILY (Liliaceae)

Trecul Yucca

Yucca treculeana Carr. [D, E, F]

Field Identification. Tree 5–25 ft, with a simple trunk or with a few stout spreading branches at the top, crowned by large symmetrical heads of radiating sharp-pointed leaves. The plant sometimes occurs as a thicket-forming shrub.

Flowers. Maturing December–April, borne in a large dense, showy glabrous or puberulous panicle 1½–4 ft long; pedicels ½–3 in.; bracts ovate to lanceolate, often spinescent at apex, varying from 1 in. at base of pedicels to 1 ft at base of main stem, becoming dry, thin, and papery; flowers creamy white, rather globose, later expanding broadly, the 6 segments ovate to ovate-lanceolate, acute to acuminate at apex, waxy, brittle, thin, 1–2 in. long; stamens 6, filaments slightly papillose above, usually finely and shortly pubescent below, about as long as the pistil; pistil ¾–1⅓ in. long, ovary slender and oblong-cylindric; style very short (⅛–⅖ in.); stigmas 3, abruptly spreading, nearly horizontal at anthesis, deeply lobed.

Fruit. Capsule indehiscent, 2–4½ in. long, about 1 in. thick, reddish brown or later black, oblong-cylindric, rather abruptly contracted at the acute or acuminate apex, surfaces often with fissures or deeply cleft, filaments and perianth often persisting, heavy and thick-walled, 3-celled, flesh sweetish and succulent; seeds numerous, flat, about ⅟₁₆ in. thick, ⅛–¼ in. broad, with a narrow border to the rim.

Leaves. In large radiating clusters, bluish green, length 2½–4 ft, 1–3½ in. wide, usually straight, concavo-convex, apex acute to short-acuminate, with a brown or black, short, sharp spine, margin entire, rigid, inner surface rather smooth, outer surface scabrous to the touch; dead leaves hanging below the crown and long-persistent.

Bark. Dark reddish brown, on older trunks ¼–½ in. thick, with shallow or deep irregular fissures. The intervening ridges broken into thin oblong plates with small appressed scales.

Wood. Light brown, spongy, fibrous, heavy, not easily cut.

Range. Well-drained hillsides, chaparral regions, or open flats near the Gulf of Mexico. From the shores of Matagorda Bay, Texas,

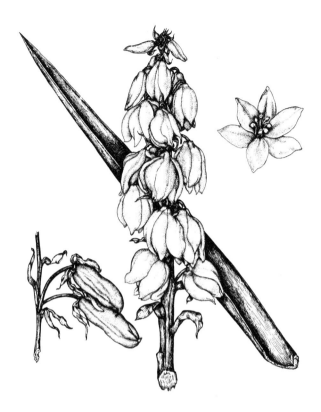

westward and southward along the coast to Brownsville. From
San Antonio in Bexar County, westward to the Rio Grande and
Pecos River. In Mexico in Nuevo León, Tamaulipas, Durango, and
Coahuila.

Remarks. The genus name, *Yucca*, is from a native Haitian name.
The species name, *treculeana*, is in honor of A. A. L. Trecul
(1818–1896), who in 1850 took the plant to France from Texas.
Also known under the vernacular names of Spanish Dagger, Spanish Bayonet, Don Quixote Lance, Pita, Palma Pita, Palma de
Dátiles, and Palma Loca. The plant is a handsome ornamental for
use in central or coastal Texas or Louisiana, and is sometimes
grown in southern Europe. The leaves are very tough and were
used in frontier days for making twine or rope. The blossoms
were made into pickles or cooked like cabbage. The spines on the
leaves are used by the Mexican people to jab the wound of a snake

bite and induce bleeding. In this manner much of the poison is carried away. The Chihuahua Indians fermented the fruit of various species of *Yucca* to make an intoxicating beverage. The trunks are sometimes used for posts, and the leaves for thatch, in making huts. It is also reported that the seeds have purgative qualities.

WILLOW FAMILY (Salicaceae)

White Poplar

Populus alba L. [D, E, F, G]

Field Identification. Tree attaining a height of 100 ft, with a trunk diameter of 3–4 ft. Sometimes spreading by root-suckers to form thickets in old fields or about abandoned dwelling sites. Recognized by the conspicuous white-tomentose undersurface of the leaves.

Flowers. Borne in pendulous catkins, pistillate about 2 in., slender, stigmas 2, each deeply 2-parted; staminate 1½–4 in.; scales dentate, fringed with long hairs; stamens 6–10 (usually about 8).

Fruit. Capsule narrowly ovoid, ⅛–⅕ in. long, tomentose, 2-valved; seeds minute, numerous, with a tuft of long silky, white hairs.

Leaves. Simple, alternate, rather variable, on vigorous shoots palmately 3–5-lobed, the lobes also coarsely toothed or with additional small lobes, base rounded to subcordate, blades 2⅓–5 in. long, upper surface dark green, lower surfaces conspicuously white-tomentose; on older branches leaves often smaller, ovate to elliptic-oblong; margin sinuate-dentate; petioles terete, densely tomentose; young twigs and branches also white-tomentose.

Bark. Greenish gray to white, usually smooth on branches or young trunks, toward the base of old trunks roughened into firm dark ridges.

Wood. Reddish to yellowish, sapwood nearly white, tough but light and soft.

Range. Adapted to many soil types, on dry, well-drained sites in the sun. Grown for ornament in Texas, New Mexico, Oklahoma, Arkansas, Louisiana, and more or less throughout the United

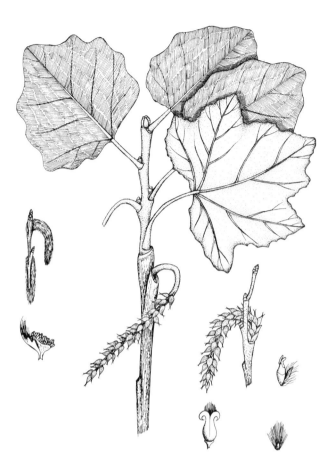

States. A native of central and southern Europe to western Siberia and central Asia.

Remarks. The genus name, *Populus*, is the ancient Latin name, and the species name, *alba*, refers to the white undersurface of the leaves. The tree is also known under the vernacular name of Abele. White Poplar has long been grown for ornament. It is very conspicuous because of the contrasting white and green leaf surfaces. However, the white undersurfaces catch soot and dust easily and become unsightly in some localities. The tree grows rapidly, transplants easily, prunes well, and has few insects or fungus pests, but is short-lived.

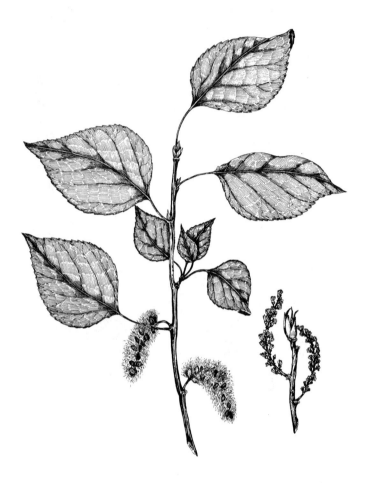

Black Poplar

Populus nigra var. *italica* Du Roi [D, E]

Field Identification. A tree 40–80 ft high with a very narrow, spirelike crown and many erect branches and twigs. The short, ridged, buttressed trunk is 2–3½ ft in diameter. Bark thick and gray-brown, or almost black on old trunks, deeply and irregularly furrowed.

Flowers. Borne in April–May before the leaves and dioecious; the staminate in sessile, dark red cylindrical catkins about 3 in. long; pistillate catkins shorter, and the staminate trees more numerous than the pistillate. Calyx none; corolla none; stamens 20–30 with white filaments and purple anthers; stigmas 2, bifid.

Fruit. Pistillate catkins to 6 in. long in fruit.

Leaves. Simple, alternate, 2–3¾ in. long, and somewhat broader than long; shape broad-deltoid; apices abruptly acuminate; margin finely but bluntly crenate-serrate; texture thick and firm; upper surface dark green and lustrous; lower surface paler; golden yellow in autumn. Petioles slender, laterally compressed, ½ in. long.

Twigs. Slender, long, flexible, glabrous, shining yellow, becoming gray. Pith rather small, 5-angled, brownish. Terminal bud conical, slightly angled, taper-pointed, glutinous, about ⅓ in. long. Lateral buds smaller, appressed. Leaf scars broad; bundle scars 3, sometimes compound; stipule scars present.

Range. A native of Europe and West Asia. Cultivated for many years in various countries.

Remarks. The genus name, *Populus*, is the classical name. The species name, *nigra*, is for the blackish trunk of old trees. The variety name, *italica*, refers to its growth in Italy on the Plains of Lombardy. Rows of these tall slender trees are conspicuous and effective in formal plantings. It is rapid growing and is sometimes used for windbreaks. The wood is light, soft, easily worked, not likely to splinter, weak, not durable, light red-brown, with thick, nearly white sapwood.

Narrow-leaf Cottonwood

Populus angustifolia James [G]

Field Identification. Western tree to 60 ft tall, 2 ft in trunk diameter. Branches slender, erect, or ascending, to form a narrowly pyramidal head.

Flowers. In drooping staminate and pistillate catkins before the leaves, length 1–4 in., pistillate longest, densely flowered, glabrous; scales brown, obovate, margins thin and fimbriate; disk shallow and irregularly lobed; ovary ovoid, style short, stigmas 2, divergent, irregularly lobed; staminate catkins 1–2½ in., disk cup-shaped; stamens 10–20, filaments short, anthers red.

Fruit. Capsule borne on pedicels about ⅓ in. long, ovoid, narrowed toward the short-pointed apex, dehiscent into 2 valves;

seeds numerous, brown, ovoid to obovoid, apex obtuse, bearing tufts of apical hairs.

Leaves. Simple, alternate, deciduous, ovate to lanceolate or elliptic, apex acute to acuminate, rarely obtuse, base cuneate or rounded, margin bluntly glandular-serrulate, or teeth acute, blade length 2–4 in., width ½–2 in. (some longer or wider on young shoots); upper surface light green and glabrous, lower surface paler green, glabrous or slightly puberulous, midrib yellowish, secondary veins slender; petiole slender, less than one-third as long as the blade, mostly terete or slightly flattened on the upper surface.

Twigs. Slender, terete, glabrous or puberulous, green to yellow or orange, eventually gray; buds resinous and aromatic, slender, ovoid, ¼–½ in. long, long-pointed, glabrous, scales thin and brown.

Bark. Green to yellowish or gray, branches and upper trunk rather smooth, lower trunk with irregular shallow fissures divided by broad flat ridges.

Wood. Pale brown, sapwood lighter colored, weak, soft, not durable, specific gravity about 0.39.

Range. Usually along streams in mountainous regions at altitudes of 2,000–7,000 ft. Trans-Pecos Texas; west to Arizona, north to British Columbia, Alberta, and Saskatchewan, and south to Chihuahua, Mexico.

Remarks. The genus name, *Populus*, is the classical Latin name. The species name, *angustifolia*, refers to the narrow leaves. Also known under the vernacular names of Black Cottonwood, Narrow-leaf Poplar, Mountain Cottonwood, and Alamo. It is a rather fast-growing tree and subject to storm damage. The wood is sometimes used for fuel or fence posts. The bark is eaten by beaver, and young branches are sometimes browsed by deer and livestock. Paul C. Standley reports that the Gosiute Indians of Utah use the young shoots for basket-making. A kind of honeydew produced on the under side of the leaves by aphids is gathered and used in much the same way as sugar. The tree was introduced into cultivation about 1893. It is sometimes planted in western cities for ornament.

Rio Grande Cottonwood

Populus fremontii var. *wislizenii* (Torr.) S. Wats. [G]

Field Identification. A large tree with a thick trunk, attaining a height of 90 ft. Branches wide-spreading to form a large crown.

Flowers. Staminate and pistillate catkins slender and elongate; pistillate catkins very slender, 3–6 in. long, longer than the staminate catkins; scales of catkins reddish, roughened, slender-lobed; staminate flower disk broad and oblique; stamens numerous, anthers large, filaments short; disk of pistillate flower cup-shaped, margin dentate, ovary rounded and long-stalked.

Fruit. Fruiting pedicels ½–¾ in., usually as long as or much longer than the capsules; capsules scattered on the glabrous pe-

duncle, about ¼ in. long, ovoid to narrowly ellipsoidal, apex acute, slightly ridged, pale, dehiscent into 3 or 4 valves.

Leaves. Simple, alternate, deciduous, broadly ovate to triangular, apex abruptly acute or long-acuminate, base subcordate to rounded or sometimes truncate, margin coarsely crenate except at apex, length or width of blades 2–4 in., surfaces yellowish green, shiny, glabrous; veins delicate, yellowish, veinlets reticulate; petioles slender and glabrous, 1¼–2 in., flattened laterally.

Twigs. Stout, yellowish to orange or gray, glabrous; buds with acute apex, resinous, shiny and puberulous; bark of trunk pale gray or light brown, fissures deep and irregular, ridges broad and flat.

Wood. Brownish, soft, specific gravity 0.46.

Range. Stream banks and valleys at altitudes of 2,500–7,000 ft. Trans-Pecos Texas along the valley of the Rio Grande; northward into New Mexico, southern Colorado, and southern Utah. In Mexico in Chihuahua and Sonora.

Remarks. The genus name, *Populus*, is the classical Latin name. The species name, *fremontii*, honors General John Charles Fremont (1813–1890), politician, soldier, and explorer of the western United States. The variety name, *wislizenii*, is for Friedrich Adolph Wislizenus (1810–1889), German-born physician of St. Louis who collected plants in Mexico and the southwestern United States in 1846–1847. The tree is sometimes listed under the species name of *P. wislizenii* (Wats.) Sarg. Also known under the vernacular names of Wislizenus Cottonwood, Valley Cottonwood, Big Bend Poplar, Alamo, and Güerigo.

The tree is rapid growing on moist sites, short-lived, and occasionally browsed by cattle. It is used for posts, fuel, rafters, and rough lumber.

Rio Grande Cottonwood is closely related to Fremont Cottonwood, *P. fremontii* S. Wats., but the former is distinguished by the very slender, elongate pistillate and staminate pedicels, and the fruit is more ellipsoid. The size and shape of the leaves are so variable that they serve as no criteria for separating the species from the variety.

Lance-leaf Cottonwood

Populus acuminata Rydb. [G]

Field Identification. A tree sometimes attaining a height of 40 ft but usually smaller, with a trunk 8–18 in. in diameter. The compact crown is formed by stout spreading branches. The bark on young trees and branches is smooth and from gray to white in color; when older the bark is gray to brown, about ½ in. thick with narrow fissures and broad flattened ridges.

Flowers. The aments slender, short-stalked, 2–3 in. long; scales scarious, light brown, glabrous, dilated, and divided into filiform lobes; disk of the staminate flower wide, oblique, and membranous; stamens many with short filaments and red anthers; pistillate flowers at maturity 4–5 in. long, disk of pistillate flowers deep cup-shaped; ovary broad-ovoid, narrowed to large, cut-lobed nearly sessile stigmas.

Fruit. Pedicellate, about ⅖–⅓ in. long; shape ellipsoid-ovoid with acute apices; thin-walled, somewhat pitted, 2–3-valved; seeds light brown, oblong-obovoid, apex rounded, about 1/12 in. long.

Leaves. Alternate, shape rhombic-lanceolate to ovate; apices acuminate; base cuneate or concave-cuneate, or sometimes rounded

and entire; margins crenate-serrate; upper surface dark green and shiny; lower surface paler; length 2–4 in.; width ¾–2 in.; midrib yellow, lateral veins remote, arcuate, and sometimes branching and joining near the margin; connected by obscure reticulate veinlets; petioles 1–3 in. long, slender.

Twigs. Slender, terete or slightly angled, color yellowish to brown; leaf scars raised, oval, horizontal. Winter buds about ⅓ in. long, acuminate, with 6–7 brown resinous scales.

Range. Arid eastern foothills of the Rocky Mountains along streams; South Dakota, Nebraska, Wyoming, Montana, Colorado, Utah, southeastern New Mexico, western Oklahoma, and adjacent Texas in the Trans-Pecos and Panhandle areas.

Remarks. The genus name, *Populus*, is the classical Latin name. The species name, *acuminata*, refers to the acuminate leaves. Some authors prefer to accept it under the name of *Populus* × *acuminata* Rydb. as a hybrid of *P. angustifolia* James and *P. sargentii* Dode. It is sometimes used for park and street planting in the Rocky Mountain area.

Great Plains Cottonwood

Populus sargentii Dode [E, F, G]

Field Identification. Tree attaining a height of 90 ft, a diameter of 6 ft. The branches erect and spreading to form a broad crown.

Flowers. In smooth staminate and pistillate catkins; staminate catkins 2–2½ in. long, scales light brown, roughened, apex

fimbriate; disk broad, oblique, margin thickened; stamens 20–25, filaments short, anthers yellow; pistillate catkins 4–8 in.; disk cup-shaped, margin slightly lobed; stigmas laciniately 3–4-lobed, ovary subglobose.

Fruit. Capsule maturing June–August, about ⅖ in. long, oblong-ovoid, apex obtuse, three to four times longer than the pedicel; seeds oblong to obovoid, apex rounded, about ¹⁄₁₆ in. long.

Leaves. Simple, alternate, deciduous, ovate to broadly deltoid; apex mostly long-acuminate; base truncate or subcordate; margin crenate-serrate; leaves slightly hairy at first; when mature glabrous, shiny, light green to yellowish green, veins rather slender and delicate; blade length 3–3½ in., width 3½–4 in.; petiole slender, laterally flattened, 2–3½ in. long, often with 2 small glands at the apex.

Twigs. Stout, glabrous, green to yellowish, somewhat angular or rounded, leaf scars rather large; buds ovoid, acute, resinous, scales puberulous and brownish.

Bark. Smooth on young trees and branches, pale gray, later with deep fissures, rounded ridges, and irregular scales closely appressed.

Range. This species is common along streams in the eastern foothills of the Rocky Mountains, 3,500–7,000 ft in Saskatchewan, the Dakotas, Wyoming, Nebraska, Kansas, Colorado, New Mexico, western Oklahoma, and the Panhandle and Trans-Pecos regions of western Texas.

Remarks. The genus name, *Populus*, is the classical Latin name. The species name, *sargentii*, honors Charles Sprague Sargent (1841–1927), American dendrologist and at one time director of the Arnold Arboretum. The wood is used for fuel, posts, veneer, and baskets.

A species once described as Texas Cottonwood, *P. texana* Sarg., is now relegated as a variety under the name of *P. sargentii* var. *texana* (Sarg.) Correll. It occurs over the same range as the species. It is a tree attaining a height of 60 ft, with a trunk sometimes to 3 ft in diameter, and pendulous branches. The twigs are yellow brown, stout, glabrous, with glabrous, acuminate winter buds.

The pistillate aments are borne on slender pedicels about ⅕ in. long. The fruit capsule is about ⅓ in. long; shape oblong-ovoid; apex acute, deeply pitted, glabrous, thin-walled, 3-valved, and a slightly lobed disk.

Leaves alternate; 3–3¼ in. long and 2¼–2½ in. wide; shape

Texas Cottonwood

broadly ovate; apices long-acuminate; margin coarsely crenate-serrate below the middle, and entire above. The slender petioles flattened and 1½–2½ in. long. There may be an abortive gland or so at the leaf base and the petiole junction, but often they are absent. This character links the variety with *P. sargentii* Dode, instead of *P. fremontii* S. Wats. and its variety *P. f.* var. *wislizenii* (Torr.) Wats. The former grows more frequently in the Texas Panhandle, and the latter two more westward along the Rio Grande and in the Trans-Pecos region.

Eastern Cottonwood

Populus deltoides Marsh.]D, E, F, G]

Field Identification. Tree to 100 ft high and 8 ft in diameter. The trunk is often rather short, the branches massive, the top rounded, and the root system spreading and shallow.

Flowers. February–May, borne in separate staminate and pistillate catkins; staminate catkins densely flowered, 1½–2 in. long, ½–¾ in. wide, disk oblique and revolute; stamens 30–60, filaments short, anthers large and red; pistillate catkins at first 3–3½ in.

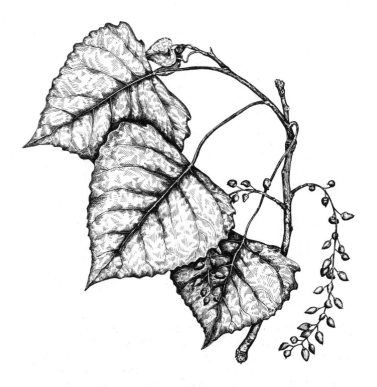

long, loosely flowered; bracts brown, glabrous, apex fimbriate; disk ovoid, obtuse, enclosing about one-third of ovary, ovary sessile, style short, stigmas 2–4, large, spreading, laciniately lobed.

Fruit. Ripening May–June, racemose, 8–12 in. long at maturity, capsules on slender pedicels ⅛–⅖ in., ovoid to conical, acute, about ¼ in. long, 1-celled, 3–4-valved; seeds numerous, small, brown, oblong-obovoid, buoyant with cottony hairs when the capsule ruptures. The minimum seed-bearing age about 10 years and maximum about 125. The seed averages 10–30 seeds per capsule, with an average of 3,032,000 seeds per lb. The commercial purity is about 40 percent, with a soundness of 95 percent. Germination averages 60–90 percent.

Leaves. Simple, alternate, deciduous, broadly deltoid-ovate, margin crenate-serrate, apex abruptly acute or acuminate, base truncate to heart-shaped or abruptly cuneate, blades 3–7 in. long, about as broad; upper surface light green, glabrous, lustrous, main vein stout, yellow to reddish; lower surface paler and glabrous with primary veins conspicuous; petiole smooth and glabrous, flattened, stipules linear.

Twigs. Yellowish to brown or gray, stout, angular, lenticels prominent; buds ovoid, acute, resinous, brown, about ½ in. long or less, laterals much flattened; leaf scars triangular or lunate, with 3 bundle marks, pith star-shaped.

Bark. Thin and smooth on young branches or trunks, green to yellow; older trunks gray to almost black with flattened, confluent broad ridges broken into closely appressed scales.

Wood. Dark brown, sapwood white, weak, soft, weighing about 24 lb per cu ft, moderately weak in bending, weak in endwise compression, low in shock resistance, moderately easy to work with tools, takes paint well, easy to glue, warps and shrinks considerably, low in durability, below average in ability to stay in place, nails easily, does not split easily.

Range. Eastern Cottonwood is found in rich, moist soil, mostly along streams. It and its varieties occur over practically the entire United States east of the Rocky Mountains. Texas, New Mexico, Oklahoma, Arkansas, and Louisiana; eastward to Florida and northward into Canada.

Remarks. The genus name, *Populus*, is the ancient name given by Pliny, and the species name, *deltoides*, refers to the triangular shape of the leaf. Other vernacular names are Carolina Poplar, Necklace Poplar, Water Poplar, Southern Cottonwood, Yellow Cottonwood, and Alamo. Alamo is the Spanish name for the tree, and was also the name given the famous Texas fort which was surrounded by the trees. "Remember the Alamo" was the battle slogan of the Texas-Mexico War. The tree is often planted for ornament and for erosion control in dune-fixing. The air-borne cottony seeds are undesirable at fruiting season. The leaves flutter rapidly and make a rustling sound in the wind because of the flexible flattened petiole. The tree sprouts from the stumps and roots, is easily storm damaged, is easily fire damaged when young, is much attacked by fungi, and grows rapidly. The foliage is known to be browsed by cattle, black-tailed deer, and cottontail. The seeds are eaten by rose-breasted grosbeak and evening grosbeak. The wood is used for paper pulp, cases and crates, tubs and pails, excelsior, veneer for plywood, musical instruments, dairy and poultry supplies, laundry appliances, and fuel.

Gulf Black Willow

Salix nigra Marsh. [D, E, F, G]

Field Identification. A rapidly growing tree sometimes attaining a height of 125 ft.

Flowers. April–May, dioecious, borne in many-flowered catkins preceding the leaves or with them; staminate catkins cylindrical, slender, 1–2 in. long; bracts obtuse, yellow, hairy below; stamens 3–7, filaments hairy below, anthers yellow; pistillate catkins 1½–3 in. long; bracts deciduous; pistil solitary, style short, the 2 stigmas thickened.

Fruit. May–June, borne on slender spreading pedicels, capsule light brown, conic-ovoid, sharp-pointed, glabrous, ¼–⅛ in. long, splitting into two valves; seeds minute, green, pilose with long hairs.

Leaves. Simple, alternate, deciduous, blades 3–6 in. long, ¼–¾ in. wide, narrowly lanceolate; apex long-attenuate and sometimes falcate; base rounded, acute; margin finely glandular-serrate; green above and paler below, glabrous or puberulent along the veins, or pubescent when young; petiole short, puberulent; stipules variable, either large, persistent, semicordate, pointed, and foliaceous, or small, ovate, and deciduous.

Twigs. Slender, brittle, reddish brown.

Bark. Light brown to black, rough, deeply fissured, ridges dividing into thick shaggy scales, rich in tannin.

Wood. Light brown, soft, light, weak, not durable, weighing 27 lb per cu ft.

Range. In wet soil, Texas, Louisiana, Oklahoma, and Arkansas. Reaching its largest size on the banks of the Brazos, San Bernard, and Colorado rivers in Texas; east to North and South Carolina, north to New Brunswick, and west to North Dakota.

Remarks. The genus name, *Salix*, is the classical Latin name, and the species name, *nigra*, refers to the black bark. Vernacular names are Scythe-leaved Willow, Swamp Willow, and Pussy Willow. The bark was formerly used as a home remedy for fever ailments. The wood is used for artificial limbs, charcoal, toys, doors, fuel, cheap furniture, boxwood, and excelsior.

Western Black Willow

Salix nigra var. *vallicola* Dudley [F, G]

Field Identification. Western tree to 45 ft, and 3 ft in diameter.

Flowers. Dioecious, staminate catkins 1–2 in. long, cylindric; scales linear-oblanceolate, apex acute, yellow, with dense long soft hairs; stamens 3–6, filaments villose; pistillate catkins 2–3½ in. long at maturity, scales early deciduous; ovary conic, apex acuminate, pubescent to glabrous; stigmas 2, short and broad.

Fruit. Capsules spread well apart on mature catkins, pedicels 1/12–⅛ in. long; capsule body ⅕–¼ in. long, conic-ovoid to lan-

ceolate, apex acute, reddish brown, pubescent at first but more glabrous later.

Leaves. Simple, alternate, deciduous, elliptic to lanceolate, some curved, long-acuminate at apex, base narrowly cuneate or attenuate, margin finely serrate, young with pale hairs, mature leaves glabrous and dull green on both sides, blade length 1½–3 in., width ¼–½ in., on young shoots considerably larger; petioles about ¼ in. long or less, pubescent to glabrous; stipules orbicular, base cordate, margin serrate, surface pubescent.

Twigs. Slender, yellow to orange or grayish, pubescent or glabrous when older.

Bark. On trunk dark gray to black, rather deeply furrowed, ridges breaking into thickish plates.

Wood. Reddish brown to pale brown, soft, weak, specific gravity 0.44.

Range. In clumps or patches along water courses at altitudes of 300–4,000 ft. In western Texas and New Mexico; west to California, north to Nevada and Utah, and south in Mexico to Chihuahua, Sonora, Sinaloa, and Baja California.

Remarks. The genus name, *Salix*, is the classical Latin name, and the species name, *nigra*, refers to the dark bark. The variety name, *vallicola*, means inhabitant of low places or valleys. Some authorities consider the tree to be a separate species instead of a variety of Black Willow and list it under the name of Gooding Willow, *S. goodingii* Ball. Leslie Newton Gooding was a botanist of the U.S. Department of Agriculture and collected the type specimen. However, the differences between the plants are so slight that a varietal name under *S. nigra* seems most fitting. The twigs of the variety are yellow to gray as compared to the reddish brown twigs of *S. nigra*; also, the leaves of the former are elliptic-lanceolate as compared to narrow-lanceolate. Also known as the Dudley Willow. The young shoots are sometimes browsed by livestock and mule deer. A decoction of the leaves is reported as being used in Chihuahua for fevers.

Sand-bar Willow

Salix interior Rowlee [D, E, F]

Field Identification. A slender, upright shrub forming thickets by stolons, or a small tree to 30 ft.

Flowers. Dioecious, April–May on leafy twigs. Staminate and pistillate catkins slender, cylindric, linear, borne on different plants; staminate catkins terminal or axillary, dense, ¾–2 in. long, about ⅓–⅜ in. broad; stamens 2, exserted, filaments distinct, hairy at base; pistillate catkins loosely flowered, 2–3 in. long and about ¼ in. broad; scales light yellow, hairy, ovate to obovate, entire or erose; ovary short-stalked, oblong-cylindric, silky-hairy when young, less hairy or glabrous later; stigmas 2, subsessile, lobed; young capsule with long white silky hairs.

Fruit. Capsule matures in April, sessile or short-peduncled, narrowly ovoid-conic, gradually narrowed to a blunt apex, ⅙–¼ in.

long, brownish, glabrous or villous, 1-celled, splitting into 2 reflexed valves; seeds minute, attached to long white hairs, buoyant
in the wind.

Leaves. Deciduous, alternate, blades 2–6 in. long, ⅛–⅓ in. wide,
linear-lanceolate, sometimes falcate, thin, apex acuminate, base
gradually narrowed into a short petiole, margin with remote, denticulate, glandular teeth, main vein prominent; upper surface dark
green and glabrous or puberulent along the main vein; paler and
pubescent beneath; petioles ⅛–³⁄₁₆ in., pubescent; stipules small
or absent. Young leaves silky-hairy beneath.

Twigs. Slender, erect, green to brown or red, glabrous or puberulent and sometimes glaucescent.

Bark. Green to gray or brown, smooth; on older trunks furrowed
and broken into closely appressed scales; lenticels sometimes
large and abundant.

Wood. Soft, light, reddish brown, sapwood pale brown, weighing 31 lb per cu ft, little used except for fuel or charcoal.

Range. The species is found in alluvial soil along streams and lakes over a wide area; Texas and Louisiana coast, and north through Arkansas and Oklahoma to Canada and Alaska. Also in northern Mexico in the states of Nuevo León, Tamaulipas, and Coahuila.

Remarks. The genus name, *Salix*, is the classical Latin name, and the species name, *interior*, refers to the plant's inland distribution along water courses. It was formerly listed under the scientific names of *S. longifolia* Muehl. and *S. fluviatilis* Sarg. Known under the vernacular names of Riverbank Willow, Osier Willow, Shrub Willow, Long-leaf Willow, Narrow-leaf Willow, Red Willow, and White Willow.

Babylon Weeping Willow

Salix babylonica L. [D, E]

Field Identification. Cultivated tree attaining a height of 50 ft. The drooping twigs give the tree its name.

Flowers. April–May, catkins small, appearing on short lateral leafy branches; staminate catkins to 1⅝ in. long and ¼–⅓ in. wide on peduncles ⅜–⅝ in. long (pistillate catkins smaller); bracts, ovate-lanceolate, yellowish, obtuse, deciduous; stamens 3–5, free, pubescent at base; style almost none.

Fruit. Capsule ovoid-conic, sessile or nearly so, glabrous, style almost absent, stigmas minute.

Leaves. Alternate, narrowly lanceolate, apex long-acuminate, base narrowed, margin serrulate, at first somewhat silky pubescent, glabrous with maturity, lower surface glaucous, blade length 3–7 in., width ¼–½ in., sometimes curling; stipules wanting or if present lanceolate and ½₂–⅓ in. long.

Twigs. Slender, glabrous, elongate, drooping, green at first, later yellowish or brownish.

Range. Grows best in damp sandy soils near water courses. In Texas, Arkansas, Oklahoma, and Louisiana eastward to Florida, northward to Virginia and Connecticut, and westward to Michigan. A native of north China, cultivated throughout North America below an altitude of 3,500 feet.

Remarks. The genus name, *Salix*, is the classical name. The species name, *babylonica*, refers to its once-presumed west Asiatic origin, but this is a misnomer because it is a native of China.

The tree of the biblical reference (Psalms 127:1–2) is now known to be the willowlike Euphrates Poplar, *Populus euphratica* Oliv. Babylon Weeping Willow sometimes escapes cultivation by the distribution of its twigs. It is known also as the Garb Willow, Napoleon Willow, and Weeping Willow.

Coastal Plain Willow

Salix caroliniana Michx. [D, E]

Field Identification. Shrub or small tree to 30 ft, and 18 in. in diameter. Branches spreading or drooping to form an open irregular crown. Closely related to Black Willow, *S. nigra* Marsh, and known to hybridize with it. However, Black Willow leaves are green beneath and Coastal Plain Willow leaves are very glaucous.

Flowers. May–June, buds single-scaled, expanding with the leaves; catkins terminal, slender, lax, narrow-cylindric, to 4 in. long; scales yellow, ovate to obovate, apex rounded or obtuse, densely villose-pubescent; glands of staminate flowers lobulate or forming a false disk; stamens 3–12, exserted, separate, filaments hairy at base, anthers yellow; gland of pistillate flower clasping the base of the pedicel; ovary stipitate, ovoid-conic, acute; style short, 2-lobed.

Fruit. Capsule ovoid-conic, ⅙–¼ in. long, granular-roughened, abruptly long-pointed, remnants of the 2 persistent stigmatic lobes almost sessile, base with pedicel to ¼ in.; seeds numerous, silky-hairy.

Leaves. Involute in the bud, simple, alternate, deciduous, length 2–7 in., width ⅜–1⅓ in., lanceolate to lanceolate-ovate, sometimes falcate, apex acuminate or acute, base gradually narrowed on young leaves, on older ones often rounded; upper surface bright green and glabrous; lower surface whitened or glaucous, somewhat puberulent when young, glabrous later, veins yellowish, delicate, margin finely serrate; petioles ⅛–½ in. long, densely hairy, glandless; stipules usually small on normal leaves, on vigorous shoots large (to ¾ in. wide), foliaceous, conspicuous, ovate to reniform, mostly serrate above the middle.

Twigs. Slender, yellowish to reddish brown or grayish, more or less pubescent, eventually glabrous; winter buds small, brown, lustrous.

Bark. Reddish brown to gray, ridges broad, fissures deep, conspicuously checkered, breaking into closely appressed scales.

Wood. Dark reddish brown, sapwood nearly white, light, soft, not strong.

Range. Mostly along gravelly banks and shores of streams or lakes or in low woods. Texas, western Arkansas, eastern Oklahoma, and Louisiana; east to Florida, north to Maryland, and west to Kansas.

Remarks. The genus name, *Salix*, is the classical Latin name, and the species name, *caroliniana*, refers to the states of Carolina. Also known under the vernacular names of Ward Willow and Carolina Willow. The scientific terminology of this willow has been very confused. The following names have been applied from time to time: *S. occidentalis* Bosc. *ex* Koch, *S. longipes* Shuttl., *S. nigra* var. *wardii* Bebb, *S. occidentalis* var. *longipes* (Anderss.) Bebb, *S. wardii* Bebb, *S. marginata* Wimm. *ex* Small, *S. amphibia* Small, *S. longipes* var. *venulosa* (Anderss.) Schneid., *S. longipes* var. *wardii* (Bebb) Schneid., *S. harbisonii* Schneid., *S. chapmanii* Small, and *S. floridana* Chapm.

Brittle Willow

Salix fragilis L. [D]

Field Identification. An introduced, rapid-growing tree 40–90 ft tall and 3 ft in trunk diameter, but usually smaller. The brown branches obliquely ascending.

Flowers. Aments appearing with the leaves, slender, lax, 1–3 in. long; ⅓–⅖ in. wide; on leafy peduncles ⅓–1¼ or 2 in. long, bearing 2–5 small leaves. Flower scales oblong, greenish yellow, crisp-villous, deciduous. The staminate tree is reported to be rare in America.

Fruit. Capsules narrowly conic, 2-valved, glabrous, 1/6–1/5 in. long; pedicels about 1/25 in. long; styles about 1/35 in. long; stigmas short, notched. The seed is often sterile.

Leaves. Simple, alternate, large, narrowly lanceolate to lanceolate; 3–7 in. long; 3/4–3 2/5 in. wide; apices long-acuminate; margin finely glandular-serrate; upper surface glabrous and dark green; lower surface glaucescent or glaucous, glabrous at maturity. Petioles 1/3–2/5 in. long, usually with 2 glands at base of blade.

Twigs. Green to dark red or brown to gray later, glabrous, very brittle at base and deciduous in winds. Stipules absent, or small, semicordate, and early deciduous. Buds medium size and pointed.

Range. Native of Europe and introduced into America in early times for ornament, hedges, shade, and gunpowder charcoal. It frequently escapes cultivation in the east, and some are found in northeast Texas.

Remarks. The genus name, *Salix*, is an ancient name. The species name, *fragilis*, refers to the brittle character of the twigs. It is reported that a stake cut from a tree and driven into the ground will soon establish itself. *S. fragilis* var. *decipiens* is a variety with yellow twigs, buds black in winter, and leaves smaller and brighter green.

Coyote Willow

Salix exigua Nutt. [F, G]

Field Identification. Shrub with spreading stems to 12 ft tall, or sometimes a tree to 25 ft and 5–6 in. in trunk diameter. The branches spreading and forming a rounded crown.

Flowers. Appearing after the leaves on glabrous twigs 1–2 in. long, catkins terminal or axillary; staminate catkins 5/8–3/4 in.; pistillate catkins 5/8–1 5/8 in. Scales hoary-pubescent, varying from lanceolate to obovate with an acute or rounded apex; stamens 2, with the filaments hairy below; ovary sessile, villose, stigma bifid, sessile, style absent.

Fruit. Capsule ovoid-lanceolate, apex acuminate, glabrous or nearly so, 1/5 in. or less long, sessile or with pedicels shorter than the gland.

Leaves. Alternate, blade linear to lanceolate or oblanceolate, apex acuminate, some curved, base gradually narrowed, margin glandular-serrate, often entire below the middle, upper surface grayish

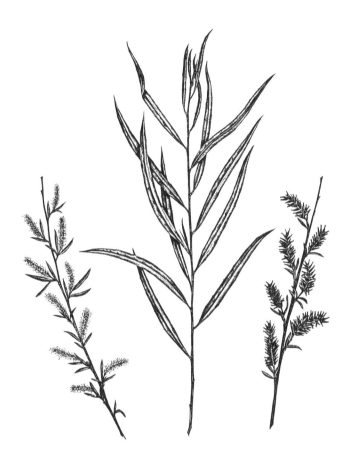

green and glabrous, lower surface with white appressed hairs (or in some forms only puberulent), length 1½–4 in., ⅛–¼ in. wide (on young growth sometimes 4½ in. long and 1½ in. wide); stipules absent or minute; sessile or nearly so.

Twigs. Slender, glabrous, reddish brown to gray.

Bark. Grayish brown, thin, longitudinally fissured, older trunks more furrowed.

Range. Along streams in mountain woodlands or desert grasslands at altitudes of 4,000–7,000 ft. Oklahoma, western Texas, and New Mexico; westward to California and northward to British Columbia. In Mexico from Chihuahua to Baja California.

Nevada Coyote Willow

Remarks. The genus name, *Salix*, is the classical name. The species name, *exigua*, refers to the small-sized leaves. Also known under the vernacular names of Basket Willow, Gray Willow, Sandbar Willow, Narrow-leaf Willow, Slender Willow, and Acequia Willow.

Narrow-leaf Coyote Willow, *S. exigua* var. *stenophylla* (Rydb.) Schneid., has very narrow leaves. It occurs in western Texas and New Mexico. Nevada Coyote Willow, *S. exigua* var. *nevadensis* (Wats.) Schneid., is segregated by having 2 glands on the glabrous ovary. From Arizona to Nevada.

Peach-leaf Willow

Salix amygdaloides Anderss. [F, G]

Field Identification. Tree to 40 ft, or rarely larger. The branches are ascending, or sometimes drooping to form an open irregular head.

Flowers. April–May, appearing with the leaves, borne on the ends of short lateral branches; staminate and pistillate catkins borne separately, glands of both elongate and free; staminate catkins 1–2 in., slender, elongate, cylindric, hairy; scales deciduous, yellowish green, hairy, ovate, apex rounded; stamens 5–9 (usually 5), filaments distinct, hairy at base, anthers yellow; pistillate catkins 1½–3 in., lax in fruit; scales narrowly oblong to obovate, early deciduous; style short, stigmas nearly sessile, bifid; ovary oblong-conic, glabrous.

Fruit. Capsules borne on the elongate catkins, about as long as the glabrous pedicels or shorter, lanceolate to narrowly ovoid or conic, ⅙–⅕ in. long, light yellow or reddish, 1-celled, valves 2–3 and recurved when ripe; seeds numerous and very small.

Leaves. Revolute in the bud, simple, alternate, deciduous, pubescent when young, lanceolate to ovate-lanceolate, some falcate, apex long-acuminate, base broad-cuneate to rounded, some inequilateral, margin finely and sharply serrate, thin, upper surface yellowish green and glabrous, lower surface paler and slightly glaucous and glabrous, veins prominent and yellowish, length of blade 2½–6 in., width ¾–1¼ in.; petiole slender, ¼–¾ in., twisted, glandless; stipules falling early, reniform, to ½ in.

Twigs. Long, slender, terete, flexible, drooping or erect, glabrous, lustrous, varying from yellow or orange to reddish brown or gray later; lenticels scattered, small and pale; buds ⅛–⅙ in. long, ovoid, shiny, light or dark brown.

Bark. Reddish brown to dark brown, fissures irregular, ridges breaking into thick flat scales.

Wood. Heartwood light brown, sapwood whitish, close-grained, soft, weak, weighing about 28 lb per cu ft.

Range. Sunny sites along margins of lakes or streams, in western areas at altitudes of 3,000–7,000 ft. In Trans-Pecos and northwestern Texas and New Mexico; east through Kentucky to Pennsylvania, north to Quebec, and west to Manitoba, Washington, and Oregon.

Remarks. The genus name, *Salix*, is the classical Latin name. The species name, *amygdaloides*, is from *amygdalus* ("peach") and refers to the peachlike leaves. Also known under the vernacular names of Almond Willow, Almond-leaf Willow, Peach Willow, Southwestern Peach Willow, Wright Willow, and Wright Peach-leaf Willow. The tree has been in cultivation since 1895 and is rapid growing and short-lived. The wood is used mostly for fuel and charcoal.

Yew-leaf Willow

Salix taxifolia H. B. K. [G]

Field Identification. Large western shrub, or tree to 50 ft, and 18 in. in diameter. Branches short and divaricate, forming a broad open crown.

Flowers. Borne March–May. Catkins on leafy branches, terminal, or axillary, usually clustered, densely flowered, staminate and pistillate catkins separate; shape of catkins subglobose to cylindric-oblong, ¼–½ in.; scales deciduous, yellowish, oblong or obovate, apex acute to rounded or apiculate, outer surface densely tomentose, inner surface glabrous or pubescent, margins ciliate; stamens 2, filaments free and pubescent below; ovary sessile or short-stalked, ovoid-conic, hairy; stigmas 2, deeply emarginate.

Fruit. Capsule sessile or short-stalked, about ¼ in. long, cylindric, ovate-conical, acuminate-pointed, reddish brown, silky-hairy at first but more glabrate later; seeds numerous, small, hairy.

Leaves. Alternate, deciduous, linear-lanceolate or oblanceolate, graduated to apices, acute and mucronate, slightly curved, margin slightly revolute, obscurely and remotely denticulate above the middle or entire, soft white-hairy when young, later grayish green and finely pubescent above, lower surface paler and somewhat more hairy, blade length ⅓–1⅓ in., width ¹⁄₁₂–⅛ in.; leaves sessile, or petioles puberulous and less than ¹⁄₁₂ in.; stipules ovate, acute, minute, early deciduous.

Bark. Light gray to brown, on the trunk of mature trees ⅓–1 in. thick, fissures deep and irregularly longitudinal, with intervening broad, flat ridges breaking into small, close scales.

Twigs. Slender, reddish brown, densely tomentose at first but glabrous later except for roughened leaf scars; buds brown, ¹⁄₁₆–⅛ in. long, ovoid, puberulous.

Range. On creek banks and in canyons at altitudes of 3,000–6,000 ft. In Trans-Pecos Texas, southwestern New Mexico, and southern Arizona. In Mexico it is widespread, especially in Sonora, Chihuahua, Coahuila, and Baja California. Also in Guatemala.

Remarks. The genus name, *Salix*, is the classical Latin name. The species name, *taxifolia*, refers to the small, narrow, yewlike leaves. Also known in the Southwest and Mexico under the vernacular names of Sauz, Sauce, Jaray, Taray, Taray de Río, and Tarais. It is considered to be a good browse for livestock. The branches are used for brooms and the bark as a remedy for malaria by the Mexican Indians.

Bonpland Willow

Salix bonplandiana H. B. K. [G]

Field Identification. Small to large tree attaining a height of 50 ft and a diameter of 4–20 in. The slender, ascending, or somewhat drooping branches form a round-topped crown.

Flowers. Borne on leafy branches, catkins dioecious, cylindric, slender; staminate catkins 1¼–2¼ in., somewhat longer than the pistillate which average ¾–1½ in.; scales obovate, apex rounded, outer surface yellow or grayish and villose, inner surface slightly villose or subglabrous; stamens 3, slightly hairy at base of filaments; ovary slender, oblong-conic, short-stalked, glabrous, stigmas much-thickened, club-shaped, nearly sessile.

Fruit. Capsule short stipitate, ovoid-conic, base rounded, yellowish to light reddish, seeds numerous and very hairy.

Leaves. Simple, alternate, deciduous, narrowly lanceolate to oblong or broadly linear, apex long-acuminate, base narrowly or

broadly cuneate, margin finely serrulate, blade length to 5 in., width ⅝–¾ in., upper surface green and glabrous, lower surface silvery white and glabrous or pubescent when younger; midrib broad and yellow; petioles ⅛–½ in., stout, grooved, glabrous or slightly pubescent; stipules ovate, entire or undulate, thin and scarious, ⅛–¼ in. broad.

Twigs. Slender, yellowish at first, later brown to reddish, slightly hairy to glabrous later.

Bark. Dark brown to black, ridges broad and flat with appressed scales, fissures narrow.

Range. At altitudes of 2,500–5,000 ft in well-drained soil in the sun. Southeastern New Mexico and central Arizona; south in Mexico from Sonora, Chihuahua, and Coahuila to Oaxaca and Guatemala.

Remarks. The genus name, *Salix*, is the classical name, and the species name, *bonplandiana*, is in honor of Aimé Bonpland (1773–1858), a French botanist. Also known under the vernacular names of Toumey Willow, Sauce, and Sauz. Cattle browse the young plants.

GARRYA FAMILY (Garryaceae)

Mexican Silktassel

Garrya ovata Benth. [F, G]

Field Identification. Western evergreen shrub or small tree 2–18 ft, all parts densely pubescent with gray or brown curled hairs.

Flowers. Dioecious, catkins axillary; staminate catkins shorter than the pistillate, bracts small; calyx with 4 linear sepals; petals absent; stamens 4, filaments distinct, anthers linear, ovary none; pistillate catkins 1–3 in., bracts large and leaflike; calyx limb abbreviated, stamens absent; styles 2, inwardly stigmatic, persistent on fruit; ovary 1-celled with 2 pendulous ovules.

Fruit. Drupe ⅙–⅓ in., sessile or short-pedicellate, globose to ovoid, bluish purple, sometimes drying brownish, eventually glabrous, stigma persistent, flesh thin; seeds 1–2, subglobose to short-oblong, one side more flattened than the other, ³⁄₁₆–¼ in. long.

Leaves. Persistent, blades 1–2½ in., opposite, leathery, variable in shape, either narrowly lanceolate to ovate, or oblong to oval or obovate, apex acute, obtuse, or rounded, usually mucronate, base broadly to narrowly cuneate or in some rounded, margin entire and sometimes irregularly thickened and muricate; young leaves densely curly-hairy on both sides; at maturity pale and densely curly-hairy beneath; becoming glabrous, or nearly so above and either dull or semilustrous, veins finely reticulate; petioles connate at base, ⅛–¾ in., at first densely curly-hairy but more glabrous later.

Twigs. Stout, 4-angled to terete later, densely curly-hairy, but eventually glabrous, reddish brown to gray; lenticels small, slitlike or elliptic.

Range. Rocky limestone hills and canyons of central Texas, and westward into the Trans-Pecos counties. In Mexico in Chihuahua, San Luis Potosí, and Puebla. The type specimens are from Guanajuato.

Remarks. The genus name, *Garrya*, is in honor of Nicholas Garry, secretary of the Hudson's Bay Company, and the species name, *ovata*, refers to the ovate leaves. A variety known as the Lindheimer Silktassel, *G. ovata* var. *lindheimeri* Coult. & Evans, has been named as occurring in central and western Texas. However, the characters by which it is described—oblong or obovate, acute, nonthickened or muricate-margined, and curly-haired leaves— do not appear distinct enough to warrant the segregation of the variety.

Wright Silktassel, *G. wrightii,* is a closely related, more glabrous species of extreme west Texas, New Mexico, and Arizona.

WAX-MYRTLE FAMILY (Myricaceae)

Southern Wax-myrtle

Myrica cerifera L. [D]

Field Identification. Crooked evergreen shrub, but sometimes a tree to 40 ft.

Flowers. Borne March–April, with staminate and pistillate catkins on different plants. Staminate catkins oblong, cylindric, ¼–¾ in.; scales acute, ovate and ciliate; stamens 2–8, yellow, anthers 2-celled, reddish yellow; pistillate catkins short, ovoid; ovary 2–4-scaled at base; stigmas 2, slender and spreading.

Fruit. Drupe maturing September–October, spikes short; bracts deciduous; drupes persistent, about ⅛ in., globose, light green, covered with granules of bluish white wax; seed pale, minute, solitary.

Leaves. Simple, alternate, tardily deciduous; 1½–5 in. long, ¼–¾ in. wide, oblanceolate to elliptic, apex acute or rounded, cuneate or narrowed at base and decurrent on the short stout petiole, margin entire or coarsely serrate above the middle, shining above, resinous with orange-colored glands beneath, aromatic when crushed.

Twigs. Reddish brown to gray, young parts with early-deciduous orange-colored glands.

Bark. Gray, or grayish green, smooth, compact, astringent.

Wood. Light, brittle, soft, fine-grained, dark brown, sapwood lighter, weighing 35 lb per cu ft.

Range. Sandy swamps or low acid prairies. Eastern Texas,

Oklahoma, Arkansas, and Louisiana; eastward to Florida and north to New Jersey.

Remarks. The genus name, *Myrica*, is the ancient name of the tamarisk, and the species name, *cerifera*, refers to the waxy fruit. Vernacular names are Waxberry, Spice-bush, Candleberry, Bayberry, Sweet-oak, and Tallow-shrub. The fruit is eaten by about 40 species of birds, especially bobwhite quail and turkey. It was first cultivated in 1699, and makes a desirable ornamental. Candles were formerly made by boiling the waxy-blue berries. The bark and leaves are reputed to have medicinal properties. Southern Wax-myrtle is closely related to the Dwarf Wax-myrtle, *M. pusilla*, which is smaller and spreads by underground runners.

WALNUT FAMILY (Juglandaceae)

Eastern Black Walnut

Juglans nigra L. [D, E, F]

Field Identification. Tree to 125 ft with a rounded crown.

Flowers. May–June, staminate and pistillate flowers on same tree; staminate catkins 2–5 in. long, stout, stamens 20–30, sessile, calyx 6-lobed, lobes oval and pubescent; bracts triangular, brown-tomentose; pistillate flowers in 2–5-flowered spikes, about ¼ in. long; stigmas 2, plumose, yellowish green; style short on a subglobose ovary; calyx-lobes acute; ovate, green, pubescent.

Fruit. Ripening September–October, solitary or clustered, subglobose; husk yellowish green, thick, papillose, indehiscent, 1½–2½ in. in diameter; nutshell hard and bony; nut dark brown to black, compressed, corrugated, 4-lobed at base, oily, sweet, edible.

Leaves. Pinnately compound, 1–2 ft long, yellowish green, deciduous; petioles puberulent; leaflets 11–23, sessile or short-stalked, ovate-lanceolate, acute or acuminate, rounded or subcordate at base, inequilateral, serrate, glabrous above, pubescent below, 3–5 in. long, 1–2 in. wide.

Bark. Grayish brown, black, or reddish, fissures deep, ridges broad, rounded, and broken into close scales.

Wood. Very beautiful, dark rich brown, sapwood white, durable, strong, heavy, hard, close-grained, is easily worked, glues well, does not warp, shrink, or swell much, takes a good polish, weighs 38 lb per cu ft. The whitish sapwood is sometimes stained to match the color of the heartwood to bring a better price.

Range. Oklahoma, Arkansas, Louisiana, and Texas; east to Florida, north to Minnesota, New York, and Ontario; and west to Nebraska.

Remarks. The genus name, *Juglans*, is from the Latin *Jovis glans*, meaning "acorn [or any nut of similar shape] of Jove," and the species name, *nigra*, refers to the dark wood. The wood is used in making superior furniture, cabinets, veneers, musical instruments, interior finish, sewing machines, caskets, coffins, posts, railroad crossties, and fuel. Large amounts were used for gunstocks during the Civil War and World War I. Trees about 12 years old begin to bear nuts. Confections and cakes are made from the

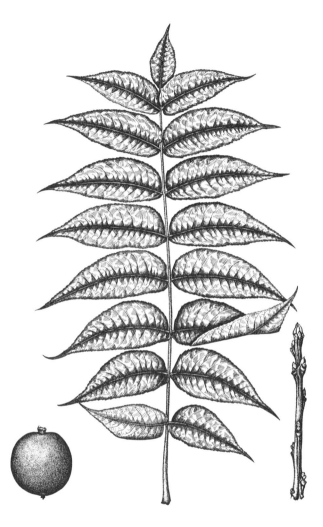

nuts, which were also a favorite with the American Indians. Squirrels are fond of the large nuts. The tree makes a fine ornamental because of its shape and beautiful large leaves. Black Walnut and English Walnut are known to hybridize. Eastern Black Walnut is sometimes planted in shelter belts, and has been cultivated since 1686. It is a rapid grower and is usually found mixed with other hardwoods.

Texas Black Walnut

Juglans microcarpa Berl. [E, F]

Field Identification. Strong-scented, many-stemmed shrub or small tree attaining a height of 30 ft, often with a number of leaning trunks from the base.

Flowers. Borne March–April in separate catkins on same tree. Staminate catkins from twigs of previous year, solitary, simple, long, slender, pendulous, pubescent at first, more glabrous later, 2–4 in. long; calyx short-stalked, greenish, puberulous, 3–6-lobed, lobes rounded; bracts densely hairy, ovate lanceolate; stamens 20–30 in several rows; anthers almost sessile, yellow, connectives somewhat lobed; pistillate catkins solitary, or several together, at the end of branches of the current year, oblong, rufous-tomentose; calyx-lobes usually 4, ovate and acute; bracts and bractlets laciniate; ovary inferior; stigmas spreading, plumose, greenish red.

Fruit. Borne solitarily, or several together, globose, ½–¾ in. in diameter; hull with persistent calyx remnants at apex, rusty-pubescent at first but more glabrous later, thin, indehiscent; nut subglobose or ovoid, deeply grooved longitudinally, 4-celled toward base, shell thick; kernel small, oily, sweet.

Leaves. Alternate, 9–12 in. long, odd-pinnately compound of 11–25 leaflets; the leaflets lanceolate to narrowly lanceolate, often scythe-shaped; margin entire or serrate with appressed teeth; apex acuminate; base cuneate or rounded, inequilateral, petiolules short; surface pubescent when young, becoming glabrous later; light green; aromatic when crushed; petiole and rachis pubescent.

Twigs. Slender, orange reddish or gray, usually pubescent, lenticels pale, pith in plates.

Bark. Gray to dark brown, fissures deep.

Wood. Dark brown, sapwood white, heavy, hard, not strong.

Range. In valleys and rocky stream beds, Texas, Oklahoma, New Mexico, and northern Mexico. In Texas from the valley of the Colorado River west into the mountains of the Trans-Pecos, passing into the closely related Arizona Black Walnut in the far West.

Remarks. The genus name, *Juglans*, is from the Latin *Jovis glans*, meaning "acorn [or any nut of similar shape] of Jove," and the species name, *microcarpa*, refers to the small fruit. Vernacular names used are Dwarf Walnut, Little Walnut, Nogal, and Nogalillo.

The wood is used for cabinet work, furniture, paneling, and veneers. The tree is sometimes cultivated for ornament in the United States and in Europe. It is also used in shelter-belt planting and has some value as a wildlife food, especially for squirrels.

Arizona Black Walnut

Juglans major (Torr.) Heller [F, G]

Field Identification. Tree attaining a height of 50 ft, with a diameter to 3–4 ft.

Flowers. Borne in spring in separate staminate and pistillate catkins; staminate catkins long, slender, pendulous, pubescent, 4–8 in. long; calyx long-stalked, 4–6-lobed; lobes greenish, ovate, acute, densely hairy; stamens 30–40, anthers yellow, almost sessile, about 1/12 in. long, with connectives; pistillate catkins shorter than the staminate catkins, solitary or a few in a cluster; ovary inferior, pistil solitary and green, stigmas 2, spreading.

Fruit. Subglobose or somewhat ovoid, 1–1½ in. in diameter; husk thin, densely rufous-tomentose; nut brown or black, ovoid, apex rounded or acute, base rounded or flattened, grooves broad and deep, shell thick; seed solitary, large, sweet.

Leaves. Alternate, 7–12 in. long, odd-pinnately compound of 9–15 (rarely 19) leaflets; leaflets ovate to lanceolate, somewhat scythe-shaped, margin coarsely serrate, apex acuminate, base cuneate or rounded or asymmetrical; surface pubescent when young, later glabrous above with scattered pubescence on midrib beneath, yellowish green, length 1½−4 in.; width 1−1½ in.; petiole and rachis slender and pubescent.

Twigs. Slender, rufous-pubescent at first, becoming reddish brown to gray later and almost glabrous, lenticels small and pale.

Bark. Gray to brownish black, deeply fissured with prominent ridges.

Range. At elevations of 2,000−7,000 ft, along rocky stream beds and canyons of west Texas, New Mexico, and Arizona; also north to Colorado. In Mexico in the states of Chihuahua and Sonora to Durango.

Remarks. The genus name, *Juglans*, is from the Latin *Jovis glans*, meaning "acorn [or any nut of similar shape] of Jove," and the species name, *major*, refers to the larger size. Vernacular names are River Walnut, Mountain Walnut, Nogal, and Nogalillo. The tree grows rapidly when young, has a well-developed taproot, and is long-lived. The wood is durable in contact with the soil and is used for posts and occasionally for furniture or veneer. A good crop of fruit is borne every 2−3 years, there being about 45 seeds per lb. The germination rate is usually less than half. It has considerable wildlife value, especially for squirrels and rodents.

Pecan

Carya illinoensis (Wangh.) K. Koch [D, E, F]

Field Identification. Tree to 150 ft, with a broad rounded crown. The largest of all hickories.

Flowers. March−May, borne in staminate and pistillate catkins on same tree, subject to frost damage; staminate in slender, fascicled, sessile catkins 3−6 in. long; calyx 2−3-lobed, center lobe longer than lateral lobes; stamens 5−6, yellowish; pistillate catkins fewer, hairy, yellow, stigmas 2−4.

Fruit. Ripening September−October, in clusters of 2−10, persistent; husk thin, aromatic, splitting along its grooved sutures into 4 valves at maturity; nut oblong to ellipsoid, cylindric, acute, bony, smooth, reddish brown, irregularly marked with darker brown, 1½−3½ in. long; seed deeply 2-grooved, convoluted on surface.

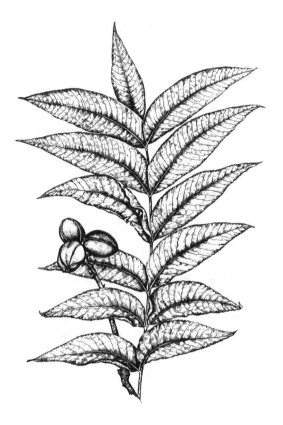

Leaves. Alternate, deciduous, odd-pinnately compound, 9–20 in. long; leaflets 9–17, sessile or short-stalked, oblong-lanceolate, falcate, acuminate at apex, rounded to cuneate and inequilateral at base, doubly serrate on margin, 4–8 in. long, 1–2 in. wide; aromatic when crushed, dark green and glabrous above, paler and glabrous or pubescent beneath; rachis slender, glabrous or pubescent.

Twigs. Reddish brown, stout, pubescent, lenticels orange-brown.

Bark. Grayish brown to light brown under scales; ridges flattened, narrow, broken, scaly; fissures narrow, irregular.

Wood. Reddish brown, sapwood lighter, coarse-grained, heavy, hard, brittle, not strong, weighing 45 lb per cu ft, inferior to other hickories.

Range. Rich river-bottom soils. Texas, Oklahoma, Arkansas, and Louisiana; eastward to Alabama, and north to Kansas, Iowa, Indiana, and Tennessee.

Remarks. The genus name, *Carya*, is the ancient name for walnut, and the species name, *illinoensis*, refers to the state of Illinois, the tree at one time having been called Illinois Nut. It is widely planted as an ornamental and for its sweet edible nuts. The wood is not important commercially but is occasionally used for furniture, flooring, agricultural implements, and fuel. The nut is valuable to wildlife, being eaten by a number of species of birds, fox squirrel, gray squirrel, opossum, raccoon, and peccary. The bark and leaves are sometimes used medicinally as an astringent. Pecan is a rather rapid grower for a hickory and is long-lived but is subject to bark beetle attacks. It has been cultivated since 1766.

Shellbark Hickory

Carya laciniosa (Michx. f.) Loud. [D]

Field Identification. Tree attaining a height of 120 ft, with short, stout limbs and a narrow crown. A specimen at Big Tree State Park, Missouri, has been reported with a circumference of 12 ft 9 in., a height of 128 ft, and a spread of 70 ft.

Flowers. April–June, borne in separate staminate and pistillate catkins on the same tree; staminate catkins in threes, 5–8 in.; bracts linear-lanceolate, acute, scurfy-tomentose; calyx 3-lobed, central lobe longer than lateral ones; stamens 3–10, hairy, yellow, anthers emarginate; pistillate in 2–5-flowered spikes, tomentose; bracts longer than calyx-lobes; stigmas short.

Fruit. Ripening September–November, solitary or 2–3 together, ellipsoid to globular, depressed at apex, 1–3 in. long; hull light to dark orange-brown, hard, woody, ¼–½ in. thick, dehiscent along the 4 ribs; nut yellowish white, ellipsoid to obovoid or globose, usually rounded and flattened at ends but sometimes pointed at apex, somewhat compressed, bony, hard, thick-shelled; kernel sweet. Largest of all hickory nuts.

Leaves. Large, 1–2 ft long, alternate, deciduous, odd-pinnately compound of 5–9, usually 7, leaflets; leaflets ovate to oblong-lanceolate or acute at apex, cuneate or rounded and inequilateral at base, finely serrate on margin; dark green, glabrous and shiny above; pale green beneath and velvety pubescent when young,

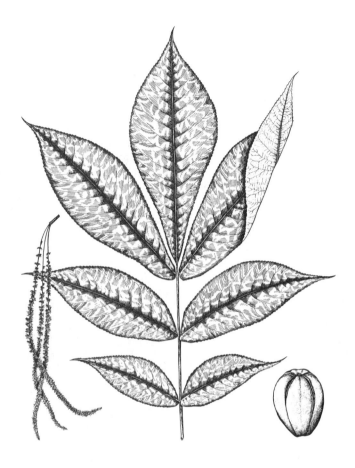

glabrous later; terminal leaflet petioled, lateral leaflets sessile or nearly so; petiole and rachis pubescent or glabrous with age.

Twigs. Stout, dark brown to reddish orange, lenticels elongate.

Bark. Gray, separating into long, thin, shaggy plates hanging loosely.

Wood. Dark brown, sapwood lighter, close-grained, hard, strong, tough, heavy, very flexible, weighing 50 lb per cu ft.

Range. Northeast Texas, Oklahoma, Arkansas, and Louisiana; east to Alabama, and north to Nebraska, Minnesota, Iowa, Kansas, Delaware, and Ontario.

Remarks. The genus name, *Carya*, is the ancient name for walnut, and the species name, *laciniosa*, refers to the deep furrowing and splitting of the bark. Vernacular names are King Nut, Bottom Shellbark, Big Shellbark, and Thick Shellbark. The wood is used as is that of other hickories, particularly for tool handles, baskets, and fuel. The large nuts are edible and sweet but are considered to lack the flavor of the Shagbark Hickory. The tree is long-lived, slow growing, hard to transplant, and subject to insect damage. It is rather similar in appearance to the Shagbark Hickory but has larger leaves and nuts and the bark is somewhat less shaggy in appearance. However, the two species are known to hybridize.

Shagbark Hickory

Carya ovata (Mill.) K. Koch [D]

Field Identification. Tree attaining a height of 100 ft, with an oblong crown and shaggy bark. A specimen in Turkey Run State Park, Indiana, has been reported with a trunk diameter of 9 ft 8 in., a height of 127 ft, and a spread of 50 ft.

Flowers. Appearing March–June, borne in separate staminate and pistillate catkins; staminate catkins in threes after the leaves appear, 4–5 in. long, slender, green, hairy-glandular; bract ovate-lanceolate and longer than the ovate and acute calyx-lobes; stamens 4, reddish yellow, hairy; pistillate catkins 2–5-flowered, rusty-tomentose.

Fruit. Ripening September–October, very variable in size and shape. Borne 1–3 together, 1–2½ in. long, oval to subglobose or obovoid, depressed at apex; hull blackish to reddish brown, glabrous or hairy, ¼–½ in. thick, splitting freely to the base into 4 valves along the grooved sutures; nut light brownish white, oblong-obovate, somewhat compressed, usually prominently 4-angled, barely acute, or rounded, or truncate at apex; rounded at base, shell thin; kernel light brown, aromatic, sweet, edible.

Leaves. Alternate, deciduous, 8–17 in. long, odd-pinnately compound of 3–5 (rarely 7) leaflets; lateral leaflets sessile or nearly so, ovate-obovate or elliptic-lanceolate, acuminate at apex, cuneate and unequal at base, serrate on margin, yellowish green and glabrous above, paler and glabrous or hairy beneath, 4–7 in. long, 2–3 in. wide; terminal leaflet stalked, terminal leaflet and the upper pair of leaflets considerably larger than the lower pairs; rachis and petiole glabrous or pubescent.

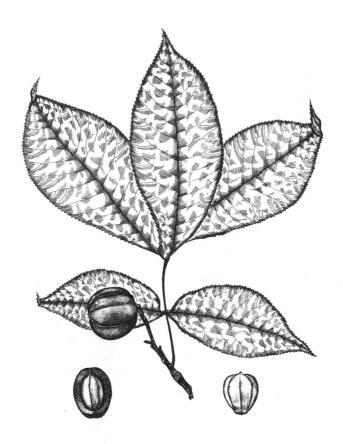

Twigs. Orange-brown, stout, glabrous or pubescent.

Bark. Gray, conspicuously exfoliating into long shaggy strips.

Wood. Light brown, sapwood lighter, close-grained, heavy, hard, strong, tough, flexible, weighing 52 lb per cu ft.

Range. East Texas, Oklahoma, Arkansas, and Louisiana; east to Alabama, north to Maine and Quebec, and west to Minnesota, Michigan, and Nebraska.

Remarks. The genus name, *Carya*, is the ancient name for walnut, and the species name, *ovata*, refers to the ovate-shaped leaflets. Vernacular names are Scaly Bark Hickory, White Hickory, Upland Hickory, Red Heart Hickory, Sweet-walnut, and White-walnut. The tree is long-lived, slow growing, and subject to insect attacks. The wood is used for fuel, tool handles, baskets, wagons, and other general uses. This nut, next to the pecan, is the best of any American tree and is the common hickory nut of commerce.

Mockernut Hickory

Carya tomentosa Nutt. [D, E]

Field Identification. Tree to 100 ft, with rather short limbs and a broad or oblong crown. A specimen has been reported from Turkey Run State Park, Indiana, with a circumference of 9 ft 6 in., a height of 146 ft, and a spread of 52 ft.

Flowers. April–May, borne in separate staminate or pistillate catkins; staminate catkins 3-branched, 4–5 in. long, yellowish green, hairy; bracts ovate to lanceolate, hairy, much longer than calyx-lobes; stamens 4, with red, hairy anthers; pistillate in 2–5-flowered hairy spikes; bracts ovate and acute, longer than bractlets and calyx-lobes; stigmas dark red.

Fruit. Ripening September–October, solitary or paired, very variable in size and shape, usually obovoid, globose, or ellipsoid, 1–3½ in. long, acute at apex, rounded or rarely with a short necklike base; hull dark reddish brown, woody, hairy or nearly glabrous with yellow resinous dots, 4-ribbed, dehiscent down the deep ribs to the middle or near the base, about ⅛–¼ in. thick; nut variable in shape, obovoid-oblong to globose or ovoid, rounded at base, acute or acuminate at apex, slightly flattened, noticeably or obscurely 4-ridged, brownish white or reddish, shell thick and hard; kernel dark brown, small, shiny, sweet, edible.

Leaves. Alternate, deciduous, 8–24 in. long, odd-pinnately compound of 5–9 (usually 7) leaflets; lateral leaflets sessile or nearly so, oblong to lanceolate or obovate, acute to acuminate at apex, rounded or broadly cuneate at base and inequilateral, serrate on margin; shiny yellowish green above, paler beneath and clothed with brownish orange hairs, glandular and resinous, fragrant when crushed, 5–8 in. long, 2–5 in. wide, terminal leaflets and upper pairs generally larger than lower pairs; rachis and petiole glandular-hairy.

Twigs. Stout, grayish brown to reddish, hairy at first but more glabrous later; buds distinctively large and tomentose.

Bark. Gray, close and rough but never shaggy, ridges rounded and netted, separated by shallow fissures.

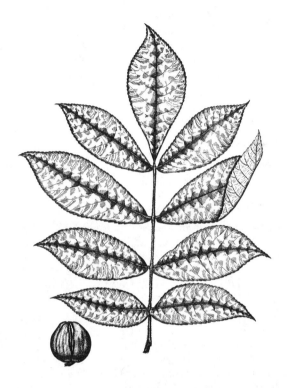

Wood. Dark brown, sapwood lighter, close-grained, heavy, hard, strong, tough, flexible, weighing 51 lb per cu ft.

Range. Texas, Louisiana, Arkansas, and Oklahoma; east to Florida, and north to Nebraska, Ontario, Iowa, Illinois, Michigan, and Maine.

Remarks. *Carya* is the ancient name for walnut, and the species name, *tomentosa*, refers to the tomentose hairs of the leaves. Vernacular names are Whiteheart Hickory, White Hickory, Red Hickory, Black Hickory, Whitebark Hickory, Hardbark Hickory, Bigbud Hickory, Bullnut Hickory, and Fragrant Hickory. It is long-lived, is a rapid grower when young, will sprout from the stump, and is subject to insect damage. The foliage is occasionally browsed by white-tailed deer. The wood is important commercially and is used for vehicle parts, handles, fuel, and agricultural implements. The nut is sweet and edible but used in smaller quantities than other edible species.

Bitternut Hickory

Carya cordiformis (Wangh.) K. Koch [D]

Field Identification. Tree attaining a height of 100 ft, with stout limbs and a broad spreading head. Tree in West Feliciana Parish, Louisiana, has been reported to be 171 ft high, with a trunk 12 ft 6 in. in circumference.

Flowers. April–May, staminate and pistillate catkins separate but on the same tree; staminate catkins in threes, 3–4 in. long, reddish-hairy, bracts ovate and acute; calyx 2–3-lobed; stamens 4, anthers yellow and hairy; pistillate catkins mostly in ones or twos, sessile.

Fruit. September–October, solitary or paired, obovoid to sub-globose, about ¾–1 in. long; husk yellow-scaled, thin, 4-winged

above the middle and splitting to somewhat below the middle; nut globose to ovate, small, smooth, white, thin-shelled, abruptly pointed into a conical beak, slightly flattened; kernel convoluted and bitter to taste.

Leaves. Alternate, deciduous, 6–12 in. long, odd-pinnately compound of 7–11 leaflets on a pubescent or glabrous rachis; leaflets ovate-lanceolate, some falcate, sessile or nearly sessile, terminal leaflets petioled, acuminate at apex, cuneate or rounded at base, serrate on margin, shiny green and glabrous above, paler and glabrous or pubescent beneath, 3–6 in. long, 1–2 in. wide; rachis slender and pubescent; leaflets are generally smaller and more slender than those of other species of hickories.

Twigs. Winter buds scurfy, bright yellow; twigs greenish brown to reddish brown, lustrous, pubescent at first and glabrous later, stout; lenticels numerous and pale.

Bark. Grayish brown, smooth for a hickory, with thin scales in the flattened ridges, furrows shallow.

Wood. Reddish brown, heavy, hard, strong, tough, weighing 47 lb per cu ft. Used for the same purposes as other hickories but wood considered to be somewhat inferior.

Range. In moist woods of bottom lands; east Texas, Oklahoma, Arkansas, and Louisiana; east to Florida, north to Minnesota, Maine, and Ontario.

Remarks. The genus name, *Carya*, is the ancient name for walnut, which is close kin to the hickories, and the species name, *cordiformis*, means "heart-shaped," in reference to either the fruit or the base of the leaflets. Vernacular names are Swamp Hickory, Pig Hickory, White Hickory, Pignut Hickory, and Red Hickory. The wood is used for wheel stock, handles, and fuel. It was first cultivated in the year 1689. It is perhaps the most rapid grower of all hickories and sprouts from the stump. It is suitable as a good park and shade tree and is often used as a potted stock for grafting pecan varieties.

Black Hickory

Carya texana Buckl. [D, E]

Field Identification. Tree attaining a height of 80 ft, with short, crooked branches forming a narrow crown.

Flowers. Borne in separate staminate and pistillate catkins, staminate catkins 2–3 in. long with acuminate bracts considerably longer than the calyx-lobes; stamens 4–5 with somewhat hairy anthers; pistillate catkins 1–2-flowered and red-hairy on all parts.

Fruit. Hull of nut 1¼–2 in. in diameter, puberulent, subglobose to obovoid, or sometimes with a short basal neck, splitting at sutures to the base with valves ¹⁄₁₂–⅙ in. thick; nut globose, or obovoid, somewhat compressed, rounded at base, suddenly narrowed to an acute apex, 4-angled along upper part especially, reddish brown, reticulate-veined, shell about ⅛ in. thick; kernel small, rounded, sweet.

Leaves. Alternate, deciduous, 8–12 in. long, odd-pinnately compound of 5–7 (usually 7) leaflets; leaflets sessile or nearly so, 4–6 in. long, lanceolate to oblanceolate or obovate, acuminate or acute at apex, cuneate and somewhat inequilateral at base, serrate on margin; dark green, shiny, and usually glabrous above; paler and rusty-pubescent below, especially when young, later becoming more glabrous; petioles rusty-hairy when young. The occurrence of rusty hairs and white scales on buds and young parts is a conspicuous feature.

Twigs. Rusty-pubescent and reddish brown at first, grayish brown and glabrous later.

Bark. Dark gray to black, ridges irregular, broken into deep fissures.

Wood. Brown, sapwood paler, hard, tough, brittle, used chiefly for fuel.

Range. The species, *texana*, and its variety, Arkansas Black Hickory, are distributed through east and south-central Texas and Louisiana; north to Oklahoma, Arkansas, Indiana, Illinois, Missouri, and Kansas.

Remarks. The genus name, *Carya*, is the ancient name for walnut, and the species name, *texana*, refers to the state of Texas. Some of the vernacular names for it are Buckley Hickory and Pignut Hickory. The thick shell makes the nut almost impossible to extract, but hogs sometimes crack them. Wood used for fuel.

BIRCH FAMILY (Betulaceae)

Hazel Alder

Alnus serrulata (Ait.) Willd. [D]

Field Identification. Irregularly shaped shrub or slender tree to 20 ft.

Flowers. Borne in separate staminate and pistillate catkins; staminate catkins in clusters of 2–5, 2–4 in. long, cylindric, drooping, bracts subtending the flowers; stamens 3–6; pistillate catkins in clusters of 2–3, about ¼ in. long, green to purple; bracts 3-lobed, each subtending 2–3 pistils.

Fruit. About ¾ in. long, ovoid, a conelike aggregation of woody bracts, each subtending a nutlet; nutlet small, ovate, flattened, sharp-margined, less than ⅛ in. long.

Leaves. Alternate, simple, deciduous, thick, blades 1–5 in. long, obovate to oval, obtuse or rounded at apex, acute or cuneate at base, sharply serrulate on margin, rather dark green on both sides, veiny and somewhat pubescent or glabrous beneath; petioles glabrous or pubescent, ⅓–½ in. long; stipules oval, deciduous.

Twigs. Reddish brown or orange, pubescent at first, glabrous later, slender.

Bark. Gray, smooth, thin, slightly roughened with age.

Wood. Light brown, soft, brittle, weighing 29 lb per cu ft.

Range. In wet soil along streams. East Texas, Louisiana, Oklahoma, and Arkansas; east to Florida, north to Maine, and west to Minnesota.

Remarks. The genus name, *Alnus*, is the classical name of the alder, and the species name, *serrulata*, refers to the finely toothed leaves. This species was formerly known as *A. rugosa* (Du Roi) Spreng., which is a name better applied to *A. incana* (L.) Moench, a European species. Vernacular names are Common Alder, Smooth Alder, Tag Alder, Green Alder, Red Alder, Speckled Alder, and American Alder. The bark yields tannic acid and is an astringent. It was formerly used in the treatment of intermittent fever. The fruit is eaten by a number of species of birds. Hazel Alder is sometimes planted to prevent erosion on stream banks.

River Birch

Betula nigra L. [D, E]

Field Identification. Tree commonly of wet ground to 90 ft high, with dull reddish brown bark peeling off in curly thin flakes.

Flowers. Staminate catkins clustered, sessile, 1–3½ in. long; scales brown and shining; stamens 2, bifid; pistillate catkins cylindric, about ½ in. long; scales ovate, green, pubescent, ciliate; ovary sessile, with 2 spreading styles.

Fruit. Strobile oblong-cylindric, about 1½ in. long and ½ in. thick, erect, borne on peduncles ½ in. long; scales 3-lobed; nutlet about ⅛ in. long, ovoid-obovate with a thin reniform wing, ripening April–June.

Leaves. Simple, alternate, deciduous, rhombic-ovate, acute, cuneate at base, doubly serrate or some lobed with double serrations,

blades 1½–3½ in. long, 1–2 in. wide, lustrous dark green above, tomentose beneath; petioles tomentose, slender, averaging about ½ in. long.

Bark. Reddish brown or grayish, marked by darker elongate lenticels, peeling into conspicuous papery strips.

Wood. Light brown, hard, strong, close-grained, weighing 36 lb per cu ft.

Range. Texas, Oklahoma, Arkansas, and Louisiana; north to Massachusetts and west to Minnesota and Kansas.

Remarks. *Betula* is the ancient classical name of the birch, and the species name, *nigra*, means "black," but no reason can be found for the name. Vernacular names are Red Birch, Water Birch, and Black Birch. The wood is used for furniture, woodenware, wagon hubs, and fuel. The seeds are sometimes eaten by birds and the foliage is browsed by white-tailed deer. Sometimes cultivated as an ornamental along streams or ponds and is also used for erosion control. It has been cultivated since 1736.

American Hornbeam

Carpinus caroliniana Walt. [D, E]

Field Identification. Small crooked tree attaining a height of 35 ft, with a fluted gray trunk and pendulous branches.

Flowers. April–June, staminate and pistillate flowers separate but on same tree; staminate flowers green, borne in linear-cylindric catkins, 1–1½ in.; scales of catkin triangular-ovate, acute, green below, red above; stamens numerous, filaments short and 2-cleft; pistillate catkins about ½ in.; flowers with hastate bracts which develop into a 3-lobed green involucre; styles slender, stigmas 2.

Fruit. August–October, nutlet about ⅓ in. long, ovoid, acute, nerved, borne at base of a 3-lobed foliaceous bract, many together forming loose pendent clusters 3–6 in. long. The middle lobe of the bract is lanceolate and entire or dentate, and much longer than the lateral lobes which are usually incised-dentate on one side.

Leaves. Simple, alternate, deciduous, sometimes falcate, acute or acuminate at apex; base rounded, wedge-shaped, or heart-shaped, often somewhat inequilateral; margin sharply double-serrate, teeth glandular except at base; dull bluish green and glabrous above, paler and hairy in axils of the veins below; petioles about

⅓ in. long, slender, hairy; stipules ovate-lanceolate, hairy, reddish green.

Twigs. Slender, zigzag, gray or red.

Bark. Smooth, tight, thin, bluish gray, sometimes blotched with darker or lighter gray (some gray blotches may be due to crustose lichens), trunk fluted into musclelike separations.

Wood. Light brown, sapwood lighter, strong, hard, tough, heavy, close-grained, weighing about 45 lb per cu ft.

Range. East Texas, Oklahoma, Arkansas, and Louisiana; east to Florida, north to Virginia, and west to Illinois.

Remarks. The genus name, *Carpinus*, is the classical name for hornbeam, and the species name, *caroliniana*, refers to the states of Carolina. Vernacular names are Blue-beech, Water-beech, Lean-tree, and Ironwood. The wood is used for golf clubs, handles, fuel, mallets, cogs, levers, and wedges. The seed is eaten by at least 9 species of birds. The tree has been cultivated since 1812.

Woolly American Hop-hornbeam

Ostrya virginiana (Mill.) K. Koch var. *lasia* Fern. [D, E]

Field Identification. Tree with grayish brown bark, attaining a height of 60 ft.

Flowers. Monoecious, staminate catkins 1–3 at ends of branches, 1½–3 in. long; scales triangular-ovate, acuminate, nerved, ciliate, green to red; stamens 3–14, filaments short and forked, anthers villous; pistillate catkins small, usually solitary, slender, about ¼ in. long; scales lanceolate, acute, ciliate, hirsute and red above, developing into pubescent-nerved bladdery sacs; ovary 2-celled.

Fruit. In conelike imbricate clusters 1½–2 in. long; peduncles hairy, about 1 in. long; each papery sac about ¾ in. long, ⅔–1 in. wide, ellipsoid, strongly tomentose at apex; nuts enclosed in the sac, small, ovoid, brown, faintly ribbed, about ¼ in. long.

Leaves. Simple, alternate, deciduous, blades 2½–4½ in. long, 1½–2½ in. wide, ovate, or oblong-lanceolate, apex acute or acuminate, base rounded, heart-shaped, or wedge-shaped, often inequilateral, margin sharply and doubly serrate, glabrous and yellowish green above, hairy and paler below, turning yellow in autumn; petioles about ¼ in. long, hairy; stipules acute, rounded, ciliate, hairy, about ½ in. long.

Twigs. Terete, crooked, slender, yellow-orange to brown, pubescent.

Bark. Grayish brown, broken into small, narrow, oblong, shreddy scales.

Wood. Hard, strong, tough, close-grained, durable, light brown to white, sapwood lighter, weighing 51 lb per cu ft.

Range. In rich, moist woods. East Texas, Oklahoma, Arkansas, and Louisiana; eastward to Florida; and the northern variety to Ontario, west to Minnesota and Nebraska. The exact overlapping distribution of the southern and northern varieties is not known.

Remarks. The genus name, *Ostrya*, is the ancient Greek name, and the species name, *virginiana*, refers to the state of Virginia. Vernacular names are Ironwood, Leverwood, Deerwood, Hardhock, and Indian-cedar. The wood is used for posts, golf clubs, tool handles, mallets, and woodenware. The fruit is eaten by at least 5 species of birds. The tree is rather slow growing but has possibilities as an ornamental; has been cultivated since 1690.

The east Texas form appears to be the southern variety, *lasia*, described by Merritt Lyndon Fernald and varying from the northern variety mostly by pubescence of leaves, petioles, and twigs. The northern variety, *O. virginiana* var. *glandulosa*, has glandular hairs on young parts.

BEECH FAMILY (Fagaceae)

The author is greatly indebted to the authors of the following two publications for much of the information on the Beech family: Cornelius H. Muller, *The Oaks of Texas, Contributions from the Texas Research Foundation*, vol. 1, part 3 (Renner, 1951); Donovan

Stewart Correll and Marshall Conring Johnston, *Manual of the Vascular Plants of Texas* (Renner: Texas Research Foundation, 1970).

American Beech

Fagus grandifolia Ehrh. [D]

Field Identification. Beautiful tree attaining a height of 120 ft, with a rounded top and spreading branches. Easily sprouting from the roots to form thickets.

Flowers. April–May after the leaves unfold in separate staminate and pistillate clusters; staminate in globose heads, about 1 in. in diameter, pendent on hairy peduncles 1–2 in. long; stamens 8–10 with green anthers; pistillate flowers in clusters of 2–4 borne on short hoary peduncles ½–1 in. long; calyx campanulate, 4–5-lobed, hairy; pistil composed of a 3-celled ovary and 3 inwardly spreading stigmatic styles.

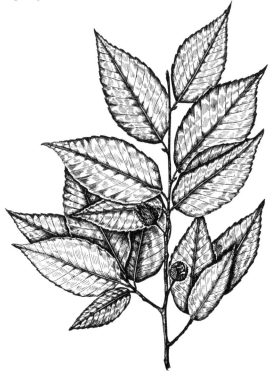

Fruit. Ripening September–November, borne on stout hairy peduncles, composed of burlike involucres ½–¾ in. long with straight or recurved prickles, full-grown at midsummer but becoming brown and persistent on the branches, splitting into 4 valves to release a pair of small brown, 3-angled, sweet nuts, dispersed after first frost, good seed crops every 2–3 years.

Leaves. Simple, alternate, deciduous, straight-veined, ovate-oblong; acuminate at apex, cuneate to rounded or cordate at base, coarsely serrate on margin; when mature glabrous and dark green above; paler and pubescent, especially in the axils of veins beneath; 3–6 in. long; petioles ⅙–½ in., hairy; stipules ovate-lanceolate to linear.

Twigs. Slender, zigzag, green and hairy at first, later glabrous and orange to yellow or reddish brown; lenticels oblong and orange-colored.

Bark. Light gray, often mottled, smooth.

Wood. Varying shades of red, sapwood lighter, close-grained, hard, strong, tough, difficult to cure, not durable, weighing 43 lb per cu ft.

Range. Eastern Texas, Louisiana, Arkansas, and Oklahoma; eastward to Florida, north to Nova Scotia, and west to Wisconsin, Michigan, Illinois, and Missouri.

Remarks. The genus name, *Fagus*, is from an old Greek word referring to the edible nuts, and the species name, *grandifolia*, refers to the large leaves. Vernacular names are Red Beech, Ridge Beech, and White Beech, also Beechnut. The tree is a very desirable one for ornamental planting, but grass has a difficult time growing under the dense foliage. It was first cultivated in the year 1800. It is long-lived, is free of disease, and sprouts easily from the roots to form thickets. The wood is sold commercially for chairs, tool handles, shoe lasts, flooring, cooperage, crates, spools, brush backs, toys, and fuel. The small sweet edible nuts are sometimes gathered and sold in the markets in the northern states and Canada and are a source of vegetable oil and swine feed. They are eaten by many species of birds and by raccoon, opossum, porcupine, gray fox, red fox, and white-tailed deer.

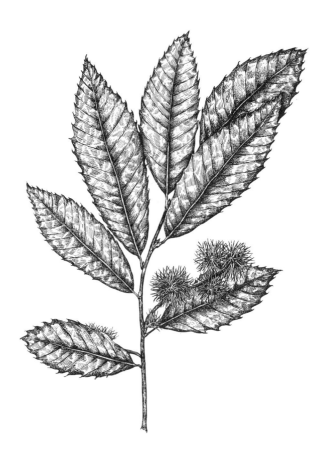

Allegheny Chinquapin

Castanea pumila (L.) Mill. [D]

Field Identification. Thicket-forming shrub or tree with slender spreading branches and a round top, sometimes attaining a height of 50 ft.

Flowers. Both staminate and pistillate catkins on same tree; some catkins all staminate, and some with both staminate and pistillate flowers; staminate catkins cylindric, slender, hoary-tomentose, 2½–6 in. long, ¼–⅓ in. in diameter; calyx small, 6-lobed; stamens 8–20 with 2-celled anthers; pistillate flowers generally in threes, or scattered toward base of catkins, and staminate flowers toward the tip; involucre prickly, sessile or short-stalked; ovary imperfectly 6-celled; styles linear, exserted with small stigmas.

Fruit. In spikelike clusters; burs formed by the prickly involucre and 1–1½ in. in diameter; spines of bur in crowded clusters, slender and basally tomentose or glabrous; bur opening by 2–3 valves to expose the nutlet; nutlet solitary, small, shiny brown, round-ovoid, pointed and somewhat pubescent at the apex; kernel sweet and edible.

Leaves. Alternate, simple, deciduous, blades 3–4 in. long, 1½–2 in. wide, elliptic-oblong to oblong-obovate, acute at the apex, unequal and rounded or broadly cuneate at the base; margins coarsely serrate with pointed teeth; upper surface glabrous, yellowish green, lower velvety-white pubescent; petioles short, stout, flattened, pubescent at first, glabrous later, ¼–½ in. long; stipules yellowish green, ovate to lanceolate or linear, pubescent.

Twigs. Green to reddish brown or orange-brown, pubescent at first, glabrous later.

Bark. Smoothish, reddish brown, furrows shallow, ridges flat with platelike scales.

Wood. Dark brown, coarse-grained, light, hard, strong, durable, weighing 37 lb per cu ft.

Range. East Texas, Oklahoma, and Louisiana; eastward to Florida, north to New Jersey, and west to Missouri.

Remarks. The genus name, *Castanea*, is for a town in Thessaly, and the species name, *pumila*, is for the tree's small stature. The tree is generally too small for commercial use but is occasionally used for posts, railroad crossties, and fuel. The sweet nuts are sometimes gathered for the market and are eaten by a number of birds and mammals.

Common Chinquapin

Castanea alnifolia Nutt. [D, E]

Field Identification. A stoloniferous shrub to 10 ft or more.

Flowers. March–June; staminate aments erect-ascending, slender, greenish yellow, pale pubescent, the small clusters interrupted and somewhat fragrant; pistillate aments as long or longer than the staminate, borne near the branch ends, with 10–12 interrupted involucres usually near the middle.

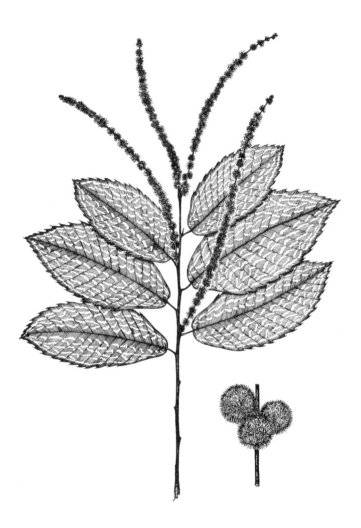

Fruit. From subglobose to short-oblong, 1–7 on a peduncle, ¾–1¼ in. in diameter, brown-tomentose to tawny, closely set; spines scattered, pubescent, divided into branches at base; scales splitting into 2–4 valves. Nuts 1–3, shape ovoid, terete, acute; color chestnut brown, shiny; about ⅓ in. in diameter; ½–¾ in. long; flesh sweet.

Leaves. Shape narrowly elliptic to oblong-obovate; apices acuminate or rounded; base narrowed to cuneate or rounded; length

3–4¾ in., width 1–2 in.; upper surface green and glabrous; lower surface light green, from tomentose at first to glabrous later; margin sinuate-toothed with apiculate teeth, the straight parallel veins ending in the teeth. Texture thin and glabrous. Petioles stout, glabrous, about ¹⁄₁₂ in. long.

Twigs. Slender, reddish brown, pilose to glabrous later.

Range. In open woodlands or in thickets. Eastern Texas, Louisiana, Mississippi, Alabama, Georgia, and Florida; northward to Arkansas, and along the coast of North Carolina.

Remarks. The genus name, *castanea*, is for a town in Thessaly. The species name, *alnifolia*, refers to the alderlike leaves. A treelike form is listed as *C. alnifolia* var. *floridana* Sarg. However, the tree form and the stoloniferous thicket-forming form seem to intergrade, and in some regions they are difficult to distinguish.

Florida Chinquapin

Castanea alnifolia var. *floridana* Sarg. [D]

Field Identification. Tree to 40 ft high, with spreading branches forming a narrow crown; often with many trunks from the base.

Flowers. Borne in 2 kinds of catkins on same tree, one kind bearing all staminate flowers, and the other bearing staminate flowers on the distal part and pistillate on the proximal; staminate catkins 4–5 in. long, cylindric, pubescent; stamens 8–20, exserted with 2-celled anthers; calyx 6-lobed; androgynous catkins with pistillate flowers below the middle, bearing prickly involucres and a 6-celled ovary terminating in linear exserted styles.

Fruit. A bur formed from the spiny involucre, ¾–1¼ in. in diameter, globose or short-oblong, tomentose; spines stout, pubescent, fascicles somewhat scattered with bald spots between; bur splitting into 2–3 valves to expose the nut; nut ovoid, shiny brown, acute, ½–¾ in. long; kernel sweet, edible.

Leaves. Alternate, simple, deciduous, oblong-obovate to elliptic, acute at apex, rounded or cuneate at base, shallowly bristle-toothed on margin, thin, dark green and glabrous above, lighter green and glabrous below, or some showing a thin tomentum, 3–4 in. long, 1–1¾ in. wide; petiole stout and glabrous.

Twigs. Reddish brown, slender, pubescent or glabrous.

Bark. Smoothish, ridges flat, furrows shallow.

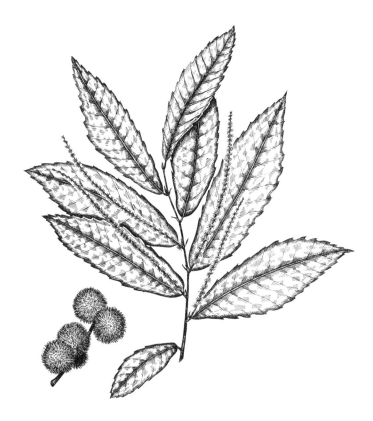

Wood. Hard, strong, durable, brownish.

Range. Rich moist soil of thickets or roadsides. Eastern Texas, Louisiana, and Oklahoma; eastward to Florida and northward to North Carolina.

Remarks. The genus name, *Castanea*, is for a town in Thessaly; the species name, *alnifolia*, refers to the alderlike leaves; the variety name, *floridana*, refers to the Floridian habitat.

Chinquapins are rather similar in appearance but may be distinguished chiefly by the leaf pubescence and spines of the fruit. The Allegheny Chinquapin has no rootstocks, it has leaves with velvety-white tomentum beneath, and the bur spines are rather long, slender, and glabrous, or sparsely pubescent. Florida Chinquapin has bur spines which are sparser and shorter, and the leaves glabrous and lustrous or only thinly tomentose beneath.

Ashe Chinquapin has even shorter, stubbier, and more pubescent spines than Florida Chinquapin, and the leaves are gray-downy beneath.

Overcup Oak

Quercus lyrata Walt. [D, E]

Field Identification. Tree attaining a height of 100 ft, and a diameter of 2–3 ft. Branches small, crooked, often drooping, forming an open, irregular head. When growing in swamps the base often buttressed.

Flowers. March–April, staminate and pistillate catkins on the same tree; staminate clusters loosely flowered, 3–6 in. long, slender, hairy; calyx yellow, hairy, irregularly lobed, lobes acute; pistillate catkins sessile, or on peduncles ⅛–¾ in., solitary or a few together; peduncles and bracts tomentose; style short, stigmas recurved.

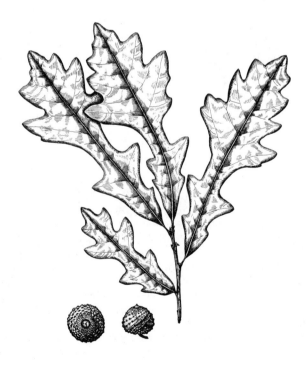

Fruit. Acorn annual, sessile or short-peduncled, solitary or in pairs, ovoid or depressed-globose, base broadly flattened, chestnut brown, ½–1 in. high, about 1 in. broad, nearly or quite covered by the cup; cup hemispheric or spheroid, depressed, ⅗–1⅕ in. broad, ⅖–⅘ in. deep, tomentose, thin, ragged, often splitting at the apex, thicker toward the base; scales reddish brown, ovate, acute, lower coarse and thickened, marginal ones small, thin, and appressed.

Leaves. Alternate, simple, deciduous, thin, obovate-oblong, blades 3–10 in. long, 1–4 in. wide, apex acute to acuminate or rounded, base cuneate or attenuate, margin with lobes very variable, usually 7–9, rounded, acute or acuminate, middle lobes generally broadest, sinuses deep and broadly rounded; upper surface dark green, glabrous and lustrous; lower surface white-tomentose or glabrate later; petioles ⅓–1 in., glabrous or pubescent.

Twigs. Slender, green and pubescent at first, later grayish brown and glabrous; buds about ⅛ in. long, ovoid, obtuse, chestnut brown; stipules deciduous and subulate.

Bark. Gray to brown or reddish, broken into irregular ridges with thin flattened scales.

Wood. Dark brown, sapwood lighter, durable, hard, strong, tough, close-grained, weighing about 51 lb per cu ft.

Range. On wet, poorly drained clay soils. East Texas, Oklahoma, and Arkansas; east to Florida, north to New Jersey, and west to Missouri.

Remarks. The genus name, *Quercus*, is the ancient classical name, and the species name, *lyrata*, refers to the lyrate-pinnatifid leaves. Other vernacular names are Water White Oak, Swamp White Oak, Swamp Post Oak, and White Oak. The wood is used for the same purpose as the true White Oak, *Q. alba*. The trees are slow growing, long-lived, generally free from insects and disease, and resistant to disease. Overcup Oak was first introduced into cultivation about 1786. The young plants are browsed by deer and cattle.

Bur Oak

Quercus macrocarpa Michx. [D, E, F]

Field Identification. Tree to 150 ft, with heavy spreading limbs and a broad crown.

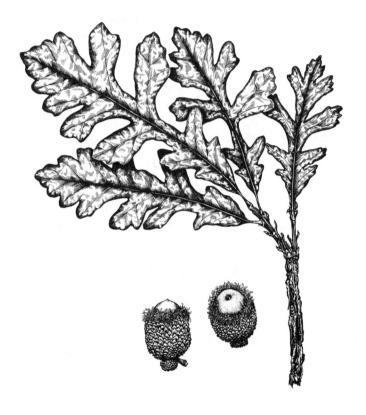

Flowers. Borne in staminate and pistillate catkins; staminate catkins 4–6 in. long, yellowish green; calyx deeply 4–6-lobed, hairy; pistillate flowers sessile or nearly so, solitary or a few together, involucral scales ovate, red, tomentose; stigmas red.

Fruit. Acorn very large, variable in size and shape, sessile or short-stalked, solitary or paired, ¾–2 in. long, ellipsoid to ovoid, apex pubescent; cup subglobose or hemispheric, thick, woody, tomentose, enclosing one-half to three-fourths of nut; scales imbricate, thick, upper scales with awnlike tips to produce a fringed border on the cup, giving a mossy appearance.

Leaves. Simple, alternate, deciduous, obovate-oblong, 5–9-lobed, lobes separated by very deep sinuses; terminal lobe usually largest and obovate with smaller lobes or coarse teeth, apex usually rounded; base cuneate from smaller lobes; blades 6–12 in. long, 3–6 in. wide; dark green, lustrous and glabrous above, paler and pubescent beneath; petioles stout, pubescent, ⅓–1 in.

Twigs. Light brown and pubescent, later becoming dark brown and glabrous, and sometimes with corky ridges; terminal buds reddish brown, pubescent, ovoid, obtuse, about ¼ in. long.

Bark. Light gray, or reddish brown, thick, deeply fissured and broken into irregular narrow flakes.

Wood. Dark or light brown, close-grained, heavy, hard, strong, tough, durable, weighing about 46 lb per cu ft.

Range. Not apparently at home on the Atlantic and Gulf Coast plains, but on higher grounds. Central and east Texas, Oklahoma, Arkansas, and Louisiana; east to Georgia, north to Nova Scotia, and west to Manitoba, Kansas, and Wyoming.

Remarks. The genus name, *Quercus*, is the ancient classical name, and the species name, *macrocarpa*, refers to the large acorn. Vernacular names are Mossycup Oak and Overcup Oak. The wood is similar to that of White Oak and is used for baskets, lumber, ties, fences, cabinets, ships, and fuel. The acorns are greedily eaten by squirrels and white-tailed deer, and young plants are browsed by livestock. A narrow-leaved and small-fruited variety of Bur Oak has been given the name of *Q. macrocarpa* var. *olivaeformis* Gray. A dwarf form of Bur Oak known as Bur Scrub Oak, *Q. macrocarpa* var. *depressa* (Nutt.) Engelm., is found in Minnesota, South Dakota, and Nebraska and has acorn cups about ⅖ in. wide, slightly fringed, innermost scales caudate-attenuate; acorns ovoid, about ⅖ in. long. It is usually 3–8 ft high with corky branches. However, many intermediate forms occur between it and the species.

White Oak

Quercus alba L. [D, E]

Field Identification. Large tree to 150 ft, with a broad open head.

Flowers. Appearing with the leaves April–May, staminate and pistillate on the same tree; staminate catkins solitary, hairy, about 3 in. long; calyx yellow, pubescent, with acute lobes; stamens 6–8; pistillate catkins usually solitary, 2–3-flowered, about ½ in. long, red; involucral scales hairy, ovate; calyx-lobes acute, ovate; styles erect, short.

A form sometimes known as *Q. alba* forma *pinnatifida*

Fruit. Ripening September–October. Acorn sessile or short-stalked, solitary or in pairs; nut ellipsoid-ovoid, light brown, lustrous, ¾–1 in. long, enclosed to one-fourth its length in cup; cup bowl-shaped, scales woody-tuberculate, thickened, somewhat fused, closely appressed, acorn maturing the first season. Minimum commercial seed-bearing age 30 years, optimum 50–100, maximum 150. Good crops about every 3 years, with light crops intervening.

Leaves. Alternate, simple, deciduous, oblong-obovate, 5–9 in. long, 7–11-lobed; lobes oblique, rounded, elongate, the terminal lobe usually shallowed, 3-parted; leaf base cuneate; bright green and glabrous above, paler or glaucous below.

Twigs. Slender, reddish brown to gray, glabrous; terminal buds about ³⁄₁₆ in. long, subglobose, glabrous, brown; leaf scars half-moon–shaped, pith stellate in cross section.

Bark. Light gray, or reddish brown beneath the flat loose ridges, which are separated by shallow fissures.

Wood. Light brown, hard, strong, heavy, close-grained, durable, weighing about 46 lb per cu ft.

Range. On bottom lands, rich uplands, and gravelly ridges. East Texas, Oklahoma, Arkansas, and Louisiana, east to Florida, north to Maine, Ontario, and Minnesota, and west to Nebraska.

Remarks. The genus name, *Quercus*, is the classical name, and the species name, *alba*, refers to the white bark. Vernacular names are Stave Oak, Fork-leaf White Oak, and Ridge White Oak. The wood is used for fuel, ties, baskets, cabinets, barrels, tools, furniture, and construction work. The dried, powdered inner bark of this and other oaks has some medicinal value because of the quercitanic acid it contains. It is used almost solely as an astringent wash, or occasionally as an injection in leucorrhea or hemorrhoids. Indians ground the acorns into meal and poured water through it to leach out the tannin before baking into bread. Squirrel, white-tailed deer, wild turkey, and bobwhite quail eat the acorns, and livestock browse the foliage. White Oak is very desirable for park and street planting and is rather free of insect pests, but is somewhat difficult to transplant. It has been in cultivation since 1724.

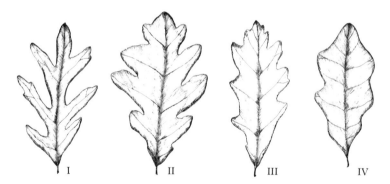

Leaf forms of *Q. alba* L., noted by William Trelease: I, *Q. alba* forma *typica*, is a widely distributed form; II, *Q. alba* forma *latiloba*, has leaves divided usually less than halfway to the midrib into broad rounded lobes and appears to be a common form from east Texas and eastward; III, *Q. alba* forma *sublyrata*, is an intermediate somewhat lyre-shaped form; IV, *Q. alba* forma *repanda*, has leaves with shallow sinuses and acorns usually short-stalked.

Chinquapin Oak

Quercus muhlenbergii Engelm. [D, E, F]

Field Identification. Narrow, round-topped tree rarely over 60 ft.

Flowers. In separate staminate and pistillate catkins on the same tree; staminate catkins 3–4 in. long, hairy; calyx 5–6-lobed, yellow, hairy, ciliate, lanceolate; stamens 4–6, filaments exserted; pistillate catkins sessile, short, tomentose; calyx 5–6-lobed; stigmas red.

Fruit. Acorns mostly solitary or in pairs, sessile or short-peduncled, broadly ovoid, brown, shiny, ½–¾ in. long, enclosed about half its length in the cup; cup thin, bowl-shaped, brown, tomentose; scales of cup appressed, obtuse to acute or cuspidate; kernel sweet, edible.

Leaves. Alternate, simple, deciduous, 4–6 in. long, 1–3½ in. wide, oblong to lanceolate or obovate, acute or acuminate at apex, cuneate to rounded or cordate at base; margin with coarse, large, acute, mucronate, often recurved teeth; dark green, lustrous and glabrous above; paler gray-tomentulose and conspicuously veined beneath; petiole slender, ½–1 in.

Twigs. Slender, hairy or glabrous, reddish brown to gray, terminal buds orange to reddish brown, ovoid, acute.

Bark. Light grayish brown, broken into narrow, loose plates.

Wood. Reddish brown, sapwood lighter, close-grained, durable, hard, heavy, strong, weighing 53 lb per cu ft.

Range. Well-drained uplands. Texas, Louisiana, Oklahoma, and Arkansas; east to Florida, north to Maine, and west to Ontario, Michigan, Wisconsin, and Nebraska. In Mexico in Coahuila and Nuevo León.

Remarks. The genus name, *Quercus*, is the classical name of the oak tree, and the species name, *muhlenbergii*, is in honor of G. H. E. Muhlenberg (1753–1815), botanist and minister in Pennsylvania. Other vernacular names are Pin Oak, Shrub Oak, Scrub Oak, Yellow Oak, Chestnut Oak, Rock Oak, and Chinkapin Oak.

Bray Chinquapin Oak

Chinquapin Oak sprouts from the stump, grows rather rapidly, and is fairly free of insects and disease. The wood is used for posts, ties, cooperage, furniture, and farm implements. Bray Chinquapin Oak, *Q. muhlenbergii* var. *brayi* (Small) Sarg., is somewhat similar and is found on the Edwards Plateau and into west Texas, and south into Mexico. It has nuts sometimes to 1¼ in. long, and deeper cups to 1 in. in diameter. However, these differences are not distinct, and it is now considered by some botanists as only a form instead of a variety.

Dwarf Chinquapin Oak

Quercus prinoides Willd. [D, E]

Field Identification. Slender shrub, or more rarely a small tree to 15 ft, with a trunk diameter of 1–4 in. Usually growing in thicket-forming clumps on rocky hillsides. Closely related to the Chinquapin Oak, *Q. muhlenbergii*, but differing in its shrubby stature, smaller leaves with generally shorter petioles, deeper acorn cups, with thicker scales, and shorter stamens.

Flowers. Borne April–May in separate staminate catkins and pistillate catkins; staminate catkins 1–2½ in. long, pendent, cylindric, loosely and remotely flowered, perianth densely hairy, lobes thin, scarious, ovate to oblong; stamens numerous, exserted, filaments short, anthers large and short-oblong; pistillate flowers solitary or paired, sessile, stigmas yellowish red.

Fruit. Ripening September–October, maturing the first season, often abundant, acorn covered one-half or more by the cup, chestnut brown, ovoid to ellipsoid, apex obtuse or rounded, ⅖–1 in. long; cup sessile or nearly so, hemispheric, thin, deep, ½–¾ in. wide; scales appressed, pale brown, densely hairy, finely tuberculate, triangular-ovate to oblong-lanceolate, apex obtuse to truncate, acorns average about 400 per lb; sweet and edible.

Leaves. Alternate, simple, deciduous, blades 2–6 in. long, width 2–3 in., obovate to oblanceolate or elliptic, apex acute or short-acuminate, base cuneate, margin undulate-serrate; teeth 3–7 to each side, large, short, acute or obtuse; upper surface olive green to bright green, lustrous, glabrous; lower surface much paler, finely gray-pubescent to tomentulose; veins conspicuous and rather straight; petiole slender, channeled, ¼–¾ in., sparsely puberulent or glabrous; leaves brilliant red in autumn.

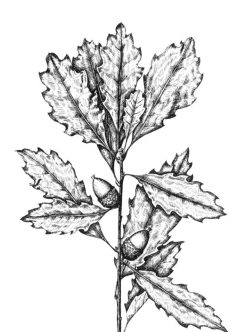

Twigs. Young reddish brown and puberulent to glabrous, older ones gray and glabrous; bark of older limbs and trunk dark brown to gray, broken into flat, scaly, checkered ridges and shallow furrows.

Range. Dwarf Chinquapin Oak is found in sunny sites, often in rocky or acid sandy soil. Northeast Texas, Oklahoma, and Arkansas; east to Alabama, north to Vermont, and west to Minnesota and Kansas.

Remarks. The genus name, *Quercus*, is the ancient classical name. The species name, *prinoides*, refers to its resemblance, especially in the leaves, to *Q. prinus*. It also has the vernacular names of Scrub Chestnut Oak, Dwarf Chestnut Oak, Running White Oak, and Chinquapin Oak. It was introduced into cultivation about 1730. The acorn is known to be eaten by a number of species of birds and mammals, including the gray squirrel and ruffed grouse, and the foliage is browsed by cottontail.

Post Oak

Quercus stellata Wangh. [D, E, F]

Field Identification. Shrub or tree to 75 ft, with stout limbs and a dense rounded head.

Flowers. Appearing with the leaves March–May, borne on the same tree in separate catkins; staminate in pendent catkins 2–4 in. long; calyx yellow, hairy, 5-lobed; lobes acute, laciniately segmented; stamens 4–6, anthers hairy; pistillate catkins short-stalked or sessile, inconspicuous; scales of involucre broadly ovate and hairy; stigmas red, short, enlarged.

Fruit. Ripening September–November. Acorns maturing the first season, sessile or short-stalked, borne solitary, in pairs, or clustered; acorn oval or ovoid-oblong, broad at base, ½–¾ in. long, striate, set in cup one-third to one-half its length; cup bowl-shaped, pale and often pubescent within, hoary-tomentose externally; scales of cup reddish brown, rounded or acute at apex, closely appressed.

Leaves. Simple, alternate, deciduous, oblong-obovate, blades 4–7 in. long, 3–4 in. wide, 5-lobed with deep rounded sinuses; lobes usually short and wide, obtuse or truncate at apex; middle lobes almost square and opposite giving a crosslike appearance to the leaf; terminal lobe often 1–3-notched; base of leaf cuneate or rounded; dark green, rough and glabrous above, paler and tomentose beneath; leathery and thick; petioles short, usually ½–1 in., pubescent.

Twigs. Brown, stout, pubescent to tomentulose, or becoming glabrous later; buds ¹⁄₁₆–⅛ in. long, subglobose, brown.

Bark. Gray to reddish brown, thick, divided into irregular fissures with platelike scales.

Wood. Light to dark brown, durable, heavy, hard, close-grained, difficult to cure, weighing about 52 lb per cu ft.

Range. Post Oak is distributed in the Edwards Plateau of Texas, adjacent Oklahoma, and Arkansas; east to Florida, north to New England, and west to Iowa and Kansas.

Remarks. The genus name, *Quercus*, is the classical name; the species name, *stellata*, refers to the stellate hairs of the leaves and petioles. Vernacular names are Iron Oak, Cross Oak, Branch Oak, Rough Oak, and Box Oak. The wood is used for railroad crossties, fuel, fence posts, furniture, and lumber; the acorns are eaten by deer, javelina, and wild turkey.

Sand Post Oak

Quercus margaretta Ashe [D, E, F, G]

Field Identification. A low, branched shrub 4–10 ft high, forming thickets in sand by means of stolons, or in other instances assuming the form of a tree to 40 ft tall. The bark light gray, thick, rough, and furrowed.

Flowers. The staminate in aments 3–4 in. long; calyx hirsute, yellowish, with 5 segments laciniately cut. Pistillate catkins sessile or short-peduncled; scales of the involucre broadly ovate, hirsute; stigmas red.

Fruit. Annual, solitary or paired, short-peduncled or sessile; acorns about one-half included in cup; ⅓–⅝ in. long; ⅓–½ in. broad, shape ovoid, color light brown, glabrous. Acorn cups ½–¾ in. broad; ¹⁄₆–⅖ in. deep, shallowly to deeply cup-shaped, with the bases rounded; scales of cup oblong to ovate to obovate; apices narrowed and loosely appressed, densely short-pubescent.

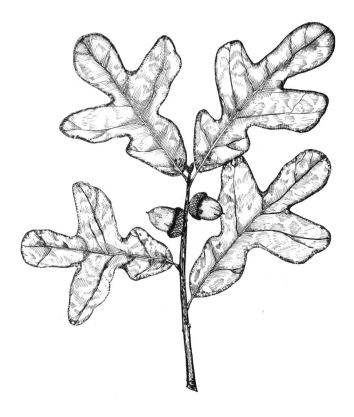

Leaves. Simple, alternate, deciduous; membranous or thickened; length 2–5¾ in.; width 1¼–4 in.; shape obovate to oblong or elliptic; apices broadly rounded; bases rounded to cuneate; margins 2–3-lobed on each side; sinuses broad or narrowed, but rounded at the bottom; lobes truncate or rounded (sometimes on same branch or tree), simple or obscurely toothed or undulate with revolute margins; upper surface glabrate or with scattered stellate hairs, shiny green; lower surface more or less densely stellate-tomentose, with age remaining pubescent or later glabrate or some slightly glaucous. Petioles ⅛–⅗ in. long, tomentose or glabrate later.

Twigs. Grooved, ¹⁄₁₅–¹⁄₁₀ in. thick, dull brown and glabrous, or when young stellate with scattered hairs; lenticels small; buds ovoid, acute, ⅛–¼ in. long; ¹⁄₁₂ in. broad; scales closely imbricated, color reddish brown, at first pubescent but later glabrate;

margins sometimes ciliate; stipules about ⅕ in. long, subulate, pubescent, soon caducous.

Range. Said to be the common Post Oak of the south Atlantic and Gulf states. In sandy soils of eastern and central Texas, western Louisiana (Natchitoches and Caddo Parishes), Mississippi, Alabama, Georgia, Florida; northward to Virginia, Oklahoma, and Arkansas.

Remarks. The genus name, *Quercus*, is an ancient name. The species name, *margaretta*, is for Margaret Henry Wilcox, the late Mrs. W. W. Ashe. In some areas the dominant form is a stoloniferous shrub, known as *Q. stellata* var. *margaretta* Sarg.; in others it is a small tree. On the areas of contact, hybrids of *Q. margaretta* and *Q. stellata* are found with intermediate characteristics.

Limestone Durand Oak

Quercus sinuata var. *breviloba* (Torr.) C. H. Mull. [D, E, F, G]

Field Identification. Straggling shrubs or small trees with gray flaking bark. This variety has been long listed under the name of *Q. durandii* var. *breviloba* (Torr.) Palmer, but it has been determined that the name of *Q. sinuata* var. *breviloba* (Torr.) C. H. Mull. has precedence. Reference is made to Muller, *The Oaks of Texas*, p. 66.

Flowers. Staminate catkins to 3¼ in. long, finely rather loosely flowered, tomentulose, the anthers moderately or only slightly exserted; pistillate catkins ⅛–⅓ in. long, 1–3-flowered, densely short-tomentose.

Fruit. Acorn annual, solitary or paired, subsessile or on a pubescent peduncle to ⅓ in. long; acorn cups to ½ in. long and ⅓ in. high, goblet-shaped or shallowly cup-shaped, base rounded or constricted; margins thin, smooth, simple; cup scales ovate, obtuse, the tomentose bases slightly or sharply keeled and thickened, the puberulent apices thin, closely appressed, dark reddish brown. Acorns to ⅝ in. long and ⅜ in. broad, ovoid to elliptic, glabrous, light brown, one-fourth enclosed in the cup.

Leaves. Simple, alternate, deciduous; texture thin to firm; to 3¼ in. long and 1½ in. broad, or often smaller; shape obovate to oblanceolate or oblong, usually broadest above the middle; apices broadly rounded; bases cuneate or obtuse or some gradually nar-

rowed; margin entire to irregularly toothed or moderately lobed;
upper surface glabrous and lustrous; lower surfaces duller, canescent with appressed, minute, stellate puberulence, or in shade
forms green and only slightly puberulent or glabrous. Petioles
1/12–1/8 in. long, glabrous or pubescent like the twigs.

Twigs. Subterete or channeled, to 1/8 in. thick; color grayish
brown, glabrous or minutely stellate-tomentulose; lenticels minute; buds 1/12–1/8 in. long, broadly ovoid, obtuse or acute, glabrous
or sparsely pubescent, dark reddish brown or grayish brown; stipules rather promptly caducous, 1/8–1/5 in. long, filiform-ligulate,
pubescent.

Range. Wooded limestone hills of central Texas and northeast
Mexico. The related species *Q. sinuata* Walt. occurs in moist
river bottoms of south and east Texas.

Remarks. The genus name, *Quercus*, is the ancient classical
name. The species name, *sinuata*, refers to the sinuate leaf margins, and the variety name, *breviloba*, to the short leaf lobes.

Other names which have been used are *Q. breviloba* (Torr.) Sarg., *Q. obtusifolia* var. *breviloba* Torr., *Q. annulata* Buckl., *Q. sansabeana* Buckl., *Q. brevilobata* Sarg., and *Q. breviloba* forma *argentata* Trel.

Mohr Oak

Quercus mohriana Buckl. [F, G]

Field Identification. Usually a thicket-forming shrub, but sometimes a small, round-topped tree to 20 ft.

Flowers. Borne in separate staminate and pistillate catkins; staminate catkins ¾–1½ in. long, loosely flowered, from sparsely to densely hairy, anthers barely exserted, red; calyx hairy, divided into ovate lobes; pistillate catkins 1–3-flowered toward the apex, hairy, ¹⁄₁₂–⅓ in.; calyx-lobes and bracts hairy.

Fruit. Acorns borne annually, solitary or 2–3, sessile, or on densely pubescent peduncles ¼–¾ in. (usually about ⅜ in.); ovoid to ellipsoid or oblong; apex abruptly rounded and apiculate; young acorns with fascicled hairs, older ones brown and lustrous; length ⅓–⅗ in., width ¼–⅓ in., enclosed one-half to two-thirds of length in cup; cup turbinate or cup-shaped, ⅕–½ in. high and ⅓–¾ in. broad, color reddish brown and tomentose; margin thin and smooth; base flattened or rounded; scales closely appressed, ovate to oblong, thickened and more tomentose toward the cup base; smaller, thinner, and more glabrous toward the cup rim; apices elongate, obtuse or acute.

Leaves. Alternate, persistent, coriaceous, oblong to elliptic to lanceolate or obovate; margin entire, or with a few, large, coarse, apiculate teeth, sometimes with a few rounded lobes, the plane surface of the margin either undulate or flattened and slightly revolute; apex acute, rounded or acuminate; base rounded or cuneate, sometimes unequal-sided; upper surface usually dark green and shiny, sparsely and minutely stellate-pubescent; lower surface usually densely gray or white-tomentose; blade length ¾–4 in., width ½–1½ in.; petiole ¹⁄₁₂–¼ in., tomentose; stipules caducous, subulate, about ⅛ in. long.

Twigs. Young parts brownish gray, tomentose, and fluted; older ones gray, smooth, and glabrous; buds reddish brown, smooth, or pubescent.

Bark. Grayish brown, thin, pale, deeply furrowed.

Range. In dry, well-drained, preferably limestone soils of the West. In west-Central Texas, southwestern Oklahoma, and Coahuila, Mexico.

Remarks. The genus name, *Quercus*, is the classical name, and the species name, *mohriana*, refers to Charles Mohr (1824–1901), German-born druggist and botanist of Alabama. Vernacular names are Scrub Oak, Shin Oak, and Limestone Oak. Mohr Oak is known to hybridize with Post Oak, Havard Oak, and Gray Oak where the contact is made. Gray Oak and Mohr Oak, especially, produce a very varied assemblage of hybrid forms. The wood of Mohr Oak, or its hybrids, has little value except as fuel or posts.

Havard Shin Oak

Quercus havardii Rydb. [E, F, G]

Field Identification. Low shrubs, hardly over 3 ft, forming thickets by underground rhizomes in deep sands. Rarely a small tree.

Flowers. Borne in separate staminate and pistillate catkins; staminate catkins pubescent, heavily flowered, ½–1½ in.; anthers pubescent, moderately exserted; pistillate catkins, ⅛–⅓ in., 1–5-flowered toward the apex.

Fruit. Acorn rather large, annual, very variable in size and shape, solitary or 2–3 in a cluster, sessile or short-peduncled, enclosed one-third to two-thirds in the cup, length ½–1 in., ½–¾ in. wide, ovoid to short-oblong, color chestnut brown, lustrous and glabrous or slightly glaucescent; cup deeply bowl-shaped to goblet-shaped, very variable in size, ½–1 in. broad and ⅖–½ in. high, base mostly rounded, margins either thin or thick; scales reddish brown, pubescent, ovate-oblong, apex long-acuminate, blunt, thinner than the base.

Leaves. Alternate, deciduous, leathery, very variable in size and shape, blades ¾–4 in. long, ¾–1½ in. wide, oblong, elliptic, lanceolate, or oblanceolate, ovate or obovate; margin entire or variously undulate, coarsely toothed or lobed, sometimes margins falcate or asymmetrical, revolute or flattened; apices broadly rounded to obtuse or acute; base cuneate or rounded; upper surface bright green, lustrous, glabrous or with minute fascicled hairs; lower surface densely brown to gray-tomentose; petioles ¹⁄₁₂–¼ in., pubescent, about ⅕ in. long.

Twigs. Rounded or sulcate, young ones densely brownish yellow-tomentose, older twigs gray to reddish brown, glabrous or nearly so. Bark gray, smooth or scaly.

Range. Across the sandy plains of the lower Texas Panhandle area into eastern New Mexico.

Remarks. The genus name, *Quercus*, is the ancient name. The species name, *havardii*, honors the botanist Valery Havard (1846–1927). Vernacular names are Shinnery Oak, Sand Oak, Panhandle Shinnery, and Sand Scrub. Also known to hybridize with Mohr Oak and with Post Oak on the eastern contact of the species. The acorns and leaves of these hybrids vary greatly in size and shape. The acorn of Havard Oak has some value to wildlife, being eaten by peccary, prairie chicken, and bobwhite. It is reported to cause some stock poisoning.

Gray Oak

Quercus grisea Liebm. [F, G]

Field Identification. Sometimes only a shrub on exposed mountain slopes, or becoming a tree to 65 ft in alluvial canyons.

Flowers. Monoecious, staminate catkins ⅔–1½ in., or rarely longer, hairy or tomentose; anthers exserted, glabrous; pistillate catkins tomentose, ⅕–1⅗ in., 1–6-flowered.

Fruit. Acorn borne annually, sessile, or peduncle to 1⅓ in. long, solitary or paired, ½–¾ in. long, ⅓–½ in. high, ellipsoid to ovoid, light brown, glabrous or puberulent, one-third to one-half included in cup; cup ⅓–½ in. broad, ⅙–⅖ in. high, cup-shaped or goblet-shaped; scales appressed, reddish brown, ovate to oblong, acute, pubescent to tomentose.

Leaves. Grayish green, entire or toothed, variable in size and toothing, thick and leathery, blades ¾–3 in. long, ⅓–1½ in.

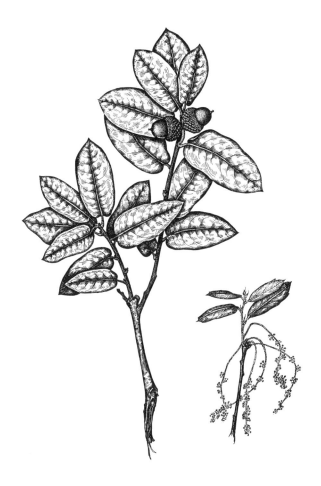

broad, ovate, oblong, or elliptic; apex acute, obtuse or rounded, mucronulate; base rounded or cordate; margin entire or with small mucronate-tipped teeth; upper surface dull grayish green, minutely stellate-pubescent; lower surface stellate-pubescent or tomentulose and conspicuously veined; petioles $\frac{1}{12}$–$\frac{2}{5}$ in., tomentose.

Twigs. Slender, grayish brown, all parts (leaves, petioles, and twigs) with a dense grayish green to buff tomentum; stipules filiform, persistent; buds small, reddish.

Bark. Dark gray, with narrow ridges and rather straight furrows.

Range. Over wide areas in the Trans-Pecos region of Texas at altitudes to 7,800 ft, also in southern New Mexico, and less abundant in Arizona. Southward it occurs in Chihuahua and Coahuila, Mexico.

Remarks. The genus name, *Quercus*, is the classical name, and the species name, *grisea*, refers to the gray appearance of the leaves. Vernacular names are Shin Oak, Scrub Oak, Encina, Prieta, and Encina Blanca. The wood is used for fuel and posts, and the leaves are browsed by livestock, deer, and porcupine. Many species of ground squirrels feed on the nut, also some birds, including Viosca's pigeon and the thick-billed parrot.

Live Oak

Quercus virginiana Mill. [D]

Field Identification. Evergreen tree to 60 ft, with a wide-spreading crown and massive limbs close to the ground.

Flowers. Staminate and pistillate borne in separate catkins on same tree; staminate catkins hairy, 2–3 in. long; calyx yellow, with 4–7 ovate lobes; stamens 6–12, filaments short, anthers hairy; pistillate catkins fewer, on pubescent peduncles ⅓ in. long; scales and calyx-lobes hairy; stigmas 3, red.

Fruit. Acorn on peduncles ¼–4 in. long, in clusters of 3–5; nut ellipsoid-obovoid, brownish black, shiny, ⅓–½ in. long; enclosed about one-half its length in the cup; cup turbinate, light reddish brown, hoary-tomentose; scales of cup ovate, acute, thin, appressed.

Leaves. Simple, alternate, persistent, coriaceous, dark green and lustrous above, paler and glabrous to pubescent beneath; very variable in size and shape, 2–5 in. long, ½–2½ in. wide, oblong or elliptic or obovate; apex rounded or acute, base cuneate, rounded or cordate, margin entire and often revolute, sometimes sharp-dentate, especially toward the apex; petioles about ¼ in. long, stout, glabrous or puberulent.

Twigs. Grayish brown, glabrous, slender, rigid; terminal buds ovate to subglobose, about ⅙ in. long, light brown; leaf scars half-moon–shaped.

Bark. Dark brown to black (in some varieties gray), furrows narrow and interlacing, scales closely appressed, small.

Wood. Light brown, sapwood lighter, close-grained, tough, hard, strong, heavy, weighing about 59 lb per cu ft, difficult to work.

Range. This species is usually found in sandy-loam soils but may also occur in heavier clays. In Texas, Oklahoma, and Louisiana. In Louisiana it reaches its largest size in the vicinity of New Orleans and the lower delta area. It extends eastward to Florida and north to Virginia.

Remarks. The genus name, *Quercus*, is the classical name, and the species name, *virginiana*, refers to the state of Virginia. The wood is used for hubs, cogs, shipbuilding, or any other purpose where a hard and strong wood is required. The tree is often planted in the southern states for ornament along avenues. It is comparatively free of insect pests and diseases and can stand considerable salinity, often growing close to the sea. The bark was formerly much used in the production of tannin, and acorn oil was much used in cooking by the Indians. Live Oak seems to be susceptible to soil types, and produces dwarf varieties and diverse leaf forms under certain conditions. The fruit seems to vary least in the varieties.

Scrub Live Oak

Quercus fusiformis Small [D, E, F, G]

Field Identification. A shrub or tree to 36 ft tall. Very similar in habit to *Q. virginiana* Mill., and, although it appears distinct in the western part of its distribution (beyond the Edwards Plateau

area and into Mexico), on its eastern range it seems to pass into this species with many intermediary variants.

Flowers. Similar to that of *Q. virginiana* Mill.

Fruit. Borne on peduncles ¾–2⅓ in. long, solitary or several together. The cups much constricted basally and flaring upward. Acorn elongate, fusiform or subfusiform, brown, shiny.

Leaves. Simple, alternate, evergreen; length ¾–2⅓ in. or more; width ⅓–1¼ in.; shape narrowly oblong; margins entire or toothed and strongly revolute.

Range. Limestone outcrops on the coastal plain uplands, abundant on the limestone hills west to the Pecos River and south along the east face of the mountains through Coahuila, Nuevo León, and Tamaulipas. The type from Kerr County, Texas.

Remarks. The genus name, *Quercus*, is the ancient Latin name. The species name, *fusiformis*, refers to the shape of the acorn. Some authors prefer to maintain it as a variety under the name of *Q. virginiana* var. *fusiformis* (Small) Sarg.

Willow Oak

Quercus phellos L. [D, E]

Field Identification. Tree to 130 ft, and 6 ft in diameter, with a rounded or broad-oblong crown.

Flowers. Borne in spring in separate staminate and pistillate catkins; moderately close-flowered, hairy, yellowish green, with 4–5 acute calyx-lobes, anthers oval and exserted; pistillate flowers usually solitary, occasionally in pairs; glabrous peduncles ¹⁄₂₅–⅛ in. long, 1–3-flowered; scales and calyx hairy; stigmas red, slender, recurved.

Fruit. Maturing in 2 years, solitary or in pairs, sessile, or on short peduncles to ⅕ in. long; acorn subglobose to ovoid, ⅖–⅗ in. long, nearly as broad as long, densely puberulent or glabrate later, yellowish to dull brown, sometimes striate, about one-fourth of base enclosed in cup; cup ⅖–⅗ in. broad, ⅙–⅓ in. high, saucershaped, shallow, margin not inrolled, enveloping only the base of the acorn; scales closely appressed, imbricate, small, thin, ovate, greenish brown, finely tomentose. Acorns averaging about 600 per lb.

Leaves. Revolute in the bud, alternate, simple, deciduous, linear-lanceolate to elliptic, entire on margin, apex acute and bristle-tipped, base cuneate or narrowly rounded; light to dark green and glabrous above, or slightly pubescent on the midrib; lower surface paler and glabrous or pubescent along the midrib, blade length 2–5 in., width ⅓–1 in.; petioles stout, ¹⁄₂₅–¼ in. long, tomentose at first and glabrate later.

Twigs. Reddish brown and pubescent at first, gray and glabrous later, slender, fluted; buds brown, ovoid to lanceolate, apex acute,

$\frac{1}{12}$–$\frac{1}{6}$ in. long, scales mostly glabrous and ciliate; stipules caducous, $\frac{1}{4}$–$\frac{1}{3}$ in. long, filiform, villous.

Wood. Light brown, close-grained, soft, moderately strong, not durable, weighing 46 lb per cu ft, of rather low quality in comparison with that of other oaks.

Range. Willow Oak grows usually on rich, wet bottom lands of clays or loams. Eastern Texas, Oklahoma, Arkansas, and Louisiana; eastward to Florida, north to New York, and west to Illinois.

Remarks. The genus name, *Quercus*, is the classical Latin name of the oaks, and the species name, *phellos* ("cork"), is the ancient Greek name of *Q. suber* L., Cork Oak. Other local names are Water Oak, Peach Oak, Sandjack Oak, Red Oak, Swamp Oak, Swamp Willow Oak, and Pin Oak. Willow Oak is often called Pin Oak in many sections of the South, but that name should apply to the true Pin Oak, *Q. palustris* Muenchh. The author has never seen the true Pin Oak in Texas outside of cultivation. However, there is a remote possibility that the true Pin Oak may extend far enough southward to reach into the northeastern corner of the state. Other oaks which are apt to be confused with the Willow Oak are Laurel Oak, Bluejack Oak, Water Oak, and Diamond-leaf Oak. Willow Oak makes an exceedingly handsome ornamental tree and has been cultivated since 1723. The wood is somewhat inferior to that of other commercial oaks but is used for fuel, charcoal, ties, shingles, sills, planks, and general construction. The acorns are eaten by wild turkey, bobwhite quail, dove, jay, gray fox, and squirrel.

Bluejack Oak

Quercus incana Bartr. [D]

Field Identification. Shrub or tree to 35 ft, with stout crooked branches.

Flowers. In spring, in staminate and pistillate catkins; staminate catkins clustered, 2–3 in. long, hairy; calyx-lobes 4–5 in. ovate, acute, red to yellowish green; stamens 4–5, yellow; anthers apiculate; pistillate catkins on stout, tomentose, short peduncles; scales and calyx-lobes of pistillate flowers tomentose, stigmas dark red.

Fruit. Maturing the second season, sessile or short-stalked, globose to ovoid, sometimes flattened, brown with grayish pubescence,

often striate, about ½ in. long, set in a shallow cup one-third to one-half its length, kernel bitter; cup shallow, saucer-shaped; scales imbricate, thin, ovate, tomentose, reddish brown.

Leaves. Alternate, simple, deciduous, entire (or rarely 3-dentate at the apex), oblong-lanceolate to elliptic, distinctly grayish green, densely tomentose beneath, smoother above, cuneate or rounded at base, acute or rounded at the apex, apiculate, 2–5 in. long, ½–1½ in. wide; petiole ¼–½ in. long, stout.

Twigs. Gray to dark brown, slender, smooth.

Bark. Grayish brown to black, broken into small blocklike plates.

Wood. Reddish brown, close-grained, hard, strong.

Range. Usually in dry sandy pinelands of east Texas, Louisiana, Oklahoma, and Arkansas; north and east to North Carolina and Virginia.

Remarks. The genus name, *Quercus*, is the ancient classical name, and the species name, *incana*, refers to the grayish green tomentum of the leaves. Vernacular names are Upland Willow

Oak, High-ground Willow Oak, Sandjack Oak, Turkey Oak, and Cinnamon Oak. The trunk is generally too small to be of much value except for fuel or posts.

Laurel Oak

Quercus laurifolia Michx. [D, E]

Field Identification. Dense, round-topped tree attaining a height of 100 ft.

Flowers. Staminate and pistillate catkins borne separately on same tree in spring. Staminate catkins clustered, red, hairy, 2–3 in. long; calyx 4-lobed, pubescent; pistillate catkins short-stalked with brown-hairy involucral scales; calyx-lobes acute; stigmas red with short spreading styles.

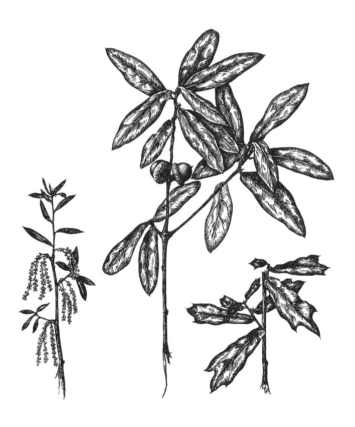

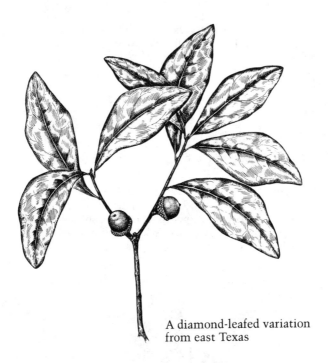

A diamond-leafed variation
from east Texas

Fruit. Acorn usually solitary, sessile or subsessile, ovoid to hemispheric, dark brown, about ½ in. long, enclosed about one-fourth
its length in the cup; cup thin, saucer-shaped, reddish brown,
with appressed ovate scales.

Leaves. Alternate, simple, deciduous in the North, half-evergreen
in the South, elliptic or oblong or occasionally obovate and lobed,
sometimes falcate; leaves on young shoots or young plants often
variously cut and lobed. Apex acute and apiculate, base narrowed,
deep shiny green and glabrous above, paler and lustrous beneath,
blades 2–6 in. long, ½–1 in. wide; petioles yellow, stout, rarely
more than ¼ in. long.

Twigs. Reddish brown to gray, glabrous, slender.

Bark. When young nearly smooth, dark brown tinged with red,
when older dark gray to black, furrows separated by flat ridges.

Wood. Reddish brown, coarse-grained, heavy, hard, strong, weighing 48 lb per cu ft, warps easily.

Range. In low grounds, eastern and coastal Texas and Louisiana; east to Florida and north to South Carolina and Virginia.

Remarks. The genus name, *Quercus*, is the classical name of the oak tree, and the species name, *laurifolia*, refers to the laurellike foliage. Vernacular names are Water Oak, Willow Oak, and Live Oak. The tree is often cultivated for ornament in the South. The wood is mostly used for fuel and charcoal.

Laurel Oak forms part of a very complex group including the Willow Oak, Water Oak, and Diamond-leaf Oak. There is considerable variation and hybridization. Botanical authors do not agree as to the exact relationship of these species. For example, the Diamond-leaf Oak, *Q. obtusa* (Willd.) Ashe, is now considered to be a broadleaf form of Laurel Oak (*Q. laurifolia* Michx.) with the leaves typically broadest across the middle (diamond-leaf) or with margins entire or slightly wavy (or short-lobed on young leaves); apex acute to rounded and apiculate and a cuneate base. Also, there is considerable diversity of opinion between the names of *Q. laurifolia* Michx. and *Q. hemisphaerica* Bartr.

Water Oak

Quercus nigra L. [D, E]

Field Identification. Tree attaining a height of 80 ft, with a round top and grayish black bark. Leaves variously shaped, wedge-shaped and entire at the apex, or 3-lobed at apex, or variously cut into oblique bristle-tipped lobes.

Flowers. Appearing with the leaves in spring in separate staminate and pistillate catkins; staminate catkins clustered, 2–3 in. long; calyx 4–5-lobed, pubescent; pistillate catkins short-peduncled, scales rusty-hairy; stigmas red.

Fruit. Ripening September–October. Acorn sessile or short-peduncled, solitary or paired, globose-ovoid, 1/3–2/3 in. high, light yellowish brown, often striate, usually somewhat pubescent, flat at base, enveloped in cup one-third to one-half its length; cup shallow, saucer-shaped, thin, reddish brown, pubescent; scales small, thin, closely appressed, imbricate.

Leaves. Simple, alternate, persistent, variously shaped; typically entire, obovate or spatulate; with a rounded or 3-lobed apex; margins on some leaves often with deep, oblique, bristle-tipped lobes,

a variety of shapes frequently appearing on the same twig or on different twigs; blades 2–4 in. long, 1–2 in. wide, upper surface lustrous green and glabrous, lower surface lighter and glabrous, or pubescent in vein axils; petioles short and stout. Leaves half-evergreen in the southern Gulf Coast area.

Twigs. Slender, glabrous, reddish gray; buds ovoid, acute, angled, reddish brown, ⅛–¼ in. long.

Bark. Grayish black to light brown, bark so tightly appressed as to appear almost smooth, ridges flattened and thin.

Wood. Light brown, sapwood lighter, close-grained, heavy, hard, strong.

Range. In low woods, or borders of streams or swamps. From the Colorado River of Texas eastward through Louisiana to Florida, northward into Oklahoma, Arkansas, and Missouri, and on the Atlantic Coastal Plain to New Jersey.

Remarks. The genus name, *Quercus*, is the classical name, and the species name, *nigra*, refers to the black bark. Vernacular names are Bluejack Oak, Duck Oak, Pin Oak, Spotted Oak, Barren Oak, Punk Oak, and Possum Oak. The wood is used for fuel, crossties, and poles. Water Oak is extensively planted as a street shade tree in the South and is subject to attack by mistletoe. Trident Water Oak, *Q. nigra* var. *tridentifera* Sarg., is a variety described as having leaves more acute at the apex, but this character does not appear to be constant, and it has been relegated to the status of a synonym of Water Oak.

Blackjack Oak

Quercus marilandica Muenchh. [D, E, F]

Field Identification. Shrub, or round-topped symmetrical tree attaining a height of 60 ft and a diameter of 2 ft.

Flowers. With the leaves in spring, in staminate or pistillate catkins; staminate catkins clustered, loosely flowered, slender, hairy, yellowish green, 2–4 in. long; stamens 3–12, filaments filiform, anthers exserted; calyx thin, pubescent, reddish green,

4–5-lobed; pistillate flowers solitary or paired, ⅛–⅕ in. long, pubescent to glabrate, peduncles rusty-tomentose and short; styles recurved, stigmas red.

Fruit. Acorn ripening in 2 years, solitary or in pairs, sessile or on peduncles ⅛–⅖ in. long; light brown, enclosed one-third to two-thirds in cup, ⅗–⅘ in. long, ½–¾ in. high, often striate, ovoid-oblong to subglobose, pubescent; cup thick, turbinate, ⅗–⅘ in. broad, bases rounded or suddenly constricted; scales of cup imbricate, loose, obtuse, ovate to oblong, thin.

Leaves. Simple, alternate, deciduous, stiff, coriaceous, broadly obovate to clavate, margin revolute; apex 3-lobed to entire or dentate, bristle-tipped, base rounded, cordate or cuneate; upper surface dark green, glossy and glabrous (or young leaves tomentose and hairy along the veins); lower surface semiglabrate or scurfy and yellow-hairy, veins conspicuous, length 3–7 in., width 2–5 in.; petioles ½–¾ in., stout, glabrous or pubescent; stipules caducous, ¼–⅓ in., glabrous or pubescent.

Twigs. Grayish brown, stout, stiff, densely tomentose at first, glabrous later; buds ⅙–⅓ in. long, ovoid to lanceolate, apex acute, reddish brown, slightly or densely tomentose.

Bark. Dark brown or black, broken into rough, blocklike plates.

Wood. Dark brown, sapwood lighter, heavy, hard, strong, weighing 46 lb per cu ft.

Range. Usually on dry, sandy, sterile soils. Central Texas, Oklahoma, and Arkansas; eastward through Louisiana to Florida, north to New York, and west to Minnesota, Michigan, Illinois, and Kansas.

Remarks. The genus name, *Quercus*, is of classical origin, and the species name, *marilandica*, refers to the state of Maryland. Also known by the vernacular names of Iron Oak, Black Oak, Jack Oak, Barren Oak, and Scrub Oak. The wood is used mostly for posts, fuel, and charcoal, and the acorns are sought by wild turkey and white-tailed deer.

Pin Oak

Quercus palustris Muenchh. [D]

Field Identification. Beautiful tree attaining a height of 120 ft, with a diameter of 5 ft. The crown oblong or broadly pyramidal. Branches numerous and spreading, the lower often pendulous.

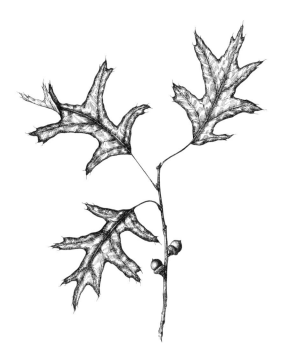

The short tough branchlets from the trunk produce a "pinlike" appearance in winter.

Flowers. Borne April–May, in separate staminate and pistillate catkins; staminate catkins slender, pubescent, 2–3 in. long, calyx-lobes 4–5, oblong, rounded at apex, denticulate on margin, shorter than the stamens, stamens exserted; pistillate flowers 1–3, on slender tomentose peduncles, scales of involucre ovate, tomentose, shorter than the acuminate calyx-lobes, styles slender, spreading, stigmas red.

Fruit. September–October, biennial, solitary or clustered, sessile or on stalks ⅖–⅗ in.; nut hemispheric or subglobose, about ½ in. in diameter, light brown, often striate, bitter, enclosed only at the base in a shallow, saucer-shaped cup; cup ⅓–½ in. broad, thin, reddish brown, scales closely appressed, ovate, acute or obtuse, puberulous, margins darker.

Leaves. Simple, alternate, deciduous, 4–6 in. long, 2–5 in. wide, 5–9-lobed, lobes with rounded sinuses cut two-thirds or more to the midrib, lobes oblong to lanceolate or triangular with apices 2–4-toothed and bristle-tipped; general shape of leaf ovate, to obovate to broadly oblong; apex acute to acuminate; base truncate to broadly cuneate; thin and firm; upper surface dark green and lustrous; lower surface paler and glabrous except for axillary tufts of hairs, scarlet in autumn; petioles slender, yellow, puberulent to glabrous, ⅝–2½ in. long.

Twigs. At first slender, tough, puberulent, green to reddish brown or orange; later brown to gray and glabrous. Older dead twigs tardily deciduous and resembling pins thrust into the tree, hence the name of Pin Oak. The twigs are subject to the attack of gall-producing insects. The small buds are about ⅛ in. long, ovoid, and reddish brown.

Bark. On young trunks and branches light brown, smooth and lustrous, later brownish gray and slightly roughened by shallow fissures and small, closely appressed scales.

Wood. Light brown, coarse-grained, heavy, hard, strong, often knotty owing to persistence of many small limbs, weighing 43 lb per cu ft.

Range. Deep rich soil of bottom lands. Oklahoma, Arkansas, and Mississippi; east through Tennessee and Kentucky to Delaware, north to Massachusetts, and west to Ontario, Wisconsin, Iowa, and Kansas.

Remarks. The genus name, *Quercus*, is an ancient classical name, and the species name, *palustris*, means "of low grounds," referring to the tree's habitat. Vernacular names are Swamp Spanish Oak, Swamp Oak, and Spanish Oak. The wood of Pin Oak is used for fuel, interior finish, crossties, construction, shingles, clapboards, and cooperage. It is similar to Northern Red Oak but inferior to it. The wood was formerly much used as wooden pins to hold together squared timbers. The trees are generally free of insects and disease.

Pin Oak is used extensively for street and yard planting in the northeastern states and in Europe, and was first cultivated in 1770. Its rapid growth, slender form, and often pendulous branches make it highly desirable. It apparently can also stand considerable amounts of dust and smoke, and it coppices fairly well. The acorns average about 400 per lb and direct seeding in spring is better than nursery planting. They should be stratified over the winter but not permitted to dry out. Storing in a cool humid place is necessary. They may be planted in rows about 12 in. apart and ½–1 in. deep. The average germination is 68 percent.

Fall beds should have a mulch of straw or leaves for protection and also be covered with hardware-cloth as a protection against rodents.

Southern Red Oak

Quercus falcata Michx. [D, E]

Field Identification. An open, rounded tree, forming a broad top and attaining a height of 80 ft. Leaves very variable, 3–7-lobed (or 5–13 lobes in some varieties), lobes often falcate, brownish white-tomentose beneath.

Flowers. March–May, staminate and pistillate catkins borne separately on same tree; staminate catkins clustered, tomentose, 3–5 in. long; calyx-lobes 4–5, round, thin, hairy; pistillate flowers

solitary or several together, borne on downy peduncles; scales of involucre with reddish tomentum; calyx-lobes acute.

Fruit. Solitary or in pairs, sessile or short-peduncled, small, globular or hemispheric, orange-brown; often striate, pubescent, about ½ in. long, enclosed to one-third its length in the shallow, saucer-shaped, thin cup; cup scales reddish, pubescent, ovate-oblong, acute or rounded at apex; matures during the second season.

Leaves. Simple, alternate, deciduous, very variable in shape and lobing, ovate-oblong to obovate, with usually 3–7 bristle-tipped lobes (usually 3-lobed in the variety *triloba*, but numerous lobes in the varieties *pagodaefolia* and *leucophylla*); lobes often falcate, slender, narrowed, rounded or cuneate at the base; dark green and lustrous above, paler with brown to grayish white tomentum beneath; leaf blades 6–7 in. long, 4–5 in. wide; petioles slender, flattened, 1–2 in.

Twigs. Reddish brown, stout, pubescent at first, later glabrous; terminal buds ⅛–¼ in. long, ovoid, acute, reddish brown.

Bark. Grayish black, broken into deep fissures and appressed scales.

Wood. Light red, sapwood lighter, coarse-grained, durable, heavy, hard, strong, weighing 43 lb per cu ft.

Range. The typical species of Southern Red Oak occur from the Brazos River of Texas eastward through Louisiana to Florida, Oklahoma, and Arkansas and northward to New York, Pennsylvania, Ohio, and Illinois.

Remarks. *Quercus* is an old classical name, and the species name, *falcata*, refers to the scythe-shaped leaves. Vernacular names are Spanish Oak, Turkey Oak, Pagoda Oak, and Cherry-bark Oak. The tree is often planted for ornament, and the wood is used for general purposes, rough lumber, and furniture (chairs and tables). The bark is excellent for tanning and is used as an astringent in medicine.

Red Oak Complex: The former name of *Q. rubra* L., meaning "Red Oak," has for many years been a vague and confusing term applying to a complex of northern and southern oaks. It was suggested that the name be replaced by *Q. falcata* Michx., as applying to Southern Red Oak, and *Q. borealis* Michx., as applying to Northern Red Oak.

Southern Red Oak, *Q. falcata*, is in itself a very variable species, and not all botanists agree as to the exact status of some of its variations. The difficulty lies in the unstable character of the species and its tendency to produce intergrading forms over wide areas.

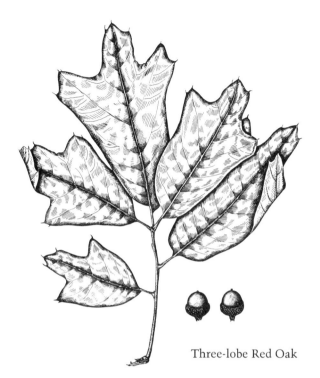

Three-lobe Red Oak

The first variety, known as the Three-lobe Red Oak, *Q. falcata* var. *triloba* (Michx.) Nutt., is a form in which the leaves are 3-lobed at the apex. Other differences between it and the species are negligible. However, the number of 3-lobed leaves on different trees varies considerably. Some trees have practically all leaves 3-lobed, some trees perhaps half, and others very few. Some botanists conclude, therefore, that this 3-lobed form is not constant enough to warrant a special varietal name.

A second variety, now known as Swamp Red Oak, *Q. falcata* var. *pagodaefolia* (Ell.) Ashe, is described by some botanists as a separate species (Pagoda Oak, *Q. pagoda* Raf.). However, a varietal standing does seem to fit the tree better than species rank. The fruit and flowers are similar to the typical species, but the leaves are distinctly pagoda-shaped, with 5–13 lobes, and have a cuneate or truncate base. Also, the bark has a tendency to be tighter and resemble the bark of Wild Cherry, hence giving it the name of Cherry-bark Oak in some areas.

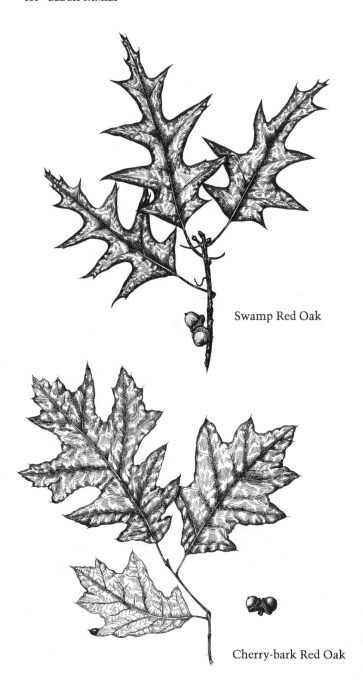

Swamp Red Oak

Cherry-bark Red Oak

The third variety, known as the true Cherry-bark Red Oak, *Quercus falcata* var. *leucophylla* (Ashe) Palmer & Steyerm., is very closely allied to the Swamp Red Oak. In fact, if the Swamp Red Oak were given a species name, then the Cherry-bark Red Oak would fall into a varietal classification under it. It has similar acorns and cherrylike bark, but the leaves have somewhat more irregular lobes and the lower surface is more or less white-tomentose. The lower leaves on Cherry-bark Oak-trees resemble those of Black Oak leaves in shape.

Black Oak

Quercus velutina Lam. [D, E]

Field Identification. Stout tree attaining a height of 90 ft, with a spreading open crown. Bark dark brownish black. Leaves cut into usually 7 oblique lobes with sinuses of different depths.

Flowers. April–May, appearing with the leaves in staminate and pistillate catkins; staminate catkins clustered, tomentose, 3–6 in. long; calyx hairy with acute lobes; stamens 4–12; pistillate catkins a few together on short tomentose peduncles; bracts ovate; stigmas red.

Fruit. Maturing September–October, acorn solitary or paired, sessile or short-stalked, ovoid-oblong or hemispheric, brown, often striate, pubescent, ½–1 in. long, one-half to three-fourths of length enclosed in cup; cup turbinate, light brown, pubescent or glabrous, ¾–1 in. broad; scales closely appressed toward base of cup but loose and spreading near the rim—a diagnostic feature distinguishing it from other similar oaks.

Leaves. Simple, alternate, deciduous, oval-obovate, usually with 7 oblique bristle-tipped lobes, middle lobes longest, apex acuminate or acute, base cuneate or truncate, surface dark green and lustrous; paler below and either pubescent or glabrous, tufts of hairs in axils of veins; 4–10 in. long, 3–7 in. broad; petioles 3–6 in., stout, yellow, glabrous or puberulous.

Twigs. Reddish brown, stout, tomentose at first, glabrous later.

Bark. Dark brown to black, ridges flattened with platelike scales between deep fissures; inner bark orange-yellow, bitter.

Wood. Reddish brown, sapwood paler, coarse-grained, strong, heavy, hard, weighing about 43 lb per cu ft, not commercially distinguished from other Red Oaks.

Range. Apparently not at home on the Gulf Coast plain. Often on poor, dry, sandy, heavy clay, or gravelly soils. Eastern Texas, Louisiana, Oklahoma, and Arkansas; eastward to Florida, north to Maine, and west to Ontario, Wisconsin, and Iowa.

Remarks. The genus name, *Quercus*, is the classical name, and the species name, *velutina*, refers to the velvety pubescence of the lower leaf surface. Vernacular names are Dyers Oak, Spotted Oak, Yellow-bark Oak, Yellow Oak, and Quercitron. The inner bark yields a tannin and a yellow dye for woolen goods. It is also a source of quercitannic acid, which has medicinal uses. However, because of the large amount of tannin, the bark is less often used in medical practice than White Oak bark. The drug is officially known as Quercus Cortex and is used mostly as a mild astringent.

The wood of Black Oak is used for rough lumber, crossties, and fuel, or generally for the same purposes as Red Oak, not generally being separated from it in the lumber trade. Black Oak is seldom used for ornamental planting because it lacks the brilliant fall coloring of some of the other oaks. It is rather slow growing and trees over 200 years of age are seldom seen. It has been cultivated since 1802.

Shumard Oak

Quercus shumardii Buckl. [D, E]

Field Identification. Tree attaining a height of 120 ft, with an open head and stout spreading branches. Leaves 5–9-lobed, usually 7-lobed, green and glabrous on both sides except for tufts of hairs in the axils of the veins beneath. Distinguished from Southern Red Oak by the smoothness and lobing, the Southern Red Oak having leaves densely pubescent beneath and irregularly lobed. Also, Southern Red Oak has much smaller acorns than Shumard Oak.

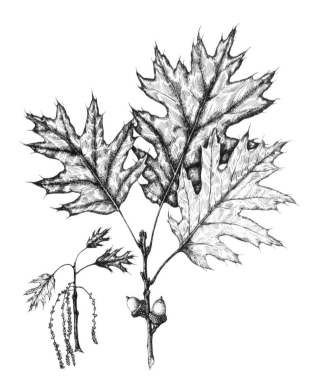

Flowers. Borne in spring on separate staminate and pistillate catkins; staminate catkins slender, 6–7 in. long, usually clustered; calyx-lobes 4–5, hairy; stamens 4–12; pistillate flowers solitary or paired, peduncles pubescent; involucral scales ovate, pubescent, brown or greenish; stigmas red.

Fruit. Acorn sessile or short-stalked, solitary or paired, ovoid to oblong-ovoid, pubescent or glabrous, sometimes striate, ¾–1 in. long, ½–1 in. wide, set only at base in shallow, thick cups; cup covering one-fourth the length of acorn; scales appressed, imbricate, thin or tuberculate, acuminate.

Leaves. Simple, alternate, deciduous, obovate, or elliptic-oblong, cut into 7–9 more or less symmetrical lobes, lobes sometimes lobulate and bristle-tipped, sinuses broad and varying in depth. The leaves of upper and lower branches often vary considerably in the number and length of lobes. Upper surface dark green, glabrous and lustrous, lower surface paler and glabrous with tufts of axillary hairs; petioles glabrous, grayish brown.

Twigs. Grayish brown, glabrous; branches smooth.

Bark. Gray to reddish brown, smooth or broken into small tight interlacing ridges.

Wood. Light reddish brown, close-grained, hard, strong, weighing 57 lb per cu ft.

Range. Moist hillsides or bottom lands in clay soils. Central Texas, Oklahoma, and Arkansas; eastward through Louisiana to Florida, northward to Pennsylvania and west to Kansas.

Remarks. The genus name, *Quercus*, is the classical name, and the species name, *shumardii*, refers to Benjamin Franklin Shumard (1820–1869), state geologist of Texas. Vernacular names are Spotted Oak, Leopard Oak, and Spanish Oak. The wood is not commercially distinguished from that of the other Red Oaks and is used for veneer, cabinets, furniture, flooring, interior trim, and lumber. It is a beautiful tree with a symmetrical leaf design and, being rather free from insects and diseases, could be more extensively cultivated for ornament.

Texas Oak

Quercus texana Buckl. [D, E, F]

Field Identification. Shrub or small tree rarely over 35 ft in height, with spreading branches. Confined mostly to the high dry uplands

of central Texas. The leaves are small, averaging about 3½ in. long.

Flowers. In catkins borne separately on same tree; staminate catkins 1⅓–3½ in. long, loosely flowered, hairy; calyx hairy-fimbriate, divided into 4–5 acute lobes, shorter than the stamens, anthers glabrous; pistillate catkins with short tomentose peduncles, catkins 1½–3½ in. long, 1–3-flowered, involucral scales reddish brown, stigmas red.

Fruit. Acorn biennial, sessile or on short peduncles ¹⁄₁₂–⅓ in. long, solitary or paired, short-oblong or ovoid, ¼–¾ in. long (mostly about ½), reddish brown, pubescent, often striate, narrowed or rounded at the apex or abruptly apiculate, rounded at the base, one-fourth to one-half included in the cup; cup turbinate, abruptly constricted at the base, reddish, densely pubescent, ⅜–½ in. high and wide; scales ovate, appressed, thin, pubescent, apex obtuse, rounded or truncate, margins darker brown and thin.

Leaves. Deciduous, turning red in autumn, 2½–5½ in. long, 2–3½ in. wide, ovate to obovate or rounded, margin with 3–7 (mostly 5) aristate lobes with intervening broad or rounded sinuses; terminal lobe often longest, entire or 2–3-lobed at the apex, acute; upper lateral lobes sometimes broad and entire or divided at the apex into lesser acuminate lobes; lower lateral lobes often much smaller (except where entire leaf is only 3-lobed); margin thin and slightly puberulent below along the veins, occasionally with tufts of hairs in the vein angles; petioles ⅓–1½ in. long, slender, glabrous, reddish yellow; lenticels small and pale; buds ⅛–⅕ in. long, lanceolate-ovoid, acute, reddish brown, tomentose; young unfolding leaves densely pubescent and reddish.

Twigs. Slender, younger ones reddish brown, mostly glabrous; older ones gray and glabrous.

Bark. Dark gray to black with thick short ridges and platelike scales, fissures deep.

Range. Common on the dry uplands of central and west Texas (Edwards Plateau), but not known to occur beyond the Pecos River. Also in southern Oklahoma in the Arbuckle Mountains.

Remarks. The genus name, *Quercus*, is the classical name, and the species name, *texana*, refers to the state of Texas, its native habitat. The first specimen described in the literature was found on limestone hills near Austin, Texas. Also known under the names of Texas Red Oak, Rock Oak, Hill Oak, Spotted Oak, Red Oak, and Spanish Oak. The wood is used locally for fuel and posts, but the tree is generally too small for lumber.

ELM FAMILY (Ulmaceae)

Sugar Hackberry

Celtis laevigata Willd. [D, E, F, G]

Field Identification. Tree attaining a height of 100 ft, with a spreading round-topped or oblong crown.

Flowers. In spring, monoecious-polygamous, small, inconspicuous, greenish, borne on slender glabrous pedicels; staminate fascicled; calyx 4–6-lobed (usually 5), lobes ovate-lanceolate, glabrous or pubescent; stamens 4–6; pistillate flowers solitary or 2 together, peduncled; ovary 1-celled, surmounted by 2 stigmas.

Fruit. Drupe ripening in late summer, pedicel ¼–½ in., sub-globose-obovoid, orange-red to black, about ¼ in. in diameter, flesh thin and dry, sweetish; seed solitary, pale brown, roughened. Fruit pedicel often longer than the leaf petiole.

Leaves. Simple, alternate, deciduous, ovate-lanceolate, often falcate, long-acuminate at apex, rounded or wedge-shaped and in-equilateral at base, entire or a few teeth near apex, thin, light green and glabrous above, paler and smooth beneath, conspicuously 3-veined at base beneath, 2½–4 in. long, 1–2½ in. wide.

Twigs. Light green to reddish brown, somewhat divaricate, lustrous, glabrous or pubescent.

Bark. Pale gray, thin, smooth or cracked, with prominent warty excrescences.

Wood. Yellowish, close-grained, soft, weak, weighing 49 lb per cu ft.

Range. The species is found in Texas, Arkansas, Oklahoma, and Louisiana; east to Florida, and north to Missouri, Kansas, Indiana, and Virginia. Also in Nuevo León, Mexico.

Remarks. *Celtis* is a name given by Pliny to a sweet-fruited African lotus. The species name, *laevigata*, means "smooth." The wood is used to a limited extent for furniture, flooring, crating, fuel, cooperage, and posts. The dry sweet fruit is eaten by at least 10 species of birds. The tree is often used for street planting in the lower South.

This species seems to present a considerable number of local variations which have caused some botanists to name a number of varieties, while other botanists feel that the distinctions are too slight. Some of these are as follows:

Texas Sugar Hackberry, *C. laevigata* var. *texana* (Scheele) Sarg., is scattered in Texas and extends over the Edwards Plateau limestone area to the west. It has leaves which are ovate-lanceolate, acuminate, mostly entire, rounded or cordate at the base, glabrous above and pubescent beneath with axillary hairs; fruit orange-red with pedicels longer than the petioles; branches gray to reddish brown and pubescent.

Uvalde Sugar Hackberry, *C. laevigata* var. *brachyphylla* Sarg., is a form with thicker and shorter leaves, found on the rocky banks of the Nueces River, Texas.

Scrub Sugar Hackberry, *C. laevigata* var. *anomala* Sarg., is a sandy-land shrub of Callahan County, Texas, having oblong-ovate, cordate leaves and dark purple, glaucous fruit.

Small Sugar Hackberry, *C. laevigata* var. *smallii* (Beadle) Sarg., is a small tree with sharply serrate, acuminate, somewhat smaller leaves. It occurs from the Gulf Coast plain north to North Carolina and Tennessee.

Arizona Sugar Hackberry, *C. laevigata* var. *brevipes* Sarg., is an Arizona variety with ovate, mostly entire leaves 1½–2 in. long, yellow fruit, and glabrous reddish brown branchlets.

Net-leaf Sugar Hackberry, *C. laevigata* var. *reticulata* (Torr.) L. Benson, is considered by some botanists as a distinct species, but others feel that it has such close affinities it should be classed as a variety of the Sugar Hackberry with xerophytic tendencies. The flowers and fruit are similar except for more pubescence on the fruit pedicel. The leaves are smaller, broadly ovate, yellowish

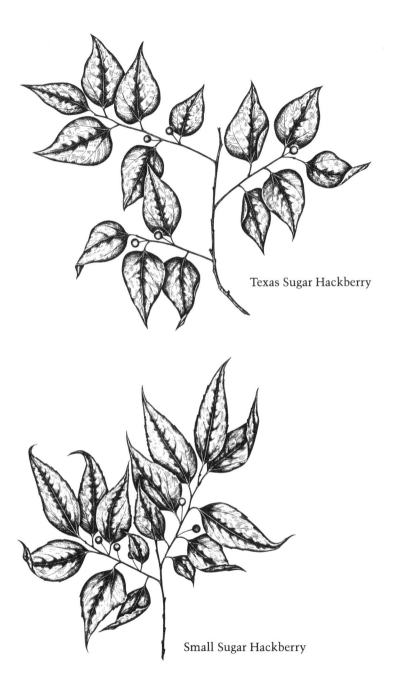

Texas Sugar Hackberry

Small Sugar Hackberry

Net-leaf Sugar Hackberry

green, stiff, coriaceous, entire or serrate, conspicuously reticulate-veined beneath, the veins are pubescent beneath, and the leaf petiole is densely pubescent. As a tree it is rarely over 30 ft and quite often it is only a large shrub. Subsequently it may be found that Arizona Sugar Hackberry is a synonym of Net-leaf Sugar Hackberry. West Texas to California; north to Colorado, Utah, Washington, and Oklahoma; and south into Mexico. In Texas generally on limestone hills west of the Colorado River. Occasionally on shell banks near the Gulf as far east as Houston.

Common Hackberry

Celtis occidentalis L. [D, E, F, G]

Field Identification. Tree attaining a height of 120 ft, with a rounded crown. The gray bark bears corky warts and ridges.

Flowers. In spring, with the leaves, perfect or imperfect, small, green, borne in axillary, slender-peduncled fascicles, or solitary; staminate fascicles few-flowered; calyx 4–6-lobed, lobes linear-oblong; stamens 4–6 (mostly 5); no petals; pistillate flowers usually solitary or in pairs; ovary sessile, ovoid, with 2 hairy reflexed stigmas.

Fruit. Drupe variable in size and color, globose or subglobose to ovoid, orange-red turning dark purple, ¼–½ in. long, persistent; flesh thin, yellow, sweetish, edible; seed bony, light brown, smooth or somewhat pitted, pedicels longer than leaf petioles.

Leaves. Simple, alternate, deciduous, ovate to elliptic-ovate, often falcate, short acuminate or acute, oblique at base with one side rounded to cuneate and the other somewhat cordate, usually coarsely serrate but less so near the base, 3-nerved at base, light green and glabrous above (or rough in var. *crassifolia*), paler green

and soft pubescent or glabrous beneath, blades 2½–4 in. long, 1½–2 in. wide; petioles slender, glabrous, about ½ in. long. The leaves are broader in proportion to width, not as long taper-pointed, more serrate on margin, and drupes larger than in Sugar Hackberry.

Twigs. Green to reddish brown, slender, somewhat divaricate, glabrous or pubescent.

Bark. Gray to grayish brown, smooth except for wartlike protuberances.

Wood. Yellowish white, coarse-grained, heavy, soft, weak, weighing 45 lb per cu ft.

Range. Texas, western Oklahoma, Arkansas, and Louisiana; eastward to Georgia, north to Quebec, and west to Manitoba, North Dakota, Nebraska, and Kansas.

Remarks. *Celtis* was a name given by Pliny to a sweet-fruited lotus, and *occidentalis* means "western." Vernacular names are Nettle-tree, False-elm, Bastard-elm, Beaverwood, Juniper-tree, Rim-ash, Hoop-ash, and One-berry. The tree is drought resistant and often planted for shade in the South and for shelter-belt planting. The wood is occasionally used commercially for fuel, furniture, veneer, and agricultural implements. The fruit is known to be eaten by 25 species of birds, especially the gallinaceous birds. It was also eaten by the Indians.

Common Hackberry is rather variable in size and shape of leaves and fruit, and botanists have described a number of varieties to fit these differences.

Big-leaf Common Hackberry, *C. occidentalis* var. *crassifolia* Gray, is perhaps the most common variety in east Texas. The leaves are large, very coarsely serrate, cordate at base, and rough to the touch above, and the hairy petioles are shorter than the fruit pedicels. It occurs mixed with the species, and intergrading forms appear to be rather common.

Dog Hackberry, *C. occidentalis* var. *canina* Sarg., is a variety with oblong-ovate acuminate leaves, abruptly cuneate at base, finely serrate and glabrous or hairy on veins beneath; petioles glabrous or rarely pubescent. Not known to occur in Texas, but common in Oklahoma and northward.

Small Hackberry

Celtis tenuifolia Nutt. [D]

Field Identification. Eastern shrub or small tree to 24 ft.

Flowers. In spring, small, axillary, 5–6-parted; staminate in small pedunculate clusters near the base of twigs of the year, calyx 5-lobed; stamens 5, opposite the calyx-lobes, exserted, usually no ovary in staminate flowers; pistillate flowers appearing with leaves, pediceled, solitary or paired from upper axils, stamens present or absent; ovary ovoid, 1-celled, 1-ovuled, ovule single and suspended; style very short, stigmas 2, elongate, subulate, recurved, divergent.

Fruit. Drupe September–October, subglobose, ⅕–⅓ in. in diameter, orange to brown or red, thin-fleshed, sweet; stone ⅕–¼ in. long, subglobose, light to dark brown, seed coat somewhat granular; peduncles ⅛–⅖ in., shorter than the subtending petioles, or longer.

Leaves. Simple, alternate, deciduous, usually broad-ovate to del-toid, apex blunt, acute or short-acuminate, base oblique and 3-nerved, mostly entire on margin (on young shoots sometimes few-toothed), blade length ¾–4 in., width ½–1¾ in., thin and smooth, surfaces grayish green but darker above, lower surfaces more or less pubescent and veiny, petioles pubescent.

Twigs. Slender, reddish brown, pubescent at first, later glabrous and darker brown to gray; bark often with corky ridges.

Range. On dry and rocky foothills. Southern to eastern Okla-homa, Arkansas, and Louisiana; eastward to northern Florida, and northward to Pennsylvania, Indiana, Kansas, and Missouri.

Remarks. *Celtis* is the name given by Pliny to a sweet-fruited African lotus. The species name, *tenuifolia*, refers to the thin leaves. It is listed as *C. pumila* by some authors. Vernacular names are Sugarberry, Nettleberry, and Nettle-tree.

Georgia Hackberry, *C. tenuifolia* var. *georgiana* (Small) Fern. & Schub., is a variety with leathery, pubescent, scabrous leaves. It was formerly listed as *C. georgiana* Small and *C. pumila* var. *georgiana* Sarg. It occurs in Arkansas, Oklahoma, Louisiana, Georgia, Missouri, Virginia, and District of Columbia.

Spiny Hackberry

Celtis pallida Torr. [D, E, F]

Field Identification. Spiny, spreading, densely branched evergreen shrub attaining a height of 18 ft.

Flowers. Axillary, inconspicuous, in 2-branched, 3–5-flowered cymes, pedicels about ½₂ in. long; flowers greenish white, polyg-amous or monoecious; corolla absent; calyx-lobes 4 or 5; stamens as many as the calyx-lobes; style absent; stigmas 2, each 2-cleft and spreading; ovary sessile, 1-celled.

Fruit. Drupe subglobose or ovoid, yellow or orange, thin-fleshed, mealy, acid, edible, ⅕–⅓ in. in diameter; stone ovoid, oval or obovoid, reticulate, acute, about ¼ in. long and ⅜ in. wide.

Leaves. Alternate, simple, small, 3-nerved, deep green, scabrous and puberulent, elliptic to oblong-ovate; rounded, acute or obtuse at the apex; oblique and somewhat semicordate at base; coarsely toothed on margin, or entire; blades ½–2¼ in. long, ½–1 in. wide; petioles pubescent, ¹⁄₁₆–³⁄₁₆ in., or longer.

Bark. Mottled gray to reddish brown, rather smooth and tight, sometimes with long, stout, gray or brown spines. Bark only rough at base of very old trunks.

Twigs. Divaricate, flexuous, spreading, smooth, gray or reddish brown, glabrous or puberulent; with stipular spines ¼–1 in., stout, straight, single or paired, often at ends of shoots; lenticels small, pale, and usually numerous.

Range. Central, western, and southern Texas, New Mexico, Arizona, and Mexico. In Mexico from Chihuahua to Baja California, and south to Oaxaca.

Remarks. The genus name, *Celtis*, is the classical name for a species of lotus, and the species name, *pallida*, refers to paleness of the branches. Commonly used vernacular names in Texas and Mexico are Desert Hackberry, Chaparral, Granjeno, Granjeno Huasteco, Capul, and Garabata.

The Indians of the Southwest are reported to have ground the fruit and eaten it with fat or parched corn. It is reported that the larvae of the snout butterfly feed upon the foliage. Spiny Hackberry is also considered a good honey plant. Many birds consume it, particularly the cactus wren, cardinal, pyrrholuxia, towhee, mockingbird, thrasher, scaled quail, Gambel's quail, and green jay. The raccoon, deer, and jack rabbit eat it occasionally. The wood is used for fence posts and fuel, and the plant is of some value in erosion control.

Slippery Elm

Ulmus rubra Muhl. [D, E, F, G]

Field Identification. Tree attaining a height of 75 ft, with spreading branches and a broad open head.

Flowers. February–April, before the leaves, borne in dense fascicles on short pedicels; perfect; no petals; calyx campanulate, green, hairy; calyx-lobes 5–9, lanceolate and acute; stamens 5–9, with elongate yellow filaments and reddish purple anthers; pistil reddish, compressed, divided into a 2-celled ovary and 2 exserted, spreading, reddish purple stigmas.

Fruit. Ripening April–June. Samara short-stalked, green, oval to orbicular, apex entire or shallowly notched, ¼–¾ in. long; seed flattened with the surrounding wing reticulate-veined; seed area reddish brown and hairy; and wing area glabrous. Minimum seed-bearing age of tree 15 years, optimum 25–125, and maximum 200 years. Good crops every 2–4 years and light crops intervening.

Leaves. Buds densely rusty-tomentose; leaves simple, alternate, deciduous, blades 4–8 in. long, 2–3 in. wide, obovate, ovate to oblong, acuminate at apex; rounded, cordate to cuneate, and inequilateral at base; margin coarsely and sharply double-serrate; dark green and very rough above because of tiny pointed tubercles, also pubescent when young and later more glabrous; paler and soft-pubescent beneath, often with axillary hairs; petioles ⅓–½ in., stout; leaves fragrant when dry.

Twigs. Gray, stout, roughened and densely pubescent when young, more glabrous later.

Bark. Gray to reddish brown, ridges flattened, fissures shallow, inner bark mucilaginous and fragrant.

Wood. Reddish brown, tough, strong, heavy, hard, compact, durable, weighing 43 lb per cu ft.

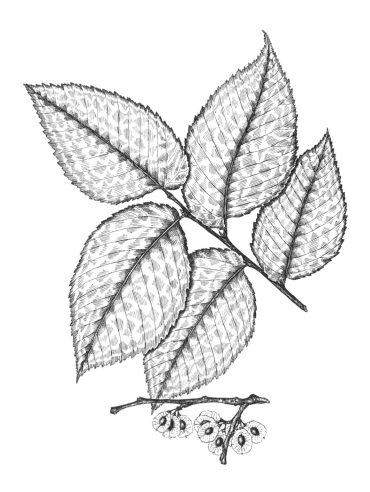

Range. Texas, Oklahoma, Arkansas, and Louisiana; eastward to Florida, north to Maine and Quebec, and west to Ontario, Minnesota, Wisconsin, and Nebraska.

Remarks. *Ulmus* is the ancient Latin name for elm, and the species name, *rubra*, refers to the reddish wood. The older name *U. rubra* Muhl. has precedence over the name *U. fulva* Michx., as used in most books. Vernacular names are Rock Elm, Red Elm, Sweet Elm, Indian Elm, Moose Elm, Gray Elm, and Soft Elm. The wood is used for making posts, ties, sills, boats, hubs, agricultural implements, furniture, slack cooperage, veneer, and sporting goods. In frontier days the bark was often chewed as a thirst quencher. White-tailed deer, rabbit, porcupine, and moose browse the twigs and foliage. The tree is rather short-lived and subject to insect damage. It has been cultivated since 1830.

American Elm

Ulmus americana L. [D, E, F]

Field Identification. Much-loved and famous American tree, admired for graceful vaselike shape. Attaining a height of 120 ft, but generally under 70 ft, and often buttressed at base. Known to reach an age of 300 years or more.

Flowers. February–April, before the leaves, in axillary, 3–4-flowered (occasionally to 12) fascicles; pedicels slender, jointed, drooping, nearly sessile or to 1 in. long; individual flowers perfect,

petals absent; calyx campanulate, red to green, lobes 7–9 and short; stamens 5–8, exserted, with slender filaments and red anthers; pistil pale green, compressed, composed of a 2-celled ovary and 2 spreading inwardly stigmatic styles.

Fruit. Ripening March–June. A samara, about ½ in. long, red to green, oval-obovate, consisting of a central flattened seed surrounded by a membranous wing; wing reticulate-veiny, glabrous but ciliate on margin, a deep terminal incision reaching the nutlet. The minimum seed-bearing age is 15 years and the maximum 300 years. Good crops occur most years.

Leaves. Simple, alternate, deciduous, 4–6 in. long, 2–3 in. wide, oval, obovate or oblong, acute or abruptly acuminate at apex; veins conspicuous to the serrations; somewhat cordate on one side at base and rounder or cuneate on the other side, giving an inequilateral shape; margin coarsely and doubly serrate, upper surface dark green and mostly smooth (occasionally scabrous on vigorous shoots); lower surface pubescent at first, but glabrate later; petioles ⅕–⅓ in., rather stout.

Twigs. Slender, varying shades of brown, pubescent at first, glabrous later.

Bark. Light to dark gray, ridges flattened and scaly, fissures deep.

Wood. Light to dark brown, sapwood whitish, coarse-grained, tough, heavy, hard, strong, weighing 40 lb per cu ft, difficult to split, durable, bends well, shrinks moderately, tends to warp and twist.

Range. Moist soils of bottom lands and upland flats. Texas, Oklahoma, Arkansas, and Louisiana; eastward to Georgia and Florida, northward to Newfoundland, and west to Ontario, North Dakota, Montana, and Nebraska.

Remarks. *Ulmus* is the ancient Latin name for elm, and the species name, *americana*, refers to its native home. Vernacular names are Rock Elm, Common Elm, Soft Elm, Swamp Elm, White Elm, and Water Elm. Known to the lumber trade as White Elm and makes up the greater part of elm lumber and logs. In most cases the trade does not distinguish between the elm species. A very desirable ornamental tree for street and park planting, attaining large size and much admired for the graceful upsweep of the branches. It is sometimes used for shelter-belt planting in the prairie states, but *U. pumila* is considered superior for that purpose. The wood is used for woodenware, vehicles, baskets, flooring, veneer, furniture, cooperage, cabinets, sporting goods, stock staves, boxes, crates, framework, agricultural implements, trunks, handles, toys, car construction, shipbuilding and boatbuilding, and fuel. It is reported that the Indians used the wood for canoes and the bast fiber for ropes. The fruit is often eaten by gallinaceous birds, and the young twigs and leaves are browsed by white-tailed deer, opossum, and cottontail. In the northern part of its range it appears to be subject to the attack of the elm-leaf beetle, *Galerucella xanthomelaena*, and in some areas large numbers of trees are killed by the Dutch elm disease, caused by a fungus, *Graphium ulmi*, and by phloem necrosis, caused by a virus. American Elm is distinguished from Slippery Elm by the former having leaves less scabrous above and the samara being ciliate on the margin.

Cedar Elm

Ulmus crassifolia Nutt. [D, E, F]

Field Identification. Tree attaining a height of 90 ft, with slender, somewhat drooping branches and a narrow or rounded crown. Twigs or branches often with lateral corky wings.

Flowers. Borne usually in July in small, 3–5-flowered fascicles; pedicels slender, ⅓–½ in.; calyx campanulate, hairy, red to green, 6–9-lobed, lobes hairy and acute; no petals; stamens 5–6, with slender filaments and reddish purple anthers; pistil green, flattened, pubescent, composed of a 2-celled ovary and 2 exserted spreading styles.

Fruit. Samara borne in late summer, small, ¼–½ in. long, oval-elliptic or oblong, green, flattened, pubescent; composed of a central seed surrounded by a wing which is deeply notched at apex and ciliate on margin.

Leaves. Simple, alternate, somewhat persistent, blades 1–2 in. long, ¾–1 in. wide, elliptic to ovate, acute or obtuse at apex, rounded or cuneate to oblique at base, doubly serrate on margin; dark green, stiff and very rough to the touch above, pubescent beneath; petiole about ⅓ in., stout, hairy.

Twigs. Reddish brown, pubescent, often with brown, thin, lateral, corky wings. The only other Texas elm with corky wings is the Winged Elm.

Bark. Brown to reddish, or gray, ridges flattened and broken into thin, loose scales.

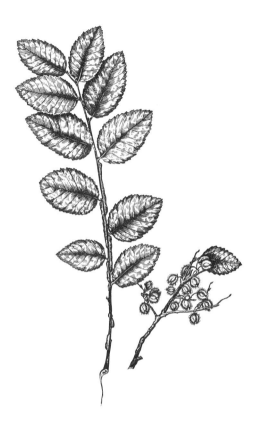

Wood. Reddish brown, sapwood lighter, brittle, heavy, hard.

Range. Often in limestone soils. Texas, Oklahoma, Arkansas, and Louisiana; east to South Carolina, north to New York, and west to Kansas.

Remarks. *Ulmus* is the ancient Latin name, and *crassifolia* refers to the rough, thick leaves. Vernacular names are Scrub Elm, Lime Elm, Texas Elm, Basket Elm, Red Elm, and Southern Rock Elm. It is often planted as a shade tree, but the wood is considered inferior to other elms because of its brittle and knotty character. It is sometimes used for hubs, furniture, and posts.

Winged Elm

Ulmus alata Michx. [D, E]

Field Identification. Tree attaining a height of 60 ft, with slender branches and a rounded or oblong crown. Often with conspicuous corky wings on the twigs and branches.

Flowers. Before the leaves in spring, borne in few-flowered drooping fascicles on filiform pedicels; flowers perfect, petals absent; calyx campanulate, red to yellow, the 5 lobes obovate and rounded; stamens 5, with long, slender filaments and reddish anthers; pistil green, hairy, flattened, composed of a tomentose 2-celled ovary tipped by 2 spreading styles.

Fruit. Samara reddish or greenish, long-stipitate, ovate to elliptic or oblong, ¼–⅓ in. long; seed solitary, flattened, ovoid; wing flat, thin, narrow, prolonged into divergent, apically incurved beaks; seed and wing hairy, especially on margin; the reddish samaras giving the tree a reddish appearance when in fruit.

Leaves. Simple, alternate, deciduous, ovate-oblong to oblong-lanceolate, occasionally somewhat falcate, blades ½–3 in. long, coarsely and doubly serrate on margin, acute or acuminate at apex, wedge-shaped or subcordate at base, pale-pubescent or glabrous beneath, with axillary hairs and prominent veins; petioles about ⅓ in. long, stout, pubescent.

Twigs. Reddish brown, slender, pubescent at first, glabrous later, often with conspicuous, opposite, thin, corky wings. The only other elms having corky wings are the Cedar Elm, September Elm, and Rock Elm.

Bark. Reddish brown to gray, ridges flat with closely appressed scales, fissures irregular and shallow.

Wood. Brown, close-grained, compact, heavy, hard, difficult to split, weighing 46 lb per cu ft, not considered as strong as other elms.

Range. Texas, Oklahoma, Arkansas, and Louisiana; eastward to Florida, north to Virginia, and west through Ohio and Indiana to Kansas and Missouri.

Remarks. *Ulmus* is the ancient Latin name, and *alata* refers to the corky wings on the twigs. Vernacular names are Cork Elm, Water Elm, Wahoo Elm, Red Elm, and Witch Elm. The Winged Elm is a favorite shade and ornamental tree. It is easily transplanted, sprouts readily from seed, is a rapid grower, and is rather free of disease and insects. The wood is generally used for the same purposes as other elms, such as tool handles, vehicle parts, and agricultural implements. Formerly the bark was used in some localities for baling twine.

Siberian Elm

Ulmus pumila L. [D]

Field Identification. Graceful cultivated shrub or small tree with slender drooping branches.

Flowers. March–April, appearing with or before the leaves, axillary, inconspicuous, greenish, clustered, short pediceled, perfect or rarely polygamous, petals absent; calyx campanulate, 4–5-

lobed; stamens 4–5, with green to violet anthers; style 2-lobed, ovary flattened and 1-celled.

Fruit. Samara April–May, clustered, ¼–½ in. long and broad, rarely more; oval to obovate, composed of a central, dry, compressed nutlet surrounded by a wing which is thin, reticulate-veined, membranous, semitransparent, apex with a notch sometimes reaching one-third to one-half way to the nutlet; pedicel ¹⁄₂₅–⅛ in.

Leaves. Simple, deciduous, alternate, oval to ovate or elliptic, blade length 1–2 in., width ½–1 in., margin doubly serrate, apex acute, base cuneate or somewhat asymmetrical, leathery and firm; upper surface olive green to dark green, glabrous, veins impressed; lower surface paler and glabrous, or somewhat pubescent when young or with axillary tufts of hair; turning yellow in autumn; petiole glabrous or pubescent, ⅙–½ in., stipules caducous.

Twigs. Slender; when young brownish and pubescent; when older brown to gray and glabrous; bark of trunk gray to brownish.

Range. A native of Asia, extensively cultivated in the United States. In its typical form a small-leaved shrub or tree from Turkistan to Siberia, Mongolia, and North China.

Remarks. The genus name, *Ulmus*, is the ancient Latin name for elm, and the species name, *pumila*, refers to its shrubby habit in some forms. Often wrongly called Chinese Elm, but that name should properly apply to *U. parvifolia* Jacq. Both the Siberian and the Chinese Elm are cultivated in the Gulf Coast states for ornament. The Siberian Elm is being extensively planted in the prairie-plains region as shelter belts, and has some use as a game cover. It is rather drought resistant and seems to be less susceptible to the Dutch elm disease, *Graphium ulmi*, than the native elm species. The wood is hard, heavy, tough, rather difficult to split, and is used in China for agricultural implements, boatbuilding, and wagon wheels. The inner bark was once made into coarse cloth.

Chinese Elm

Ulmus parvifolia Jacq. [D]

Field Identification. A cultivated, attractive, semievergreen tree, attaining a height of 45 ft or more, but usually smaller. The branches slender to form a broad-rounded, open crown. Bark usually smooth, thin and pale gray; young trees often marked with white blotches, or circular, white bands; older trunks developing irregular shallow fissures with thin, small scales, which exfoliate to expose an orange-red inner bark.

Flowers. Borne August–September in axillary clusters on short pedicels, on twigs of the preceding season; bisexual or more rarely unisexual; corolla absent; calyx campanulate; the 4–5 lobes (or sometimes more) divided below the middle; stamens as many as the calyx-lobes and opposite them, the filaments straight, long-exserted; ovary superior, 1-celled, 1-ovuled; styles 2.

Fruit. Samara flat, oval to ovate or elliptic, with a broad, narrow, membranous wing surrounding the seed and notched at apex; from about ⅓ in. long and glabrous.

Leaves. Simple, alternate; texture subcoriaceous; shape elliptic to ovate; apices acute to obtusish; margin mostly simply serrate; base rounded to cuneate or somewhat unequal sided; length ¾–2½ in. Upper surface glabrous or somewhat roughened with minute papilla; lower surface glabrous or with pale pilose scattered hairs, but more so on the venation; color rather lustrous, olive green to dark green above, but somewhat paler beneath; venation with 8–10 straight, lateral veins to a side, and each ending in a tooth. Stipules linear-lanceolate, narrow at the base. Petioles very short, ½₅–¼ in. long, pale strigose-hairy.

Twigs. Slender, gray to brown, pubescent when young, more glabrous later.

Range. A native of China, Korea, and Japan. Cultivated in the Gulf Coast states and occasionally escaping. In Houston, Texas, a considerable number cultivated on the grounds of the Town and Country Shopping Center on Katy Freeway.

Remarks. The genus name, *Ulmus*, is an ancient Latin name. The species name, *parvifolia*, refers to the small leaves. Closely related species have been described as *U. sieboldii* Daveau, *U. shirasawana* Daveau, and *U. coreana* Nakai, but they differ little from *Ulmus parvifolia*. Chinese Elm is also sometimes confused with Siberian Elm, *U. pumila* L.

Water Elm

Planera aquatica (Walt.) Gmel. [D]

Field Identification. Contorted shrub or tree to 40 ft, growing in swampy ground.

Flowers. Three kinds of flowers on the same tree—male, female, and perfect. Staminate flowers fascicled, 2–5-flowered; petals none; calyx 4–5-lobed, bell-shaped, greenish yellow, lobes ovate and obtuse; stamens 4–5, filaments filiform, exserted; pistillate flowers 1–3 together, perfect; ovary ovoid, stalked, tubercular, 1-celled; styles 2, reflexed, stigmatic along inner side.

Fruit. Peculiar, covered with irregular warty excrescences, leathery, oblong-ovoid, compressed, ridged, about ⅓ in. long, short-stalked; seed ovoid.

Leaves. Elmlike, alternate, deciduous, blades 2–4 in. long, ½–1 in. wide, ovate or oblong-lanceolate, crenulate-serrate, acute to obtuse at apex, cordate or oblique at base, dark green, paler below; petioles stout, puberulent, about ¼ in. long; stipules lanceolate, caducous.

Bark. Light reddish brown or gray, dividing into large shreddy scales.

Wood. Soft, weak, light, close-grained, light brown, weighing 33 lb per cu ft.

Range. In swamps or river-bottom lands. Texas, Oklahoma, Arkansas, and Louisiana; eastward to Florida, northward to North Carolina, and west through Kentucky and Illinois to Missouri.

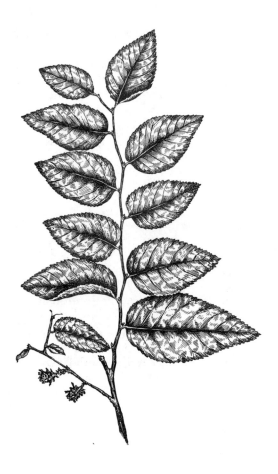

Remarks. The genus name, *Planera*, is in honor of the German botanist Johann Jakob Planer (1743–1789), a professor at the University of Erfurt, and the species name, *aquatica*, refers to the swampy habitat of the tree. The peculiar little warty fruit is considered to be an important duck food in swampland areas. Squirrels also eat the fruit. The wood has no commercial importance.

MULBERRY FAMILY (Moraceae)

Common Paper Mulberry

Broussonetia papyrifera (L.) Vent. [D, E]

Field Identification. Small tree, rarely to 50 ft, with irregular spreading branches.

Flowers. Dioecious, staminate catkins peduncled, cylindric, pendulous, 2½–3½ in. long; no petals; stamens 4; calyx 4-lobed;

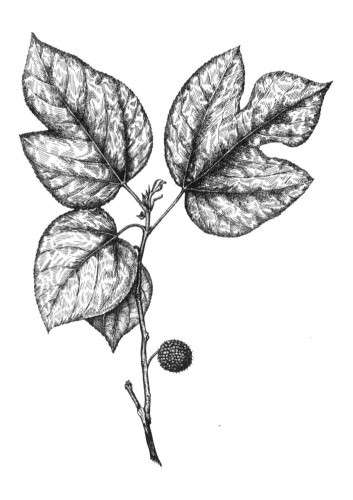

pistillate in globose heads with a tubular perianth; ovary stipitate, stigma filiform and slender.

Fruit. Globose, about ¾ in. across, a multiple fruit composed of many 1-seeded drupelets which are reddish orange and which protrude from the persistent calyx.

Leaves. Alternate, deciduous, long-petiolate, blades 3–8 in. long, ovate, margin coarsely dentate and often deeply lobed; apex acuminate; base cordate or rounded; rough above, conspicuously veined and velvety-pubescent beneath; stipules ovate-lanceolate, deciduous.

Twigs. Stout, hirsute, tomentose.

Bark. Smooth, tight, reticulate, green to yellow.

Wood. Coarse-grained, soft, light, easily worked.

Range. Texas, New Mexico, Oklahoma, Arkansas, and Louisiana; eastward to Florida, and northward to Missouri and New York. A native of Asia. Cultivated and escaping to grow wild in some areas in the United States.

Remarks. The genus, *Broussonetia*, is named in honor of Auguste Broussonet, a French naturalist; and the species name, *papyrifera*, refers to the use of the inner bark in papermaking. The inner bark is also used for making cloth in the tree's native home of Japan and China. The famous tapa cloth of the South Pacific islands is also made from the bark by macerating it and pounding with a wooden mallet. It is often planted for ornament in the United States, being drought resistant and a rapid grower, and sprouting freely from the root. The fruit is also eaten by a number of species of birds.

Red Mulberry

Morus rubra L. [D, E, F]

Field Identification. Handsome tree to 70 ft, with a rather broad, spreading crown.

Flowers. With the leaves in spring, green; petals absent; staminate spikes cylindric, 2–3 in. long; stamens 4, green; filaments flattened; calyx with 4 ovate lobes; pistillate spikes about 1 in., cylindric, sessile; calyx 4-lobed; styles 2; ovary ovoid, flat, 2-celled, 1 cell generally atrophies.

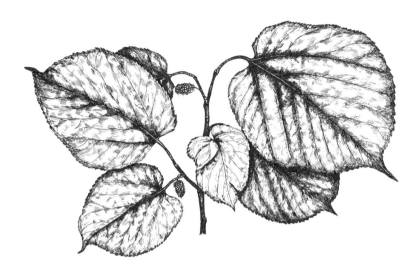

Fruit. Ripening May–August, a cylindric syncarp ¾–1¼ in. long, resembling a blackberry, red at first, becoming purplish black, juicy, edible; achene ovoid, acute, light brown, covered by the succulent calyx. Minimum seed-bearing age of the tree 10 years, optimum 30–85 years, maximum about 125 years.

Leaves. Simple, alternate, deciduous, 3–9 in. long, ovate or oval, or 3–7-lobed, doubly serrate, rough and glabrous above, soft pubescent beneath, very veiny, acute or acuminate at apex, cordate or truncate at base, turning yellow in autumn; petiole 1–2 in.; stipules lanceolate and hairy. The lobing of the leaves varies considerably on different trees or even on the same tree; some are only serrate, while others have numerous lobes.

Bark. Dark brown to gray, ½–¾ in. thick, divided into irregular, elongate plates separating into appressed flakes.

Wood. Light orange, sapwood lighter, durable, close-grained, light, soft, weak, weighing about 45 lb per cu ft, used for boats, fencing, cooperage, and railroad crossties.

Range. Usually in rich moist soil. Does not grow well on thin, poor soil. Texas, Oklahoma, Arkansas, and Louisiana; eastward to Florida, north to Vermont, and west to Ontario, Wisconsin, Michigan, Minnesota, Nebraska, and Kansas.

Remarks. The genus name, *Morus*, is the classical name of the mulberry, and the species name, *rubra*, a Latin word for "red," has reference to the red, immature fruit. The fibrous bark was used to make cloth by early Indians. The fruit is known to be eaten by at least 21 kinds of birds, fox squirrels, and human beings. Although the fruit is sweet, it does not seem to be very much in demand for culinary uses. For fruit-bearing purposes the trees may be planted 20–40 ft apart. Trees should not be planted next to walks because the abundant ripe fruit mashes readily underfoot. Often planted for ornament and known in cultivation since 1629.

Black Mulberry

Morus nigra L. [D, E, F]

Field Identification. Cultivated shrub or tree attaining a height of 30 ft, or occasionally larger. The trunk is short and the wide-spreading branches form a broad, rounded, or irregularly shaped crown.

Flowers. Staminate flowers in cylindrical spikes ⅓–1 in., longer than the peduncles; stamens 4, inserted opposite the sepals under the ovary, filaments filiform; sepals 4; pistillate spikes cylindric-oval, ⅓–¾ in., shorter than the pubescent peduncles; sepals 4, lateral ones largest, sepals enclosing the fruit at maturity and becoming succulent; ovary sessile, 1-celled, style terminal and short, stigmas 2 and ascending.

Fruit. Syncarp dark red or black, fleshy, oval-oblong, ⅓–1 in. long, achenes included in calyx and tipped by persistent stigmas.

Leaves. Simple, alternate, deciduous, thin, ovate to oval, blades 1½–6 in. long, apex acute or short-acuminate, margin coarsely toothed or sometimes with one or more lobes, base rounded, cordate or semitruncate, upper surface dull dark green, usually rough and becoming glabrous, lower surface paler and sparingly pubescent on the veins to glabrous; young foliage pubescent; petioles usually shorter than the blade, one-fourth to one-half as long.

Twigs. Young ones green to brown and pubescent, older ones darker brown to gray or glabrous.

Range. Old gardens, roadsides, thickets, and waste grounds. Cultivated in Texas, Louisiana, Oklahoma, and Arkansas; eastward to Florida and north to New York. A native of western Asia.

Remarks. The genus name, *Morus,* is the classical Latin name of mulberry, and the species name, *nigra,* refers to the black color of the fruit. It is sometimes grown for fruit or for shade. Although

Black Mulberry is sometimes reported as being cultivated in the Southwest, many times incorrect identifications are made because of its close resemblance to a black-fruited race of White Mulberry, *M. alba* var. *tatarica* (L.) Ser.

White Mulberry

Morus alba L. [D, E, F, G]

Field Identification. An introduced tree to 40 ft, and attaining a diameter of 3 ft.

Flowers. Staminate and pistillate catkins axillary, borne on the same tree or on different trees; staminate catkins ⅜–1 in., cylindric, slender, drooping; calyx 4-parted, lobes ovate; stamens 4, elastically expanding; pistillate catkins drooping, oblong or oval to subglobose, cylindric, ½–⅔ in. long, about ¼ in. in diameter; calyx 4-parted, lateral sepals largest, calyx greatly enlarging to envelop the achene at maturity; ovary sessile, 2-celled, 1 cell atrophies; styles 2, linear, stigmatic down the inner side.

Fruit. Borne June–August on slender, glabrous or pubescent peduncles ¼–⅔ in. long, pendent, subglobose to oval or oblong, white to pink (rarely black), ½–¾ in. long and about ¼ in. wide, sweet; fruit a syncarp, or an aggregation of ovate, compressed achenes each covered by the succulent, thickened calyx, the whole fruit as a unit thus juicy and elongate.

Leaves. Alternate, deciduous, ovate to oval or asymmetrical, heart-shaped, blades 2½–8 in. long, 1–4½ in. wide; margin with blunt, crenate teeth or often also 1–6-lobed, apex acute or short-acuminate; base semicordate, rounded or truncate, 3-veined; thin and smooth; upper surface olive green, lustrous and glabrous, paler and glabrous beneath; petiole ½–1½ in., shorter than the blade, slender, glabrous or slightly pubescent.

Twigs. When young reddish brown, glabrous to slightly pubescent, when older slender, glabrous, gray.

Bark. Light to dark gray, broken into narrow furrows and irregular, often twisted, ridges.

Range. Escaping cultivation to roadsides, fields, and thickets. Naturalized Texas, Oklahoma, Arkansas, and Louisiana; north to Maine, and west to Minnesota and Wisconsin. Native home not positively known, either Europe or China, but most authorities cite an Asiatic origin. A cosmopolitan plant, known in nearly all parts of the world.

Remarks. The genus name, *Morus*, is the classical Latin name, and the species name, *alba*, refers to the white fruit. It is also known under the names of Silkworm Mulberry, Russian Mulberry, Morera, and Morea. The fruit is not as juicy as the native Red Mulberry and is somewhat smaller. It also seems to vary as to sweetness, on some trees being very sweet and on others so insipid and dry as to be hardly edible. Although the fruit of the species is most commonly white or pink, some varieties produce red or black fruit. The fruit has some wildlife value, being eaten readily by a number of species of birds, opossum, and raccoon, as well as by poultry and hogs. The wood is hard and durable and is used for furniture, utensils, and boatbuilding.

Texas Mulberry

Morus microphylla Buckl. [D, E, F, G]

Field Identification. Shrub, or sometimes a small, scraggy tree to 20 ft.

Flowers. Dioecious, small, green, inconspicuous, borne in ament-like spikes; staminate spikes on short pedicels, many-flowered, ½–¾ in. long; petals absent; calyx hairy, 4-lobed, lobes rounded, green to reddish; stamens 4, filaments filiform, anthers yellow with dark green connectives; pistillate sessile, drooping in short-oblong, few-flowered spikes rarely over ½ in. long; calyx hairy, 4-lobed, lobes thick, rounded, 2 larger than the others; ovary green and glabrous, 2-celled at first with one soon atrophying; stigmas 2, short, spreading.

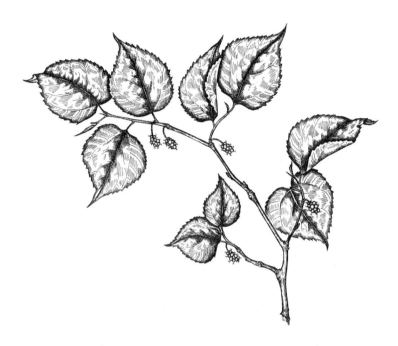

Fruit. A syncarp (multiple fruit) ripening in May, subglobose or short-ovoid, red at first to black later, sweet or sour, with scant juice, edible. Syncarp composed of numerous small, 1-seeded drupes; drupes about ⅙ in. long, ovoid, rounded at ends, containing a thick-walled, crustaceous, brown nutlet; seed pendulous, ovoid, pointed, pale yellow.

Leaves. Simple, alternate, petioled, blades 1½–2½ in. long, ¾–1 in. wide; ovate to oval; margin coarsely serrate, sometimes 3-lobed; base truncate, rounded or semicordate; apex acute to short-acuminate; thin but firm; upper surface dull green, somewhat pubescent, tubercular-roughened, veins inconspicuous; lower surface paler, glabrous to somewhat hairy, veins delicate-reticulate, 3-veined at base; petioles slender, pubescent, about ⅓–¾ in., stipules linear-lanceolate, somewhat falcate, apex acute, white-tomentose, about ½ in.

Twigs. Slender, white-hairy at first, glabrous later, light reddish brown to gray; lenticels small, round, pale.

Bark. Light gray or tinged with red, smooth, tight, shallowly furrowed and broken on the surface into narrow ridges and broad, flat fissures with slightly appressed scales.

Wood. Dark orange or brown, sapwood lighter, heavy, hard, elastic, close-grained, specific gravity 0.77.

Range. Texas, New Mexico, Arizona, and Mexico. In Texas generally west of the Colorado River on dry limestone hills. In Mexico in the states of Chihuahua to Durango.

Remarks. The genus name, *Morus*, is the classical name, and the species name, *microphylla*, refers to the small leaves. Vernacular names are Mexican Mulberry, Dwarf Mulberry, Wild Mulberry, Mountain Mulberry, Tzitzi, Hamdek-kiup, and Mora. The Indians of Arizona and New Mexico are reported to have grown the tree for its fruit and made bows from the wood. In Mexico the wood is used occasionally in carpentry. The fruit is rather small and dry but edible. It is consumed by a number of species of birds, including mockingbird, cardinal, mourning dove, Mearns's quail, scaled quail, and Gambel's quail, and is sometimes browsed by the white-tailed deer. Texas Mulberry is easily distinguished from Red Mulberry by much smaller leaves and fruit. Texas Mulberry is generally found on dry, limestone soils. At one time the botanist E. L. Greene split the species into a number of segregates. However, most of these divisions are not constant in character, so the recent tendency is to regard them as geographical forms of the same species, *M. microphylla* Buckl.

Osage-orange

Maclura pomifera (Raf.) Schneid. [D, E, F, G]

Field Identification. Tree attaining a height of 60 ft, with a milky sap and bearing stout thorns.

Flowers. April–June, dioecious, green, staminate in long-peduncled axillary racemes, 1–1½ in. long; petals none; stamens 4, exserted; calyx 4-lobed; pistillate in globose dense heads about 1 in. in diameter; calyx 4-lobed, thick, enclosing the ovary; ovary ovoid, compressed, 1-celled; style filiform, long, exserted.

Fruit. September–October, a syncarp, or aggregation of 1-seeded drupelets, globose, yellowish green, 4–5 in. in diameter; achenes surrounded by enlarged fleshy calyx; juice of fruit milky and acid.

Leaves. Deciduous, alternate, entire, broad-ovate to ovate-lanceolate, rounded or subcordate at base, or broadly cuneate, acuminate at apex, 3–6 in. long, tomentose at first, lustrous later, yellow in autumn, petioles ½–2 in., stipules triangular, small, early deciduous.

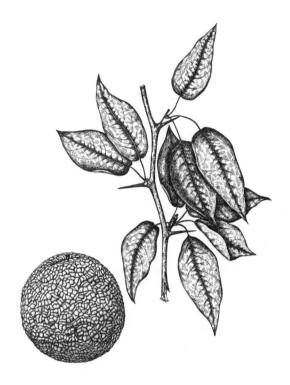

Bark. Brown to orange, deeply furrowed, ridges rounded and interlacing.

Wood. Bright orange or yellow, heavy, hard, durable, strong, weighing 48 lb per cu ft.

Range. Arkansas, Oklahoma, Louisiana, Missouri, and south into Texas. Well developed in the Oklahoma Red River Valley. Also escaping cultivation throughout eastern United States.

Remarks. The genus name, *Maclura*, is in memory of William Maclure, an early American geologist, and the species name, *pomifera*, means "fruit-bearing." The name Bois d'Arc was given to it by the French, meaning "bow-wood," with reference to the fact that the Osage Indians made bows from the wood. Vernacular names are Hedge-apple, Horse-apple, Mock-orange, and Yellow-wood. Yellow dye was formerly made from the root bark. Also the bark of the trunk was used for tanning leather. Squirrels feed on the little achenes buried in the pulpy fruit, and black-tail deer browse the leaves. The tree was formerly much planted as wind-breaks or hedgerows, and has been cultivated since 1818.

Common Fig

Ficus carica L. [D, E]

Field Identification. Deciduous spreading shrub or tree to 30 ft. Branches numerous, stout, glabrous, spreading or ascending, forming a rounded or flattened crown. Sap thick and milky.

Flowers. Borne inside a hollow pear-shaped receptacle with a narrow orifice, axillary, solitary, greenish or brown to violet, length 1½–3⅓ in., staminate flowers nearly sessile, with 2–6 sepals and 1–3 stamens; pistillate flowers short-stalked; style lateral and elongate; ovary sessile, 1-celled.

Fruit. Synconium obovoid to ellipsoid, fleshy, achenes small, numerous, included in fruit; taste mild, sweet, mucilaginous; firm and leathery.

Leaves. Simple, alternate, ovate to oval, usually 3–7-lobed, some leaves lobed a second time; lobes obovate or obtuse at apex and irregularly dentate, blades 4–8 in. long and about as broad, base cordate or truncate, scabrous above and below with stout, stiff hairs, venation palmate; petioles ¾–2 in., usually one-half to two-thirds as long as the blade, lightly to densely pubescent.

Twigs. Smooth, stout, gray, pubescent at first, branches glabrous later.

Range. Cultivated in Texas, Oklahoma, Arkansas, and Louisiana; eastward to Florida and Tennessee, and northward along the Atlantic coastal plain as far north as New York. Not escaping cultivation readily because of frost kill. In old gardens, fields, and along roadsides. A native of western Asia. Cultivated since ancient times.

Remarks. The genus name, *Ficus*, is the ancient Latin name. The species name, *carica*, is from Caria in Asia Minor.

MAGNOLIA FAMILY (Magnoliaceae)

Southern Magnolia

Magnolia grandiflora L. [D, E]

Field Identification. Large evergreen tree attaining a maximum height of 135 ft, but usually not over 50 ft. Possibly one of the largest trees known has been recorded from Pascagoula, Mississippi, with a trunk circumference of 13 ft 7 in., height of 52 ft, and spread of 92 ft.

Flowers. April–August, solitary on short pedicels, terminal, cup-shaped, 6–9 in. across; petals 6–18, rounded or obovate, white, often purple at base, arranged in a series; sepals 3, petallike; stamens numerous, short, filaments purple; anthers linear, opening on the inner side; pistils numerous, coherent along a prolonged receptacle to form a fleshy cone, ovules 2.

Fruit. Ripening July–October, cone ovoid to cylindric, rose-colored, fleshy, rusty-hairy, imbricate, 2–4 in., 1½–2 in. wide.

Each carpel splits dorsally to expose 1 or 2 red, obovoid seeds suspended on thin threads. From 40–60 seeds per cone.

Leaves. Very variable, alternate, simple, evergreen, coriaceous, blades 4–9 in. long, 2–3 in. wide, elliptic or oval, acute or obtuse at apex, cuneate at base, margin entire, shiny and dark green above, rusty-tomentose beneath; petioles stout, tomentose, about ¾ in.; stipules foliaceous, deciduous.

Twigs. Green to olive, stout, hairy, or glabrous later.

Bark. Aromatic, bitter, grayish brown, breaking into small, thin scales.

Wood. Creamy white, hard, weak, not durable, fairly heavy.

Range. In rich, moist soil; Texas, Oklahoma, Arkansas, and Louisiana; eastward to Florida and north to North Carolina. Cultivated for ornament as far north as Washington, D.C.

Remarks. The genus name, *Magnolia*, is in honor of Pierre Magnol, professor of botany at Montpellier, and the species name, *grandiflora*, refers to the large flowers. Vernacular names are Bullbay, Great Laurel Magnolia, and Loblolly Magnolia. The seeds are eaten by at least 5 species of birds and by squirrels. The wood is used for fuel, baskets, crates, woodenware, furniture, and shades. This species and others of the same genus are widely cultivated for their beautiful flowers and showy leaves, both in the United States and in Europe. It has been cultivated since 1734. Horticulturists have also developed a number of clones from the Southern Magnolia, among which are the Exmouth, Gallisson, Glorious, Goliath, Narrow-leaf, and Round-leaf.

Sweet-bay Magnolia

Magnolia virginiana L. [D]

Field Identification. Swamp-loving shrub or tree attaining a height of 30 ft. The largest specimen ever recorded is in Cambden, South Carolina. This tree has a height of 67 ft and a circumference of 6 ft. One of the field marks for identification is the conspicuous white undersurface of the leaves.

Flowers. Borne on short slender pedicels, very fragrant, depressed-globose, 2–3 in. broad; petals 8–12, elliptic, obovate or oval, obtuse; sepals 3, obtuse, shorter than petals, obovate or oblong; stamens short-filamented, numerous on a prolonged receptacle.

Fruit. Pistils coherent to form an ellipsoidal, imbricate, fleshy, red cone 1–2 in. long; cone splitting at maturity to discharge from each carpel 1–2 red, oval seeds suspended on thin threads.

Leaves. Scattered, alternate, simple, undulate, oblong, elliptic or oval, obtuse at apex, broad-cuneate at base, green above, white or pale glaucous beneath, blades 3–6 in. long, 1–2½ in. wide; petioles slender, smooth, about 1 in.

Twigs. Slender, bright green, glabrous or hairy.

Bark. Pale gray to brown, smooth, aromatic, bitter.

Wood. Pale brown, sapwood white, soft, weighing 31 lb per cu ft.

Range. Usually in low, wet, acid, sandy soil. Texas, Oklahoma, Arkansas, and Louisiana; eastward to Florida, northward to Pennsylvania, and in isolated stations to Massachusetts.

Remarks. The genus name, *Magnolia*, is in honor of the botanist Pierre Magnol, and the species name is for the state of Virginia. Vernacular names are Swamp-bay, Beaver-tree, White-bay, White-laurel, Swamp Magnolia, Swamp-sassafras, and Indian-bark. This species is easily identified by the white undersurface of the leaves. Although deciduous in the North, the leaves tend to be evergreen in the South. It is reported that the flowers have been used in perfume manufacture, and the leaves as a flavoring for meats. The tree is sometimes confused with the Red Bay, *Persea borbonia*, which also has leaves used for flavoring purposes. Sweet-bay Magnolia is occasionally cultivated for ornament and is thicket forming by sprouts from the roots. The flowers are small, but have a penetrating fragrance. The wood is used for making light woodenware articles.

CUSTARD-APPLE FAMILY (Annonaceae)

Common Pawpaw

Asimina triloba (L.) Dunal [D]

Field Identification. Spreading shrub or broad-crowned tree attaining a height of 40 ft.

Flowers. Axillary, solitary, perfect, on stout rusty-hairy pedicels, 1–2 in. across, appearing with or before the leaves; petals 6, purplish green, veiny, the 3 outer ovate-obovate or orbicular, larger than the 3-pointed, erect, glandular inner ones; stamens many, short; pistils few to many; style inwardly stigmatic; ovary 1-celled, ovules numerous; calyx of 3 ovate, acuminate, pale green sepals, much smaller than petals.

Fruit. Bananalike, borne singly, or in oblique clusters of 2–4, oblong-cylindric, often falcate, apex and base pointed or rounded, 2–7 in. long, 1–2½ in. thick, green when young, brown or black when mature; pulp sweet, white or yellow, aromatic, edible; seeds several, dark brown, large, bony, rounded, flat, horizontal, about 1 in. long and ½ in. broad.

Leaves. Deciduous, alternate, simple, oblong-obovate abruptly pointed or acute at apex, obtuse or cuneate at base, entire, thin, rusty-pubescent when young, globous later, blades 4–11 in. long, 2–6 in. broad, odorous when bruised; petioles ⅓–1 in., stout.

Twigs. Slender, olive brown, often blotched, smooth, rougher when older, and often with warty excrescences.

Bark. Dark brown, thin, smooth, later with shallow fissures.

Wood. Pale yellow, coarse-grained, soft, weak, weighing 24 lb per cu ft.

Range. Rich soil of bottom lands. East Texas, Arkansas, and Louisiana; eastward to Florida, and north to New York, Michigan, and Nebraska.

Remarks. The genus name, *Asimina*, is from the early French name *Asiminier*, which in turn was derived from the Indian *Arsimin*. The species name, *triloba*, refers to the petals, which are in sets of 3. Vernacular names are Fetid-shrub and Custard-apple. Pawpaw fruit falls to the ground in autumn and must be stored until ripe. It may be baked into pies, made into dessert, or eaten raw with cream as a breakfast food. When eaten raw it is cloying-

ly sweet with a custardlike flavor. Seemingly a taste for it must be cultivated because some consider it nauseating. The food value is largely carbohydrate. The fruit varies greatly in size and flavor. Some are large, yellow fleshed, highly flavored, and early ripening. Others are white fleshed, mildly flavored, and late ripening. Handling the fruit is known to produce a skin rash on some people. The rough bark is sometimes used as a rope substitute. Birds are fond of the fruit, and it is also eaten by gray fox, opossum, raccoon, and squirrel. The seeds of the Pawpaw contain an alkaloid, asiminine, which is reported to have emetic properties. The bark was once used as a medicine and contains the alkaloid analobine.

LAUREL FAMILY (Lauraceae)

Common Spice-bush

Lindera benzoin (L.) Blume [D]

Field Identification. Stout, glabrous, aromatic shrub of damp woods. Attaining a height of 20 ft, with usually several stems from the base.

Flowers. Appearing before the leaves, polygamodioecious, yellow, fragrant, ¼–⅓ in. broad, in lateral, almost sessile, dense, um-

Hairy Common Spice-bush

bellike clusters of 3–6 flowers; involucre of 4 deciduous scales; petals absent; sepals 6, thin, obovate to elliptic, apex obtuse to retuse or truncate; staminate flowers with 9 stamens (in 3 series), some filaments glandular at base, anthers introrse, 2-celled and 2-valved; pistillate flowers with 12–18 rudimentary stamens in 2 forms (glandular and glandless); ovary globose, style slender and columnar.

Fruit. Ripening August–September, drupes solitary or in small clusters on pedicels 1/12–1/5 in., orbicular to obovoid, elongate, about 2/5 in. long, red, fleshy, spicy; 1-seeded, seeds light brown, speckled darker brown.

Leaves. Leaf buds scaly, leaves simple, alternate, deciduous, obovate to oval or elliptic, apex acute or short-acuminate, base acute or acuminate, margin entire, thin, bright green above, glaucous, beneath glabrous, more rarely pubescent, blade length 2–4¾ in., width 1–2½ in.; petioles ³⁄₁₆–¾ in. Twigs often with 2 leaf sizes, much smaller ones sometimes at base of larger ones.

Twigs. Slender, glabrous, smooth, brittle, bark with corky lenticels, spicy to the taste.

Range. Sandy or peaty soils in low woods or swamps. Central Texas, Oklahoma, Arkansas, and Louisiana; eastward to Florida, north to Maine, and west to Ontario, Michigan, and Kansas.

Remarks. The genus name, *Lindera*, is for John Linder, a Swedish physician (1676–1723). The species name, *benzoin*, denotes its similarity, in odor, to the true balsamic resin of *Styrax benzoin*, an Asiatic tree. Vernacular names are Benjamin-bush, Spice-wood, Fever-bush, Snap-bush, and Wild Allspice. There are also a few varieties of Common Spice-bush, such as the Hairy Common Spice-bush, *L. benzoin* var. *pubescens* (Palm. & Steyerm.) Rehd., which has pubescent and ciliate leaves and petioles. Some authorities list the Common Spice-bush under the scientific name of *Benzoin aestivale* (L.) Nees.

The leaves, twigs, bark, and fruit contain an aromatic oil which was made into a fragrant tea by the pioneers. The bark is aromatic, tonic, astringent, stimulant, and pleasant to chew. A substitute for allspice was once made from the dry, powdered drupes. Twenty-four species of birds are known to feed upon the fruit, also rabbit and white-tailed deer nibble the leaves.

Common Sassafras

Sassafras albidum (Nutt.) Nees [D, E]

Field Identification. Tree attaining a height of 90 ft, with a flattened oblong crown, and short, crooked branches.

Flowers. March–April, dioecious, axillary, in racemes about 2 in. long; calyx yellowish green, of 6 spreading sepals; corolla absent; stamens in 3 sets of 3 each, the inner set glandular at the base; anthers 4-celled, with flattened, elongate filaments; pistillate flowers with an erect columnar style and depressed stigma, also 6 sterile stamens.

Fruit. Drupaceous, blue, lustrous, ½ in. long, oblong or spherical, borne on a thickened red pedicel, pulpy; stone solitary, light brown, dispersed chiefly by birds.

Leaves. Alternate, simple, deciduous, thin, aromatic, blades 3–5 in. long, ovate or elliptic, entire on the margin, or divided into 2–3 mitten-shaped lobes, lobes acute or obtuse; cuneate at base, bright green above, glabrous and glaucous beneath, often hairy on the veins; petioles about 1 in.

Twigs. Yellowish green, mucilaginous, pubescent at first, turning glabrous and orange-red later.

Bark. Reddish brown to gray, aromatic, irregularly broken into broad flat ridges.

Wood. Orange-colored, aromatic, durable, close-grained, soft, weak, brittle, weighing 31 lb per cu ft.

Range. Texas, Oklahoma, Arkansas, and Louisiana; eastward to Florida, north to Maine, and west to Ontario, Michigan, and Iowa.

Remarks. The genus name, *Sassafras*, is a popular one derived from the word *salsafras*, which was given by early French settlers, with reference to its medicinal properties; and the species name, *albidum*, refers to a light-colored condition of the wood. Other commonly used vernacular names are Ague-tree, Cinnamon-wood, Smelling-stick, Saloop, and Gumbo-file. The tree is long-lived and rather free of diseases. The fruit is known to be eaten by 28 species of birds, and the leaves browsed by woodchuck, white-tailed deer, marsh rabbit, and black bear. The wood is used for posts, rails, buckets, cabinets, and interior finish.

Silky Sassafras, *S. albidum* var. *molle* (Raf.) Fern., is a variety with buds and twigs pubescent, leaves glaucescent and silky pubescent beneath, at least while young. Texas to Florida; north to Ontario and Michigan. In Texas west to the Brazos River.

JUNCO FAMILY (Koeberliniaceae)

Spiny Allthorn

Koeberlinia spinosa Zucc. [F, G]

Field Identification. Much-branched, usually leafless shrub or tree attaining a height of 24 ft, and consisting of a tangled mass of stiff green spines.

Flowers. Borne on slender pedicels $\frac{1}{12}-\frac{1}{3}$ in. long in lateral racemes, each flower small, perfect, and about $\frac{1}{4}$ in. across; petals 4, greenish white, linear to oblong, apex obtuse or sometimes notched, longer than sepals; stamens 8, filaments flattened in the middle and somewhat petaloid, anthers large, sagittate and deciduous; ovary 2–5 united carpels, styles united; calyx of 4 ovate, deciduous sepals about $\frac{1}{25}$ in. long. In some flowers it is difficult to distinguish between the petals and petaloid stamens with deciduous anthers.

Fruit. Borne in clusters about 1 in. long, peduncles clavate and about $\frac{1}{3}$ in. long; berry black, subglobose, apiculate, $\frac{3}{16}-\frac{1}{4}$ in. in diameter, fleshy, 2-celled; seeds 1–4, about $\frac{1}{8}$ in. long, curled, wrinkled, and striate.

Leaves. Alternate, consisting of minute scales which are early-deciduous, thus leaving the plant barren most of the year.

Twigs. Green, smooth, stout, stiff, divaricate, all ending in large, sharp thorns.

Bark. Smooth, green to brown or gray on young trunks, older with small scales and shallow fissures.

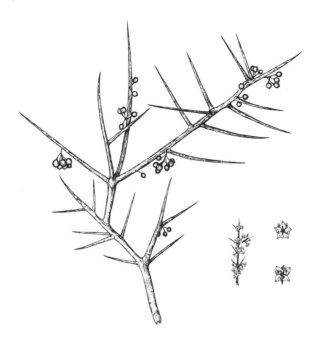

Wood. Black or brown, hard, resinous, close-grained, with a specific gravity of 1.12, emitting a disagreeable odor when burned.

Range. Arid places in western and southwestern Texas; west through New Mexico to Arizona, and south into Mexico in Sonora to Tamaulipas and Hidalgo.

Remarks. The genus name, *Koeberlinia*, is in honor of C. L. Koeberlin, German clergyman and amateur botanist. The species name, *spinosa*, refers to the abundant spines. Common names for the plant are Junco, Corona de Cristo, and Crucifixion Thorn. Scaled quail have been seen to eat the fruit, as has the jack rabbit. The plant is perhaps of some value in erosion control. It is a perfect example of adjustment to desert conditions, with the green thorns and twigs carrying on the photosynthetic process. Being thicket-forming, it presents an impenetrable green mass of thorns to any intruder.

WITCH HAZEL FAMILY (Hamamelidaceae)

American Sweetgum

Liquidambar styraciflua L. [D, E]

Field Identification. Large tree, attaining a height of 150 ft, with palmately lobed, serrate, alternate leaves. The branches and twigs are corky-winged, or wingless on some trees.

Flowers. March–May, monoecious, very small, greenish; perianth none; staminate flowers in terminal, erect, tomentose racemes 2–3 in. long; stamens numerous, set among tiny scales, filaments slender and short; pistillate flowers in axillary, globose, long-peduncled, drooping heads; styles 2, inwardly stigmatic, sterile stamens 4.

Fruit. September–November, persistent, globular, spinose, lustrous, 1–1½ in. in diameter, long-peduncled, resulting from the aggregation of the many 2-celled ovaries which are tipped by the 2-beaked or hornlike styles; ovules many, but maturing only 1–2 flat-winged seeds, the rest abortive, light brown; good seed crops every three years, light years in between.

Leaves. Simple, alternate, deciduous, petioled, broader than long, blades 3–9 in. wide, with 3–7 acuminate lobes; lobes oblong-triangular, glandular-serrate; slightly cordate or truncate at base; glabrous and glossy above, pubescent along the veins beneath, aromatic when bruised; petioles 2–4¾ in., slender, stipules falling away early.

Twigs. At first with rusty-red tomentum, later glabrous and with wide corky wings, or some trees without wings.

Bark. Very rough, deeply furrowed, ridges rounded, brown to gray.

Wood. Fine-grained, fairly hard, not strong, heartwood reddish brown, takes a high polish, sapwood white or pinkish, weighing about 37 lb per cu ft.

Range. Usually in low bottom-land woods. In east Texas, Oklahoma, Arkansas, and Louisiana; eastward to Florida, north to New York and Connecticut, and west to Illinois and Missouri; also in mountains of Mexico.

Remarks. The genus name, *Liquidambar*, refers to the amber-colored liquid sap, and the species name, *styraciflua*, is from *styraci* ("storax") and *flua* ("fluidus"). Vernacular names are White Gum, Alligator-tree, Opossum-tree, Red Gum, Bilsted, Stain-walnut, Gum-wood, California Red Gum, and Star-leaf Gum. Medicinally the tree is known as "copalm balsam," and the resinous gum is used extensively in Mexico and Europe, especially as a substitute for storax. Various ointments and syrups are prepared from it and are used in the treatment of dysentery and diarrhea. The gum is sometimes chewed by children. It is also used as a perfuming agent in soap, and as an adhesive. It is reported as excellent for healing wounds. The reddish brown wood is used for flooring, furniture, veneers, woodenware, general construction, boxes, crossties, barrels, sewing machines, cabinets, molding, vehicle parts, conveyors, musical instruments, tobacco boxes, and other articles. At least 25 species of birds are known to feed upon the fruit, as well as the gray squirrel and Eastern chipmunk. The autumn foliage is conspicuous because of its beautiful color variations of red and yellow. It has been cultivated since 1681, and is highly ornamental. It is rapid growing, long-lived, and relatively free from insects and disease damage. Perhaps it could be used more extensively in reforestation projects because of its rapid growth in cutover lands.

SYCAMORE FAMILY (Platanaceae)

American Plane-tree (Sycamore)

Platanus occidentalis L. [D, E]

Field Identification. Tree attaining a height of 170 ft, with reddish brown bark which scales off to expose the white, smooth, new bark.

Flowers. April–May, monoecious, the separate heads globose and peduncled; staminate head red, with 3–8 short-filamented stamens accompanied by tiny, club-shaped scales; pistillate heads solitary, green at first, brown when mature, composed of angular ovaries set among tiny scales; ovary linear, 1-celled; style elongate, threadlike; carpels mingled with staminodia.

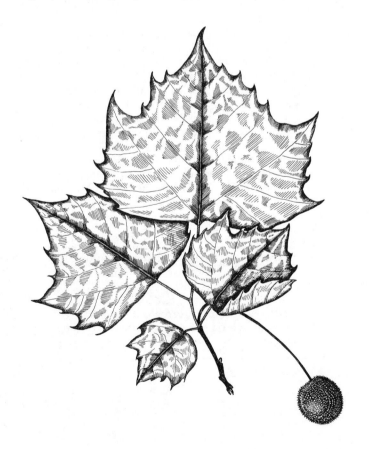

Smooth American
Plane-tree

Fruit. Ripe September–October, borne on peduncles 3–6 in. long,
usually solitary, persistent, globose, 1–1½ in. in diameter, light
brown; achenes numerous, obovoid, small, leathery, obtuse at the
apex, hairy at base, 1-seeded.

Leaves. Simple, alternate, deciduous, thin, broadly ovate, 4–12 in.
across; margin usually set with 5 short, sinuate, acuminate lobes
with large teeth between; truncate or heart-shaped at the base;
bright green above, paler and densely pubescent along the veins
beneath; stipules sheathing, conspicuous, toothed, 1–1½ in.; petiole stout, woolly, shorter than the blade, 3–5 in.

Twigs. Slender, shiny, tomentose at first, glabrous later, orange-
brown to gray.

Bark. Reddish brown, scaling off in thin plates to expose the conspicuous white, or greenish, new bark.

Wood. Light brown, rather weak, close-grained, hard, weighing 33
lb per cu ft, difficult to work.

Range. In rich bottom-land soils, mostly along streams. Texas, Oklahoma, Arkansas, and Louisiana; east to Florida, and north to Maine, Minnesota, Nebraska, and Ontario.

Remarks. The genus name, *Platanus*, is the classical name of the Plane-tree, and the species name, *occidentalis*, means "western." Vernacular names are Button-wood, Buttonball-tree, and Water-beech. The wood is used for crates, interior finishing, furniture, cooperage, rollers, butcher blocks, and tobacco boxes. It attains the largest size of any deciduous tree in the United States and is often planted for ornament. It is slow-growing, but long-lived, and old trees are often hollow with decay. It was first cultivated in 1640. The seeds are eaten by a number of species of birds and sometimes by muskrat.

Smooth American Plane-tree, *P. occidentalis* var. *glabrata* (Fern.) Sarg., is a variety with less numerous and more angular teeth to the leaves. It occurs in Texas on limestone soils from the Colorado River westward to the Devils River and the Rio Grande. Also in Coahuila and Nuevo León, Mexico.

ROSE FAMILY (Rosaceae)

Genus *Crataegus*
The *Crataegus* Problem

The genus *Crataegus* with its numerous variations and hybrids represents a very difficult taxonomic complex. One of the difficulties appears to be in the separation of the so-called successful hybrid misfits from the normal, well-distributed, sexual, diploid species. To make the matter more complicated, many of the non-hybrid good species cannot be determined with certainty by any one set of parts or characters. It is evident that too many species have been described. Most of the 1,100 specific names given during the last 25 years were applied by the authors C. S. Sargent, W. W. Ashe, and C. D. Beadle. Many of these have been, and more probably will be, reduced to synonymy as a better knowledge of the group is achieved.

Faced with the very difficult problem of choosing the tree and shrub species of the southwestern United States, the author has turned to Dr. Ernest J. Palmer of Webb City, Missouri, for advice. Dr. Palmer is the leading authority on this group and has done much to clarify many problems concerning its species. He has studied the group closely for more than thirty years and has contributed a monographic treatment in the 1950 edition of *Gray's Manual of Botany* by M. L. Fernald. Dr. Palmer has graciously provided a list of those southwestern species which he considers to be valid and also has contributed a key to both the series and the species.

Using these keys and list as a basis of approach, the author has carefully reviewed all of the original descriptions of Palmer, Sargent, Ashe, and Beadle. This was supplemented by inspection of all of the type material available at the Missouri Botanical Garden, the New York Botanical Garden, the Smithsonian Institution, and the Arnold Arboretum. Although five years were spent in the study of this complex group, the author makes no claim to having clarified all the problems concerning the southwestern species. The last word has certainly not been said, and the material presented is only broadly interpreted. Changes and corrections will undoubtedly have to be made when the species become better known.

The key is in two parts: a Key to the Series of *Crataegus* and a Key to the Species under the Series. In the Key to the Series, the characters of the series are outlined in contrasting pairs of statements or, occasionally, groups of three contrasting statements. Always choose the statement which most closely describes the plant you have to identify. For example, first compare the two statements designated as (a). If the first (a) is the one which seems to apply to the plant in question, then choose between the two (b) characters. It will be noted that the first (b) requires a further choice between (c) and (c), whereas the second (b) leads to the number and name of a series. Whenever a sequence of choices leads to the name of a series, turn to the Key to the Species under the Series and proceed in the same manner.

The reader will note that both the series and the species sections of the following keys refer to all of the species of *Crataegus* in Texas and adjacent states. However, only the north Texas species are marked D, E, F, or G in the species key.

Key to the Series of *Crataegus*

(a) Veins of the leaves running to the sinuses as well as to the points of the lobes
   (b) Leaves thin but firm, early deciduous; fruit ⅛–⅕ in. thick; nutlets 3–5; native species
      (c) Leaves mostly 1¼–1⅞ in. wide, ovate or deltoid in outline; flowers opening in May; fruit with deciduous calyx exposing tips of nutlets .... 1. **Cordatae** Beadle

(c) Leaves mostly ⅝–1½ in. wide, narrowly obovate to deltoid in outline; flowers opening in March or April; fruit with persistent calyx .... 2. **Microcarpae** Loud.

(b) Leaves thick, persistent until late in the season; fruit ⅜–¼ in. thick; introduced species .... 3. **Oxyacanthae** Loud.

(a) Veins of the leaves running only to the points of the lobes

(d) Fruit red or yellow or remaining green at maturity; thorns usually long and slender, to 1¾–2½ in. long, or rarely thornless

(e) Flowers single or 2–5 in simple clusters; stamens 20–25

(f) Leaves mostly 1⅜–2½ in. long; petioles slender, ⅜–⅝ in. long; sepals not foliaceous, entire or serrate; fruit ½–¾ in. thick, becoming mellow or succulent, edible; arborescent shrubs or small trees in wet or swampy ground .... 5. **Aestivales** Sarg.

(f) Leaves mostly ⅝–1¼ in. long; petioles stout, ⅛–⅕ in. long; sepals foliaceous, pectinate or deeply glandular-serrate; fruit ⅜–⅞ in. thick, remaining firm or hard, scarcely edible; slender shrubs 1½–6 ft tall, in dry or sandy ground .... 6. **Parvifoliae** Loud.

(e) Flowers more numerous, usually 5–20 in simple or compound cymes or corymbs; stamens 5–20

(g) Flowers opening in late March through April according to latitude; nutlets plane on ventral surfaces

(h) Foliage and inflorescence glandular, usually conspicuously so

(i) Leaves mostly narrowly obovate or spatulate, broadest above the middle except at the ends of branchlets where sometimes broadly oval or suborbicular; fruit red or orange-red, becoming mellow; arborescent shrubs or small trees .... 7. **Flavae** Loud.

(i) Leaves mostly ovate, oblong-ovate, or rhombic in outline, broadest at or below the middle, gradually or abruptly narrowed at base, usually lobed, especially at the ends of branchlets; fruit bronze-green or dull red, remaining firm or hard; shrubs usually less than 9 ft tall .... 8. **Intricatae** Sarg.

(h) Foliage and inflorescence eglandular, or if slightly glandular, the glands small and soon deciduous

(j) Leaves mostly narrowly obovate, cuneate or oblong-obovate, unlobed or very obscurely lobed except at the ends of branchlets, where sometimes broadly obovate to oval or suborbicular

(k) Leaves thick or firm, glossy above in most species; fruit remaining hard and often green at

maturity; nutlets 1–3 (or rarely 2–5 in a few
species) .... 10. **Crus-galli** Loud.

  (k) Leaves thin to firm, not coriaceous, dull green
above; fruit becoming soft or mellow; nutlets
usually 3–5

    (l) Leaves relatively thin, the veins obscure, most-
ly 1¾–2½ in. long, quite variable in shape,
often oblong-obovate or rhombic, unlobed or
slightly lobed except at the ends of branchlets
where broadly oval or ovate and more deeply
lobed; fruit ¼–⁷⁄₁₆ in. thick; bark thin, exfoliating from orange-brown inner bark ....
.... 9. **Virides** Beadle

    (l) Leaves firm, more uniform in shape, mostly
oblong-obovate, unlobed or with small shallow
lobes above the middle; veins distinctly impressed above, mostly 1¼–2 in. long; fruit usually ³⁄₈–⁵⁄₈ in. thick; bark gray, thick, slightly
scaly or ridged .... 11. **Punctatae** Loud.

 (j) Leaves mostly oblong-ovate to rhombic, or broadly
ovate to suborbicular at the ends of branchlets, all
sharply lobed; New Mexico ....
.... 12. **Rotundifoliae** Egglest.

 (j) Leaves mostly ovate or deltoid in outline, broadest
below the middle, often rounded, truncate, or subcordate at base; Arkansas and eastward, except
some species in 16 and 19

  (m) Sepals entire or serrate, not pectinate or deeply
glandular-serrate; filaments as long or nearly as
long as the petals; nutlets 3–5, usually less than
5

    (n) Leaves thin, glabrous except for short pilose
hairs above while young; stamens about 10;
fruit less than ⁷⁄₁₆ in. thick, becoming succulent
.... 13. **Tenuifoliae** Sarg.

    (n) Leaves firm or thick; fruit usually ⁷⁄₁₆ in. or
more thick, remaining firm or hard

      (o) Young leaves scabrate with sparse hairs
above, becoming glabrous; fruiting calyx
small and sessile .... 14. **Silvicolae** Beadle

      (o) Young leaves glabrous above, glabrous or
rarely pubescent beneath; fruiting calyx elevated and usually prominent ....
.... 15. **Pruinosae** Sarg.

(m) Sepals conspicuously glandular-serrate or pectinate; filaments distinctly shorter than the petals; nutlets usually 5

(p) Foliage and inflorescence pubescent; flowers ¾–⅞ in. wide; fruit pubescent at least while young, ripening in August or early September .... 16. **Molles** Sarg.

(p) Foliage and inflorescence glabrous; flowers ¾–1 in. wide; fruit glabrous, ripening in October .... 17. **Dilatatae** Sarg.

(d) Fruit blue or black at maturity; thorns short and stout, usually less than ¾ in. long

(q) Leaves mostly abruptly pointed or rounded at the apex, lustrous above; fruit blue at maturity (except in rare form), glaucous; eastern Texas and eastward .... 4. **Brevispinae** Beadle

(q) Leaves mostly acute or acuminate at the apex, dull green above; fruit turning from purple to black, lustrous but not glaucous; New Mexico and westward .... 18. **Douglasianae** Egglest.

(q) Flowers opening late, April or May according to latitude; nutlets pitted on ventral surfaces .... 19. **Macracanthae** Loud.

Key to the Species under the Series

1. **Cordatae** (only one species in this area) ... 1. *C. phaenopyrum*
2. **Microcarpae**
   a. Leaves mostly broadly ovate in outline, often as broad or broader than long, deeply incised, rounded to cordate at base; anthers red; fruit oblong .... 2. *C. marshallii* [D]
   a. Leaves mostly narrowly obovate or spatulate, unlobed or nearly so except at the ends of branchlets, cuneate or attenuate at base; anthers pale yellow; fruit subglobose .... 3. *C. spathulata* [D, E]
3. **Oxyacanthae** (only one species in this area) .... 4. *C. monogyna*
4. **Brevispinae** (only one species in this area) .... 5. *C. brachyacantha* [D]
5. **Aestivales**
   a. Pubescence on the under surface of the leaves rusty brown, mainly along the veins; fruit ripening in May .... 6. *C. opaca* (typical) [D]
   a. Pubescence on the under surface of the leaves gray, mainly in the axils of the veins; fruit ripening in June .... 6a. *C. opaca* var. *dormanae*

6. **Parvifoliae** (only one species in this area) . . . . 7. *C. uniflora*
7. **Flavae** (only one species in this area) . . . . 8. *C. pearsonii*
8. **Intricatae**
  a. Foliage and inflorescence glabrous or essentially so
    b. Leaves mostly 1⅝–2½ in. long, 1–2 in. wide; flowers
      ⅝–¾ in. wide
      c. Fruit remaining dry and hard; sepals glandular-serrate
        d. Terminal leaves often ovate and deeply lobed near the
          base; fruit remaining green or yellowish green
          e. Anthers white or pale yellow (rarely pink) . . . .
            . . . . 9. *C. intricata* var. *straminea*
          e. Anthers pink or red (rarely white); fruit subglobose
            or short-oblong; nutlets 2–4, usually 2–3 . . . .
            . . . . 9a. *C. neobushii*
        d. Terminal leaves usually oblong-ovate or broadly ellip-
          tic, not deeply lobed; fruit becoming dull red
          f. Fruit subglobose; nutlets 3–5 . . . . 10. *C. buckleyi*
          f. Fruit obovoid or oblong; nutlets 2–5, usually less
            than 5 . . . . 11. *C. rubella*
      c. Fruit becoming mellow or juicy; sepals entire or finely
        glandular-serrate . . . . 12. *C. padifolia* var. *incarnata*
    b. Leaves mostly 1–1⅝ in. wide; flowers ½–⅝ in. wide . . . . . .
      . . . . 13. *C. pagensis*
  a. Foliage and inflorescence pubescent, at least while young;
    young leaves and inflorescence sparsely pilose, becoming
    glabrous or nearly so; stamens about 20; anthers red; fruit
    usually less than 7/16 in. thick, glabrous
    g. Leaves mostly 1⅝–2 in. long, 1¼–1⅝ in. wide; flowers
      mostly 6–12 in corymb; fruit subglobose, about 7/16 in.
      thick, orange-colored; arborescent shrub or small tree . . . . .
      . . . . 16. *C. harveyana*
    g. Leaves mostly ¾–1⅝ in. long and wide; flowers mostly
      3–8 in corymb; fruit oblong or pyriform, about ⅓ in.
      thick, dull red; widely branching shrub 3–6 ft tall . . . .
      . . . . 14. *C. ouachitensis*
  a. Foliage and inflorescence pubescent throughout the season;
    stamens about 10; anthers cream-white or pale yellow; fruit
    pubescent while young . . . . 15. *C. biltmoreana*
9. **Virides**
  a. Mature leaves and inflorescence glabrous or essentially so
    (except in variety of no. 17)
    b. Leaves firm but comparatively thin at maturity, dull green
      above; nutlets normally 5
      c. Leaves variable in shape, mostly oblong-ovate or oblong-
        elliptic, glabrous (except in variety); anthers pale yellow
        or rarely pink . . . . 17. *C. viridis* [D, E, F]

  c. Leaves more uniform in shape, mostly ovate or oblong-
   ovate, pubescent above as they unfold, soon glabrous;
   anthers pink .... 22. *C. sutherlandensis*
 b. Leaves thick or subcoriaceous at maturity, glossy above,
  nutlets 3–5
  d. Leaves mostly 2–2¾ in. long; terminal leaves broadly
   ovate and sharply lobed; fruit ¼–⁷⁄₁₆ in. thick ....
   .... 18. *C. nitida*
  d. Leaves mostly 1⅝–2½ in. long; terminal leaves broadly
   ovate to suborbicular; fruit about ⅓ in. thick ....
   .... 23. *C. glabriuscula* forma *desertorum*
a. Foliage and inflorescence conspicuously pubescent while
 young, the leaves more or less pubescent throughout the
 season
  e. Mature leaves comparatively thin; flowers mostly 8–15 in
   corymb; fruit subglobose
   f. Leaves pubescent beneath throughout the season;
    flowers ½–⅝ in. wide .... *C. viridis* var. *velutina*
   f. Leaves strongly pubescent while young, becoming nearly
    glabrous; flowers about ¾ in. wide ...... 19. *C. anamesa*
  e. Mature leaves thick or subcoriaceous, pubescent while
   young, becoming glabrous and glossy above and slightly
   hairy along the veins beneath
   g. Flowers ¾ in. or more wide, mostly 10–20 in corymb;
    sepals narrowly lanceolate, long-acuminate ....
    .... 20. *C. stenosepala*
   g. Flowers ⅝–¾ in. wide, mostly 5–15 in corymb; sepals
    lanceolate or deltoid-lanceolate, broad based
    h. Leaves mostly 1¼–1¾ in. long; fruit subglobose or
     ovoid, orange-red, becoming mellow ....
     .... 21. *C. poliophylla*
    h. Leaves mostly 1–1¼ in. long; fruit subglobose, dull
     red, remaining hard and dry .... 24. *C. amicalis*
10. **Crus-galli**
 a. Foliage and inflorescence glabrous or essentially so, except in
  no. 30 and in var. of no. 32, in which the young leaves are
  more or less pubescent
  b. Mature leaves thick or subcoriaceous and glossy above (except sometimes in shade)
   c. Leaves mostly obovate or spatulate, distinctly longer
    than broad, broadest above the middle, except some-
    times at the ends of branchlets
    d. Serration of the leaves sharp with acute teeth; fruit
     usually ⅓–½ in. thick; nutlets 1–3, usually 1 or 2
     e. Terminal shoot leaves unlobed or rarely very

obscurely lobed; flowers $\frac{7}{16}$–$\frac{5}{8}$ in. wide; stamens
about 10 (except in var. *leptophylla*) ....
.... 25. *C. crus-galli* [D, E]
  e. Terminal shoot leaves often slightly lobed; flowers
    about ¾ in. wide; nutlets usually 2 ...26. *C. bushii*
 d. Serration of the leaves shallow or crenate; fruit ¼–⅖
   in. thick; nutlets usually 2 ....
   .... 34 and 34a. *C. pyracanthoides* vars. [D]
c. Leaves broader, mostly broadly obovate, oblong-obovate
  or oval, only slightly longer than broad or often as broad
  as long at the ends of shoots
  f. Young leaves quite glabrous; terminal shoot leaves
    usually broadly ovate to suborbicular
    g. Flowers ½–⅝ in. wide; fruit $\frac{7}{16}$ in. or less thick;
      nutlets usually 3; terminal leaves broadly ovate or
      oblong-ovate, sometimes slightly lobed toward the
      base .... 27. *C. palmeri*
    g. Flowers ⅝–¾ in. wide; fruit $\frac{7}{16}$–½ in. thick (or
      smaller in varieties); terminal leaves broadly oval or
      suborbicular, often with several small shallow lobes
      .... 29. *C. reverchonii* [D, E]
    g. Flowers about ½ in. wide; corymbs glabrous; sta-
      mens 10, anthers red or pink; fruit ellipsoidal; leaves
      oblong .... 29a. *C. cherokeensis*
  f. Young leaves sometimes slightly villous, soon gla-
    brous (except in var. of no. 32 where they are perma-
    nently pubescent)
    h. Leaves mostly obovate or oblong-obovate; terminal
      leaves incisely lobed; flowers usually 8–15 in lax
      corymbs
      i. Leaves sharply and deeply serrate; terminal shoot
        leaves mostly oval with 2–3 pairs of small shal-
        low lobes; stamens about 10; fruit $\frac{7}{16}$–½ in. thick,
        dull red; nutlets 2–3 .... 32. *C. regalis*
      i. Leaves with sharp but shallow serrations terminal
        leaves mostly elliptic, sometimes slightly lobed
        toward the apex; flowers about ¾ in. wide; sta-
        mens about 10; fruit about $\frac{7}{16}$ in. thick, bright
        orange or orange-red; nutlets usually 3 ....
        .... 30. *C. mohrii*
    h. Terminal shoot leaves broad-obovate to elliptic,
      glabrous at maturity, unlobed but deeply and irreg-
      ularly serrate; flowers mostly 5–6 in compact cor-
      ymbs; stamens 20, anthers pink ....
      .... 36. *C. sublobulata*

    h. Terminal shoot leaves ovate to oval or obovate, pale villose below at maturity . . . . 36a. *C. warneri*

  b. Mature leaves comparatively thin, not subcoriaceous, yellowish green, slightly lustrous but not glossy above

      j. Leaves mostly elliptic or oblong-obovate, longer than wide except sometimes at the ends of shoots, the veins obscure; fruit subglobose or slightly obovoid, dull red at maturity . . . . 28. *C. acutifolia*

      j. Leaves mostly broadly obovate or rhombic, nearly or sometimes quite as broad as long, the veins slightly impressed above; fruit oblong, green or yellowish flushed with red at maturity . . . . 33. *C. sabineana*

 a. Foliage and inflorescence pubescent while young and usually throughout the season

    k. Leaves mostly obovate or oblong-obovate, broadest above the middle except sometimes at the ends of shoots

      l. Fruit 7/16 in. or less thick, remaining dry and hard

        m. Flowers 7/16–5/8 in. wide; fruit red or orange at maturity, not lustrous

          n. Flowers mostly 4–5 in compact corymbs; stamens about 20; anthers pale yellow . . . 38. *C. berberifolia*

          n. Flowers mostly 8–12 in loose corymbs; stamens about 10; anthers usually pink, rarely white . . . . 39. *C. engelmannii* [D, E]

      l. Fruit 1/2–3/4 in. thick, becoming mellow or succulent; flowers 5/8–3/4 in. wide . . . . 31. *C. palliata*

    k. Leaves broader, mostly oblong-obovate, oval or elliptic, usually broadest about the middle

 a. Leaves pubescent beneath throughout the season; flowers flattish, not noticeably cup-shaped

    o. Leaves mostly broadly obovate or oval, those at the ends of shoots similar but larger and relatively broader; sepals entire or minutely serrate; anthers yellow

      p. Flowers about 5/8 in. wide; stamens about 20; fruit subglobose or short-oblong . . . . 40. *C. subpilosa*

      p. Flowers about 3/4 in. wide; stamens about 10; fruit ovoid . . . . 32a. *C. regalis* var. *paradoxa*

    o. Leaves mostly rhombic or oval, those at the ends of shoots broadly oval to suborbicular; sepals conspicuously glandular-serrate; anthers pink or red . . . . 41. *C. traceyi*

 a. Leaves slightly pubescent on both sides while young, becoming glabrous at maturity; flowers cup-shaped . . . 30. *C. mohrii*

11. **Punctatae**

 a. Leaves mostly obovate or oblong-obovate, or at the ends of shoots elliptic or oval; flowers 5–12 in villose corymbs

  b. Flowers mostly 5–8 in corymbs; usually less than ¾ in.
     wide; stamens 10–20, usually 10–15; anthers white or pale
     yellow .... 42. *C. collina*
  b. Flowers mostly 8–12 in corymbs, usually ¾ in. or more
     wide; stamens about 20; anthers pink or rose ....
     .... 44. *C. verruculosa*
 a. Leaves mostly broadly oval or ovate; flowers mostly 8–15 in
    glabrous corymbs .... 43. *C. fastosa*
 a. Leaves oval to obovate, acute or acuminate at apex; fruit
    often rather longer than broad, bright canary yellow; flowers
    in broad 7–8-flowered, slightly villose corymbs ....
    .... 43a. *C. brazoria*
12. **Rotundifoliae**
 a. Leaves elliptic, oval or suborbicular, usually slightly lobed,
    more or less pubescent while young; fruit about ⁷⁄₁₆ in. thick,
    dark red or rarely dull yellow at maturity ....
    .... 45. *C. chrysocarpa*
 a. Leaves mostly ovate or obovate, glabrous; fruit about ⅓ in.
    thick, orange-red or reddish orange at maturity ....
    .... 46. *C. erythropoda*
13. **Tenuifoliae** (only one species in this area) ....
    .... 47. *C. macrosperma*
14. **Silvicolae** (only one species in this area) ....
    .... 48. *C. iracunda* var. *silvicola*
15. **Pruinosae**
 a. Flowers ½–¾ in. wide; fruit ⁷⁄₁₆–⅝ in. thick with prominent
    elevated calyx
   b. Leaves of flowering spurs mostly 1–1¾ in. wide; terminal
      shoot leaves larger, ovate or deltoid, sharply lobed
     c. Leaves mostly abruptly narrowed or rounded at the base;
        fruit usually pruinose .... 49. *C. pruinosa*
     c. Leaves mostly rounded, truncate or subcordate at base;
        fruit not pruinose
   b. Leaves of flowering spurs mostly 1–1⅜ in. wide, the ter-
      minal lobe often conspicuously elongate especially at the
      ends of shoots .... 51. *C. gattingeri*
     d. Leaves with shallow or obscure lobes, mostly rounded or
        abruptly narrowed at base; fruit with a narrow slightly
        elevated calyx .... 51a. *C. disjuncta*
   b. Leaves of flowering spurs mostly 1⅜–1¼ in. wide; termi-
      nal shoot leaves sometimes as broad as long or broader,
      the terminal lobe not conspicuously elongate
     e. Leaves glabrous or essentially so from the first ....
        .... 50. *C. mackenzii*
     e. Leaves short villose above while young, and pubescent

along the veins beneath throughout the season . . . .
. . . . 50a. *C. mackenzii* var. *aspera*
  a. Flowers ¾–1 in. wide; fruit ⅝–¾ in. thick, subglobose or
    depressed-globose, often wider than long, with a broad,
    slightly elevated, calyx . . . . 53. *C. platycarpa*

16. **Molles**
  a. Leaves of flowering spurs mostly oval or ovate, rounded at
    base; terminal shoot leaves broadly ovate, often truncate or
    subcordate at base
    b. Fruit bright red at maturity
      c. Leaves longer than broad except rarely at the ends of
        shoots
        d. Mature leaves firm but comparatively thin; flowers
          numerous, to 15–20 in corymb
          e. Fruit ripening in August or September; flesh suc-
            culent and edible; nutlets 4–5, usually 5 . . . .
            . . . . 54. *C. mollis* [D, E]
          e. Fruit ripening in October; flesh dry and mealy; nut-
            lets 3–5 . . . . 57. *C. limaria* [D, E]
        d. Mature leaves thick or subcoriaceous; flowers mostly
          5–12 in corymb
          f. Leaves bluish green; flowers mostly 5–12 in com-
            pound corymbs; stamens about 20 . . . .
            . . . . 60. *C. lanuginosa*
          f. Leaves dull yellowish green; flowers mostly 5–8 in
            simple corymbs . . . . 64. *C. greggiana*
      c. Leaves often as broad as long, comparatively small; ter-
        minal shoot leaves sometimes broader than long . . . .
        . . . . 62. *C. brachyphylla*
    b. Fruit bright yellow at maturity . . . . 63. *C. viburnifolia*
  a. Leaves of flowering spurs mostly elliptic or oblong-ovate,
    noticeably longer than broad, gradually or abruptly narrowed
    at base; terminal shoot leaves broader, usually rounded or
    rarely truncate at base; fruit red at maturity; sepals glandu-
    lar-serrate
    b. Stamens 10 or less; nutlets 3–5 . . . . 56. *C. noelensis*
    b. Stamens about 20; nutlets 4–5, usually 5, except in no. 58
      c. Mature leaves thick; sepals foliaceous, deeply glandular-
        serrate; anthers large, dark red; fruit with thick mellow
        flesh, edible . . . . 55. *C. texana*
      c. Mature leaves relatively thin; sepals not foliaceous,
        more or less glandular-serrate; fruit with thin dry or
        mealy flesh, scarcely edible
        d. Anthers white or pale yellow; sepals laciniately glan-
          dular-serrate; nutlets 3–5 . . . . 58. *C. invisa*

d. Anthers pink or rose, or sometimes white in no. 59;
nutlets 4–5, usually 5
e. Flowers about 1 in. wide; sepals glandular-serrate;
fruit bright red or crimson and lustrous at maturity
.... 59. *C. dispessa*
e. Flowers about ¾ in. wide; sepals sparingly and irregularly glandular-serrate; fruit dull dark red at maturity .... 61. *C. dallasiana* [D, E]
17. **Dilatatae** (only one species in this area) ... 66. *C. coccinioides*
18. **Douglasianae** (only one species in this area) ....
.... 67. *C. rivularis* [F, G]
19. **Macracanthae**
a. Leaves relatively large, those of the flowering spurs mostly
2–4 in. long, 1¾–3¼ in. wide; flowers mostly 8–20 in loose
compound corymbs
b. Mature leaves dull yellowish green above; anthers pink or
rarely pale yellow in variety; arborescent shrubs or small
trees to 18–24 ft .... 68. *C. calpodendron* [D]
b. Mature leaves bright green, glossy above; anthers pale
yellow; diffuse shrubs 6–9 ft tall ...... 70. *C. carrollensis*
a. Leaves relatively small, those of the flowering spurs mostly
1–1¾ in. long, ¾–1¼ in. wide; flowers mostly 5–8 in compact corymbs; low branching shrubs 3–4½ ft ....
.... 69. *C. thermopegaea*

Parsley Hawthorn

Crataegus marshallii Egglest.—Series **Microcarpae** (2) [D]

Field Identification. Shrub or small tree attaining a height of 20 ft,
with smooth gray bark and spreading crooked branches.

Flowers. Borne in villose corymbs of 3–12; petals 5, white,
spreading, rounded, inserted on the disk margin; calyx 5-lobed,
lobes lanceolate, acuminate, often glandular-serrate; stamens
about 20, with red anthers; styles 1–3; nearly the whole of the
inflorescence white-pubescent.

Fruit. Pome oblong or ovoid, about ⅓ in. long, bright red, shiny,
slightly pubescent; flesh thin, yellow, edible; nutlets 1–3, usually
2, smooth, rounded.

Leaves. Simple, alternate, deciduous, ovate to orbicular, ¾–1½ in.
long; acute at the apex; truncate, cuneate, or subcordate at base;
incised into 5–7 deep clefts and serrate on the margin; pubescent

on both faces when young, when older more glabrous above but hairy along veins beneath; petioles 1–2 in., slender, tomentose.

Twigs. Brown to gray, pubescent when young, smooth later, crooked; bearing stout, straight, brown, scattered spines 1–2 in. long.

Bark. Gray to brown, smooth, scaling off in large thin plates to expose reddish brown inner bark.

Wood. Reddish brown, heavy, hard, strong, weighing 46 lb per cu ft, of no particular commercial value.

Range. Texas to Florida; north to Oklahoma, Arkansas, Missouri, and Virginia.

Remarks. *Crataegus* is a Greek word meaning "strong," in reference to the tough wood, and the species name, *marshallii*, is in honor of the botanist Humphrey Marshall. Parsley Haw could be more extensively cultivated for its beautiful foliage, white flowers, and scarlet fruit.

Little-hip Hawthorn

Crataegus spathulata Michx.—Series **Microcarpae** (2) [D, E]

Field Identification. Shrub or small tree to 25 ft, with a broad open head and bearing sparse straight spines.

Flowers. March—May, borne in glabrous, many-flowered corymbs; individual flowers about ½ in. in diameter on slender pedicels; petals 5, white, rounded, spreading, inserted on the margin of the disk; stamens about 20. Calyx-tube obconic, glabrous, with 5 lobes; lobes deltoid, entire, minutely glandular at apex.

Fruit. Pome ripe in October, globose or nearly so, bright red, ¼ in. or less in diameter, tipped with the persistent reflexed calyx-lobes; flesh dry, thin, and mealy; nutlets 3–5, slightly ridged or smooth on back.

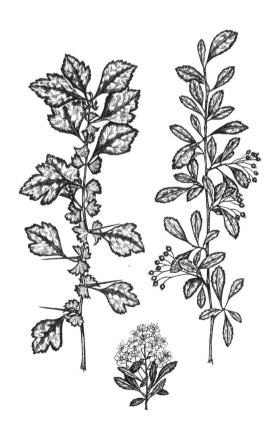

Leaves. Simple, alternate, deciduous; spatulate to oblanceolate, sometimes 3–5-lobed at the apex; crenate-serrate on the margin, the cuneate base entire and tapering to a winged petiole; apex acute or rounded; hairy when young on both sides, at maturity becoming firm, glabrous, shiny and dark green above, and glabrous or villose on the veins beneath; 1–2 in. long, 1–1½ in. wide; terminal leaves with stipules stalked, foliaceous, falcate, serrate, and to ½ in. wide.

Twigs. Reddish brown, glabrous, crooked, armed or unarmed; spines sparse, slender, more or less straight, brown, 1–1½ in. long.

Bark. Light brown to gray, smooth, flaking off.

Wood. Reddish brown, heavy, hard, strong, weighing 45 lb per cu ft, not large enough for commercial use.

Range. Oklahoma, Arkansas, and eastern Texas; eastward to Florida and northward to South Carolina and Virginia.

Remarks. *Crataegus* is a Greek word meaning "strong," in reference to its tough wood, and the species name, *spathulata*, refers to the spathe- or spoon-like shaped leaves.

Blueberry Hawthorn

Crataegus brachyacantha Engelm. & Sarg.—Series **Brevispinae** (4) [D]

Field Identification. Beautiful round-topped tree attaining a height of 40 ft, armed with short-curved spines.

Flowers. Borne in many-flowered glabrous corymbs; flowers about ⅓ in. across, white at first and orange with age; petals 5, borne on the edge of the disk, rounded, spreading; stamens 15–20, anthers yellow; styles 3–5; calyx-tube obconic, glabrous, 5-lobed; lobes triangular to lanceolate, gland-tipped, entire.

Fruit. Ripe pomes borne a few in a cluster on erect pedicels in August; depressed, subglobose or obovoid, bright blue or black and glaucous, ⅓–½ in. long, flesh thin; nutlets 3–5, round at apex, acute at base, rounded or with 2 slight grooves on the back, about ¼ in. long, light brown.

Leaves. Simple, alternate, deciduous, those on vigorous shoots often quite distinct from those on slow-growing spurs, oblong-obovate or oblong-lanceolate or ovate-rhombic, leathery; acute or obtuse at apex; cuneate to truncate or cordate at the base; crenate-

serrate on margins and lobed on some; when lobed usually 3-lobed with the middle lobe longest and somewhat shallowly cleft again, or only serrate; dark green, glabrous and lustrous above; paler, and glabrous or pubescent beneath, ¾–3½ in. long, about ½–2 in. wide; petiole ½–¾ in., slender, sometimes winged; stipules foliaceous, ovate-triangular, asymmetrical, broader than long, elongate and acuminate pointed on one side, the other side shortened and coarsely toothed also across the apex, to 1 in. long.

Twigs. Green and minutely pubescent at first, glabrous and reddish brown to gray later; spines short, ⅓–⅔ in. long, stout, usually curved but some straight, gray to brown.

Bark. Smooth and gray on young trunks, on old trunks gray to brown and divided into narrow flattened ridges and shallow furrows, loosening with age into thin scales to expose reddish brown inner bark.

Wood. Hard, strong, heavy, not large enough to be commercially usable.

Range. Margins of streams and swamps, Texas and Louisiana; east to Georgia and north to Arkansas. In Texas west to the Trinity River. Locally abundant between Hull and Saratoga, Texas.

Remarks. *Crataegus* is from an ancient Greek word and means strength in reference to the tough wood, and the species name, *brachyacantha*, refers to the short thorns. The French gave the tree the name of Pomette Bleu in reference to the blue fruit, which is unusual for a hawthorn.

May Hawthorn

Crataegus opaca Hook. & Arn.—Series **Aestivales** (5) [D]

Field Identification. Shrub or small tree up to 30 ft, with slender erect branches and a rounded head.

Flowers. Borne before the leaves in February or March, in 2–5-flowered glabrous corymbs, corolla about ¾ in. across; petals 5, white, spreading, rounded, inserted on the margin of the disk; stamens about 20 with rose-purple anthers; styles 3–5; calyx-tube obconic, glabrous, 5-lobed; the calyx-lobes triangular, acute and gland-tipped, entire or serrulate on margin, often reddish-colored.

Fruit. Pome borne in May, large, ½–¾ in. across, red, dotted, fragrant, globose, somewhat depressed, calyx persistent; flesh juicy, sweet-acid; nutlets 3–5, rounded.

Leaves. Simple, alternate, deciduous, oblong to obovate or elliptic, acute or rounded at the apex, cuneate at the base, margin crenate-serrate or often 3-lobed, 1–2½ in. long, ½–1⅓ in. wide; dark green and usually glabrous above; lower surface clothed with dense rusty brown pubescence, especially on the veins; petioles slender, rusty-pubescent.

Twigs. Brown to gray, hairy at first, glabrous later; unarmed, or bearing stout, straight, brown spines ½–1 in.

Bark. Dark reddish brown, deeply fissured into persistent scales.

Wood. Heavy, hard, strong, not large enough for commercial use.

Range. The species is found in wet soil in Texas, Arkansas, Louisiana, and north to South Carolina.

Remarks. *Crataegus* is from an ancient Greek word meaning "strength," in reference to the wood, and the species name, *opaca*, refers to the dull fruit. It was formerly listed under the name of *C. aestivalis* (Walt.) Torr. & Gray, but this name now applies to an-

other species. Also known as the Riverflat Hawthorn. This is the famous May Haw of the South, from which preserves are made. The large size and acid character of the pomes make it particularly desirable for that purpose.

Green Hawthorn

Crataegus viridis L.—Series **Virides** (9) [D, E, F]

Field Identification. Tree attaining a height of 35 ft and forming a broad rounded crown. The trunk is often fluted, and the twigs are sparsely spined, or not at all.

Flowers. Opening March–April. Borne in many-flowered, glabrous corymbs; individual flowers on slender pedicels, about ¾ in. in diameter; petals 5, rounded, spreading, inserted on the disk margin in the calyx-throat; stamens 15–20, anthers yellow; styles

2–5, hairy at the base; calyx-tube obconic, glabrous, with lobes entire, lanceolate, glabrous or puberulent, or pubescent to villose in some varieties.

Fruit. Pome globose or depressed-globose, in drooping clusters, red to orange and often glaucous (sometimes remaining greenish), ⅙–¼ in. in diameter; calyx-lobes 5, small, often dropping away early from the fruit; nutlets 4–5, obscurely ridged or grooved on the back, ⅙–⅛ in. long.

Leaves. Simple, alternate, deciduous, ovate-oblong, acute to acuminate or rarely obtuse at the apex, cuneate or rounded at the base; serrate to doubly serrate and often shallowly lobed toward the apex, teeth usually few or none at the cuneate base; dark green and shiny above and becoming glabrous later, paler beneath with axillary tufts of white hairs, blades ¾–3½ in. long, ½–2 in. wide; petiole slender and glabrous.

Twigs. Gray or reddish, with or without spines; spines when present slender, pale, sharp, ¼–1 in.

Bark. Gray to reddish brown, shedding in small scales.

Wood. Reddish brown, heavy, hard, tough, weighing about 40 lb per cu ft, not large enough to be commercially valuable.

Range. The species is known from Texas in the eastern and upper coastal regions; Louisiana, Arkansas, and eastern Oklahoma; eastward to Florida, northward to southeastern Virginia, and westward to southwestern Indiana, Kansas, and Missouri.

Remarks. The genus name, *Crataegus*, is from an ancient Greek word meaning "strength," in reference to the tough wood, and the species name, *viridis*, means "green." Vernacular names are Green Thorn and Southern Thorn.

Cock's-spur Hawthorn

Crataegus crus-galli L.—Series **Crus-galli** (10) [D, E]

Field Identification. Shrub or tree to 30 ft, and 6–12 in. in diameter. The branches are stout, rigid, horizontal or drooping, forming a round-topped or broadly depressed crown.

Flowers. Opening May–June after the leaves, in lax, many-flowered, glabrous corymbs; pedicels slender and glabrous, corolla ½–⅗ in. broad, petals 5, white, reflexed after anthesis; calyx-tube narrow and obconic, glabrous, sepals 5, ⅛–⅕ in. long, linear-lanceolate, entire or glandular-serrate; stamens 10, anthers pink or white; styles 2, hairy at the base.

Fruit. Maturing in October, persistent over winter, short-oblong to subglobose or ovoid (occasionally slightly 5-angled), dull red, ⅓–½ in. long, with a terminal depression, flesh thin and dry; nutlets 2 (rarely 1 or 3), ridged dorsally, ends rounded, about ¼ in. long.

Leaves. Simple, alternate, deciduous, thick and leathery at maturity, mostly obovate to oblanceolate, apex obtuse to rounded or acute, base gradually cuneate, margin sharply and minutely toothed above the middle, teeth often glandular; upper surface dark green and lustrous, lower surface paler and reticulate-veined, blade length ⅗–4 in., width ½–1⅓ in., turning yellow, orange, or red in the fall; petiole ½–¾ in. long, stout, winged above; leaves on young shoots often longer and apex acute or acuminate.

Twigs. Stout, reddish brown to gray, glabrous, armed with sharp,

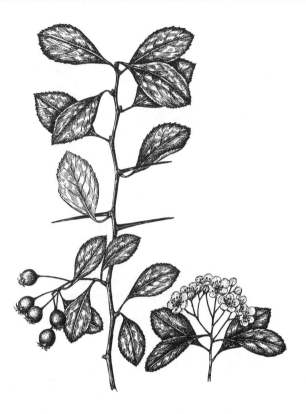

straight or slightly curved spines 2–8 in. long, sometimes with lateral spines; bark of trunk dark brown to gray, breaking into small scales with irregular, moderately deep fissures.

Wood. Heavy, hard, fine-grained, suitable for tool handles.

Range. Fence rows, woods, and thickets. The species and varieties are widespread. East Texas, Oklahoma, Arkansas, and Louisiana; east to Georgia, north to Michigan, Kansas, and southern Quebec, and west to Ontario.

Remarks. The genus name, *Crataegus*, is the classical Greek name for hawthorn. The species name, *crus-galli*, refers to the long thorns which resemble the spurs of a fowl. Cock's-spur Hawthorn is very desirable for cultivation because of the rounded crown, shiny leaves, and conspicuous flowers. It is perhaps the most widely planted hawthorn in the United States and Europe.

Unique Pyracantha Hawthorn

Crataegus pyracanthoides var. *uniqua* (Sarg.) Palmer—Series **Crus-galli** (10) [D]

Field Identification. Slender tree to 20 ft, with wide-spreading branches forming a flat head.

Flowers. Opening in April, in 5–8-flowered, glabrous corymbs, pedicels slender; calyx-tube narrowly obconic, the 5 lobes short, broad and acuminate, margin entire or slightly dentate, somewhat hairy within, later reflexed; stamens 20, anthers white; styles 2–3.

Fruit. Ripening in October, on slender drooping pedicels, short-oblong, rounded at the ends, dull red, ⅜–½ in. long and about ⅓ in. thick; calyx conspicuous with a deep wide cavity broad in the bottom; sepals 5, reflexed, appressed, slightly hairy within, persistent; flesh thin, dry, hard; nutlets 2 or 3, broad and rounded at the base, keeled on the back with a high wide-grooved ridge, ¼–⅓ in. long and about ⅛–⅙ in. wide; hypostyle conspicuous and broad, extending to below the middle of the nutlet.

Leaves. About half-grown when the flowers open, simple, alternate, deciduous, oblong-obovate; apex acute or occasionally rounded, base gradually narrowed or cuneate; teeth on margin straight, incurved and glandular, usually above the middle, length ¾–1¾ in., width ⅜–¾ in., on vigorous shoots broadly obovate, acute or rounded at base, more closely serrate, 2–2½ in. long and 1–1⅓ in. wide; surfaces when young glabrous except along the veins; at maturity glabrous, thin but firm, upper surface dark green and shiny, paler beneath, midrib and veins rather slender.

Twigs. Slender, slightly divaricate, yellow to orange or reddish brown, armed or unarmed, spines straight or slightly curved, shiny brown, ⅜–¾ in.

Range. In southwestern Arkansas, eastern Texas, and northwestern Louisiana. This tree is found in Texas in low rich woods near Marshall, Harrison County; Louisiana at the marble quarry near Winnfield, Winn Parish.

Remarks. The genus name, *Crataegus*, is the classical name of the hawthorn. The variety name, *uniqua*, means "unique." This hawthorn has been variously described under the synonyms of *C. uniqua* Sarg., *C. arioclada* Sarg., and *C. cocksii* Sarg.

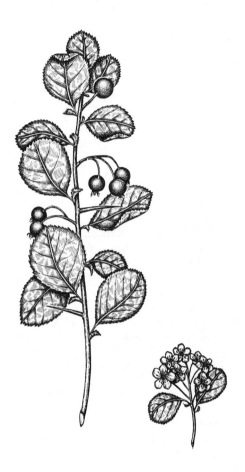

Reverchon Hawthorn

Crataegus reverchonii Sarg.—Series **Crus-galli** (10) [D, E]

Field Identification. Shrub 3–9 ft, usually with many stems from the base, or occasionally a small thorny tree to 26 ft.

Flowers. April–May, borne in slender pediceled, compact, glabrous, few-flowered corymbs; each flower about ⅓ in. in diameter, petals 5, white, rounded; calyx-tube narrowly obconic, 5-lobed, lobes slender, apices acuminate with a small red gland, margins entire or obscurely serrate; stamens 10–15, styles 3–5, usually 5.

Fruit. Maturing in September on drooping few-flowered corymbs, with slender pedicels; subglobose, some slightly broader than long, light scarlet, shiny, marked by occasional large dots, about ⅓ in. in diameter; flesh sweet, juicy, yellow, thick; nutlets usually 4, dorsally and prominently ridged, about ¼ in. in diameter; calyx-lobes slender and deciduous.

Leaves. Simple, alternate, deciduous, oval to obovate, margin finely crenate-serrate with gland-tipped teeth above the base; at first yellowish green and mostly glabrous above, lower surface slightly hairy on the midrib and veins; mature leaves leathery, dark green and shiny above, lower surface paler; blade length 1¼–1½ in., width ¾–1 in.; midrib stout, yellow, primary veins 5–6 pairs; petioles stout, about ⅓ in., grooved, wing-margined almost to the base; stipules minute, linear, reddish later, falling early; leaves on vigorous shoots rounded, less often ovate or elliptic, margin coarsely serrate or slightly lobed, about 1½ in. in diameter, petioles short-glandular, broad-winged.

Twigs. Erect, divaricate, glabrous, lustrous, orange-brown to reddish brown, lenticels small, pale, and numerous; older twigs gray, armed with spines 1½–3 in. long (occasionally to 5 in.), slender, nearly straight, lustrous, reddish brown or purple.

Range. Southwestern Oklahoma, Arkansas, northern and central Texas (Dallas County), Missouri, and eastern Kansas.

Remarks. The genus name, *Crataegus*, is the classical name of the hawthorn, and the species name, *reverchonii*, honors Julien Reverchon (1837–1905), a Texas plant collector of French birth. Charles Sprague Sargent remarks that the Reverchon Hawthorn is one of the most typical species of the Crus-galli group.

Engelmann Hawthorn

Crataegus engelmannii Sarg.—Series **Crus-galli** (10) [D, E]

Field Identification. Tree 15–20 ft, with a diameter of 5–6 in. Branches usually wide-spreading and usually horizontal, forming a low flat-topped or rounded head.

Flowers. April–May, flowers white, 5-petaled, about ¾ in. in diameter, in wide 8–12-flowered, slender-branched cymes thickly coated with long pale hairs; bracts about ½ in. long, linear-lanceolate, tomentose or villous; calyx tomentose, villous, or nearly glabrous, the lobes narrow, acuminate, entire, glabrous on

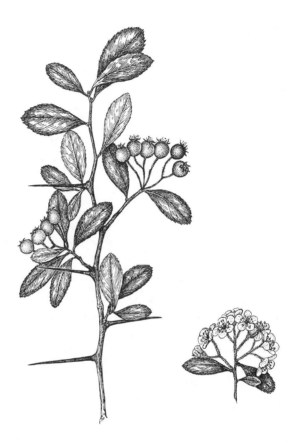

the outer surface, and usually more or less pubescent on the inner surface, reflexed after anthesis, often deciduous before the ripening of the fruit; stamens 10; filaments slender; anthers small, rose-colored; styles 2–3.

Fruit. Ripening early in November, globose, about ⅓ in. in diameter, bright orange-red with a yellow cheek and thin dry green flesh; tube of the calyx prominent, the cavity broad in proportion to the size of the fruit, shallow, nutlets 2 or 3, thick, prominently ribbed on the back with high rounded ridges, ¼ in. long.

Leaves. Simple, alternate, deciduous, broadly obovate or rarely elliptic, apex rounded or short-pointed, gradually narrowed below into short glandular pilose petioles, coarsely glandular-serrate with incurved teeth usually only above the middle and generally only at the apex, coriaceous, dark green, lustrous and roughened on the upper surface with short rigid pale hairs, pale on the lower surface, pilose above and below on the slender midribs and on the thin obscure primary veins and veinlets, 1–1½ in. long, ½–1 in. broad; stipules linear-lanceolate, light red, ⅓ in. long, caducous.

Twigs. Slightly zigzag, marked with large scattered white lenticels, at first clothed with pale hairs, becoming nearly glabrous and reddish brown during the first season, and lighter colored and gray or gray tinged with red during their second year, and armed with remote slender straight or slightly curved chestnut brown spines 1½–2½ in. long.

Range. Dry hillsides and slopes of limestone soil. East and north-central Texas, Oklahoma, Kansas, Missouri, Arkansas, Tennessee, Kentucky, Alabama, Mississippi, and Illinois.

Remarks. The genus name, *Crataegus*, is the classical name of the hawthorn. The species name, *engelmannii*, honors George Engelmann (1809–1884), a German-born American physician and botanist of St. Louis, Missouri, who first collected it.

Downy Hawthorn

Crataegus mollis (Torr. & Gray) Scheele—Series **Molles** (16) [D, E]

Field Identification. Tree attaining a height of 40 ft and a diameter of 12–18 in., branches stout and spreading to form a round-topped crown.

Flowers. Opening April–May, corymbs many-flowered and broad, pedicels densely hairy; bracts and bractlets conspicuous; corolla white, 5-petaled, about 1 in. across; calyx-tube narrowly obconic, densely tomentose, lobes 5, linear to lanceolate, apex acuminate, margin serrate and red-glandular, externally villose, tomentose within; stamens 20, anthers large, light yellow; styles 4–5, basally hoary-tomentose.

Fruit. Maturing in September, corymbs hairy, few-fruited, drooping, subglobose or short-oblong, terminally rounded, somewhat pubescent, scarlet, some dark dotted, ⅔–1 in. in diameter; flesh yellow, dry, mealy; nutlets 4–5, light brown, dorsally rounded and lightly ridged, about ¼ in. long; fruiting calyx-lobes deciduous when fruit half grown, at first erect, incurved, and hairy.

Leaves. Simple, alternate, deciduous, broad-ovate, apex acute, base rounded or cordate, margin doubly serrate, and also with 4–5

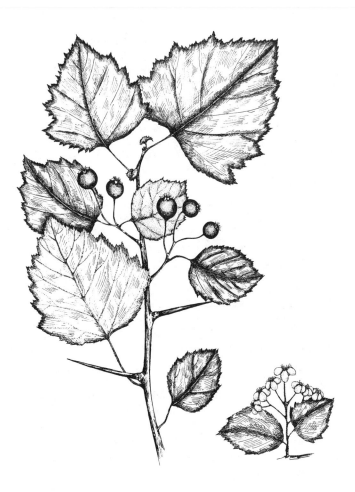

lateral acute or rounded lobes on each side; mature leaves with upper surfaces dark yellowish green; lower surface paler and pubescent, particularly along the midrib, lateral veins 4–5 pairs, length and width of blades 3–4 in.; leaves on young shoots larger, lobes and basal sinus deeper; petioles ½–1¼ in. long, stout, densely hairy at first, later pubescent, some with minute dark glands.

Twigs. Stout, densely white-villose at first, when older becoming glabrous, gray, bearing stout, shiny, chestnut-brown spines 1–2 in. long.

Range. In rich bottom lands. In Texas in Dallas, Grayson, and Lamar counties, and Oklahoma; east to Alabama, north to Ontario, and west to Minnesota and South Dakota.

Remarks. The genus name, *Crataegus*, is the classical name for hawthorn, and the species name, *mollis*, refers to the soft-hairy foliage. Downy Hawthorn has also been listed in the literature under the names of *C. arkansanum* Sarg., *C. lasiantha* Sarg., and *C. gravida* Beadle. Vernacular names in use are Red Haw and Downy Thorn.

Shiny Hawthorn

Crataegus limaria Sarg.—Series **Molles** (16) [D, E]

Field Identification. Tree 20–30 ft, with a trunk 6–12 in. in diameter, the branches forming an irregular crown.

Flowers. March–April, borne in white-hairy corymbs of 12–20 flowers; petals 5, white, rounded, when spread the flower to 1 in. in diameter; stamens 15–18, anthers white; styles 3–5, hairy at base; calyx-tube obconic, white-hairy, the 5 sepals narrow, acuminate at apex, margin cut into glandular serrations.

Fruit. Maturing September–October, few in a cluster, pedicels hairy, body ovoid to ellipsoid or short-oblong, base truncate or rounded, apex rounded, red, sometimes with pale spots, hairy at first, later glabrous, ½–⅗ in. in diameter; calyx with the 5 sepals hairy, reddish and persistent; flesh yellowish, mealy, insipid; nutlets 3–5, obscurely grooved dorsally, ends rounded, ⅕–¼ in. long.

Leaves. Simple, alternate, young ones white-hairy above and densely tomentose beneath; mature leaves with upper surfaces light green and roughened, lower surface paler and tomentose, blade ovate, margin singly or doubly serrate (or 3–4-lobed on each margin), apex acute, base rounded to cordate or concave-cuneate, length 2½–3 in., width 1½–2 in.; petioles ¾–1½ in., slender, villose.

Twigs. Young ones yellow to orange-brown and densely white-hairy, older ones brown to gray and eventually glabrous, spines purple to gray, sharp, slender, straight or slightly curved.

Range. Bottom lands of the Guadalupe, Cibolo, and San Antonio rivers in Texas. In Arkansas on the Red River near Fulton in Hempstead County. Also in southeastern Oklahoma.

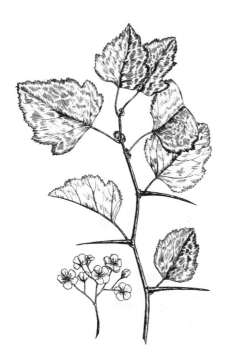

Remarks. The genus name, *Crataegus*, is from an ancient Greek word referring to the strength of the wood. The species name, *limaria*, refers to the lustrous, or shiny, fruits. The tree is listed by some authors under the name of *C. mackensenii* Sarg.

Dallas Hawthorn

Crataegus dallasiana Sarg.—Series **Molles** (16) [D, E]

Field Identification. Tree attaining a height of 25 ft and a diameter of 4–10 in. The branches ascending or erect to produce an irregularly shaped crown.

Flowers. Opening in April, corymbs many-flowered with slender, very hairy pedicels; corolla white, 5-petaled, each about ⅝ in. across; calyx-tube densely hairy; lobes 5, hairy, long-acuminate, margin with a few glandular serrations; stamens 20, anthers pink; styles 5.

Fruit. Maturing in July, corymbs few-fruited, pedicels pubescent and mostly erect, shape of fruit globose, dark red, ⅜–½ in. in diameter; nutlets 5, ends acute, body flattened, dorsally grooved or ridged, ¼–⁵⁄₁₆ in. long; calyx persistent, conspicuous, lobes spreading and green or reddish.

Leaves. Simple, alternate, deciduous, blades 1¾–2½ in. long, 1¼–1½ in. wide, oblong to ovate, apex acuminate or rounded, base cuneate to concave, margin doubly serrate except at base, sometimes shallowly lobed above; young leaves densely villose and tomentose; at maturity yellowish green, upper surface shiny and glabrous, lower surface paler and pubescent along the veins; petioles ¼–⅔ in. long, slender, tomentose at first but glabrous later, somewhat winged toward the blade.

Twigs. Slender, rather divaricate, at first densely tomentose and reddish brown, later gray and shiny, bearing slender spines 1¼–2¼ in. long.

Range. Northeastern Texas and adjacent Oklahoma.

Remarks. The genus name, *Crataegus*, is the classical name, and the species name, *dallasiana*, is for Dallas County, Texas, where it occurs along bottom-land streams.

River Hawthorn

Crataegus rivularis Nutt.—Series **Douglasianae** [18] [F, G]

Field Identification. Small western tree 9–20 ft, with erect, ascending branches forming a narrow open head.

Flowers. Opening in May, borne in compact glabrous corymbs on long slender pedicels; corolla about ½ in. in diameter, petals 5, white, rounded; calyx-tube broadly obconic, slightly hairy at first but glabrous later, 5-lobed; lobes slender, entire or minutely glandular, glabrous externally, hairy within, sometimes reddish; stamens 10–20, anthers rose-colored; styles usually 5.

Fruit. Ripening in September, corymbs drooping, few-fruited, long-pediceled; fruit body short-oblong, ends full and rounded, dark red to almost black, lustrous, usually white-dotted, length ⅓–½ in.; flesh yellow, thin, dry, mealy; nutlets 3–5, about ¼ in. long, apices narrowed or rounded, dorsally ridged, ventral cavities broad and shallow; calyx persistent, rather closely appressed, outer surface reddish and some slightly hairy below.

Leaves. Simple, alternate, deciduous, lanceolate to narrowly oblong-obovate or elliptic, apices acute or abruptly acuminate, base gradually narrowed and cuneate to concave, entire, margin irregularly and crenately serrate above, with glandular teeth, rarely lobed; young leaves reddish and pale-hairy; mature leaves rather dull green, thin, smooth and glabrous above, paler and yellowish green beneath, blade length 1½–2 in.; about ¾ in. wide, some twice as long as wide; midrib yellow, slender, primary veins obscure and 3–4 pairs; petiole about ½ in. long, slender, slightly winged above, hairy at first but reddish and glabrous later; young leaves almost round, coarsely toothed, some slightly incised-lobed, leathery, often to 3 in. long and 2 in. wide, petiole broadly winged.

Twigs. Slender, reddish brown, lustrous, glabrous, lenticels numerous and pale, spineless, or spines straight, slender, blackish, ¼–1¼ in. long, bark on older stems or trunk dark brown and scaly.

Range. At altitudes of 3,000–8,500 ft, borders of streams. Arizona, New Mexico, and northwestern Texas; northward to Idaho and Wyoming.

Remarks. The genus name, *Crataegus*, is the classical name for the hawthorn, and the species name, *rivularis*, refers to its preference for the moist banks of small rivulets or streams.

Pear Hawthorn

Crataegus calpodendron (Ehrh.) Medic.—Series **Macracanthae** (19) [D]

Field Identification. Shrub or small tree attaining a height of 15–18 ft, the scaly branches thorny or thornless.

Flowers. In many-flowered villose or tomentose corymbs; petals 5, white, rounded, corolla ⅜–⅝ in. wide when spread; stamens about 20, anthers pink or rarely white; calyx-tube pubescent, the 5 lobes glandular-serrate or pectinate.

Fruit. Oblong or obovoid, occasionally subglobose, about ⅓ in. thick, at first pubescent, later glabrous, bright red or orange-red; flesh thin, sweet, and succulent; nutlets 2–3, deeply pitted on the inner surface.

Leaves. Simple, alternate, deciduous, blade oblong-elliptic or rhombic, margin coarsely serrate, except near the base, often with 3–5 pairs of irregular lateral lobes above the middle (sometimes lobed only on the vegetative shoots), young leaves short-villous above; when mature, pubescent beneath, dull yellowish green, firm, veins impressed above; petioles stout, ⅜–⅝ in. long, sometimes wing-margined nearly to the base.

Twigs. Young ones tomentose, reddish brown, later glabrous and gray, bark on old trunks and limbs furrowed and thick; spineless, or spines ½–2 in. long, stout, slender, sharp, straight or slightly curved.

Range. The species and its varieties occur in open woods and thickets, often along small rocky streams. East Texas and Arkansas; east to Georgia, north to New York and Ontario, and west to Minnesota.

Remarks. The genus name, *Crataegus*, refers to the hard wood of some species. The species name, *calpodendron*, means "urn-tree" and refers to the shape of the fruit.

Carolina Cherry-laurel

Prunus caroliniana (Mill.) Ait. [D]

Field Identification. Evergreen tree attaining a height of 40 ft, with alternate, leathery, entire or toothed leaves.

Flowers. In short, axillary racemes; flowers perfect, white, pedicels about ½ in. long with acuminate bracts; calyx-tube narrow-obconic, 5-lobed; lobes suborbicular, reflexed, deciduous; petals 5, white, boat-shaped, erect, smaller than the sepals; stamens numerous, exserted, orange, longer than the petals; filaments dis-

tinct; ovary sessile, small, 1-celled; style simple and slender; stigma club-shaped; ovules 2.

Fruit. Drupe conic-ovoid or oval, abruptly pointed, black, lustrous, persistent; about ½ in. long, skin thick, flesh thin and dry, not edible; seed ovoid, acute, rounded at base, about ½ in. long, dorsal groove prominent.

Leaves. Alternate, simple, persistent, coriaceous, shiny, margin entire or a few with remote spine-tipped teeth, oblong-lanceolate, apex acute or acuminate, mucronate, base wedge-shaped, glabrous and dark green above, paler beneath, 2–4½ in. long, ¾–1½ in. wide, aromatic when crushed, taste bitter because of prussic acid; petioles stout, about ⅓ in. long; stipules lanceolate.

Twigs. Slender, glabrous, green to red or grayish brown.

Bark. Gray, thin, smooth, or later irregularly roughened, marked with blotches.

Wood. Reddish brown, hard, heavy, strong, close-grained.

Range. In Texas, extending from the valley of the Guadalupe River, eastward through eastern Texas and Louisiana to Florida, northward to the Carolinas.

Remarks. The genus name, *Prunus*, is the classical name. The species name, *caroliniana*, refers to the Carolina region. Vernacular names are Wild Peach, Cherry-laurel, Carolina Cherry, and Mock-orange. The leaves contain prussic acid which is injurious to livestock. A number of birds feed on the seeds. The tree is widely cultivated as a popular ornamental and can be trained into hedges.

Black Cherry

Prunus serotina Ehrh. [D]

Field Identification. Tree to 100 ft, with oval-oblong or lanceolate leaves which are finely callous-serrate on the margin.

Flowers. March–June, racemes in spring with immature but nearly expanded leaves; individual flowers white, about ¼ in. in diameter, borne on slender pedicels; petals 5, obovate; stamens numerous, in 3 ranks; stigmas flattened; calyx-tube saucer-shaped, the lobes short, ovate-oblong, acute.

Fruit. Ripening June–October, drupe borne in racemes, thin-skinned, black when mature, juicy, bitter-sweet, ⅓–½ in. in diameter; stone oblong-ovoid, about ⅓ in. long. The commercial seed-bearing age is about 10 years, with 25 to 75 as the most prolific and 100 as the maximum. Good crops are borne almost annually.

Leaves. Simple, alternate, finely callous-serrate, apex acuminate, base cuneate, oval-oblong or oblong-lanceolate, firm, dark green and lustrous above, glabrous or hairy on midrib beneath, blades

Escarpment Black Cherry

2–6 in. long, 1–2 in. broad, with one or more red glands at base, tasting of hydrocyanic acid.

Bark. Reddish brown, gray or white, striped horizontally with gray to black lenticels, smooth when young, broken into small plates later, bitter to the taste.

Wood. Rich reddish brown, sapwood whitish or light brown, heavy, moderately hard, strong, bends well, shock resistance high, works well, finishes smoothly, glues well, seasons well, shrinks moderately, moderately free from checking and warping, weighing about 36 lb per cu ft, taking a beautiful polish.

Range. Texas, Oklahoma, Arkansas, and Louisiana; eastward to Florida, north to Nova Scotia, west to North Dakota, Nebraska, and Kansas, and southward in Mexico.

Remarks. *Prunus* is the ancient classical name, and the species name, *serotina*, means "late-flowering." It is also known under the vernacular names of Mountain Black Cherry and Rum Cherry. The bark is used medicinally as a cough remedy. The fruit is used as a basic flavoring extract, and is also eaten raw by man. It is eaten by a wide variety of wildlife, including 33 birds, raccoon, opossum, squirrel, bear, and rabbit. The foliage is considered to be poisonous to livestock. The wood is used for furniture, cabinet-making, printer's blocks, veneer, patterns, panels, interior trim, handles, woodenware, toys, and scientific instruments. The tree has been cultivated for ornament since 1629.

Escarpment Black Cherry, *P. serotina* var. *eximia* (Small) Little, has flowers 35–60 on the rachis, pedicels ⅛–⅕ in. (or ⅙–¼ in. in fruit); the 5 petals ⅒–⅙ in. long or wide; calyx segments ¹⁄₂₅–¹⁄₁₅ in. long; drupe about ⅜ in. across; leaves 2–3½ in. long, 1¼–1¾ in. wide, margin with 4–6 teeth every ⅜ in., surfaces glabrous or some with axillary red tufts of hairs; petioles ⅝–¾ in. (to 1¼ in. sometimes). In Texas in the valley of the Colorado River, in San Saba and Burnet counties; south to Comal and Medina counties; west to the south fork of the Llano River in Kimble County and to the west fork of the Nueces River in Kinney County.

Common Choke Cherry

Prunus virginiana L. [D, E, F, G]

Field Identification. Large shrub or small tree to 30 ft, with erect or horizontal branches.

Flowers. April–July, in short, dense, cylindric racemes 3–6 in. long; flowers ¼–⅓ in. in diameter, borne on slender, glabrous pedicels from the axils of early-deciduous bracts; corolla small, white, 5-merous; petals rounded, short-clawed; filaments glabrous; style thick, short, with orbicular stigmas; calyx-tube 5-lobed, lobes short, obtuse at apex, glandular-laciniate on the margin.

Fruit. Ripening July–September, cherry ¼–⅓ in. thick, globose, lustrous, dark red, scarlet, or nearly black; skin thick, flesh juicy, acidulous and astringent, barely edible; stone oblong-ovoid, one suture ridged, the other suture acute. Good crops are borne almost annually.

Leaves. Alternate, simple, deciduous, thin, blades ¾–4 in. long, ½–2 in. wide, oval to oblong or obovate, abruptly acuminate or acute at the apex, rounded to cuneate or somewhat cordate at the base, sharply serrate on the margin, dark green and lustrous above, paler on the lower surface, sometimes pubescent on veins, turning yellow in autumn, strong odor when crushed; petioles slender, ½–1 in., 2 glands at the apex.

Twigs. Reddish brown to orange-brown, glabrous, slender, lenticels pale.

Bark. Dark gray to brown or blackish; old trees somewhat irregularly fissured into small scales with paler excrescences, smoother and tighter when young, inner bark ill-scented.

Wood. Light brown, sapwood lighter, close-grained, moderately strong, hard, heavy, weighing 36 lb per cu ft.

Range. The species and its varieties rather widespread. Texas, New Mexico, Oklahoma, Arkansas, and Louisiana; eastward to Georgia, northward to Maine and Newfoundland, and west to British Columbia, Washington, Oregon, and California.

Remarks. The genus name, *Prunus*, is the classical name, and the species name, *virginiana*, refers to the state of Virginia. Vernacular names are Wild Black Cherry, Cabinet Cherry, Rum Cherry, Whiskey Cherry, Black Chokeberry, California Chokeberry, Eastern Chokeberry, Eastern Choke Cherry, Western Choke Cherry, and Caupulin. The tree is sometimes planted for ornament and for erosion control. It has been in cultivation since 1724. It has a tendency to form thickets of considerable extent from root sprouts. The fruit is used to make jellies and jams, and is eaten by at least 40 species of birds, and browsed by black bear and cotton-tail. The bark is sometimes used as a flavoring agent in cough syrup.

Oklahoma Plum

Prunus gracilis Engelm. & Gray [D, E, F, G]

Field Identification. Straggling thicket-forming shrub 1–15 ft.

Flowers. Opening in March, usually before the leaves, borne in sessile lateral umbels, 2–4 in a cluster; pedicels slender, pubescent ⅓–⅖ in. long; corolla ¼–⅓ in. broad; petals 5, white,

rounded, imbricate, spreading, inserted in the throat of the hypanthium; stamens numerous, inserted with the petals, filaments filiform and distinct; ovary sessile, 1-celled, ovules 2 and side by side, pendulous; style simple and terminal; calyx with 5 imbricate sepals which are spreading, deciduous, ovate to ovate-lanceolate, obtuse to acute, entire or denticulate, and finely pubescent.

Fruit. Drupe maturing June–August, subglobose or ovoid to somewhat pointed at the ends, to ⅝ in. in diameter, usually red with a slight bloom, pulpy; stone oval, indehiscent, obtuse at ends, bony, nearly smooth, slightly flattened; seed with membranous testa.

Leaves. Simple, alternate or fascicled, deciduous, length 1–2 in., elliptic to oval or ovate, margin finely and sharply serrate with appressed teeth, apex acute or obtuse, base gradually narrowed, thickish, upper surface slightly pubescent to glabrous when mature, lower surface reticulate-veined and densely pubescent; winter buds with imbricate scales; petioles short, pubescent, glandless.

Twigs. Slender, slightly divaricate, soft-pubescent, reddish brown, later gray and glabrous.

Range. On dry sandy soils in the sun. North Texas, Oklahoma, and western Arkansas, to Tennessee and Kansas.

Remarks. The genus name, *Prunus*, is the ancient Latin name, and the species name, *gracilis*, refers to the slender branches. The plant was introduced into cultivation in 1916. It is susceptible to black-knot fungus disease on the limbs and twigs. The fruit is edible but not of particularly good quality. Also known as the Sour Plum.

Chickasaw Plum

Prunus angustifolia Marsh. [D, E, F, G]

Field Identification. Twiggy shrub forming dense thickets, or a short-trunked, irregularly-branched tree to 25 ft.

Flowers. March–April, in lateral 2–4-flowered umbels borne before the leaves on slender, glabrous pedicels ¼–½ in.; corolla white, about ⅓ in. across; petals 5, obovate, rounded at apex, somewhat clawed at base; calyx-tube campanulate, glabrous, 5-

lobed; lobes ovate, obtuse, ciliate, pubescent within; stamens usually 15–20, filaments free with oval anthers; ovary 1-celled.

Fruit. May–July, drupe globose, ½–¾ in. in diameter, red or yellow, yellow-dotted, lustrous, little bloom if any, skin thin with juicy, edible, subacid flesh; stone ovoid to oblong, about ½ in. long, rounded, somewhat grooved on the dorsal suture, rugose and turgid.

Leaves. Alternate, simple, deciduous, 1–2 in. long, ⅓–⅔ in. wide, lanceolate or oblong-lanceolate, acuminate to acute and apiculate at the apex, rounded or broadly cuneate at the base, troughlike, glabrous and lustrous green above, paler and glabrous or pubescent beneath, sharply serrate with small glandular teeth; petioles slender, glabrous or puberulous, ¼–½ in. long, glandless or with 2 red glands near the apex.

Twigs. Reddish brown, lustrous, hairy at first but glabrous later, slender, zigzag, often with spinescent spurlike lateral divisions; lenticels horizontal, orange-colored.

Bark. Reddish brown to dark gray, scales thin and appressed; lenticels horizontal and prominent.

Wood. Reddish brown, sapwood lighter, rather soft, not strong, fairly heavy, weighing 43 lb per cu ft.

Range. Thought to be originally native in Texas and Oklahoma but now rather rare in a wild state. Arkansas and Louisiana; eastward to Florida, northward to New Jersey, and west to Illinois.

Remarks. The genus name, *Prunus*, is the classical name for the European plum, and the species name, *angustifolia*, refers to the narrow foliage. Often called Mountain Cherry in some localities. Seldom found in a wild state but most often around dwellings. It is sometimes used in shelter-belt planting.

Wild-goose Plum

Prunus munsoniana Wight & Hedrick [D, E]

Field Identification. Thicket-forming shrub or small round-topped tree to 25 ft.

Flowers. In 2–4-flowered corymbs; pedicels slender, glabrous, ⅔–1 in., bearing flowers ½–⅗ in. in diameter; calyx-tube obconic, with 5 sepals which are ovate-oblong, acute or obtuse, glandular on the margin, glabrous or pubescent; petals about ¼ in. long, white, oblong-obovate, abruptly contracted into a short claw, entire or somewhat erose; stamens usually 15–20, filaments with oval anthers; ovary 1-celled, with 2 ovules, style terminal.

Fruit. Drupe globose to oval, about ¾ in. long, red or yellow, white-dotted, bloom light, skin thin, flesh yellow and juicy; stone oval, pointed at the apex, truncate at the base, grooved on the sutures, roughened.

Leaves. Alternate, simple, deciduous, blades 2½–4 in. long, ¾–1¼ in. wide, lanceolate to oblong-lanceolate, acute or acumi-

nate at the apex, cuneate or rounded at the base, finely glandular-serrate on the margin, bright lustrous green above, sparingly pubescent, especially along the veins beneath; petioles slender, glabrous or pubescent, biglandular at the apex.

Twigs. Reddish brown, shiny, glabrous; lenticels pale and numerous.

Bark. Reddish or chestnut brown, thin, smooth.

Range. Texas, Oklahoma, Arkansas, and Louisiana; north to Kansas, Kentucky, and Illinois.

Remarks. The genus name, *Prunus*, is the classical name of a European plum, and the species name, *munsoniana*, refers to T. V. Munson (1823–1913), American botanist. The tree is grown both for ornament and for its fruit.

Mexican Plum

Prunus mexicana Wats. [D, E]

Field Identification. Shrub or small tree to 25 ft, with an irregular open crown.

Flowers. White, ¾–1 in. in diameter, borne on slender glabrous pedicels in 2–4-flowered umbels; petals 5, ovate-oblong, rounded, narrowed into a claw, entire or crenulate, pubescent, much longer than the calyx-lobes; stamens 15–20; style elongate, ovary 1-celled; calyx-tube obconic, puberulous on the exterior, tomentose within, 5-lobed; lobes ovate to oblong, entire or serrate, ciliate and glandular on the margin, about as long as the tube.

Fruit. Drupe subglobose to short-oblong, dark purplish red with a bloom, 1¼–1⅓ in. in diameter; flesh juicy, of varying palatability; stone ovoid to oval, dorsal edge ridged, ventral edge grooved, smooth, turgid.

Leaves. Alternate, simple, deciduous, thickish, blades 1¾–3½ in. long, 1–2 in. wide, ovate to elliptic or obovate, abruptly acuminate at the apex; cuneate or rounded at the base; singly or doubly serrate with apiculate teeth; upper surface yellowish green, glabrous, shiny, hairy below especially on the veins; prominently reticulate-veined both above and below; petioles stout, pubescent, hardly over ⅗ in. long, glandular at the apex.

Twigs. Slender, stiff, glabrous, or pubescent early, shiny, grayish brown.

Bark. Gray to black, exfoliating in platelike scales when young, when older rough and deeply furrowed.

Range. Texas, Louisiana, Arkansas, and Oklahoma; north to Missouri, Tennessee, and Kentucky, and southward into northeastern Mexico.

Remarks. The genus name, *Prunus*, is the ancient classical name for a plum of Europe, and the species name, *mexicana*, refers to this species' southwestern distribution. It is sometimes known as Big-tree Plum, because of the fact that it is treelike and does not sucker to form thickets. It is rather drought resistant and has been used as a grafting stock.

Hortulan Plum

Prunus hortulana Bailey [D]

Field Identification. Many-stemmed shrub or small tree to 30 ft, with a broad round-topped crown.

Flowers. Maturing late March–early May. Borne in 2–3-flowered umbels on slender, puberulous or glabrous pedicels ⅕–½ in. long; flower white, ⅔–1 in. in diameter; petals 5, oval-oblong, rounded at the apex, long-clawed, entire or erose; stamens numerous; ovary short; calyx-tube obconic, glabrous, 5-lobed; lobes glabrous, oblong-ovate, acute or obtuse, glandular-ciliate, pubescent, about as long as the tube.

Fruit. Maturing August–October. Drupe globose to ellipsoid, ¾–1 in. long, red or yellow-red, white-dotted, lustrous, little or no bloom, thin-skinned; stone turgid, reticulate, ⅔–¾ in. long,

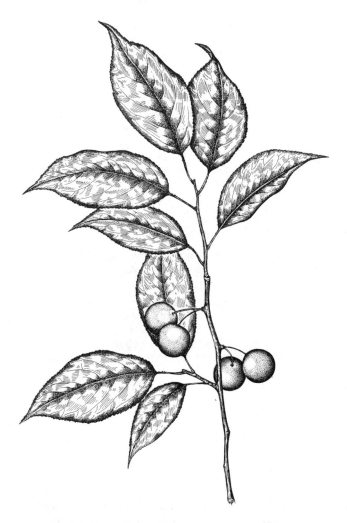

rounded or short-pointed at the apex, rounded or truncate at the base, grooved on the dorsal suture.

Leaves. Alternate, simple, deciduous, blades 4–6 in. long, 1–1½ in. wide, oblong-obovate to oblong-oval, acuminate at the apex, cuneate or rounded at the base; upper surface glabrous, dark green, lustrous; lower surface glabrous or slightly pubescent; finely glandular-serrate on the margin; petiole slender, orange-colored, 1–1½ in. long, glandular.

Twigs. Dark reddish brown, stout, rigid, glabrous, or pubescent, occasionally somewhat spinescent.

Bark. Dark or light brown, exfoliating into large thin plates.

Range. Texas, Oklahoma, Arkansas, and Louisiana; northward to Missouri, Iowa, Kansas, Kentucky, and Tennessee.

Remarks. The genus name, *Prunus*, is the ancient Latin name, and the species name, *hortulana*, means "of gardens" and refers to its value in horticulture.

American Plum

Prunus americana Marsh. [D, E]

Field Identification. Shrub propagating by root sprouts to form thickets, or a tree to 35 ft, with spreading, pendulous, more or less thorny branches.

Flowers. March–May, borne in 2–5-flowered umbels on slender, glabrous pedicels ⅓–⅔ in. long; flowers ¾–1¼ in. broad, perfect, white; petals 5, narrowly obovate, rounded or erose at the apex, narrowed into a claw which is red at base, about ½ in. long; stamens about 20, in numerous rows; pistil with a 1-celled ovary; calyx-tube obconic, glabrous or pubescent, red or greenish; lobes of calyx 5, lanceolate, acute or obtuse at the apex, entire or toothed toward the apex, glabrous or puberulous on the exterior, usually pubescent within.

Fruit. Ripening June–October, variable in size, usually ¾–1 in. long, subglobose, red or sometimes yellow, somewhat glaucous or not at all, conspicuously marked with pale dots; skin tough; flesh yellow and succulent, varying in flavor, sometimes hardly edible, bittersweet, acid, very suitable for preserves; stone oval, rounded at apex, somewhat narrowed at base, smooth to slightly rugose, turgid, somewhat compressed, obscurely ridged on one suture and grooved on the other.

Leaves. Alternate, simple, deciduous, 2½–4 in. long, 1½–2 in. wide, ovate to obovate or oblong, acuminate at apex, rounded or cuneate at the base; sharply and singly or doubly serrate on the margin; thick, firm, more or less rugose; dark green and glabrous above; paler and reticulate-veined, and glabrous or slightly pubescent along the veins beneath; petioles ½–¾ in. long, slender, glabrous or puberulous, eglandular or glandular at the apex.

Twigs. Slender, glabrous, green to orange to reddish brown; lateral branchlets spurlike, sometimes spinescent; lenticels circular, raised, minute.

Bark. Dark brown to reddish, breaking into thin, long, persistent plates.

Wood. Dark brown, with lighter colored sapwood, close-grained, strong, hard, weighing 45 lb per cu ft, of no commercial importance because of small size of trunks.

Range. Texas, New Mexico, Oklahoma, Arkansas, and Louisiana; eastward to Florida, northward to Massachusetts, New York, and southern Ontario, and west to the Rocky Mountains.

Remarks. The genus name, *Prunus*, is the classical name for a European plum, and the species name, *americana*, is of obvious meaning. Other vernacular names are Horse Plum, Hog Plum, Goose Plum, Native Plum, River Plum, Wild Yellow Plum, Red

Plum, and Thorn Plum. The fruit makes excellent jellies and preserves or may be eaten raw or cooked. The fruit is also eaten by many species of birds. Many horticultural varieties have been developed. It is probably the best fruit plum for the Middle West and North.

Peach

Prunus persica Batsch [D, E]

Field Identification. Tree attaining a height of 24 ft, with a rounded crown and spreading branches.

Flowers. Usually expanding before the leaves March–May, subsessile, solitary or 2 together, fragrant, perfect, 1–2 in. across; petals 5, pink, spreading, rounded; calyx with the 5 sepals exter-

nally pubescent; stamens 20–30, filaments usually colored like the petals, exserted, slender, distinct; ovary tomentulose, 1-celled and sessile, the 2 ovules pendulous; pistil solitary with a simple terminal style.

Fruit. Drupe maturing July–October, subglobose, grooved on one side, velvety-tomentose, 2–3⅓ in. in diameter, fleshy, separating in halves at the sutures; stone elliptic to ovoid-elliptic, usually pointed at distal end, deeply pitted and furrowed, very hard; fruit of escaped trees usually harder and smaller.

Leaves. Numerous, conduplicate in the bud, almond-scented, impregnated with prussic acid, simple, alternate, some appearing clustered, elliptic-lanceolate to oblong-lanceolate, broadest at the middle or slightly above the middle, 3–6 in. long, apex long-acuminate, base varying from acute to acuminate or broad-cuneate, margin serrate or serrulate, surfaces glabrous and lustrous, bright green, thin; petioles glandular, ⅜–⅝ in.

Range. A native of China but extensively cultivated from Texas eastward to Florida and northward to New York and southern Ontario. Sometimes escaped from cultivation in the southeastern United States.

Remarks. The genus name, *Prunus*, is the classical Latin name of a plum of Europe. The species name, *persica*, means "Persian" and is also an old generic name for peach. The genus name of *Amygdalus* L. is used by some authors.

Common Pear

Pyrus communis L. [D, E, F]

Field Identification. Tree generally pyramidal and upright, living to an old age. Attaining a height of 75 ft and 2–3 ft in diameter. The branches are stiff, upright, and sometimes thorny.

Flowers. March–May, with or before the leaves; cymes simple, terminal, 4–12-flowered, borne on short twigs of the preceding year; pedicels ½–2 in., pubescent at first, glabrous later; corolla white or pink, 1–2 in. broad, 5-petaled, petals broad-oblong, rounded, short-clawed; stamens numerous, exserted; anthers yellow, small, 2-celled, sacs longitudinally dehiscent; styles 5, distinct to the base, stigma small, ovules 2 in each cavity, cavities as many as the styles; disk cushionlike; calyx urn-shaped, the 5 acute lobes about as long as the tube.

Fruit. Ripening July–October, pome pear-shaped, tapering to the base, in the wild form about 2 in. long, much longer in cultivated forms, yellow to reddish, flesh with abundant grit cells; seeds small, smooth, brown to black, endosperm none, cotyledons fleshy, the pome consisting of the thickened calyx-tube and receptacle enclosing the carpels.

Leaves. Simple, alternate, deciduous, usually on short lateral spurs, ovate to elliptic or obovate, margin finely serrate to entire, apex acute or acuminate, sometimes abruptly so, base usually rounded, blade length 1½–4 in., young leaves downy and ciliate, mature leaves lustrous, dark green to olive green above, lower surface paler, both sides glabrous or nearly so; petioles 1¼–3 in., as long as the blades or longer.

Twigs. Somewhat pubescent at first, glabrous later, reddish brown to gray or black.

Wood. Reddish brown, hard, fine-grained, 51 lb per cu ft.

Range. Common Pear is a native of Europe and Asia and escapes cultivation in some areas in the Southwest and elsewhere in North America. It is often cultivated in Texas, Oklahoma, Arkansas, and Louisiana.

Remarks. The genus name, *Pyrus*, is the classical name for the pear tree, and the species name, *communis*, means "common." The tree is sometimes used for shelter-belt planting and for wildlife food.

Prairie Crab-apple

Pyrus ioensis (Wood) Bailey [D, F]

Field Identification. Tree attaining a height of 28 ft and a trunk diameter of 18 in., the numerous rigid, crooked branches forming a rounded spreading crown.

Flowers. Borne April–June, fragrant, in 2–5-flowered clusters on very hairy pedicels 1–1½ in.; calyx-lobes 5, lanceolate-acuminate, longer than the tube, densely white-tomentose; petals 5, white or pink, about ½ in. wide, obovate, base narrowed into a slender claw; stamens numerous, shorter than the petals; styles 5, joined below and white-hairy.

Fruit. Maturing September–October, peduncles ¾–1½ in. long, globose, somewhat depressed, apical and basal depressions shallow, greenish to yellow, sometimes with minute, yellow dots, surface waxy and greasy to the touch, length ¾–1¼ in., width ¾–1½ in., flesh sour and astringent.

Leaves. Simple, alternate or clustered, deciduous, length and width variable on weak and vigorous shoots, blades 1½–5 in. long, ¾–4 in. wide, elliptic to oblong or obovate-oblong, apex acute or obtuse to rounded, base cuneate or rounded, margin singly or doubly crenate-serrate, or on some deeply lobed as well; at maturity coriaceous, dark green, lustrous and glabrous above, lower surface varying from almost glabrous to densely white-tomentose, turning yellow in autumn; petioles slender, at first with hoary-white tomentum, becoming pubescent or glabrous later.

Twigs. Reddish brown to gray, densely tomentose at first but with age less so, finally glabrous, lenticels small and pale; twigs often set with numerous short lateral shoots bearing thorns terminally; winter buds small, obtuse, pubescent.

Bark. Reddish brown to dark gray, about ⅓ in. thick, scales small, narrow, persistent.

Range. In Texas, Oklahoma, Arkansas, and Louisiana; eastward to Alabama and north to Minnesota.

Remarks. The genus name, *Pyrus*, is the classical name for the pear tree, and the species name, *ioensis*, refers to the state of Iowa where it was first described. Other vernacular names are Iowa Crab, Prairie Crab, and Western Crab-apple. The flesh of this crab-apple is sour and inedible, but is sometimes used for making vinegar. It has been cultivated for ornament since 1885. It is of considerable value as food for wildlife, the fruit known to be eaten by at least 20 species of birds and mammals, including bobwhite quail, ruffed grouse, ring-necked pheasant, gray and red fox, skunk, opossum, raccoon, cottontail, woodchuck, red squirrel, and fox squirrel.

Red Chokeberry

Pyrus arbutifolia (L.) L. f. [D, E]

Field Identification. Deciduous, swamp-loving shrub to 12 ft. Sometimes the young shoots overtop the compound flower clusters.

Flowers. Borne March–May, in terminal compound cymes ¾–2½ in. wide; axillary branches short, persistently villous, 9–20-flowered, sometimes overtopped by the sterile shoots; flowers small, white to pink, ⅓–½ in. broad; calyx urn-shaped, sepals 5, ovate to triangular, apex acute to obtuse, usually glandular, tomentose; petals 5, ⅙–¼ in. long, spreading, obovate to oval, concave, apex rounded, base short-clawed; stamens numerous (about 20), exserted, filaments shorter than the petals, anthers reddish or purplish; ovary woolly above, styles 5 and united at base, persistent.

Fruit. Pome ripening September–October, globose or short pear-shaped, ⅙–¼ in. in diameter, conspicuously bright red at maturity, hairy at first, glabrous later, long persistent, carpels leathery; seeds 1–5, some usually abortive.

Leaves. Convolute in the bud, simple, alternate, deciduous, oval to elliptic or oblong to obovate; apex obtuse or acute to short-acuminate and apiculate; base cuneate or narrowed; margin serrulate-crenulate, the teeth rounded, incurved, and glandular, blade 1–3 in. long; upper surface usually glabrous, midrib sometimes glandular; lower surface densely gray-tomentose; petioles ⅛–⅖ in., semiglabrous to tomentose; stipules narrow, early deciduous. Leaves turning red in autumn.

Twigs. Brown to gray, persistently tomentose-hairy, older glabrate.

Range. Wet woods and swamps. East Texas, Oklahoma, Arkansas, and Louisiana; eastward to Florida, northward to Nova Scotia, and west to Minnesota.

Remarks. The genus name, *Pyrus*, is the classical name of the pear tree. The species name, *arbutifolia*, refers to the *Arbutus*-like leaves. Also known under the vernacular names of Choke-pear and Dogberry. The fruit is a valuable wildlife food in fall and winter, being eaten by at least 13 species of birds, including bob-white quail, ruffed grouse, ring-necked pheasant, and cedar wax-wing. It has been cultivated since 1700. Red Chokeberry is some-what subject to blight and borer attacks, withstands city smoke, and the leaves are tardily deciduous. It could be more extensively cultivated for its attractive flowers, brilliant fruit, and colorful autumn leaves.

Shadblow Service-berry

Amelanchier arborea (Michx. f.) Fern. [D]

Field Identification. Slender shrub or small round-topped tree seldom over 25 ft.

Flowers. March–May, racemes 3–7 in. long, rather dense, erect or nodding, silky-hairy, fragrant, 6–12-flowered; calyx 5-cleft, campanulate, glabrous or hairy, sepals triangular-ovate; petals 5, white, elliptic to obovate, ½–1 in. long; stamens about 20; ovary 5-celled, terminating in 2–5 styles with broad stigmas.

Fruit. June–July, on long pedicels, subglobose, ¼–½ in. in diameter, dry, reddish purple, tasteless or sweetish; seeds small and numerous (4–10, some abortive), usually dispersed by birds and animals.

Leaves. Alternate, simple, deciduous, oval to oblong or obovate, acute or acuminate at the apex, rounded or cordate at the base, sharply and finely serrate on the margin, glabrous or nearly so above, paler and pubescent beneath or finally glabrous, blades 2–5 in. long, 1–2 in. wide; petioles 1½–2 in., slender, hairy at first but glabrous later.

Twigs. Reddish brown to black, slender, rather crooked, somewhat hairy when young but glabrous later; lenticels numerous and pale.

Bark. Gray to black, thin, smooth, in age becoming shallowly fissured with scaly longitudinal ridges.

Wood. Brown, close-grained, hard, strong, tough, elastic, weighing 49 lb per cu ft.

Range. Oklahoma, Arkansas, Louisiana, and northeast Texas; eastward to Florida and northward to Quebec, Ontario, and Newfoundland.

Remarks. The genus name, *Amelanchier*, is derived from the French name of a European species. The species name, *arborea*, refers to the treelike character of this species. Vernacular names are Boxwood, Bill-berry, June-plum, Indian-cherry, Swamp Shadbush, Indian-pear, Juice-pear, Sugar-pear, Plum-pear, and Berry-pear. It is occasionally cultivated in gardens for the showy white flowers. Dwarf plants are often found growing in sterile ground. The berries may be eaten uncooked or made into pies. Shadblow Service-berry is a valuable wildlife plant, its fruit being eaten by at least 35 species of birds, and its foliage browsed by cottontail and white-tailed deer. The wood is sometimes used for making handles.

Narrow-leaf Firethorn

Pyracantha angustifolia (Franch.) Schneid. [D, E]

Field Identification. Cultivated, half-evergreen shrub with diffusely spreading, irregular, spiny branches, or sometimes a tree to 20 ft. Occasionally almost prostrate in form.

Flowers. April–May, corymbs axillary, pubescent, many-flowered, ½–3 in. broad; calyx 5-lobed, lobes short, about ¹⁄₁₆ in. long, broadly obtuse to acute, white-hairy; margins thin and whitened, glandular or glandless, ciliate; corolla about ⅜ in. across, white, 5-petaled; petals spreading, suborbicular, narrowed to a broad

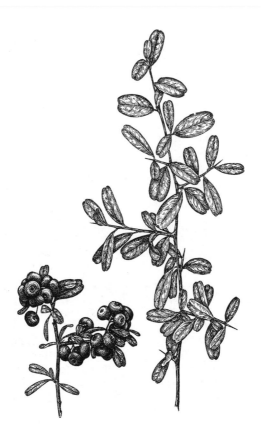

base; stamens exserted, numerous, spreading, filaments white, anthers yellow; carpels 5, spreading, free on the ventral side, on the dorsal side partially connate with the calyx-tube.

Fruit. Pomes persistent in the winter, numerous, red to orange, ⅕–⅜ in. across, depressed-globose, fleshy, calyx remnants persistent; seeds 5, about ⅛ in. long, black, lustrous, 2 surfaces plane, dorsal surface rounded, one end rounded, the other abruptly apiculate-pointed.

Leaves. Simple, alternate, or somewhat clustered on short, lateral, spinescent branches, half-evergreen, leathery, oval-oblong to oblanceolate, apex obtuse to rounded or notched, base cuneate, margin entire, length ½–1¾ in.; upper surface dark green, shiny, apparently smooth (but often with scattered, white, cobwebby hairs under magnification); lower surface much paler, glabrous, or with a few white hairs along the main vein, obscurely reticulate-veined; petioles ¹⁄₁₆–¼ in., pubescent to glabrous; stipules minute, caducous; buds small and pubescent.

Twigs. Green to grayish with dense fine pubescence; secondary twigs almost at right angles, and usually short and spiniferous; spines straight, ⅛–½ in. long, often pubescent at the base with apex reddish brown and more glabrous.

Range. Cultivated in gardens in Texas, Louisiana, Arkansas, Oklahoma, and elsewhere, sometimes escaping. Hardy as far north as Massachusetts. A native of southwest China.

Remarks. The genus name, *Pyracantha*, is from the Greek words *pyr* ("fire") and *akanthos* ("thorn"), alluding to the bright red fruit. The species name, *angustifolia*, refers to the narrow leaves. The plant is often cultivated for ornament. Robin and cedar waxwing, as well as other birds, eagerly devour the fruit. Other closely related species, such as the Scarlet Firethorn, *P. coccinea* Roem., with crenate more glabrous leaves, are also cultivated extensively.

Loquat

Eriobotrya japonica Lindl. [D]

Field Identification. Evergreen tree often planted for ornament in the warmer parts of the United States. Persistent in abandoned gardens for many years. Attains a height of 25 ft with an open but rather rounded crown.

Flowers. August–November, fragrant, borne in terminal woolly panicles 4–7½ in. long, buds with conspicuously rusty-woolly tomentum, flowers about ½ in. across; calyx-lobes 5, ⅛–¼ in. long, acute, densely rusty-woolly; petals 5, white, oval to suborbicular, short-clawed; stamens 20; styles 2–5, connate below, ovary inferior, 2–5-celled, cells 2-ovuled.

Fruit. In spring, pome edible, small, pear-shaped or spherical, yellow, 1½–3 in. long, endocarp thin; seeds large, ovoid, solitary or a few.

Leaves. Simple, alternate, sessile or very short-petioled, crowded terminally and whorled to give a rosettelike appearance, rather stiff and firm, large and ornamental, 4–12 in. long, oval to oblong or obovate, margin with remote slender teeth but entire toward

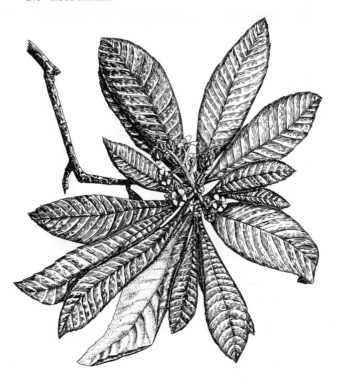

the base; upper surface with veins deeply impressed, dark green, lustrous, at maturity glabrous; lower surface much paler and densely feltlike with rusty tomentum.

Twigs. Stout, green to brown, densely woolly-tomentose, when older brown to dark gray and glabrous; leaf scars large, half-round, bundle scars 3.

Range. A native of China and Japan, much planted for ornament in Texas, Louisiana, and other Gulf states. Grown as a pot plant in the North.

Remarks. The genus name, *Eriobotrya*, is the Greek word for "woolly cluster," referring to the hairy panicles. The species name, *japonica*, is for Japan, its original home. It is also known as Japanese-plum and China-plum. The fruit may be eaten raw or prepared as jelly, jam, pies, and preserves. It has an agreeable acid flavor.

True Mountain Mahogany

Cercocarpus montanus Raf. [G]

Field Identification. Western shrub or small tree to 12 ft, with upright or spreading branches. The present taxonomical treatment follows that of Floyd L. Martin, "A Revision of *Cercocarpus*," *Brittonia* 7, no. 2 (March 1950): 91–111.

Flowers. Often crowded on short spurlike branchlets, solitary or fascicled; pedicels to ⅛ in., to ⅓ in. long in fruit; floral tube ⅕–⅓ in. long, elongate, cylindrical, spreading-villous or appressed-silky, usually somewhat enlarged below, and at apex abruptly widened into a campanulate deciduous limb; sepals 5, ⅛–⅕ in. wide; corolla absent; stamens 22–44, filaments distinct, inserted in 2–3 rows, anthers hairy, emarginate at both ends, affixed dorsally above the base; pistil solitary, inserted in the bottom of the

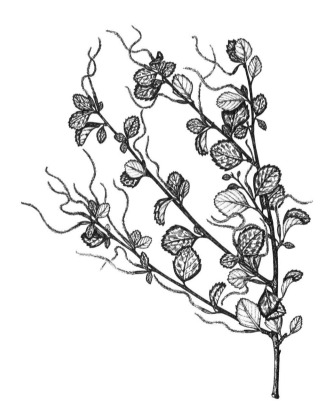

floral tube; ovary cylindric-fusiform, sessile; style terminal, elongate, exserted, silky-plumose; ovules solitary, ascending, affixed above the middle.

Fruit. Length ⅓–⅖ in., appressed silky-hairy, cylindric-fusiform, about one-third exserted from the floral tube at maturity; tail 1¾–2½ in. long, densely spreading, silky-plumose, testa membranaceous, seed cylindric; cotyledons linear, elongate, hypocotyl very short.

Leaves. Simple, alternate, or somewhat fascicled on short spurlike branchlets, blade ovate to oval or obovate (in some varieties lanceolate, oblanceolate, or elliptic), apex acute to rounded, base usually cuneate, margin usually with coarse ovate to triangular teeth but sometimes entire, length ⅝–1¼ in., to ¾ in. wide; thin but firm, upper surface green to grayish green above, lower surface lighter and varying from glabrous to short villous or rather densely appressed-silky; lateral veins 3–6, parallel or somewhat curved toward the margins, prominent to less noticeable; petiole to ⅓ in. long; stipules adnate to petiole at base, lanceolate to ovate, acute, brown, scarious.

Twigs. Rather stout, rigid, terete, roughened by leaf scars, often with short lateral spurs, gray to brown, pubescent, later roughened and fissured on old branches or trunk; wood hard and dark colored.

Range. Dry rocky bluffs or mountainsides at altitudes of 3,500–9,000 ft. In New Mexico in the Zuni, Jemez, Sandia, and Sangre de Cristo mountains; west to Arizona and northward to Wyoming and South Dakota.

Remarks. The genus name, *Cercocarpus*, refers to the long tail of the fruit. The species name, *montanus*, is for the mountainous habitat.

Silver Mountain Mahogany, *C. montanus* var. *argenteus* (Rydb.) F. L. Martin, is a shrub 4–15 ft, with ascending branches; flowers June–July, floral tube ⅕–⅛ in. long (in fruit to ⅖ in. long), appressed-silky; calyx-limb ⅛–⅖ in. wide; pedicel ¹⁄₂₅ in. or less in length in flower (in fruit ⅛–⅙ in. long); leaves oblanceolate, narrowly obovate to narrowly elliptic; margin set with short, broad, triangular teeth which are apiculate-tipped or entire, length ¾–1½ in., width ⅜–¾ in., surfaces white, appressed-silky, rarely sparsely villous or nearly glabrate, veins 5–6. In New Mexico and Texas. In Texas in Hutcheson, Randall, Lubbock, Presidio, Brewster, Pecos, Edwards, Kimble, Real, and Uvalde counties. In New Mexico in Sandoval, Santa Fe, San Miguel, Lincoln, and Otero counties. Rocky hillsides, canyons, mountains at altitudes of 4,000–8,500 ft. (Listed elsewhere as *C. argenteus* Rydb.)

Shaggy Mountain Mahogany, *C. montanus* var. *paucidentatus* (Wats.) F. L. Martin, is a shrub 3–15 ft; flowers May–November, floral tube ⅛–¼ in. long (in fruit ⅛–⅓ in. long), spreading villous or appressed-silky; calyx-limb 1/12–⅕ in. wide; pedicel very short in flower, in fruit 1/12–⅙ in. long; tail of fruit ⅝–2 in. long; leaves lanceolate, oblanceolate or narrowly obovate, margin entire or with 3–5 short teeth at apex, short-villous, appressed-silky or glabrate, lateral veins 3–5 (rarely 6), length ⅜–¾ in. (rarely to 1¼ in.), width ¼–⅓ in. In Arizona, New Mexico, Texas, and Mexico. In New Mexico south to the Mexican border. In Texas in El Paso and Jeff Davis counties. In Mexico in Sonora, Chihuahua, Coahuila, San Luis Potosí, and Hidalgo. Rocky hills at altitudes of 4,500–8,500 ft.

LEGUME FAMILY (Leguminosae)
Subfamily Mimosoideae

Silk-tree Albizia

Albizia julibrissin (Willd.) Durazz. [D, E]

Field Identification. Cultivated tree attaining a height of 40 ft, with a flat top and widely spreading branches, often broader than high.

Flowers. May–August, on the upper ends of the branches, in axillary, tassellike, capitate clusters on slender, pubescent peduncles ½–2 in. long; heads 1½–2 in. broad, flowers perfect; stamens numerous, conspicuous, long-exserted, filamentous, 1–1½ in. long, pink distally, whitish proximally, united at base; pistils considerably longer than stamens, style white or pink, filiform, stigma minute, ovary short-stalked; corolla tubular, greenish, pubescent, ⅛–¼ in. long, 5-lobed, lobes oblong or ovate, obtuse or acute; calyx tubular, 1/12–⅛ in. long, shallowly 5-lobed, pubescent.

Fruit. Legume on a pubescent peduncle 1–2½ in. long, oblong to linear, 5–8 in. long, ¾–1 in. wide, margin straight or wavy, apex gradually or abruptly narrowed into a long spinose point, base cuneate; valves thin, flattened papery, yellowish brown, not separating on margin, without partitions between the seeds; seeds

brown, lustrous, flattened, rounded or obtuse at the ends, about ¼ in. long, averaging 11,000 seeds per lb, one-fourth to one-third germinating.

Leaves. Alternate, deciduous, twice-pinnately compound, 10–15 in. long; rachis green to brown, smooth or striate, pubescent, often glandular near the base; pinnae 2–6 in. long, 5–12 pairs, rachilla pubescent; leaflets 8–30 pairs per pinna, sessile or nearly so, ¼–⅜ in. long, oblong, slightly falcate, oblique; margin entire, ciliate, straighter on one side than the other; apex half-rounded and mucronulate; base truncate or rounded, attached to the rachilla on one side; main vein parallel to and close to the margin on one side; glabrous to puberulent.

Twigs. Green to brown or gray, somewhat angular or rounded, glabrous, lenticels small but numerous.

Bark. Smooth, tight, blotched gray, sometimes brownish on young trunks or limbs.

Range. A native of Asia, cultivated from Washington, D.C., Philadelphia, and Indianapolis; and Maryland, south to Florida and west into Texas. Commonly planted on the streets of Houston and other Gulf Coast cities.

Remarks. The genus, *Albizia*, was named after F. Degli Albizzi, an Italian nobleman and naturalist. The tree is often called Mimosa in the southern states. Silk-tree was first introduced into cultivation in 1745 and is considered a top ornamental for the South, being somewhat drouth resistant and fairly free from disease and insects. However, it has been reported that specimens in Georgia and the Carolinas have been very susceptible to the killing attacks of the root fungus *Fusorium perniciosum*. The tree does not seem to escape cultivation and reproduce readily. The seeds may furnish a limited amount of food for birds, squirrels, and other wildlife. The wood is used for cabinetmaking in its native Asiatic home.

Sweet Acacia

Acacia farnesiana (L.) Willd. [D, E]

Field Identification. Shrub with many stems from the base, or a thorny tree to 30 ft, and 18 in. in diameter. With either a flat top in coastal specimens, or round-topped with pendulous branches.

Flowers. February–March, very fragrant, solitary, or 2–5 heads together on puberulous peduncles 1–1½ in. long; bracts 2, minute; heads about ⅔ in. in diameter; stamens numerous, yellow, with distinct filaments (about 20), much longer than the corolla; corolla tubular-funnelform, shallowly 5-lobed, lobes as high as broad, about 1⁄12 in. long; calyx about half as long as corolla-lobes, somewhat hairy; ovary short-stipitate and hairy, style filiform.

Fruit. Legume persistent, tardily dehiscent, cylindric, oblong, thick, woody, stout, straight or curved, 2–3 in. long, ½–⅔ in. broad, short-pointed, reddish brown to purple or black, partitions thin and papery, pulp pithy; seeds in solitary compartments, transverse, ovoid, brown, shining, flattened on one side, about ¼ in. long, peduncles stout and short.

Leaves. Pinnately compound, alternate, deciduous, 1–4 in. long; pinnae 2–8 pairs; leaflets 10–25 pairs, linear, apex acute or obtuse, or with a minute mucro, base inequilateral, length about 1⁄12–¼ in., width about 1⁄25 in., sessile or short-petioled, bright green and glabrous or puberulent.

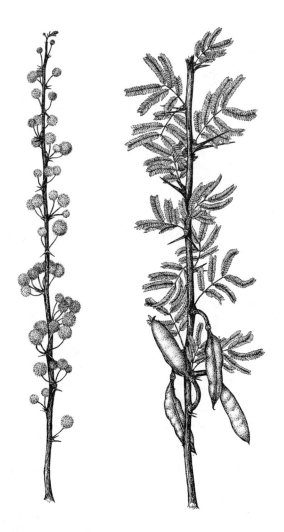

Twigs. Ascending, pendulous or horizontal, slender, terete, striate, angled, glabrous or puberulent, armed with paired straight, rigid, stipular spines to 1½₂ in. long.

Wood. Reddish brown, sapwood paler, hard, heavy, durable, close-grained, specific gravity 0.83.

Range. Cultivated in tropical and semitropical regions of both hemispheres. In Texas and Louisiana; eastward to Florida, northward in New Mexico and Arizona, southward on the Texas coast through Mexico, through Central America and northern South America to the Guianas.

Remarks. The genus name, *Acacia*, refers to the hard sharp spinescent stipules of some species. The species name, *farnesiana*, honors Cardinal Odoardo Farnese (1573–1626) of Rome. This species was the first introduced to his gardens in 1611. Our species is cultivated in France under the name of Cassie, but is usually known in Texas as Huisache; however, because of confusion with other acacias, it seems best to apply the name of Sweet Acacia. Vernacular names in the United States and Latin America are Acacia-catclaw, Honey-ball, Opopanax, Yellow-opopanax, Popinach, Hinsach, Binorama, Vinorama, Huisache (from the Nahuatl *huitz-axin*), Guisache Yondino, Guisache, Huisache de la Semilla, Huixachin, Uisatsin, Xkantiriz, Matitas, Finisache, Bihi, Espiño, Aroma, Zubin, Zubin-ché, Gabia, Gavia, Subin, Aroma Amarilla, Espiño Blanco, Cacheto de aroma, Cuji Cimarrón, Pelá, Uña de Cabra, and Espinillo.

Sweet Acacia is commonly cultivated as a garden ornamental in tropical countries. The wood is used for many purposes, including posts, agricultural instruments, and woodenware articles. It is considered a good winter forage plant and a desirable honey plant in semiarid areas, being resistant to drought and heat. The bark and fruit are used for tanning, dying, and ink-making. Glue from the young pods is used to mend pottery.

Wright Acacia

Acacia wrightii Benth. [E, F]

Field Identification. Spiny shrub, or sometimes a tree attaining a height of 30 ft, and to 1 ft in diameter. The glabrous, spreading branches form a wide irregular-shaped crown.

Flowers. March–May, or at odd times after rains, in cylindric spikes ¾–1½ in. long which are sometimes interrupted; peduncles slender, glabrous or pubescent, solitary or clustered; individual flower pedicels slender, subtended by minute caducous bracts; calyx minutely 5-toothed, pubescent on the outer surface; petals spatulate, slightly united at base, margin ciliate; stamens exserted, about ¼ in. long; ovary hairy, long-stalked.

Fruit. Ripe June–September, legume often abundant and conspicuous, borne on peduncles ¾–2 in. long; legume 2–4 in. long, 1–1¼ in. wide; margin thick, straight or irregularly contracted or

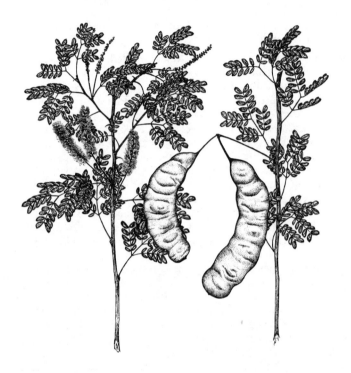

curved; apex rounded and usually short-pointed; base round or oblique and short-stipitate; valves much flattened, papery, thin, finely reticulate-veined, glabrous; seeds compressed, narrow-obovoid, light brown, sometimes marked with oval depressions, length about ¼ in.

Leaves. Solitary or fascicled, 1–2 in. long, petiole and rachis pubescent, petiole ¼–1⅓ in. long, sometimes with a solitary gland near the apex; pinnae 1–3 pairs, each pinna with 2–6 pairs of leaflets obovate to oblong, apex obliquely rounded to obtuse or retuse, often apiculate; base sessile or short-petiolulate; length ¼–⅚ in.; surface 2–3-nerved and reticulate-veined, glabrous or pubescent, paler green on the lower surface.

Twigs. Gray to brown or yellowish, mostly glabrous and some-what striately angled; spineless, or armed with brown, recurved, flattened, sharp pointed infrastipular spines about ¼ in. long.

Bark. Rather thin, gray to brown, divided into broad ridges and shallow fissures, the ridges separating into thin, narrow scales on old trunks.

Wood. Pale brown to reddish brown, sapwood white to yellow, close-grained, heavy, hard.

Range. On dry, rocky, prairie soils. In Texas from the valley of the Guadalupe River westward. Assuming tree habit and of greatest abundance in the vicinity of Brackettville, Uvalde, Sabinal, and Montell. In Mexico in Sonora, Tamaulipas, and Nuevo León.

Remarks. The genus name, *Acacia*, refers to the sharp, pointed spinescent stipules of some species. The species name, *wrightii*, is in honor of Charles Wright, who collected plants in Texas in 1847–1848 while with the military forces at the western forts. Wright Acacia can be transplanted or grown from seed and makes an excellent ornamental tree in the drier areas of the state. A few horticultural varieties have been developed. The legume is borne abundantly and is conspicuous. The spikes of yellow flowers make a good bee food, and the wood is sometimes used for fuel and posts. Vernacular names are Tree Catclaw, Texas Catclaw, Uña de Gato, and Negra. Wright Acacia can be distinguished from Catclaw Acacia, *A. greggii*, by the wider legume and leaflets which are twice as large.

Catclaw Acacia

Acacia greggii Gray [E, F, G]

Field Identification. Thorny, thicket-forming shrub or small tree to 30 ft, and 12 in. in diameter. The numerous slender, spreading, thorny branches are almost impenetrable.

Flowers. Usually April–October; spikes 1¼–2½ in. long, about ½ in. in diameter, dense, oblong, creamy yellow, fragrant, peduncle usually about one-half the length of the spike, sometimes a number of spikes clustered together at the ends of the twigs; calyx green, about ¹⁄₁₂ in. long (half as long as the petals), obscurely 5-toothed, puberulous on the outer surface; petals 5, ⅛–⅙ in. long, greenish, yellowish, and hairy on the margins; stamens numerous, exserted, about ¼ in. long, filaments pale yellow; ovary long-stalked, hairy.

Fruit. Persistent from July through the winter, legume 2–5½ in. long, ½–¾ in. wide, compressed, straight, curved, or often curling and contorted, constricted between the seeds, apex acute or rounded, sometimes mucronulate, base obliquely narrowed into a short stalk, margins thickened, light brown or reddish, reticulate-veined, valves thin and membranous; seeds dark brown, shiny,

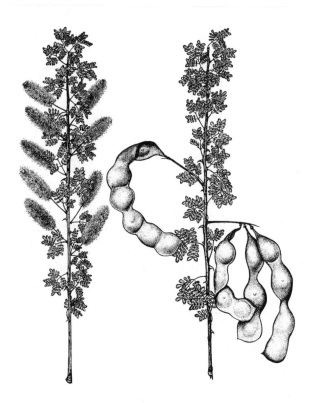

almost orbicular, compressed, ¼–⅓ in. long, germination about 60 percent.

Leaves. Bipinnate, 1–3 in. long; pinnae short-stalked, 1–3 pairs, petiole with a minute brown gland near the middle; leaflets 3–7 (usually 3–5) pairs, obovate to oblong; apex rounded, obtuse or truncate, apiculate; base unequally contracted into a short petiolule; blade surface 2–3-nerved, lightly reticulate-veined, pubescent, length ⅙–¼ in.

Twigs. Pale brown to reddish or gray, pubescent or glabrous; spines ⅛–¼ in. long, dark brown or gray, stout, recurved, flat at base, infrastipular.

Bark. Gray to black, about ⅛ in. thick, furrowed, the surface separating into small thin scales on older trunks.

Wood. Brown to reddish, sapwood light yellow, close-grained, hard, heavy, strong, durable.

Range. At altitudes of 1,000–5,000 ft, on dry gravelly mesas, sides of canyons, and banks of arroyos. In west Texas there are two more or less disjunct ranges. The more southerly of these extends southward from Bexar County to Willacy County; the other from Taylor County southwestward, with heavy concentration in the Big Bend area. Also in New Mexico, Arizona, and Colorado; north to Nevada and Utah, west to California, and south into the Mexican states of Coahuila, Chihuahua, Sonora, and Baja California.

Remarks. The genus name, *Acacia*, means "hard-pointed" and refers to the spinescent stipules of some of the species. The species name, *greggii*, honors Josiah Gregg (1806–1850), early botanist who collected in the Southwest and northern Mexico. Vernacular names used are Devil Claws, Texas Mimosa, Paradise Flower, Gregg Acacia, Long-flowered Acacia, Huajilla, Chaparral, Gatuña, and Uña de Gato.

Catclaw Acacia often grows in almost impenetrable thickets, furnishing shelter for various birds and mammals. The seeds are eaten by scaled quail, and the leaves are nibbled by jack rabbit when other food is scarce. The wood is used for fuel, small household articles, and singletrees. Cattle browse on the young foliage when grass is scarce, but is not palatable. It apparently stands heavy grazing well and is drought resistant. The fragrant yellow flowers furnish an excellent bee food, and honey from it is of light yellow and of good flavor. The Indians of west Texas, New Mexico, and Arizona made a meal, known as "pinole," from the legumes, which was eaten in the form of mush or cakes. It is also reported that the lac insect, *Tachardia lacca* Kerr., feeds on the sap and exudes the substance from its body. This substance is used as commercial lac. However, the infestation does not appear to be abundant enough to make the gathering of the lac commercially profitable on Catclaw Acacia.

Roemer Acacia

Acacia roemeriana Scheele [E, F, G]

Field Identification. Prickly, round-topped shrub with many spreading branches. More rarely a small tree to 15 ft or more, with a maximum trunk diameter to 16 in.

Flowers. Heads mostly axillary; borne on slender, glabrous peduncles ⅓–1⅓ in. long; flowers white to pale greenish yellow, ¼–½ in. in diameter; calyx small, 5-lobed; corolla 5-lobed; stamens numerous, exserted, distinct, anthers small; ovary stalked.

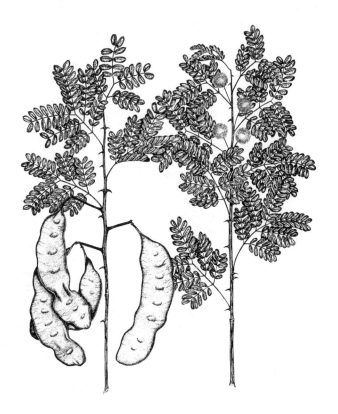

Fruit. Legume oblong to linear, 2−5 in. long, ¾−1¼ in. broad, straight or somewhat curved, compressed, leathery, margin entire to lobed or constricted, apex obtuse, base rounded to cuneate and stipitate, surface red or pink at maturity, glabrous and prominently nerved on the edge of the valves.

Leaves. Bipinnate, 1⅓−4 in. long, pinnae 1−3 pairs, leaflets 3−8 pairs, each leaflet ⅓−⅗ in. long, oblong to oval or cuneate, oblique, obtuse to retuse and often apiculate, glabrous or nearly so, veins prominent beneath.

Twigs. Gray to brown, smooth, with short curved prickles.

Bark. Gray to brown, smooth on young trunks, breaking into thin, small scales on old trunks.

Range. In dry, limestone soil, or on gravelly bluffs or banks. From the valley of the Colorado River south and west to El Paso County, Texas. The type specimen was collected at Austin. Abundant in the vicinity of New Braunfels, San Antonio, Langtry, and Del Rio, Texas. To altitudes of 4,500 ft in the foothills of the Chisos Mountains in Brewster County, Texas. In the lower Rio Grande Valley in Cameron and Hidalgo counties. Also in southern New Mexico near Carlsbad, and in Mexico in the states of Coahuila, Chihuahua, and Baja California.

Remarks. The genus name, *Acacia*, refers to the sharp-pointed, spinescent stipules of some species. The species name, *roemeriana*, honors Ferdinand Roemer, a German geologist and naturalist who collected specimens, 1845–1847, in the vicinity of New Braunfels, Texas. Vernacular names for the plant are Round-flowered Acacia and Round-flowered Catclaw. It is sometimes planted for ornament and is an important source of honey.

Golden-ball Lead-tree

Leucaena retusa Benth. [F, G]

Field Identification. Shrub or small tree to 25 ft, and 8 in. in diameter.

Flowers. April–October, borne on stout, single or fascicled, axillary peduncles, 1½–3 in. long and subtended by 2 villose bracts; bracts ⅙–¼ in. long, apex subulate; flower heads yellow, globose, dense, ¾–1¼ in. in diameter; calyx tubular, minutely 5-toothed, membranous, 1/12–⅛ in. long; petals 5, free, narrowly oblong, barely longer than the calyx; stamens 10, distinct, free, exserted, ¼–⅓ in. long; filaments filiform, anthers glabrous and oblong; ovary stipitate, style slender, stigma minute and terminal.

Fruit. Generally mature in August, solitary or clustered, borne on stout puberulous peduncles 1½–5 in. long; pods 3–10 in. long, ⅓–½ in. wide, stipitate, narrowly linear, flattened, somewhat constricted on the thickened margin, apex acute or acuminate, base cuneate; rigid, thin, papery, glabrous; light to dark brown; seeds numerous, obliquely transverse, compressed, about ⅓ in. long and ¼ in. wide; seed coat thin, crustaceous, brown and lustrous.

Leaves. Alternate, bipinnate, stipellate, 3–8 in. long, 4–5 in. wide, petiole and rachis slender; pinnae 2–5 pairs (usually 3–4), long-stalked and distant; leaflets 3–8 pairs (usually 3–6 per pinna), short-stalked; oblong to elliptic, or the upper obovate, basally asymmetric; apex rounded or obtuse to retuse, mucronu-

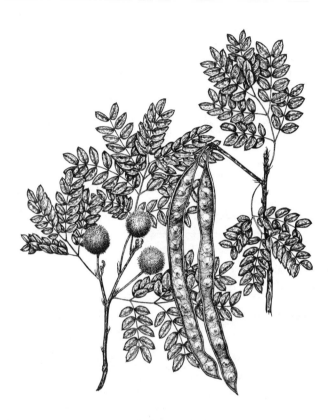

late; base rounded or cuneate; margin entire; length ⅓–1 in., width ⅓–½ in.; surface glabrous or pubescent, reticulate-veined, bluish green, thin; glands usually solitary and elevated, borne between the pinnae or leaflets; stipules ovate to lanceolate, subulate-tipped, ⅖–⅗ in. long.

Twigs. Slender, grooved, brown to reddish, pubescent or puberulous, lenticels numerous and oval.

Bark. Light gray to brown, broken into small thin scales on old trunks, smooth on young branches.

Range. Mostly on dry, well-drained, rocky, limestone soils in central Texas and the Trans-Pecos area. Also in New Mexico and Mexico.

Remarks. The genus name, *Leucaena*, refers to the white flowers of some species, and the species name, *retusa*, refers to rounded, sometimes concave-tipped, leaflets. It is apparently not abundant enough to warrant the application of other vernacular names except that of Mimosa and Wahoo-tree. Much browsed by cattle. Worthy of cultivation in the central and west Texas limestone areas because of the attractive flowers, fruit, and leaves.

Honey Mesquite

Prosopis glandulosa Torr. [D, E, F, G]

Field Identification. Thorny shrub or small tree to 30 ft, with crooked, drooping branches and a rounded crown. Trunk dividing into branches a short distance above the ground. Root system radially spreading and deep.

Flowers. May–September, perfect, borne in yellowish green, cylindric, axillary, pedunculate spikelike racemes; calyx bell-shaped, minute, 5-lobed, with lobes triangular; corolla greenish white, small, with 5 linear petals which are erect, pubescent within, and much longer than the calyx-tube; stamens 10, exserted, with filiform filaments and oblong anthers; ovary stipitate, pubescent; style filiform; stigma small.

Fruit. August–September, legumes in loose clusters, 4–9 in. long, somewhat flattened, glabrous, linear, straight or curved, somewhat constricted between the seeds, indehiscent; seeds oblong, compressed, shiny, brown, set in spongy tissue.

Leaves. Alternate, deciduous, long-petioled, bipinnately compound of 2 (rarely 3 or 4) pairs of pinnae; with 12–20 leaflets; leaflets smooth, dark green, linear, acute or obtuse at apex, about 2 in. long and ¼ in. wide.

Twigs. Zigzag, armed with stout straight spines to 2 in. long, or sometimes spineless.

Bark. Rough, reddish brown, with shallow fissures and thick scales.

Wood. Reddish brown, heavy, hard, durable, close-grained, sapwood yellow.

Range. Honey Mesquite is distributed from Kansas and New Mexico east into Oklahoma and Arkansas, and across Texas into Louisiana.

Remarks. The genus name, *Prosopis*, is the old Greek name for the burdock. The species name, *glandulosa*, is for the glandular anther connectives of the flowers. Mesquite is often shrubby, forming thickets in dry areas and taking over grasslands rapidly. It readily sprouts from the stump, is very deep rooted, and is not easily damaged by disease or insects. The wood is used for charcoal, fuel, furniture, building blocks, crossties, and posts and is often the only wood available in regions in which it grows. Mesquite foliage and pods are eaten by livestock, and the seeds pass through the digestive tracts and grow where they fall. This fact has been responsible for much of its rapid distribution. The seeds are also considered an important wildlife food, being eaten by Gambel's quail, scaled quail, white-winged dove, rock squirrel, ground squirrel, coyote, skunk, jack rabbit, and white-tailed and mule deer. Mesquite beans played an important part in the diet of the southwestern Indian. The legumes contain as high as 30 percent sugar, and a meal known as "pinole" was prepared from them and made into bread. Fermentation of the meal also produced an intoxicating beverage. Exudation of gum from the

Torrey Mesquite

branches and trunk offers possibilities as a substitute for gum arabic and is used locally in candy. It also produces a black dye and a cement for mending pottery.

It had been considered at one time by various authors, that the species *P. juliflora* (Swartz) DC. was centered in distribution in Mexico and Central and South America. Those in the Texas area were therefore reported as *P. juliflora* var. *glandulosa* (Torr.) Cockrell, *P. juliflora* var. *velutina* (Woot.) Standl., and *P. juliflora* var. *torreyana* L. Benson. It is now interpreted (Correll and Johnston, *Manual of the Vascular Plants of Texas*, p. 783) that *P. glandulosa* Torr. is the common species of Texas, and that the only valid variety is *P. glandulosa* var. *torreyana* (L. Benson) M. C. Johnst. This variety has leaflets ⅖–1⅓ in. long, about 5–8 times as long as broad, with 8–20 (average 10–15) pairs per pinna. Common in Trans-Pecos region. Also occurring along the Rio Grande, and then along the Gulf in the vicinity of Corpus Christi, Texas. Also in the Mexican states of Nuevo León, Coahuila, Chihuahua, and Sonora; and New Mexico and Arizona.

Subfamily Caesalpinioideae

Eastern Redbud

Cercis canadensis L. [D, E, F]

Field Identification. Shrub or small tree to 40 ft, trunk usually straight, branching usually 5–9 ft from the ground, top broadly rounded or flattened. Distinctly ornamental in spring with small, clustered, rose-purple flowers covering the bare branches before the leaves.

Flowers. March–May, before the leaves, in clusters of 2–8, on pedicels ¼–¾ in. long; flowers ¼–⅖ in. long, perfect, imperfectly papilionaceous, rose-purple, petals 5, standard smaller than the wings; keel petals not united, large; stamens 10, shorter than the petals; ovary pubescent, short, stipitate, style curved; calyx campanulate, 5-toothed.

Fruit. September–October, persistent on the branches, often abundant, peduncles divaricate and reflexed, ⅓–⅗ in. long; legume 2–4 in. long, about ½ in. wide or less, tapering at both ends, flat, leathery, reddish brown, upper suture with a somewhat winged margin; valves 2, thin, reticulate-veined; seeds several, oblong, flattened, ⅙–⅕ in. long.

Leaves. Simple, alternate, deciduous, 2–6 in. long, 1¼–6 in. broad, ovate to cordate or reniform, apex usually abruptly obtuse or acute, base cordate or subtruncate, margin entire, palmately 7–9-veined; upper surface dull green and glabrous; lower surface paler and glabrous or somewhat hairy along the veins, membranous at first but firm (not coriaceous) later; petioles 1¼–5 in. long, essentially glabrous, stipules caducous.

Twigs. Slender, glabrous, somewhat divaricate, brown to gray, when young lustrous, when older dull.

Bark. Reddish brown to gray, thin and smooth when young, older ones with elongate fissures separating long, narrow plates with small scales, lenticels numerous.

Wood. Reddish brown, sapwood yellowish, close-grained, hard, weak, weighing 30 lb per cu ft.

Range. Eastern Redbud is found in rich soil along streams or in bottom lands from central Texas, Oklahoma, Arkansas, and Louisiana; eastward to Florida, northward to Connecticut and Ontario, and west to Michigan, Missouri, Nebraska, and Kansas.

Remarks. The genus name, *Cercis,* is the ancient name of the closely related Judas-tree of Europe and Asia. According to tradition Judas hung himself from a branch of the tree. The species name, *canadensis,* literally means "of Canada," where it is rather uncommon. Or perhaps the Linnean name refers to northeastern North America, before political boundaries were set up. The tree is a very handsome ornamental and has been in cultivation since 1641. It is reported that the acid flowers are sometimes pickled for use in salad, and in Mexico they are fried. The seeds are eaten by a number of species of birds and the foliage browsed by the white-tailed deer. Eastern Redbud also has some value as a source of honey.

Two native varieties of Redbud of Texas, Oklahoma, and Mexico are Texas Redbud, *C. canadensis* var. *texensis* (S. Wats.) Hopkins, and Mexican Redbud, *C. canadensis* var. *mexicana* (Rose) Hopkins.

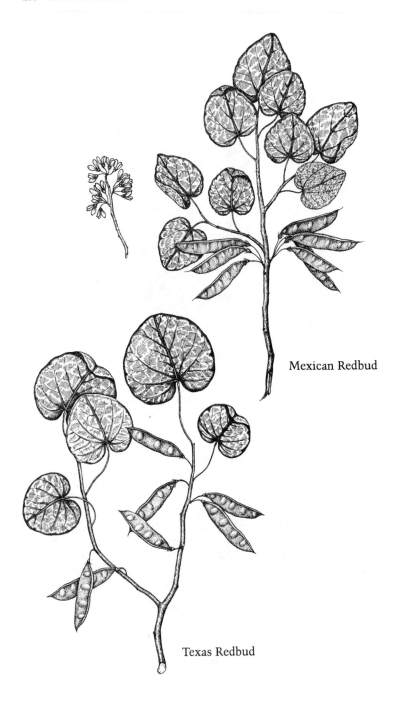

Mexican Redbud

Texas Redbud

Both the Texas and Mexican varieties differ from the Eastern Redbud by having conspicuously shiny and stiffly coriaceous leaves (leaves of the Eastern Redbud are dull green and not distinctly coriaceous). The leaf shapes of the species and the 2 varieties are rather similar, varying from cordate with an acute apex to reniform or rounded with the apex obtuse or emarginate.

The Texas and Mexican varieties are separated from each other on the dubious characters of the amount of hairs present on various parts. Texas Redbud has pedicels, young branchlets, and leaves glabrous or nearly so. Mexican Redbud has pedicels and young branchlets densely woolly-tomentose and leaves slightly so. These distinctions are so close that some botanists consider the Mexican Redbud to be only a hairy form of the Texas Redbud, instead of a distinct variety of the Eastern Redbud. However, since forms closely resembling *C. canadensis* var. *mexicana* have been found in northeast Texas, it is more likely that the latter is derived from *C. canadensis*.

Texas Redbud has been collected on limestone areas in Texas in Val Verde, Kerr, Austin, Comal, Erath, Brown, Dallas, and Hood counties. It is known in Oklahoma near Turner Falls Park in the Arbuckle Mountains, in Platt National Park at Antelope Springs, and in Mexico in Nuevo León and Tamaulipas.

Mexican Redbud has been collected on limestone areas in Texas in Brown, Dallas, Terrell, Nolan, Brewster, and Austin counties. It is the prevalent form in Trans-Pecos Texas, and occurs in Mexico in Coahuila, Nuevo León, and San Luis Potosí.

Flowering Senna

Cassia corymbosa Lam. [D]

Field Identification. Cultivated shrub or small tree to 12 ft, with a trunk 2−5 in. in diameter. The numerous elongate, erect or spreading branches form a rounded crown.

Flowers. Blooms in late summer. Borne in corymbose panicles from the leaf axils; primary peduncles glabrous, 1−2½ in. long; secondary flower-bearing pedicels to ¾ in. long; petals 5, bright yellow, nearly equal, obovate, ⅜−½ in. long; stamens 7, 3 of them long-exserted, upcurved, anthers large with oblique cup-like apices; 4 of the stamens more erect with anthers shorter; staminodia 2−3, short and flattened somewhat; style elongate, exserted, upcurved, short white-hairy; calyx of 5 sepals, green or yellowish, unequal in shape, narrowly elliptic to ovate, ¼−⅜ in. long.

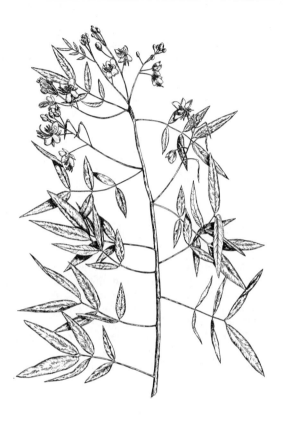

Fruit. Legume stout, thick, 1¾–6 in. long, sides convex and sutures furrowed, indehiscent.

Leaves. Evenly pinnately compound, rachis averaging about 2 in. long, mostly glabrous; leaflets 4–6, 1–2 in. long, terminal pair longest, lanceolate to linear-elliptic or elliptic-lanceolate, apex long-acute or acuminate, base rounded and often asymmetrical, margin entire, upper surface dull green and glabrous, lower surface paler and glabrous; petiolules ¹⁄₁₆–⅛ in. long, glabrous or with a few sparse white hairs, or a few dark, stalked glands in the axils.

Twigs. Young ones elongate, slender, green, glabrous; older ones brown and glabrous.

Bark. On older branches and trunk smooth, dark brown to light or dark gray, marked with numerous pale, linear, horizontal lenticels.

Range. A native of Argentina, cultivated in gardens in many cities along the Gulf Coast. Occasionally escaping cultivation, or persistent about abandoned gardens of eastern Texas and Louisiana; eastward to Tennessee, Georgia, and Florida.

Remarks. The genus name, *Cassia*, is the ancient name of an aromatic plant. The species name, *corymbosa*, is for the flower arrangement. It is listed by some authors under the name of *Adipera corymbosa* Britt. & Rose. This garden shrub is gaining in popularity because of its dense foliage, bright yellow flowers, and freedom from disease.

Common Honey-locust

Gleditsia triacanthos L. [D, E, F]

Field Identification. Tree to 100 ft, with a thorny trunk and branches and a loose, open crown.

Flowers. May–June, perfect or imperfect, borne in axillary, dense, green racemes; racemes of the staminate flowers often clustered, pubescent, 2–5 in. long; calyx campanulate; lobes of calyx 5, elliptic-lanceolate, spreading, hairy, acute; petals 4–5, longer than calyx-lobes, erect, oval, white; stamens 10, inserted on the calyx-tube, anthers green, pistil rudimentary or absent in the staminate flower; pistillate racemes 2–3 in. long, slender, few-flowered, usually solitary; pistil tomentose, ovary almost sessile, style short, stigma oblique, ovules 2 or many; stamens much smaller and abortive in pistillate flower.

Fruit. Ripening September–October, legume ½–1½ ft long, ½–1½ in. wide, borne on short peduncles, usually in twos or threes, dark brown, shiny, flattened, often twisted, falcate or straight, coriaceous, pulp succulent and sweetish between the seeds, occasional sterile legumes are seedless and pulpless, some trees with rather small legumes, others with large legumes, and some with a mixture of small, intermediate, and large; seeds about ⅓ in. long, oval, hard, compressed. The minimum commercial seed-bearing age is 10 years and the maximum 100 years.

Leaves. Alternate, deciduous, once- or twice-pinnate (the twice-pinnate usually on more vigorous shoots), 5–10 in. long; pinnae 4–8 pairs; leaflets 15–30, alternate or opposite, almost sessile, ¾–2 in. long, ½–1 in. wide, oblong-lanceolate, rounded or acute at apex, cuneate or rounded or inequilateral at base, crenulate or entire on margin, dark green and lustrous above, paler and often pubescent beneath; rachis and petioles pubescent.

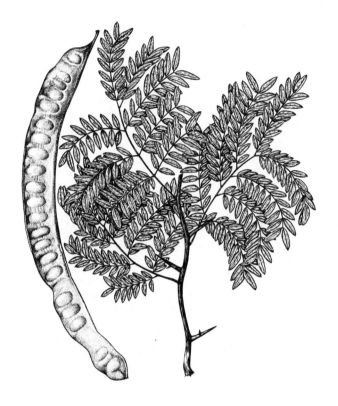

Twigs. Greenish or reddish brown, lustrous, stout, armed with solitary or 3-branched thorns which are rigid, sharp, straight, shiny, purplish brown.

Bark. Grayish brown to black, on older trees with fissures deep and narrow, separating into scaly ridges, often bearing heavy simple to multibranched thorns.

Wood. Brown to reddish, sapwood yellowish, coarse-grained, strong in bending and end compression, stiff, highly shock resistant, tools well, splits rather easy, shrinks little, does not glue satisfactorily, rather hard, moderately durable, weighing 42 lb per cu ft.

Range. In moist fertile soil. Texas, Oklahoma, Arkansas, and Louisiana; eastward to Florida, northward to Pennsylvania and New York, and west to Nebraska.

Remarks. The genus name, *Gleditsia*, is a contraction and is in honor of Johann Gottlieb Gleditsch, an eighteenth-century German botanist. The species name, *triacanthos*, refers to the commonly 3-branched thorns. Other vernacular names are Honey-shucks, Sweet Locust, Thorn-tree, Thorny Locust, Three-thorned-acacia, and Sweet-bean. It has been known in cultivation since 1700 and is often planted for ornament, particularly the thornless form. The tree has few diseases or insect pests. The wood is used for farm implements, fuel, lumber, posts, vehicles, furniture, and railroad crossties. The flowers are reported to be a good bee food, and the Indians ate the fleshy sweet pulp of the young pods, older pods turning bitter. The pods are also eaten by cattle, white-tailed deer, gray squirrel, and cottontail.

Jerusalem-thorn

Parkinsonia aculeata L. [D, E, F, G]

Field Identification. Green-barked, thorny shrub or tree to 36 ft. Branches slender, spiny, spreading, often pendulous to form a rounded head.

Flowers. Fragrant, borne in spring or throughout the summer especially after rains. Racemes 5–6 in. long, axillary, solitary or fascicled, pedicels ⅓–½ in. long; petals 5, imbricate in the bud, yellow, about ½ in. long, spreading, oval, clawed at the base, margin erose or entire; one petal larger than the others and bearing a gland at base, becoming red-dotted or orange with age; stamens 10, shorter than the petals, filaments distinct and hairy below, anthers yellow to reddish, opening lengthwise; ovary pubescent; calyx glabrous or nearly so, tube short, lobes oblong and reflexed, longer than the tube.

Fruit. On pedicels ½–¾ in. long; a linear legume, 2–4 in. long, brown to orange or reddish, puberulent or glabrous, leathery, ends attenuate, constricted between the seeds, swollen portions almost terete, constrictions flattened; seeds 1–8, about ⅓ in. long, oblong, seed coat green to brown.

Leaves. Bipinnate or rarely pinnate, petioles short, alternate or fascicled, linear, 8–16 in. long, rachis flat and winged; leaflets numerous (25–30 pairs), remote, linear to oblanceolate, about ⅓ in. long or less, inequilateral, dropping away early and leaving the persistent, flat, naked, photosynthetic rachis, petiolules slender; stipules spinescent; rachis terminating with a weak spine.

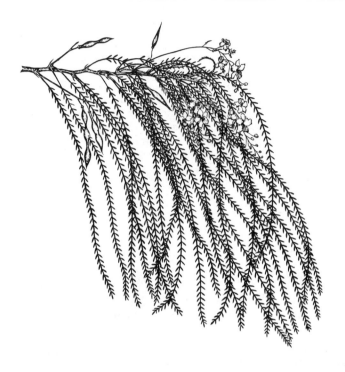

Twigs. Somewhat divaricate, green to yellowish, puberulent to glabrous; later gray to brown or orange; spines green, brown or black, to 1 in. long.

Bark. Thin, smooth, green, later brown to reddish with small scales on old trunks.

Wood. Light brown to yellow, hard, heavy, close-grained, specific gravity 0.61.

Range. Usually in moist sandy soils, but resistant to saline situations. In the southern half of Texas; west through New Mexico to Arizona and southward through Mexico to northern South America. Probably an escape from cultivation in California, Florida, and the West Indies.

Remarks. The genus name, *Parkinsonia*, refers to John Parkinson, an English botanical author. The species name, *aculeata*, refers to the spines. Other vernacular names are Horsebean, Cloth-of-Gold, Crown-of-thorns, Barbados Fence Flowers, Paloverde, Lluvia de Oro, Cambrón, Espilla, Espinillo, Espinillo de España, Junco,

Junco Marion, Palo de Rayo, Flor de Rayo, Yabo, Calentano, Espiño Real de España, Acacia de Aguijote, Guichi-belle, Mesquite
Extranjero, Guacopano, Retama de Cerda, and Retama. A grove of
trees is known as a "retamal" by the Mexican people. The tree is
a rapid grower and is generally free of diseases and insects. It is
often grown for ornament and hedges. The wood is occasionally
used as fuel and was formerly used for papermaking. An infusion
of the leaves is used in tropical America as a febrifuge, for diabe-
tes, for epilepsy, and as a sudorific and abortifacient. The leaves
and pods are eaten by horses, cattle, and deer, particularly in
times of stress. The Indians formerly pounded the seeds into flour
to make bread. The flowers are sometimes important as a bee
food.

Paradise Poinciana

Caesalpinia pulcherrima (L.) Swartz [D, E, F]

Field Identification. An attractive tropical shrub or irregularly
branched small tree to 15 ft. The large beautiful flowers have 5
petals which are red, orange, yellow, or mottled.

Flowers. In upright racemes 5–20 in. long, pedicels ⅓–3 in. long
and glabrous; sepals 5, about ⅗ in. long, imbricate, petaloid,
oblong to oblanceolate, apex rounded, much shorter than the petals (one sepal larger than the others, concave and overlapping the
others in the bud); corolla of 5 unequal petals ¾–1¼ in. long, the
standard petal generally the longest with a revolute, almost tubular claw, the other petals with shorter claws, blades flabellate,
margin erose and crisped, variously colored red, orange, yellow, or
blotched; stamens 10, long-exserted, up-curved, filaments filiform, red, distinct, about 1⅗ in. long, anthers opening lengthwise;
style long-exserted, filiform, stigma minute.

Fruit. Legume 3–5 in. long, ½–¾ in. wide, broadly linear, greatly
flattened, one margin straight, the other margin slightly undulate,
base inequilateral, apex abruptly one-sided into an apiculate
point, surface dark brown or black when mature; seeds 5–9, flattened, impressed on the flattened surface of the legume; peduncle
2–3 in. long, glabrous.

Leaves. Spreading, bipinnate, 8–15 in. long, rachis green and
glabrous or brownish, pinnae 3–9 pairs, each about 3½–6 in.
long; leaflets 7–12 pairs per pinna, oblong to elliptic or cuneate,
apex rounded or slightly notched with a minute mucro, base

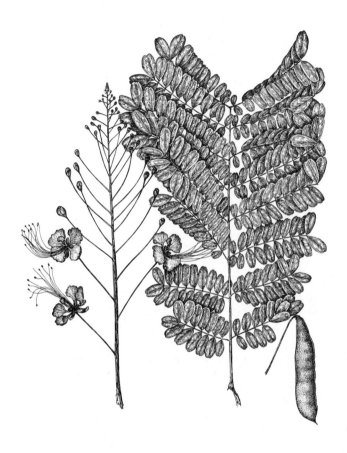

rounded and inequilateral, length ⅗–1 in., width ⅕–½ in., upper surface light green, glabrous, veins obscure; lower surface paler green, glabrous, delicately reticulate-veined; petiolules ⅟25–⅟16 in. long, glabrous or slightly puberulent.

Twigs. Green, becoming dark brown or black with age, glabrate to slightly glaucous, finely grooved.

Range. In sandy soils, widely distributed and naturalized in tropical areas. In Texas in the lower Rio Grande area. Often planted in gardens in Brownsville, Texas, sometimes escaping cultivation to grow on the edges of old resacas. Also in southern Florida, southern California, and Mexico; southward to West Indies and continental tropical America.

Remarks. The genus name, *Caesalpinia*, is in honor of Andreas Caesalpinus, chief physician to Pope Clement VIII. The species name, *pulcherrima*, means "very beautiful." Other vernacular names are Barbados-flower, Barbados-Pride, Flame-tree, and Dwarf Poinciana.

A variety with yellow flowers is known as *C. pulcherrima* var. *flava* Hort. The Paradise Poinciana is a popular plant in gardens in frostless areas. It is usually grown from seeds or, occasionally, greenwood cuttings.

Subfamily Papilionoideae

Texas Sophora

Sophora affinis Torr. & Gray [D, E, F]

Field Identification. A shrub or small tree to 25 ft, with spreading branches and a rounded head.

Flowers. In June, arranged in simple axillary racemes 2–6 in. long; pedicels slender, finely tomentose, about ½ in. long, subtended by small deciduous bracts; corolla bonnet-shaped, about ½ in. long, pink to white, somewhat fragrant; petals short-clawed, standard large, nearly orbicular, somewhat notched, reflexed, ⅜–⅝ in. long; wing and keel petals ovate to oblong and auriculate at base; stamens 10; ovary hairy and stipitate, stigma capitate; calyx campanulate, short, about ¼ in. long, abruptly narrowed at the base, obscurely 5-toothed with teeth triangular to ovate, somewhat pubescent.

Fruit. Fruiting peduncle 2–4 in. long; legume ½–3½ in. long, abruptly constricted between the seeds, terete, black, often hairy, especially on the strictures, coriaceous, indehiscent, tipped with the prolonged style remnants, flesh thin, persistent; seeds 1–8 (mostly 4–8), ovoid or oval, seed coat brown. Constrictions between the seeds give the pod a beadlike appearance.

Leaves. Alternate, odd-pinnately compound, deciduous; rachis lightly tomentose, 3–9 in. long, leaflets 9–19 (usually 13–15); leaflets elliptical or oval, margin entire; apex obtuse, acute, retuse and mucronulate; base rounded or cuneate, contracted into short stout petiolules ⅛–¹⁄₁₆ in. long; upper surface dark green to yellowish green, lustrous, glabrous or slightly hairy; lower surface slightly paler and pubescent; thin and soft; ¾–1½ in. long, about ½ in. wide; young leaves hoary-pubescent.

Twigs. Slender, green to brown or streaked with lighter brown, nearly glabrous or puberulent, somewhat divaricate, somewhat swollen at the nodes.

Bark. Gray to reddish brown, broken into small, thin, oblong scales.

Wood. Light red, sapwood yellow, heavy, strong, and hard.

Range. Usually on limestone soils of northwestern Louisiana and southwestern Oklahoma, down through central Texas. Occurs at Dallas, Kerrville, Austin, and San Antonio, Texas. Often in small groves on hillsides or along streams.

Remarks. The genus name, *Sophora*, is from the Arabic word *Sophero*, which was applied to some tree of the same family, and the species name, *affinis*, means "related to." Another vernacular name is Eve's Necklace. The plant could be more extensively cultivated for ornament.

Mescal-bean Sophora

Sophora secundiflora (Ortega) Lag. [D, E]

Field Identification. Evergreen shrub, or sometimes a tree to 35 ft, with a narrow top, upright branches and velvety twigs.

Flowers. With the young leaves March–April; racemes densely flowered, terminal, 2–4¾ in. long, showy, violet, fragrant; pedicels ¼–⅖ in. long, subtended by subulate bracts about ½ in. long; calyx campanulate, ⅓–⅖ in. long, oblique, the 2 upper teeth almost united throughout, the lower 3 teeth triangular to ovate; corolla bonnet-shaped, violet; standard petal erect, broad,

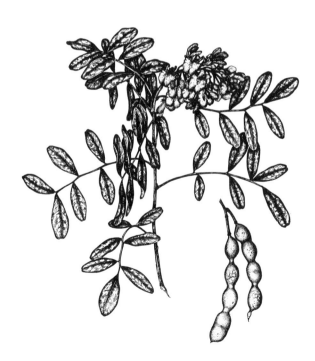

suborbicular to ovate, crisped, notched, ⅗–⅔ in. long, somewhat spotted at the base within; wing and keel petals oblong to obovate; stamens 10; ovary white-hairy.

Fruit. Pod in September, on pedicels ¼–1 in. long, woody, hard, oblong, terete, densely brown-pubescent, somewhat constricted between the seeds, apex abruptly prolonged by persistent style remnants, indehiscent, 1–5 in. long, about ¾ in. wide, walls about ¼ in. thick; seeds red, 1–8 (usually 3–4), about ½ in. long, globose to oblong, often flattened at one end, hard, bony; hilum small, pale and about ⅛ in. long.

Leaves. Odd-pinnately compound, 4–6 in. long, rachis grooved above; leaflets 5–13 (usually 5–9), persistent, elliptic-oblong or oval; apex rounded or obtuse, notched, or mucronulate; base gradually narrowed; margin entire; upper surface lustrous, leathery, reticulate, dark green, hairy when young but glabrous later; lower surface paler, glabrous or puberulent; 1–2½ in. long, ½–1½ in. wide; petioles stout, puberulous, sometimes leaflets sessile or nearly so.

Twigs. With fine velvety tomentum at first, later becoming glabrous, or nearly so, green to orange-brown.

Bark. Dark gray to black, broken into shallow fissures with narrow flattened ridges and thin scales.

Wood. Heartwood orange to red; sapwood yellow, hard, heavy, close-grained, specific gravity about 0.98, said to yield a yellow dye, otherwise of no commercial value.

Range. Usually on limestone soils in central, southern, and western Texas, New Mexico, and northern Mexico. In Texas from the shores of Matagorda Bay, almost at sea level, west into the Chisos and Davis mountains to altitudes of 5,000 ft. Frequent on the limestone hills around Austin, Texas. In Mexico from Nuevo León to San Luis Potosí.

Remarks. The genus name, *Sophora*, is from the Arabic name *Sophero*, and the species name, *secundiflora*, refers to the one-sided inflorescence. Other vernacular names are Texas Mountain-laurel, Frigolito, Frijollito, Frijolillo, Coral Bean, Big-drunk Bean, and Colorín.

Although called Mountain-laurel in Texas this plant is not a member of the Laurel family (Lauraceae). However, neither is the so-called Mountain-laurel of the eastern states, which is *Kalmia latifolia*, a heath. The true laurel, or Poet's Laurel, *Laurus nobilis*, is a native of Asia and south Europe. American representatives of the true Laurel family native to our area are the Red Bay, *Persea borbonia*, and the Sassafras, *Sassafras albidum*.

The persistent, shiny leaves of Mescal-bean give a lustrous effect when seen in mass at a distance. The beautiful violet flowers are very fragrant, in fact offensively so to some people. A volatile liquid alkaloid, sophorine, which is identical with cytisine, exists in many species of *Sophora*, including *S. secundiflora*, *S. tomentosa*, and *S. sericea*. Other sophoras, including *S. angustifolia*, *S. alopecuroides*, and *S. pachycarpa*, contain the alkaloids matrine and sophocarpine.

The narcotic properties of the red seeds of Mescal-bean Sophora were well known to the Indians. A powder from them, in very small amounts, was mixed with the beverage mescal to produce intoxication, delirium, excitement, and finally a long sleep. The seeds are poisonous to both humans and livestock. They were frequently used as a trade article by the Indians in the form of necklaces. The red seeds of *Erythrina herbacea* were also used for this purpose, and the two plants are often confused, but *Erythrina* has 3 leaflets only, and the pod is dehiscent at maturity. Mescal-bean is rather difficult to transplant, but this can be done if sufficient calcium is in the soil. The shrub is rather slow growing.

Drummond Rattlebox

Sesbania drummondii (Rydb.) Cory [D]

Field Identification. A short-lived shrub of low, wet grounds to 15 ft, with many stems from the base, or sometimes a small tree to 20 ft.

Flowers. Racemes 2–6 in. long, shorter than the leaves, showy, loosely flowered, slender, axillary peduncles slender upper one-third to one-half flowered, the perfect bonnet-shaped flowers on slender pedicels ¼–½ in. long; standard petal larger than the others, about as broad as long, ½–¾ in. long, orbicular, notched at the apex, base clawed, yellow and streaked with red; wing petals oblong, obtuse, yellow, ½–¾ in. long; keel petals ½–¾ in. long; stamens 10, 9 united and one free; pistil with a slender style and glabrous, stalked ovary; calyx minute, campanulate, somewhat 2-lipped with 5 short, acute, apiculate lobes.

Fruit. Pod 4-sided and 4-winged, 2½–3½ in. long, on a stipe ⅜–⅝ in. long, persistent, leathery, indehiscent, constricted somewhat between the seeds; the several seeds separated by partitions, rattling when dry.

Leaves. Folding in the hot sun, even-pinnately compound, 5–8 in. long, leaflets 12–60 (usually 13–40); blades narrowly oblong or

elliptic, ⅜–1 in. long, base cuneate, apex rounded and mucronate; upper surface dull green, glabrous, and inconspicuously veined; lower surface paler and glabrous or somewhat glaucescent beneath; petiolules about ⅟₁₆ in. long.

Stems. When young green and smooth, when older light brown; bark tight, on older stems separating into small, thin scales.

Wood. Green to yellowish or white, pith large, of no commercial value.

Range. In low wet places. Arkansas, Texas, and Louisiana; eastward to Florida and southward into Mexico.

Remarks. The genus name, *Sesbania*, is the Latinized version of the old Adansonian name, *Sesban*, which has presumably an Arabic origin. The species name, *drummondii*, is from Thomas Drummond, an English botanist, who collected in Texas, 1833– 1834. He collected extensively in the vicinity of Galveston, Texas, where the plant is abundant. Other common names for the Drummond Rattlebox are Siene Bean, Rattle-bush, Rattle Bean, Coffee Bean, and Senna. The seeds of the Drummond Rattlebox are poisonous to livestock, especially sheep and goats, and death may follow if a quantity is eaten. The symptoms are diarrhea, extreme weakness, and lethargy from one to two days after eating. It is reported that the seeds were used as a substitute for coffee during the Civil War period. However, because of their toxic properties this seems to be open to question. The extent to which this toxicity is reduced by boiling has not been determined. Until suitable studies are made, its use for human consumption seems unwise and is not recommended.

Drummond Rattlebox has some ornamental value for planting along the edges of streams or lakes. Some closely related tropical species are now being introduced into cultivation in the Gulf Coast states and seem to do well, occasionally escaping to grow wild.

Black Locust

Robinia pseudo-acacia L. [D, E]

Field Identification. Spiny tree attaining a height of 100 ft, with a trunk diameter of 30 in. Trees rapid-growing, reaching maturity in 30–40 years.

Flowers. May–June, attractive, fragrant, in loose, pendent racemes 4–5 in. long; individual flowers perfect, bonnet-shaped, about 1 in. long; corolla white, petals 5; standard petal obcordate, rounded, a yellow blotch often on inner surface; wing petals 2, free; keel petals incurved, obtuse, united below; stamens 10, in 2 groups, 9 united and one free, the group forming a tube; pistil superior, ovary oblong, style hairy and reflexed, stigma small; ovules numerous; calyx 5-lobed, lower lobe longest and acuminate; pedicels about ½ in. long.

Fruit. A legume, ripe September–October; brown, flattened, oblong-linear, straight or slightly curved, 2–5 in. long, about ½ in. wide, 2-valved, persistent; peduncle short and thick; seeds 4–8, hard, flat, mottled-brown, kidney-shaped, seed dispersed September–April from the persistent legume.

Leaves. Pinnately compound, alternate, deciduous, 8–14 in. long; leaflets 7–19, each one ½–2 in. long and ½–1 in. wide, sessile or short-stalked; rounded at both ends or sometimes wedge-shaped at base; ovate-oblong or oval, entire, mature leaves bluish green and glabrous above, usually paler and glabrous except on veins beneath; young leaves silvery-hairy, mature leaves turning yellow in autumn; stipules becoming straight or slightly curved spines; leaves folding on dark days or in the evenings.

Twigs. Stout, zigzag, brittle, greenish brown, glabrous, somewhat angular, stipules modified into sharp spines.

Bark. Gray to reddish brown, ½–1½ in. thick, rough, ridged, deeply furrowed, sometimes twisted, inner bark pale yellow, thorns paired and scattered.

Wood. Greenish yellow or light brown, sapwood white and narrow, durable, hard, heavy, strong, stiff, close-grained, weighing about 45 lb per cu ft, is shock-resistant, shows little shrinkage, is very resistant to decay, but is difficult to hand-tool.

Range. Prefers deep, well-drained calcareous soil, probably originally native to the high lands of the Piedmont Plateau and Appalachian Mountains. Georgia; west to Oklahoma and Arkansas and northeast to New York. In other areas probably introduced and escaped from cultivation. Not native to Texas but persistent along fence rows, abandoned fields, and old home sites. Now commonly distributed by nurserymen in the Gulf Coast states.

Remarks. The genus name, *Robinia*, is in honor of Jean and Vespasian Robin, herbalists to Henry IV of France, and the species name, *pseudo-acacia* ("false-acacia"), refers to its resemblance to an acacia. Other vernacular names are White Locust, Yellow Locust, Red Locust, Red-flowering Locust, Green Locust, Honey Locust, Silver Locust, Post Locust, Pea-flower Locust, Silverchain, and False-acacia Locust. The wood is highly resistant to decay.

CALTROP FAMILY (Zygophyllaceae)

Texas Porlieria

Porlieria angustifolia (Engelm.) Gray [E, F]

Field Identification. Shrub or tree to 21 ft, often in clumps, scrubby, compact, stiff, evergreen, the branches thick and stubby.

Flowers. Terminal, clustered or solitary, violet or purple, ⅓–¾ in. across, fragrant, attractive; petals 5, short-clawed, elliptic, apex often notched; sepals 5, shorter than petals, suborbicular, concave; stamens 10, as long as the petals, with scalelike appendages at the base; anthers yellow; ovary densely villous, 2–5-celled.

Fruit. Capsule heart-shaped, mostly 2-lobed, somewhat winged on margin, apex abruptly attenuate-apiculate, surface reticulate, ⅓–⅔ in. broad; seeds 2 (sometimes 1 or 3), beanlike, large, shiny, red, yellow, or orange.

Leaves. Often half-folded in the heat of the day, opposite or alternate, abruptly pinnate, rachis pubescent, composed of 4–8 pairs of leaflets; leaflets sessile or nearly so, about ⅔ in. long or less,

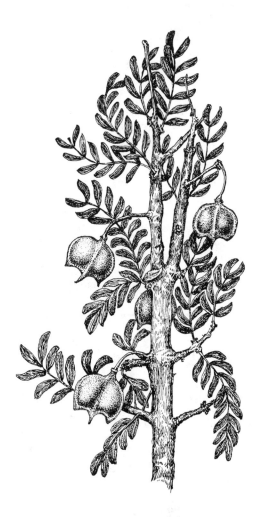

entire, linear to oblong, leathery, lustrous, reticulate, dark green, acute and apiculate at the apex, oblique at the base, persistent; stipules persistent, somewhat spiniferous.

Twigs. Short, stout, stiff, knotty, and gray.

Bark. Gray to black, broken into rough scales on old trunks and branches.

Range. From central through western and southwestern Texas; Mexico in Coahuila to Tamaulipas.

Remarks. The genus name, *Porlieria*, is in honor of Porlier de Baxamar, Spanish patron of botany. The species name, *angusti-folia*, refers to the narrow leaflets. Vernacular names for the plant are Soap-bush, Guayacán, and Guajacum. Texas Porlieria has pos-sibilities as an ornamental. It is a good honey plant, and the wood is used for fence posts in some localities. The bark of the roots is sold in the Mexican markets as a soap for washing woolens. Ex-tracts of the root are used to treat rheumatism and venereal dis-ease, and they are also used as a sudorific.

RUE FAMILY (Rutaceae)

Trifoliate Orange

Citrus trifoliata L. [D, E]

Field Identification. Green, aromatic, spiny tree to 30 ft, with stiff, flattened branches.

Flowers. Borne on the bare branches of old wood in spring, axil-lary, subsessile, white, spreading, 1½–2 in. across, perfect; petals 5, flat, thin, oblong-obovate to spatulate, at first imbricate but later spreading, base clawed, much longer than the sepals; sepals ovate-elliptic; stamens 8–10 free; ovary pubescent, 6–8-celled, ovules in 2 rows; style stout and short.

Fruit. Berry September–October, yellow, aromatic, densely downy, globose, 1½–2 in. across; pulp thin, acid, rather sour; seeds numerous, large, taking up the greater part of the berry, ¼–½ in. long, flattened, obovate, rounded at one end and acute at the other, white to brown, smooth, often ridged or grooved on one side.

Leaves. Trifoliate, about 3½ in. long or less; petiole broadly winged, ⅓–1 in. long or less; leaflets 3, aromatic, elliptic, oblong, oval or obovate; margin crenate-toothed; apex obtuse, rounded or emarginate; base often cuneate or rounded (in lateral leaflets often asymmetrical); sessile or very short-petioled; terminal leaflet 1–2½ in. long, laterals usually smaller; olive green, glabrous, with pellucid dots above; lower surface paler, glabrous or puberulent along the veins.

Twigs. Dark green, glabrous, divaricate, conspicuously flattened at the nodes to flare out into heavy, green, sharp, flattened spines ⅓–2¾ in. long.

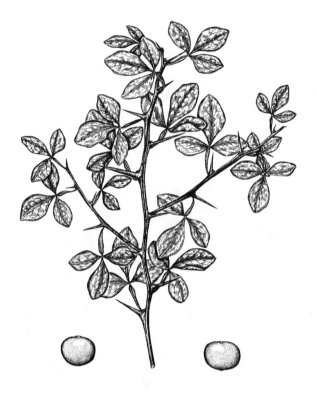

Bark. Green or brown-streaked, smooth, often with thorns.

Range. Frequently planted for ornament and hedges from Texas to Florida, escaping cultivation in some areas. Hardy as far north as Washington, D.C. Native of China and Korea. Often planted for ornament in Japan.

Remarks. The genus name, *Citrus*, is from the Greek and was given by Pliny the Elder (A.D. 23–79), a Roman naturalist. The species name, *trifoliata*, is for the trifoliate leaves. Some authors use the name of *Poncirus trifoliata* (L.) Raf. *Poncirus* is from the French word *poncire*, a kind of citrus. Some vernacular names are Bitter Orange and Limoncito. Oil from the fruit has a rancid flavor, and the pulp is aromatic.

Common Hop-tree

Ptelea trifoliata L. [D, E]

Field Identification. Usually a rounded shrub, but occasionally a small tree to 25 ft. Leaves divided into 3 leaflets which are very unpleasantly scented. This is an extremely variable species in both form and habit of growth, and in the size and shape of the leaflets. Numerous varieties, forms, and species have been segregated by various authors. The entire genus *Ptelea* should be revised.

Flowers. March–July, polygamous, in terminal cymes; flowers small, borne on slender pedicels ¼–1½ in. long; calyx-lobes 4–5, obtuse, pubescent; petals 4–5, greenish white, oblong, somewhat puberulent, exceeding the calyx-lobes; stamens 4–5, alternating with the petals, filaments hairy, anthers ovoid; pistillate flowers with a raised pistil and abortive anthers; style short, sometimes glandular-dotted, stigma 2–3-lobed, ovary puberulous.

Fruit. Ripening August–September, samaras borne in drooping clusters on slender reflexed pedicels; reticulate-veined, membranous, compressed, thin, waferlike, suborbicular or obovate, ¾–1 in. across, persistent in winter, unpleasantly scented, 2–3-celled; seeds 2–3, oblong-ovoid, acute, leathery, reddish brown,

Showing leaf variation
on the same plant

Leaves. Alternate or opposite, trifoliate; leaflets sessile or nearly so, entire or finely serrulate, ovate-oblong, acute or acuminate, wedge-shaped at base with lateral leaflets often oblique, more or less pubescent and glandular below (in *P. trifoliata* var. *mollis* densely woolly beneath), darker green and lustrous above, unpleasantly scented, 4–6 in. long, 2–4 in. wide; petiole stout, base swollen, pubescent.

Twigs. Slender, green, yellowish or reddish brown, pubescent, unpleasantly scented when bruised.

Bark. Thin, smooth, light to dark gray or brown, numerous excrescences, bitter to the taste.

Wood. Yellowish brown, close-grained, hard, heavy, weighing about 51 lb per cu ft.

Root. Taste bitter, pungent, slightly acid, aromatic.

Range. Common Hop-tree, with its many varieties and closely related species, is distributed over a rather wide territory, growing in various types of soil; Texas, Louisiana, Arkansas, Oklahoma, and New Mexico; eastward to Florida, westward into Arizona and California, northward into Colorado, Utah, Nebraska, Minnesota, Michigan, Illinois, and continuing on east to Ontario, New York and Quebec.

Remarks. The genus name, *Ptelea*, is the classical name for the elm. The species name, *trifoliata*, refers to the three leaflets. Vernacular names are Three-leaf Hop-tree, Shrubby-trefoil, Swamp Dogwood, Wafer-ash, Skunk-bush, Potatochip-tree, Quinine-tree, Ague-bark, Pickaway-anise, Prairie-grub, Cola de Zorillo, and Wingseed. All parts of the plant emit a disagreeable odor. The fruit was once used as a substitute for hops in beer brewing.

Baldwin Hop-tree

Baldwin Hop-tree, *P. baldwinii* Torr., has somewhat larger flowers in smaller corymbs; fruit ⅜−⅝ in. across and apiculate; leaves 1−2½ in. long, narrowly elliptic-ovate or oblong-ovate, pubescent beneath; branches dark brown. It occurs from central and southern Texas to New Mexico, Colorado, Utah, northern California, and Arizona; also in Mexico.

Hercules-club

Zanthoxylum clava-herculis L. [D, E]

Field Identification. Small tree with a broad, rounded crown, easily recognized by the corky-based prickles on the trunk and branches.

Flowers. Dioecious, greenish white, in large terminal cymes; petals 4−5, oblong-ovate, obtuse, ⅛−¼ in. long, stamens 4−5, filaments slender and exserted, longer than the petals; pistils 2−3, styles short, with a 2-lobed stigma; calyx of 4−5 ovate or ovate-lanceolate, obtuse sepals.

Fruit. Follicles 2−5 together, globose-obovoid, brownish, rough, pitted, apiculate, ⅙−¼ in. long, 2-valved; seed solitary, wrinkled, black, shining, persistent outside of follicle after dehiscence.

Leaves. Alternate, 5–15 in. long, odd-pinnately compound of 5–19 leaflets, ½–4½ in. long, subsessile, sometimes falcate, ovate or ovate-lanceolate, acute or acuminate at apex, somewhat oblique and cuneate at base, crenate-serrulate, leathery, glabrous, lustrous above and more or less hairy below, spicy and dotted with pellucid glands, bitter-aromatic, stinging the mouth when chewed; petioles somewhat spiny, stout, hairy or glabrous.

Twigs. Brown to gray, stout, hairy at first, glabrous later, often somewhat glandular, spinescent.

Wood. Light brown or yellow, light, soft, close-grained, weighing 31 lb per cu ft.

Bark. Light gray, thin, covered with conspicuous, conelike corky tubercles.

Range. Texas, Louisiana, Oklahoma, and Arkansas; eastward to Florida and northward to Virginia.

Remarks. The genus name, *Zanthoxylum*, comes from an erroneous rendering of the Greek word *xanthos* ("yellow") plus *xylon* ("wood"); the species name, *clava-herculis*, means "club of Hercules" and refers to the trunk's thorny character. Vernacular names are Toothache, Sea Ash, Pepperwood, Prickly Yellowwood, Yellow Prickly-ash, Tongue-bush, Rabbit Gum, Wild Orange, Sting Tongue, Tear Blanket, Pillenterry, and Wait-a-bit. A number of species of birds eat the fruit.

Texas Hercules-club

Zanthoxylum hirsutum Buckl. [D, E, F]

Field Identification. Thorny shrub 3–15 ft, aromatic in all parts.

Flowers. Borne in early spring, dioecious, in cymes ⅓–2 in. long, 1–1½ in. wide; pedicels ¹⁄₁₂–⅛ in. long; sepals 5, minute, linear to subulate, acute; petals 5, greenish, elliptic, concave, about ¹⁄₁₂ in. long; stamens 5, exserted on filiform filaments about as long as the petals or shorter, but shorter than the anthers, wanting or rudimentary in the pistillate flowers; pistils 2–3, ovary sessile, style short, stigma entire or slightly 2-lobed.

Fruit. Capsule borne in clusters ⅓–2 in. long on red, pubescent pedicels ¼–½ in., body of fruit subglobose, asymmetrical, glandular-dotted, apiculate, green at first, reddish brown later, about ¼ in. long, splitting into valves; seed black, shiny, obliquely ovoid, persistent to one valve.

Leaves. Odd-pinnately compound, 1½–2½ in. long (more rarely to 4 in.); rachis red, pubescent, bearing reddish brown, straight, sharp thorns to ¼ in. long; leaflets 3–7 (usually 5), ½–1½ in. long, elliptic to oblong or oval, leathery, aromatic, glandular-dotted especially on the margin, crinkled, crenate, apex obtuse, base cuneate, lustrous above, dull beneath; lateral leaflets short-petioluled or sessile, the petiolule of the terminal leaflet longer.

Twigs. Young ones greenish, pubescent; older ones gray and armed with stout, straight, gray or brown spines to ½ in. long.

Bark. Smooth, mottled light to dark gray; spines straight, or slightly curved, to 1 in. long, not built up on conspicuous corky bases as in *Z. clava-herculis.*

Range. On sandy or gravelly soil of central west Texas. Sandy areas south of San Antonio, also between Utopia and Tarpley. Reported from Arkansas.

Remarks. The genus name, *Zanthoxylum*, comes from an erroneous rendering of the Greek word *xanthos* ("yellow"), plus *xylon* ("wood"). The species name, *hirsutum*, refers to the hirsute twigs and leaves. It has also been listed under the names of *Z. carolinianum* var. *fruticosum* Gray and *Z. clava-herculis* L. var. *fruticosum* Gray.

QUASSIA FAMILY (Simarubaceae)

Tree-of-heaven

Ailanthus altissima (Mill.) Swingle [D, E]

Field Identification. Cultivated tree attaining a height of 100 ft, and a diameter of 3 ft. Handsome and rapid-growing with a symmetrical open head and stout branches.

Flowers. April–May, borne in clusters of 1–5 in large, loose, terminal panicles 6–12 in.; pedicels subtended by small bracts or none; staminate and pistillate panicles on different plants or polygamous; flowers small, ⅕–⅓ in. across, yellowish green; staminate flowers unpleasantly scented; calyx regular, sepals 5, valvate in the bud, oval to oblong, spreading, ⅛–⅙ in. long, villous near the base, inserted at the base of the small 10-lobed disk; stamens 10 (in perfect flowers), staminate flowers with or without a rudimentary pistil; pistillate flowers smaller than staminate with 2 or 3 imperfect stamens or none; ovary deeply 2–5-cleft, the lobes flat and cuneate, ovules solitary in each cavity.

Fruit. September–October, in persistent clusters of 1–5, samara linear-elliptic; ½–1½ in. long; flattened, thin, membranous, veiny, dry, twisted at the apex, sometimes curved, notched on one side, brownish red, the single flattened seed in the center, albumen thin.

Leaves. Alternate, deciduous, odd-pinnately compound, length 8 in.–2½ ft, rachis pubescent or glabrous, unpleasantly odorous when bruised; leaflets 11–41; petiolules ⅛–⅓ in., pubescent or glabrous, leaflets ovate to oblong or lanceolate, sometimes asymmetrical, apex acute or acuminate, base cordate or truncate and often oblique, margin entire except for 2–4 coarse, glandular

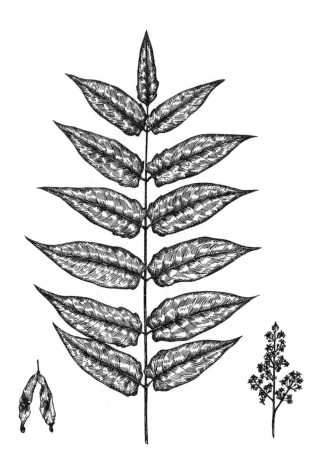

teeth at the base, length 2–5 in., upper surface dull dark green, glabrous or slightly hairy, lower surface paler and glabrous or with a few hairs on the veins; petiole swollen at base.

Twigs. Coarse, blunt, yellowish orange or brown, younger ones pubescent, older ones glabrous, leaf scars large and conspicuous, pith reddish.

Bark. Pale grayish brown, fissures shallow.

Wood. Pale yellowish brown, medium hard, not durable, weak, coarse, open-grained, said to make fairly good fuel, and sometimes used in cabinet work.

Range. A native of China, cultivated for ornament in the United States and sometimes escaping cultivation in our area. Very hardy, seemingly growing well under adverse conditions of dust, smoke, and poor soil. Often found in waste places, trash heaps, vacant lots, cracks of pavement, crowded against buildings, and other situations. Does best on light, moist soils. In Texas, New Mexico, Oklahoma, Arkansas, and Louisiana; east to Florida and north to Massachusetts. Also cultivated westward throughout the interior to the Pacific coast.

Remarks. The genus name, *Ailanthus*, is from a Chinese name, *Ailanto*, meaning "tree-of-heaven" and referring to its height. The species name, *altissima*, means "very tall." Vernacular names for the tree are Copal, Tree-of-the-Gods, Chinese Sumac, Heaven-ward-tree, False Varnish-tree, and Devil's Walkingstick.

The tree was introduced into the United States from China by William Hamilton in 1784. It is a very rapid grower, spreads freely from suckers and by seed, is rather free of insects, but is easily storm damaged. It was once used in erosion control work in the dune areas of the Black Sea and was planted for timber in New Zealand. The seeds are known to be eaten by a number of birds, including the pine grosbeak and crossbill, and occasionally browsed by white-tailed deer. The tree is sometimes planted in China as host to a species of silkworm, *Attacus cynthia*, which produces a coarse inferior silk.

MAHOGANY FAMILY (Meliaceae)

China-berry

Melia azedarach L. [D]

Field Identification. Tree to 45 ft; rounded crown; twice-compound leaves sometimes 2 ft long.

Flowers. March–May, panicles 4–6 in., loose, open, fragrant, showy, individual flowers about ½ in. across; sepals 5–6, lobes acute; petals 5–6, purplish, oblanceolate to narrow-oblong, obtuse; staminal tube with 10–12 stamens and sagittate anthers; ovary 5-celled, style elongate, stigma 3–6-lobed.

Fruit. Ripening September–October, persistent, drupe ½–¾ in. in diameter, subglobose, coriaceous, fleshy, translucent, smooth, yellow, indehiscent, borne in conspicuous drooping clusters;

stone ridged, seeds 3–5, smooth, black, ellipsoid, asymmetrical, acute or obtuse at ends, dispersed by birds or mammals.

Leaves. Large, alternate, deciduous, twice-compound, to 25 in., long-petioled; leaflets numerous, ovate-elliptic, serrate or lobed, some entire, acute at apex, 1¼–2 in. long, mostly glabrous.

Wood. Color variegated, durable, somewhat brittle.

Range. A native of Asia, introduced into the United States as an ornamental, and escaping to grow wild over a wide area. Texas; east to Florida, and north to Oklahoma, Arkansas, and North Carolina.

Remarks. The genus name, *Melia*, is an old Greek name. The species name, *azedarach*, is from a Persian word meaning "noble-tree." Vernacular names are China-tree, Bead-tree, Indian-lilac, and Pride-of-India. The fruit is eaten by birds and swine, but if fermented it sometimes has a toxic effect. The fruit pulp is also used as an insect repellent and vermifuge. In some countries the hard seeds are made into rosaries. The wood was formerly used in cabinet work. China-berry grows rapidly, is rather free of insects, but cannot stand excessive droughts or much cold below zero. It is desirable as a shade tree and was formerly much planted in the South. The northern limit of hardiness is probably Virginia. Besides the species, there occurs an umbrella-shaped variety known as the Texas Umbrella China-berry, *M. azedarach* forma *umbraculiformis* Berckm., which was reported to be found by botanists originally near San Jacinto Battlefield, Houston, Texas.

EUPHORBIA FAMILY (Euphorbiaceae)

Chinese Tallow-tree

Sapium sebiferum (L.) Roxb. [D, E]

Field Identification. Small cultivated tree with a rounded crown, attaining a height of 30 ft.

Flowers. Male and female together on a yellowish green terminal spike, the pistillate below the staminate; calyx of staminate flowers 2–3-lobed, the lobes imbricate; petals absent; stamens 2–3, filaments free, anthers opening lengthwise; pistillate calyx of 2–3 sepals; ovary 1–3-celled, styles 2–3.

Fruit. Capsule 3-lobed, lobes rounded externally and flattened against each other, ⅓–½ in. in diameter, dehiscent by the valves of the capsule falling away to expose the 3 white seeds; seed solitary, crustaceous.

Leaves. Alternate, or rarely opposite, entire, rhombic-ovate, abruptly long-acuminate, base broadly cuneate, 1–3½ in. long, 1–3 in. broad, widest across the middle, deep green and glabrous above, paler below, turning deep red in winter; petiole slender, usually shorter than the blade, 2 glands at the apex.

Twigs. Young twigs slender and green, older grayish brown and marked with numerous small lenticels.

Bark. Brownish gray, broken into appressed ridges, fissures shallow.

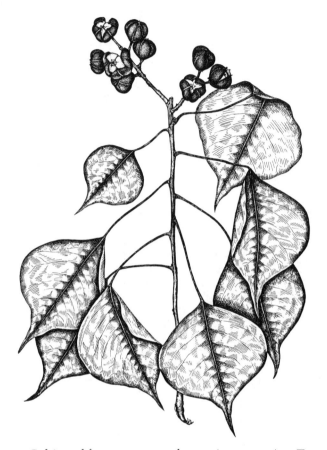

Range. Cultivated for ornament and sometimes escaping. Texas, Oklahoma, Arkansas, and Louisiana; eastward to Florida, along the Atlantic coast to South Carolina. A native of China.

Remarks. The genus name, *Sapium*, was given by Pliny to a resinous pine, and the species name, *sebiferum*, refers to the vegetable tallow, or wax, of the fruit. Another vernacular name is Vegetable Tallow-tree. The milky sap is poisonous, but the tree is cultivated in China for the wax of the seed covering which is used for soap, candles, and cloth-dressing. The wax was formerly imported into the United States, but mineral waxes have almost entirely taken its place. The tree is easily propagated by seeds and cuttings and is attractive with white seeds and red leaves in the fall.

SUMAC FAMILY (Anacardiaceae)

European Smoke-tree

Cotinus coggygria Scop. [D]

Field Identification. A cultivated, deciduous dense shrub or small tree to 15 ft tall, often wider than high. Bark gray to brown, with resinous, odorous sap. Cultivated since 1656.

Flowers. Blooming in June–July, very showy; polygamous or dioecious. Panicles terminal, loose, to 8 in. long, densely plumose, usually purplish or greenish (the pedicels of numerous sterile

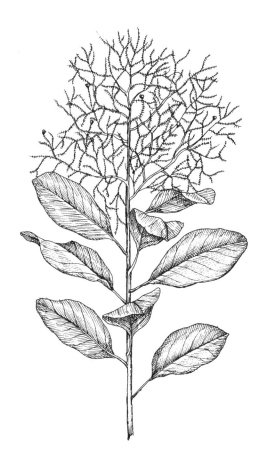

flowers, elongated and with spreading hairs). Flowers few, regular, yellowish to greenish, about ⅛ in. long. Petals 5, oblong, twice as long as the lance-ovate sepals; stamens 5, filaments separate, shorter than the petals, inserted at base of annular disk between the lobes. Ovary superior, 1-celled, with 1 ovule in each cell, placentation axile; with 3 lateral styles.

Fruit. Drupe small, dry, obliquely obovoid (kidney-shaped), reticulate, compressed, ⅛–⅙ in. across. Embryo with flat cotyledons.

Leaves. Simple, alternate, shape mostly oval; apices rounded or slightly emarginate; margin entire; base abruptly narrowed; surfaces glabrous; length 1½–3 in. Petioles slender. Buds with several imbricate, dark, red-brown scales.

Range. Southern Europe to central China and the Himalayas. Cultivated for the feathery panicles, smaller more oval leaves, which are more attractive than the native American species, *C. obovatus* Raf. The loose plumose pedicels give the appearance of smoke at a distance.

Remarks. The genus name, *Cotinus*, is an ancient Greek name of the wild olive. The species name, *coggygria*, is from the ancient Greek. Also known under the name of *Rhus cotinus* L.

Evergreen Sumac

Rhus sempervirens Scheele [D, E, F]

Field Identification. Western evergreen shrub to 12 ft, forming rounded clumps. Branches spreading and often the lower ones touching the ground.

Flowers. Appearing irregularly during the summer after rains, borne in terminal or axillary, thyrsoid panicles ¾–2 in. long, shorter than the leaves; panicles subtended by persistent bracts which are ovate, acute to rounded at the apex, ¹⁄₂₅–¹⁄₁₂ in. long, upper surface glabrous or nearly so, lower surface hairy, margin ciliate; sepals 5, oval, ovate or triangular, obtuse at apex, about ¹⁄₁₂ in. long, glabrous above and somewhat hairy beneath, the ciliate marginal hairs simple or glandular; petals 5, white or greenish, oblong-ovate to obovate, obtuse at apex, base obtuse or truncate, ⅛–⅙ in. long and ¹⁄₁₂ in. broad, glabrous above and hairy beneath; stamens 5, filaments as long as the sepals with anthers about ¹⁄₂₅ in. long and broad; pistil with a slightly lobed stigma.

Fruit. Maturing usually by September, subglobose, lenticular, oblique, ⅓–⅖ in. long, covered with red hairs which are simple and glandular; seed lenticular, broader than long, smooth.

Leaves. Alternate, evergreen, 2–5½ in. long, odd-pinnately compound of 5–9 leaflets on a softly pubescent rachis, oblong, oval, ovate or lanceolate, apex acute, base cuneate, margin entire or subrevolute, leathery; upper surface dark green, lustrous and glabrous to puberulent; lower surface paler dull green with simple or glandular hairs; lateral leaflets ½–1½ in. long, ⅜–¾ in. broad, petiolules about 1/12 in. long; segments of rachis between leaflets ¼–½ in. long; terminal leaflet ¾–1½ in. long, ⅜–¾ in. wide, long-petiolulate; petioles about ⅝ in. long. Leaves turning red, yellow, or brown in autumn.

Twigs. Brown to gray, slender, stiff, young puberulent, older glabrous.

Bark. Gray to brown, rough with small loose scales.

Range. In central and western Texas, New Mexico, and Mexico. On rocky hillsides, cliffs, and slopes at altitudes of 2,000–7,500 ft. In Mexico in the states of Nuevo León, Coahuila, Chihuahua, San Luis Potosí, Zacatecas, Durango, and Hidalgo.

Remarks. The genus name, *Rhus*, is the ancient Latin name, and the species name, *sempervirens*, refers to the evergreen habit. It has also been listed by some authors under the name of *R. virens* Lindh. Vernacular names in English, Spanish, and Indian dialects are Tobacco Sumac, Capulín, Lambrisco, Lantrioco, Ayume, Kinnikinnick, and Tamaichia. Tamaichia was the name given by the Comanche Indians, who gathered the leaves in the fall, sun-cured them, and mixed them with tobacco for smoking. It is also reported that the leaves were used in domestic medicine for relieving asthma. The acid, red fruit steeped in water makes a cooling drink. The red fruit and evergreen, lustrous leaves suit the plant for use in horticulture.

A closely related species of Arizona is *R. choriophylla* Woot. & Standl., which has longer, more glabrous leaves and axillary inflorescence. However, some authors feel that it is only a geographical variation of *R. sempervirens*.

Flame-leaf Sumac

Rhus copallina L. [D, E]

Field Identification. Slender-branched shrub or small tree to 25 ft.

Flowers. Polygamo-dioecious, about ⅛ in. across, borne in a densely pubescent, terminal thyrse about 4¾ in. long and 4 in. broad; pedicels about 1/12 in. long, pubescent; bracts very small, lanceolate, about 1/12 in. long; sepals 5, deltoid, pubescent, glandular-ciliate, 1/12–⅛ in. long, about 1/25 in. broad; stamens 5, anthers lanceolate; pistil 1, sessile, ovary pubescent, stigmas 3, styles 3; disk annular. Petals greenish white, 1/12–1/10 in. long, 1/25 in. broad, glabrous externally, a few hairs on the inner side, margin ciliate and glandular, deciduous.

Fruit. In compact panicles, erect or drooping, persistent; drupe subglobose, flattened, red, glandular-hairy, ⅛–⅙ in. in diameter; seeds solitary, smooth.

Leaves. Deciduous, alternate, pinnate, 5–12 in. long, rachis pubescent, broadly winged; leaflets 7–17, subsessile, inequilateral, elliptic or ovate to lanceolate, acute or acuminate at the apex, asymmetrical and obtuse, or rounded to subcuneate at the base,

entire or few-toothed, lustrous, glabrous to pubescent above, hairy and glandular beneath; lateral leaflets sessile, 1–3½ in. long, ½–1¼ in. broad, terminal leaflet petiolulate or sessile.

Twigs. Green to reddish brown, pubescent at first, glabrous later; lenticels dark.

Bark. Thick, greenish brown, excrescences circular, scales thin.

Wood. Light brown to greenish, coarse-grained, soft, weighing 32 lb per cu ft, sometimes used for small posts.

Range. Moist soil in shade or sun. Texas, Oklahoma, Arkansas, and Louisiana; eastward to Georgia, northward to New Hampshire, and west to Michigan and Missouri.

Remarks. The genus name, *Rhus*, is the ancient Latin name, and the species name, *copallina*, means "copal gum." Vernacular names for this plant are Mountain Sumac, Smooth Sumac, Black Sumac, Shining Sumac, Dwarf Sumac, Upland Sumac, and Winged Sumac.

The bark and leaves contain tannin and are used in the tanning industry. The crushed acrid fruit of this and other species was added to drinking water by the Indians to make it more palatable.

According to stomach records, the fruit has been eaten by at least 20 species of birds, and white-tailed deer occasionally browse it. It is propagated by seed. It is conspicuous in fall because of the brilliant red leaves.

Flame-leaf Sumac is generally replaced in central Texas by the Prairie Flame-leaf Sumac, *R. copallina* L. var. *lanceolata* Gray, which has narrower and more falcate leaves, larger clusters of fruit, and a more treelike rounded form. It is thought that the two may hybridize in their overlapping areas.

White Flame-leaf Sumac, *R. copallina* var. *leucantha* (Jacq.) DC., is a variety with white flowers found near New Braunfels, Texas.

A variety with 5–13 broader oblong to narrow-ovate leaflets has been described from Oklahoma, Texas, Arkansas, and Louisiana as *R. copallina* L. var. *latifolia* Engl., but other authors have relegated it to the status of a synonym of the species.

Prairie Flame-leaf Sumac

Rhus copallina L. var. *lanceolata* Gray [D, E, F]

Field Identification. Clumpy shrub or small tree to 30 ft, with a rounded top.

Flowers. Borne in terminal panicles 4–6 in. long and 2–3 in. wide, peduncle pubescent, secondary pedicels about ⅙ in. long or flowers almost sessile; individual flowers yellowish green to white, about ⅛ in. long; bracts deciduous, ovate ¹⁄₂₅–¹⁄₁₂ in. long, apex rounded, glabrous above, hairy below, margin ciliate; sepals 5, erect, ovate-triangular, acute or obtuse, ¹⁄₂₅–¹⁄₁₂ in. long, glabrous above, hairy beneath, margin ciliate with glandular or simple hairs; petals 5, yellowish green to white, about ⅛ in. long and ¹⁄₂₅ in. wide, oblong-ovate, obtuse, reflexed, smooth above, hairy beneath, margin ciliate; stamens 5, exserted, filaments elongate; anthers lanceolate, yellow, conspicuous, about ¹⁄₂₅ in. long and wide; ovary 1-celled, stigmas 3, styles 3.

Fruit. In terminal showy panicles, drupe about ³⁄₁₆ in. long, subglobose, flattened, dark red, glandular-hairy, the stigma persisting; seeds about ⅛ in. long and ¹⁄₁₂ in. broad, smooth, oval to obovate.

Leaves. Alternate, 5–9 in. long, odd-pinnately compound of 9–21 leaflets; rachis between the leaflets narrowly winged, green to reddish, pubescent; leaflets sessile or short petioluled, 1–3 in. long, ¼–½ in. wide, lanceolate to linear, falcate, apex acuminate, base cuneate or rounded, asymmetrical, margin entire or with coarse teeth, thin, subrevolute; upper surface dark green, lustrous, glabrous; lower surface duller, paler, pubescent or glandular-hairy, veins rather conspicuous; petiole 1–1½ in. long.

Twigs. Slender, all young parts hairy, green to red; older twigs gray, glabrous, lenticels small.

Bark. Gray to brown, smooth when young, with small scales when older, excrescences lenticular, numerous, horizontal.

Range. Usually on dry and rocky soil of the Texas Edwards Plateau area; north into Oklahoma, northwest into New Mexico, and south into Mexico. In Mexico in the states of Coahuila, Puebla, and Tamaulipas.

Remarks. The genus name, *Rhus*, is the ancient Latin name; the species name, *copallina*, means "gum copal," and the variety name, *lanceolata*, refers to the lanceolate-shaped leaflets. Vernacular names are Lance-leaf Sumac, Tree Sumac, Limestone Sumac, Mountain Sumac, Black Sumac, and Prairie Shining Sumac.

Prairie Flame-leaf Sumac is considered by some authorities to be a distinct species instead of a variety of the Flame-leaf Sumac, *R. copallina*. However, later classification takes into account the considerable variation of the Flame-leaf Sumac and has assigned the Prairie Flame-leaf Sumac as a variety of it. The Prairie Flame-leaf Sumac, in its most typical form, seems most abundant on the dry stony hills of central and west Texas. It has longer panicles of flowers and larger fruit than the Flame-leaf Sumac. The leaflets tend to be narrower, entire or remotely serrate, and falcate, and the rachi wing narrower. The habit approaches that of a small rounded tree instead of a straggling shrub.

The leaves of both the Flame-leaf and Prairie Flame-leaf Sumac contain considerable amounts of tannin and have been used as a substitute for oak bark in tanning leather. The acrid drupes, when crushed in water, produce a cooling drink known as "Sumac-ade" or "Rhus-ade." The drupes also produce a black dye for woolen goods. Because of the brilliant fall coloring of its red, purple, and orange leaves, Prairie Flame-leaf Sumac is being adapted to horticulture.

It has considerable wildlife value, the drupe being eaten particularly by the gallinaceous birds, such as various species of quail, grouse, prairie chicken, and ring-necked pheasant. It is also browsed by white-tailed deer and mule deer.

Smooth Sumac

Rhus glabra L. [D, E, F]

Field Identification. Thicket-forming shrub or small tree attaining a height of 20 ft. Leaves pinnate, bearing 11–31 elliptic or lanceolate, sharply serrate leaflets.

Flowers. June–August, in a terminal thyrse, 5–9 in. long; bracts narrowly lanceolate, about ⅟₂₅ in. long; calyx of 5 lanceolate sepals, each about ⅟₁₂ in. long; petals 5, white, spreading, lanceolate, ⅙ in. long or less; stamens 5; pistil 1, ovary 1-seeded, stigmas 3.

Fruit. Ripening September–October, drupe subglobose, about ⅙ in. long, covered with short, red-velvety hairs; 1-seeded, stone smooth, seed dispersed by birds and mammals.

Leaves. Alternate, pinnately compound, 11–31 leaflets which are elliptic, lanceolate, oblong or ovate, acuminate at the apex; rounded, subcordate, cuneate or oblique at the base, sharply serrate, usually dark green above, lighter to conspicuously white

beneath; lateral ones sessile or almost so, 2½–4¾ in. long, ½–1¼ in. broad; terminal one sessile or petiolulate, 2–3¾ in. long, ½–1½ in. broad.

Wood. Orange, soft, brittle.

Range. In moist, rich soil. Texas, New Mexico, Oklahoma, Arkansas, and Louisiana; eastward to Florida, northward to Quebec, and westward to British Columbia, Washington, Oregon, Utah, Colorado, and Missouri.

Remarks. The genus name, *Rhus*, is the ancient Latin name, and the species name, *glabra*, refers to the plant's smoothness. Vernacular names are Scarlet Sumac, Red Sumac, White Sumac, Shoe-make, Vinegar-tree, Senhalanac, Pennsylvania Sumac, Upland Sumac, and Sleek Sumac. The leaves are reported to have been mixed with tobacco and smoked. The twigs, leaves, and roots contain tannin and were used for staining and dyeing. Smooth Sumac is now used extensively for ornament. Its red clusters of fruit and long graceful leaves which turn brilliant colors in the autumn are its attractive features. It should be more extensively cultivated for ornament. Records show that the date of earliest cultivation was 1620. It is occasionally planted for erosion control and used for shelter-belt planting in the prairie states. Thirty-two species of birds are known to feed on it. Wild turkey, bobwhite, cottontail, and white-tailed deer eat it eagerly.

HOLLY FAMILY (Aquifoliaceae)

Yaupon Holly

Ilex vomitoria Ait. [D]

Field Identification. An evergreen, thicket-forming shrub with many stems from the base, or a tree to 25 ft, and a diameter of 12 in. The crown is low, dense, and rounded.

Flowers. April–May on branchlets of the previous year, solitary or fascicled in the leaf axils, polygamo-dioecious, pedicels slender, $\frac{1}{25}$–$\frac{1}{6}$ in. long; staminate glabrous, 2–3-flowered; pistillate puberulent, 1–2-flowered; calyx-lobes 4–5, glabrous, ovate or rounded, obtuse, about $\frac{1}{25}$ in. long; corolla white, petals 4–5, united at base, elliptic-oblong, $\frac{1}{12}$–$\frac{1}{8}$ in. long, about $\frac{1}{12}$ in. wide; stamens 4–5, almost as long as the petals, anthers oblong and cordate; staminodia of the pistillate flowers shorter than the petals; ovary ovoid, $\frac{1}{25}$–$\frac{1}{12}$ in. long, 1–4-celled, stigma flattened and capitate.

Fruit. Often in abundance, drupe shiny red, semitranslucent, subglobose, about $\frac{1}{4}$ in. long, often crowned by the persistent stigma, nutlets usually 4, to $\frac{1}{6}$ in. long, obtuse, prominently ribbed.

Leaves. Evergreen, simple, alternate, elliptic-oblong to oval, margin crenate and teeth minutely mucronulate, apex obtuse or rounded and sometimes minutely emarginate and mucronulate, base obtuse or rounded, thick and coriaceous; upper surface dark lustrous green and glabrous, veins obscure; lower surface paler, glabrous, or with a few hairs on veins; petioles $\frac{1}{25}$–$\frac{1}{4}$ in. long, grooved, glabrous or puberulent. Leaves vary considerably in size and shape on different plants.

Twigs. Gray to brown, terete, stout, rigid, crooked, short, glabrous or puberulent; winter buds minute, obtuse, scales brown.

Bark. Averaging ¹⁄₁₆–¹⁄₈ in. thick, brownish to mottled gray or almost black, tight, smooth except for lenticels, or on old trunks eventually breaking into thin, small scales.

Wood. White, heavy, hard, strong, close-grained, weighing about 46 lb per cu ft, sometimes used for turnery, inlay work, or woodenware.

Range. Low moist woods, mostly near the coast. Texas, Oklahoma, Arkansas, and Louisiana. Evidently reaching its largest size in the east Texas bottom lands. Eastward to Florida and northward to Virginia.

Remarks. The genus name, *Ilex*, is the ancient name for the Holly Oak, and the species name, *vomitoria*, refers to its use as a medicine. Local names in use are Cassena, Cassine, Cassio-berry-bush, Evergreen Cassena, Yapon, Yopan, Youpon, Emetic Holly, Evergreen Holly, South-sea-tea, Carolina-tea, Appalachian-tea, Yopon del Indio, Chocolate del Indio, Indian Blackdrink, Christmas-berry.

The fruit is known to be eaten by at least 7 species of birds. In regions where it grows it is often used as a holiday decoration. Although yellow-fruited plants have been given variety names from time to time, they do not apparently reproduce true to color and are therefore to be regarded only as unstable forms.

American Holly

Ilex opaca Ait. [D]

Field Identification. An evergreen tree to 70 ft, with short, crooked branches and a rounded or pyramidal crown.

Flowers. April–June, in short-stalked, axillary, cymose clusters; polygamo-dioecious, staminate in 3–9-flowered cymes, small, white, petals 4–6; stamens 4–6, alternating with the petals; pistillate flowers solitary or 2–3 together; ovary 4–8-celled, style short with broad stigmas; pistil rudimentary in the staminate flowers; calyx 4–6-lobed, lobes acute, ciliate; peduncles with 2 bracts.

Fruit. Maturing November–December, spherical or ellipsoid, mostly red, more rarely yellow or orange, ¼–½ in. long, nutlets prominently ribbed.

Leaves. Variable in shape, size, and spines, simple, alternate, persistent, ovate to oblong or oval, flattened, keeled or twisted, stiff and coriaceous, margins wavy, set with sharp, stiff, flat or divaricate spines, sometimes spineless; apex acute, spinose; base cuneate or rounded; upper surface dark to light green, lustrous or dull, paler and glabrous to somewhat puberulous beneath, length 2–4 in., width 1–1½ in.; petioles short, stout, grooved, sometimes puberulent; stipules minute, deltoid, acute.

Twigs. Stout, green to light brown or gray, glabrous or puberulous.

Bark. Light or dark gray, often roughened by small protuberances.

Wood. White or brownish, tough, close-grained, shock resistance high, works with tools well, shrinks considerably, checks or warps

badly unless properly seasoned, not durable under exposure, rather heavy, specific gravity when dry about 0.61. It is used for cabinets, interior finish, novelties, handles, fixtures, and scientific instruments.

Range. Texas, Oklahoma, Arkansas, and Louisiana; eastward to Florida, north to Massachusetts and New York, and westward through Pennsylvania, Ohio, Indiana, and Illinois to Missouri.

Remarks. The genus name, *Ilex*, is the old name for Holly Oak, and the species name, *opaca*, refers to the dull green leaf. Vernacular names are Yule Holly, Christmas Holly, and White Holly. The foliage and fruit are often used for holiday decorations and are sometimes browsed by cattle. At least 18 species of birds eat the fruit.

Possum-haw Holly

Ilex decidua Walt. [D, E, F]

Field Identification. Usually a shrub with a spreading open crown, but sometimes a tree to 30 ft, with an inclined trunk to 10 in. in diameter.

Flowers. Borne March–May with the leaves, polygamo-dioecious, solitary or fascicled, borne on slender pedicels; pedicels of staminate flowers to ½ in. long, that of the pistillate flower generally shorter than the staminate; petals 4–6, white, united at the base, oblong to elliptic, ⅛–⅙ in. long; calyx-lobes 4–6, lobes ovate to triangular, acute or obtuse, entire to denticulate, sometimes ciliolate; stamens 4–6, anthers oblong and cordate, fertile stamens as long as the petals or shorter; staminodia of pistillate flowers shorter than the petals; ovary ovoid, about ¹⁄₁₂ in. long, 4-celled, stigma large, capitate and sessile.

Fruit. Ripe in early autumn, persistent on branches most of the winter after leaves are shed, drupe globose or depressed-globose, orange-red, ¼–⅓ in. in diameter, solitary or 2–3 together; nutlets usually 4, crustaceous, ovate or lunate, longitudinally ribbed, up to ⅕ in. long.

Leaves. Simple, deciduous, alternate or often fascicled on short lateral spurs, obovate to spatulate or oblong, margin crenate-serrate with gland-tipped teeth; apex acute to obtuse, rounded or emarginate; base cuneate or attenuate, membranous at first but firm later; upper surface dark green and glabrous or with a few hairs, main vein impressed; lower surface paler and glabrous or pubescent on ribs, blade length 2–3 in., width ½–1½ in.; petiole slender, grooved, glabrous to densely puberulent, length ¹⁄₁₂–½ in.; stipules filiform, deciduous.

Twigs. Elongate, slender, often with many short spurlike lateral twigs, light to dark gray, glabrous or puberulent, lightly lenticellate, leaf scars lunate, buds small and obtuse.

Bark. Smooth, thin, mottled gray to brown, sometimes with numerous warty protuberances.

Wood. White, close-grained, weighing 46 lb per cu ft, of no commercial value.

Range. In rich, moist soil, usually along streams or in swamps. Texas, Louisiana, Oklahoma, and Arkansas; eastward to Florida, and northward to Tennessee, Kentucky, Indiana, Illinois, Kansas, and Missouri.

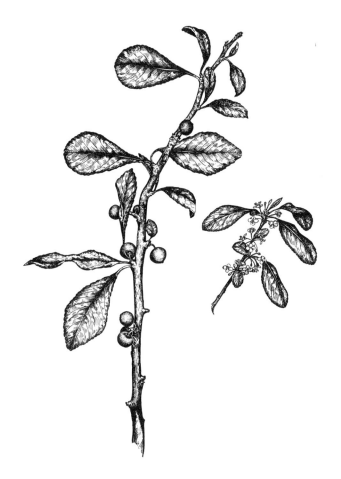

Remarks. The genus name, *Ilex*, is the ancient name of the Holly Oak, and the species name, *decidua*, refers to the autumn-shed leaves. Local names are Deciduous Holly, Meadow Holly, Prairie Holly, Welk Holly, Bearberry, and Winterberry. It is occasionally planted for ornament and is attractive in winter because of the persistent orange-red drupes. It is sometimes mistaken for a hawthorn in fruit, and possums are fond of it, hence the name, Possum-haw. At least 9 species of birds are known to feed upon the fruit, including the bobwhite quail.

STAFF-TREE FAMILY (Celastraceae)

Eastern Wahoo

Euonymus atropurpureus Jacq. [D]

Field Identification. Usually a shrub, but sometimes a small tree to 25 ft, with spreading branches and an irregular crown.

Flowers. May–June, borne in 7–15-flowered, axillary, trichotomous cymes; peduncles slender, 1–2 in. long, with individual perfect flowers about ½ in. wide; petals 4, purple, obovate, undulate or obscurely toothed, borne on the edge of a 4-angled disk; stamens 4, short, with 2-celled purple anthers; ovary 4-celled, style short, stigma depressed.

Fruit. September–October, capsule deeply 3–4-lobed, smooth, about ½ in. across, persistent on long peduncles; valves purple or red, splitting open to expose brown seeds about ¼ in. long enclosed by a scarlet seed coat.

Leaves. Opposite, petioled, deciduous, 2–5 in. long, 1–2 in. wide, ovate-elliptic, acuminate or acute at the apex, acute or cuneate at the base, finely crenate-serrate on the margin, bright green above, pale and puberulent beneath; petioles ½–1 in. long.

Twigs. Slender, somewhat 4-angled, purplish green to brownish later; lenticels pale and prominent.

Bark. Smooth, thin, gray, with minute scales.

Wood. Almost white, or tinged with yellow or orange, close-grained, heavy, hard, tough, weighing 41 lb per cu ft.

Range. Eastern Texas and Arkansas; east to northern Alabama, north to New York, and west to Ontario, Montana, Nebraska, and Kansas.

Remarks. The genus name, *Euonymus*, is a translation of an ancient Greek term meaning "true name," and the species name, *atropurpureus*, refers to the purple flowers and fruit. Vernacular names are Spindle-tree, Burning-bush, Bleeding-heart, Arrow-wood, Indian-arrow, Bitter-oak, and Strawberry-tree. The tree is sometimes used as an ornament because of its beautiful scarlet fruit in autumn, although it is subject to scale and fungus diseases. It is known to be purgative to livestock. The seeds are eaten by a number of species of birds.

MAPLE FAMILY (Aceraceae)

Red Maple

Acer rubrum L. [D]

Field Identification. Beautiful tree attaining a height of 100 ft, with a narrow, rounded crown.

Flowers. Borne in early spring before the leaves, in staminate and pistillate axillary fascicles on the same tree, or on different trees, red to yellowish green; petals 5, same length as the calyx-lobes, linear-oblong; stamens 5–8, anthers red; pistil short, ovary glabrous; styles 2, stout and spreading; calyx campanulate, 5-lobed.

Fruit. Ripening March–June, borne on slender, drooping pedicels 2–4 in.; composed of a pair of winged, red, yellowish green or brown, flattened samaras, with a seed at the base; wings spreading, ½–1 in. long.

Leaves. Opposite, simple, deciduous, blades ovate to oval, 2–6 in. long, 3–5-lobed; lobes acuminate or acute, irregularly serrate, sinuses angular; base truncate or somewhat cordate; bright green and glabrous above, whitish beneath; turning beautiful shades of yellow, orange, or red in autumn; petioles slender, 2–4 in., green to red.

Twigs. Slender, glabrous, reddish, lenticels pale.

Bark. Light gray and smooth at first, becoming darker, furrowed and flaky on old trunks.

Wood. Light reddish brown, close-grained, hard, heavy, weak, weighing 38 lb per cu ft.

Range. In Texas, Oklahoma, Arkansas, and Louisiana; eastward to Florida, northward to Newfoundland, and west to Ontario, Minnesota, Wisconsin, and Missouri.

Remarks. The genus name, *Acer*, is the ancient Celt name, and the species name, *rubrum*, may refer to the red flowers, fruit, or autumn leaves. Vernacular names are Scarlet Maple, Shoe-peg

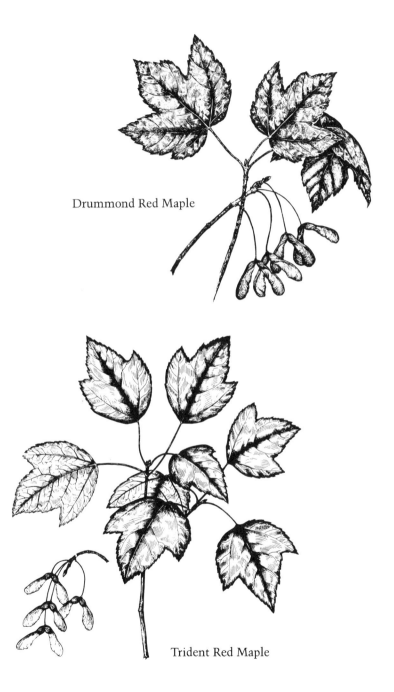

Drummond Red Maple

Trident Red Maple

Maple, Swamp Maple, Soft Maple, and Hard Maple. The wood is used for furniture, turnery, fuel, gunstocks, and woodenware. The seeds are eaten by squirrel and chipmunk, and the foliage browsed by cottontail and white-tailed deer.

Red Maple is subject to considerable variation, and some of the more constant varieties are as follows:

Drummond Red Maple, *A. rubrum* var. *drummondii* (Hook. & Arn.) Sarg., is perhaps more common in east Texas than the species, with 3–5-lobed leaves which are generally broader than long, woolly white-hairy beneath, and the scarlet fruit is somewhat larger than in the species.

Trident Red Maple, *A. rubrum* var. *tridens* Wood, has smaller 3-lobed leaves, obovate, narrowed and rounded, and sparingly toothed or entire below the 3 short lobes; dark green above, white-tomentose beneath; flowers often yellowish green.

Pale-flower Red Maple, *A. rubrum* var. *pallidiflorum* Pax, has yellow flowers. A number of horticultural clones, which reproduce asexually, have been developed. The most popular are the Column (*columnare*), Dwarf (*globosum*), and Schlesinger (*schlesingeri*).

Sugar Maple

Acer saccharum Marsh. [D]

Field Identification. Large, broad, round-topped tree attaining a height of 100 ft, and a diameter of 2½ ft.

Flowers. Borne March–May, polygamous, pedicels slender, hairy, ¾–3 in. long, together forming a greenish yellow corymb; petals absent; calyx campanulate, 5-lobed, lobes obtuse and hairy; stamens 7–8, filaments slender and glabrous in the staminate flower, and shorter in the pistillate; ovary pale green, hairy, with 2 long-exserted stigmas.

Fruit. Ripening September–October, borne in clusters; samara double, reddish brown, 1–1½ in. long, winged; wings ¼–½ in. wide, flat, thin, parallel or angle of divergence exceeding 45°; seeds at the samara base smooth, red, about ¼ in. long, easily wind-borne because of the attached wing, good seed crops every 3–7 years.

Leaves. Simple, opposite, deciduous, blades 3–6 in. long and as wide, usually 5-lobed, but occasionally 3-lobed; lobes entire or irregularly toothed or lobed, apex acuminate; base cordate,

rounded, or truncate; upper surface at maturity dark green, paler
and whitish to glaucous beneath; leaf turning beautiful shades of
yellow, orange, or red in autumn; petioles slender, glabrous, 1½–
3 in.

Twigs. Slender, lustrous, glabrous, green at first, reddish brown
later; lenticels conspicuous, pale, oblong; buds conical, reddish
brown, ⅛–⅕ in. long.

Bark. Light gray to brown, smooth when young, on older trees
darker and fissured with irregular scaly plates.

Wood. Reddish brown, sapwood white, close-grained, straight- or
curly-grained, hard, strong, tough, stiff, odorless, strong in bending and endwise compression, shock resistance high, tools well,

stays smooth under abrasion, takes a high polish, stains well, holds nails well, fair in gluing, dries easily, shrinks moderately, not durable when exposed to decay conditions.

Range. Almost the entire eastern half of the United States; west to east Texas, Arkansas, Oklahoma, Louisiana, Kansas, Nebraska, North Dakota, and South Dakota. In Canada in Manitoba, Ontario, Quebec, New Brunswick, and Newfoundland.

Remarks. The genus name, *Acer*, is the ancient name of a maple of Europe, and the species name, *saccharum*, refers to the sugar content of the sap. Vernacular names are Hard Maple, Black Maple, and Sweet Maple. This tree is considered by many to be the most valuable hardwood tree in America. The wood is used for furniture, shoe lasts, turnery, pegs, shipbuilding, fuel, crossties, veneer, athletic equipment, musical instruments, boxes, woodenware, handles, shuttles, toys, and general millwork. Individual trees produce the bird's-eye and curly grains used in furniture. The wood is also rich in potash, and the sap is a source of the sucrose-rich maple sugar which is produced mostly in the northern states and Canada. It is usually not refined but owes its flavor to impurities in the crude product.

Silver Maple

Acer saccharinum L. [D]

Field Identification. Tree to 100 ft, with a rounded crown and slender spreading branches.

Flowers. Before the leaves in spring, from imbricate involucres in sessile, or short-stalked, axillary clusters, greenish yellow, polygamo-dioecious; no petals; stamens 3–7, exserted; filaments slender with red anthers; pistil short, with a pubescent ovary and 2 spreading stigmatic styles; calyx obscurely 5-lobed, narrower in the staminate than in the pistillate flower, greenish yellow, pubescent.

Fruit. Ripe when the leaves are almost mature, and pendent on slender pedicels, composed of 2 samaras with nutlets at the base and thin, widely divergent wings; samaras rather large, 1½–2 in. long, hairy at first but glabrous later, flattened, reddish brown or green, wrinkled, thin, falcate, dispersed April–June, good seed crops nearly every year.

Leaves. Opposite, simple, deciduous, blades 6–7 in. long, borne on red, drooping petioles about 4 in., truncate or somewhat cor-

date at the base, 5-lobed; lobes deep, narrow, acuminate, variously toothed and cut, sinuses acute or rounded; upper surface pale green, lower surface silvery white, turning yellow in autumn.

Twigs. Slender, brittle, shiny, reddish brown.

Bark. At first smooth and gray, later breaking into loose flakes.

Wood. Pale brown, close-grained, somewhat brittle, even-textured, moderately strong, easily worked, decaying rapidly on exposure, weighing 32 lb per cu ft.

Range. East Texas, Oklahoma, Arkansas, and Louisiana; eastward to Florida, north to New Brunswick, and west to Ontario, the Dakotas, Nebraska, and Kansas.

Remarks. *Acer* is the ancient Celt name, and the species name, *saccharinum*, refers to the sweet sap. Vernacular names are White Maple, Soft Maple, River Maple, Creek Maple, and Swamp Maple. The tree is brittle and subject to wind damage. It is also rather susceptible to insect and fungus diseases. Although short-lived it is a rapid grower and is often planted for ornament and occasionally for shelter-belt planting and stream-bank protection. Sugar is made from the sap occasionally, and the wood is made into flooring and furniture and used for fuel. The fruit is eaten by a number of species of birds, and by squirrel and chipmunk.

Big-tooth Maple

Acer grandidentatum Nutt. [G]

Field Identification. Western shrub or tree to 50 ft, and a diameter of 8–10 in. The branches rather stout and usually erect to form an open rounded crown.

Flowers. Appearing with the leaves April–May, axillary, corymbs short-stalked or almost sessile, hairy, yellow, few-flowered; pedicels slender, drooping, hairy; calyx persistent, campanulate, about ¼ in. long, lobes broad, rounded, and pale-hairy; corolla absent; stamens 6–8, elongate in the staminate flower; ovary superior, glabrous, 2-carpellate, 2-lobed, and 2-celled.

Fruit. A double samara, mature in September, green or rose-colored; wings ¾–1¼ in. long, usually divaricate, glabrous or nearly so, reticulate; seed reddish brown, smooth, about ¼ in. long, calyx persistent.

Leaves. Simple, alternate, deciduous, 2–5 in. wide, 3–5-lobed, the lobes acute or obtuse and usually sinuate-dentate, more rarely entire, sinuses broad and rounded, base of leaf cordate or truncate, coriaceous; upper surface dark green, lustrous and glabrous; lower surface paler, glaucescent, and somewhat pubescent, turning red or yellow in autumn; petiole stout, 1¼–2 in. long.

Twigs. Slender, reddish to brown, gray later; lenticels pale, small, numerous; leaf scars narrow, almost circular; buds reddish brown, about ¹⁄₁₆ in. long, scales ovate to obovate, puberulous and ciliate.

Bark. Thin, dark brown to gray with narrow fissures and flat ridges separating into platelike scales.

Wood. Heart brown, sapwood nearly white, and wide, heavy, hard, close-grained, often used for fuel.

Range. Valleys, canyons, banks of mountain streams, at altitudes of 4,000–6,000 ft. In Trans-Pecos Texas in the Guadalupe, Davis, and Chisos mountains. In New Mexico in the Organ, White, and Sacramento mountains. In Oklahoma in the Wichita Mountains; also in Arizona, north to Idaho, Utah, Colorado, and Wyoming.

Remarks. The genus name, *Acer*, is the classical name of maple; the species name, *grandidentatum*, refers to the large teeth, or lobes, on the leaf margin. It is reported that the sap is sometimes used for sugar-making, and the foliage occasionally browsed by deer and livestock.

BUCKEYE FAMILY (Hippocastanaceae)

Texas Buckeye

Aesculus arguta Buckl. [D, E]

Field Identification. Usually a shrub, but under favorable conditions a tree to 35 ft. The branches are stout and the crown is rounded to oblong.

Flowers. Inflorescence a dense, yellow panicle, borne after the leaves, 4–8 in. long, 2–3½ in. broad, primary peduncle of panicle densely brown-tomentose, secondary racemes ¾–½ in. long, 3–15-flowered, tomentose; individual flower pedicels ⅛–¼ in., densely tomentose; calyx campanulate, ⅕–¼ in. long, brown-tomentose, 4–5-lobed above, lobes imbricate in the bud, lobes unequal, apices obtuse to rounded or truncate; petals 4, pale yellow, some reddish at the base, ⅓–¾ in. long, upright, parallel, clawed, thin, deciduous, densely hairy, margin ciliate; upper pair oval to broadly oblong; lateral pair elongate, oblong to spatulate, long-clawed, apex rounded to truncate or notched; disk hypogynous, annular, depressed; stamens 7–8, inserted on the disk, long-exserted, upcurved, unequal, filiform, hairy, longer than the petals; anthers yellow, ellipsoid, introrse, 2-celled, opening longitudinally; style 1, slender, elongate, curved; stigma terminal and entire; ovary 3-celled, sessile, cells often 1-ovuled by abortion.

Fruit. Maturing May–June, peduncles stout, hairy at first, glabrate later; capsule ¾–1¾ in. in diameter, subglobose to obovoid or asymmetrically lobed, armed with stout warts or prickles or occasionally smooth, light brown, dehiscent into 2–3 valves at maturity; seeds usually solitary and rounded, if 2, usually flattened by pressure, coriaceous, smooth, lustrous, brown, ⅝–¾ in. in diameter.

Leaves. Deciduous, opposite, palmately compound of 7–9 leaflets (often 7), sessile or nearly so, narrowly elliptic to lanceolate, or more rarely obovate, apex long-acuminate (less often broader and abruptly acuminate), base attenuate to narrowly cuneate, margin finely serrate or occasionally incised above the middle, blade length 2½–5 in., width ½–2 in.; upper surface olive green, lustrous, a few fine hairs mostly along the veins; lower surface paler and more pubescent; petioles slender, 3–5 in., grooved, woolly-hairy.

Bark. Gray to black; fissures narrow, short and irregular; ridges broken into small short, rough scales.

Twigs. Tough, stout, terete, the young ones green and glabrous to somewhat hairy, the older ones gray to reddish brown, lenticels small; leaf scars lunate or horseshoe-shaped, fibrovascular marks 3–6.

Range. Texas Buckeye is found on limestone or granite soils in the Edwards Plateau area of Texas, north to southern Oklahoma, and in Missouri.

Remarks. The genus name, *Aesculus*, is the old name for a European mast-bearing tree, and the species name, *arguta*, means "sharp-toothed," perhaps referring to the foliage. Texas Buckeye is closely related to Ohio Buckeye, *A. glabra* Willd., and at one time was listed as a variety of it under the name of *A. glabra* var. *arguta* (Buckl.) Robinson. Although listed only as a shrub in most literature, Texas Buckeye becomes a tree to 35 ft and 18 in. in diameter on the Texas Edwards Plateau. The leaves and flower parts of Texas Buckeye appear to be only lightly pubescent on some specimens and heavily tomentose on others.

Red Buckeye

Aesculus pavia L. [D, E]

Field Identification. Shrub with an inclined stem, or more rarely a tree attaining a height of 28 ft and a diameter of 10 in. The crown is usually dense and the branches short, crooked, and ascending.

Flowers. March–May, panicles narrow to ovoid, erect, pubescent, 4–8 in. long; 1–numerous-flowered, pedicels slender, ¼–½ in.; flowers red, ¾–1½ in. long; calyx tubular, ⅜–⅝ in. long, dark

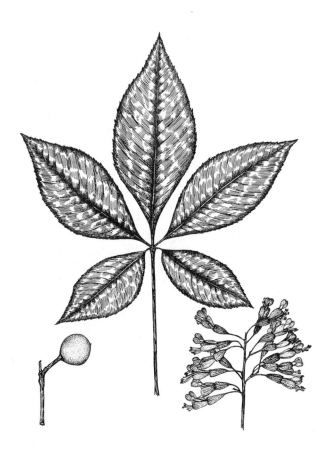

red, tube about five times as long as the rounded lobes; petals 4, red, connivent, ⅝−1 in. long, oblong to obovate, apex rounded, base narrowed into a claw, limbs of the 2 superior petals shorter than the 2 lateral pairs; stamens about equaling the longest petals, exserted, usually 8 in number, filaments filiform and villous below; ovary sessile, villous, 3-celled (or by abortion fewer), style slender.

Fruit. Capsule 1−2 in. in diameter, subglobose or obovoid, light brown, smooth but finely pitted, dehiscent into 2−3 valves; seeds 1−3, rounded, or flattened by pressure against each other, lustrous, light to dark brown, about 1 in. in diameter.

Leaves. Deciduous, opposite, palmately compound of 5 leaflets (rarely, 3 or 7), leaflets oblong to elliptic or oval to obovate, apex acute to short-acuminate, base gradually narrowed, margin coarsely serrate, leaflet length 3–6 in., width 1–1½ in., firm; upper surface lustrous, dark green, glabrous except a few hairs on the veins; lower surface paler, almost glabrous to densely tomentose; petiole nearly glabrous or with varying degree of hairiness, red, 3–7 in.

Bark. Gray to brown, smooth on young branches, on old trunks roughened into short plates which flake off in small, thin scales.

Twigs. Green to gray or brown, crooked, stout, smooth; lenticels pale brown to orange; leaf scars large and conspicuous, with 3 fibrovascular bundles.

Range. Mostly along streams of the coastal plains. East and central Texas to the Edwards Plateau, Oklahoma, and Arkansas; eastward through Louisiana to Florida, north to southern Illinois, and west to southeast Missouri.

Remarks. The genus name, *Aesculus,* is the ancient name for an old mast-bearing tree, and the species name, *pavia,* honors Peter Paaw (d. 1617) of Leyden. Some vernacular names in use for the plant are Scarlet Buckeye, Woolly Buckeye, Firecracker-plant, and

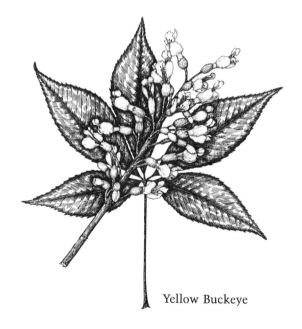

Yellow Buckeye

Fish-poison–bush. It is reported that the powdered bark is used in domestic medicine for toothache and ulcers, the roots are used for washing clothes, and the crushed fruit is used for fish poison.

At one time the common east Texas Buckeye (*A. pavia* L.) and the Woolly Buckeye (*A. discolor* Pursh, *A. discolor* var. *mollis* [Raf.] Sarg., *A. discolor* var. *flavescens* Sarg., and *A. austrina* Small) of the Edwards Plateau area of central Texas were considered as separate species. However, they have now been combined under the name of *A. pavia* L. Also, a yellow-flowered variation of the Edwards Plateau has been relegated to the position of a variety as *A. pavia* var. *flavescens* (Sarg.) Correll. It occurs mostly on the Edwards Plateau of Edwards and Kinney counties, especially near San Marcos, New Braunfels, Boerne, Comfort, and Kerrville.

On the edges of contact of the yellow and red forms, plants with yellow flowers deeply tinged or marked with red are found (see Correll and Johnston, *Manual of the Vascular Plants of Texas*, p. 1005).

SOAPBERRY FAMILY (Sapindaceae)

Western Soapberry

Sapindus saponaria L. var. *drummondii* (H. & A.) L. Benson
[D, E, F, G]

Field Identification. Tree attaining a height of 50 ft, with a diameter of 1–2 ft. The branches are usually erect to form a rounded crown.

Flowers. May–June, in large, showy panicles 5–10 in. long and 5–6 in. wide; perianth about ⅕₅ in. across; petals 4–5, obovate, rounded, white; sepals 4–5, acute, concave, ciliate on margin, shorter than the petals; stamens usually 8, inserted on the disk; style single, slender, with a 2–4-lobed stigma; ovary 3-lobed and 3-celled, each cell containing 1 ovule.

Fruit. September–October, globular, fleshy, from white to yellowish or blackish, translucent, persistent and shriveled; seed 1, obovoid, dark brown, the other 2 seeds seeming to atrophy.

Leaves. Short-petiolate, deciduous, alternate, 5–18 in. long, abruptly pinnate; leaflets 4–11 pairs, 1½–4 in. long, ½–¾ in. wide, falcate, lanceolate, acuminate at the apex, asymmetrical at

base, veiny, yellowish green, glabrous above, soft pubescent or glabrous beneath.

Bark. Gray to reddish, divided into narrow plates that break into small reddish scales.

Twigs. Yellowish green to gray, pubescent to glabrous, lenticels small.

Wood. Light brown or yellowish, close-grained, hard, strong, weighing 51 lb per cu ft.

Range. In moist soils along streams; Texas, New Mexico, Arizona, Oklahoma, and Arkansas; eastward into Louisiana, north to Missouri and Kansas, and south into Mexico.

Remarks. The genus name, *Sapindus*, is from *sapo* ("soap") and *Indus* ("Indies"), referring to the fact that some of the West Indian species are used for soap. The variety name, *drummondii*, is in honor of the botanist Thomas Drummond. Vernacular names are Amole de Bolita, Tehuistle, Palo Blanco, Jaboncillo, Wild China-tree, and Indian Soap-plant.

The fruit of this tree, and related species, contains the poisonous substance saponin, which produces a good lather in water. It is used in Mexico as a laundry soap. The fruit is also used medicinally as a remedy for renal disorders, rheumatism, and fevers. Buttons and necklaces are made from the seeds. The wood is of little value except for making baskets and frames and as fuel. Soapberry makes a desirable shade tree and could be more extensively planted for ornament. It has been cultivated since 1900 and is sometimes used for shelter-belt planting.

Mexican-buckeye

Ungnadia speciosa Endl. [D, E, F]

Field Identification. Western shrub or tree to 30 ft, and 10 in. in trunk diameter. Branches small and upright to spreading with an irregularly shaped crown.

Flowers. Borne in pubescent fascicles in spring, appearing with the leaves, or just before them; polygamous and irregular, about 1 in. across, fragrant; petals usually 4 or occasionally 5, rose-colored, deciduous, obovate, erect, clawed, margin crenulate, somewhat tomentose, with a tuft of fleshy hairs; disk 1-sided, oblique, tongue-shaped, connate with the ovary base; calyx campanulate, 5-lobed, lobes oblong-lanceolate; stamens 7–10, unequal, exserted, inserted on edge of disk, filaments filiform and pink, anthers oblong and red; ovary ovoid, stipitate, hairy, 3-celled, rudimentary in the staminate flower, ovules 2; style subulate, elongate, filiform, slightly upcurved; stigma terminal, minute.

Fruit. Capsule stipitate, broad-ovoid, crowned by the style remnants, about 2 in. broad, leathery, roughened, reddish brown, 3-celled and 3-valved, dehiscent in October while still on the trees, but hardly opening wide enough to release the large seeds; seeds usually solitary because of the abortion of the others, about ½ in. in diameter, round, smooth, shining, black or brown, hilum scar broad.

Leaves. Odd-pinnately compound, alternate, deciduous, 5–12 in. long, leaflets 5–7 (rarely, 3), ovate to lanceolate, apex acuminate, base rounded or cuneate, margin crenate-serrate, 3–5 in. long, 1½–2 in. wide, rather leathery, upper surface dark green, lustrous and glabrous, lower surface paler and pubescent to glabrous; petiole 2–6 in.; petiolule of terminal leaflet ¼–1 in.; lateral leaflets sessile or very short-petioluled.

Twigs. Buds imbricate, ovate to almost globose, leaf scars large and obcordate, twigs slender, terete, brown to orange and pubescent at first, later reddish brown and glabrous.

Bark. Mottled gray to brown, thin, tight, smooth, broken into shallow fissures on old trunks.

Wood. Reddish brown, sapwood lighter, brittle, soft, close-grained.

Range. Usually in limestone soils of stream banks, moist canyons, or on bluffs. In Texas, New Mexico, and Mexico. In Texas of greatest abundance west of the Brazos River. A few trees found as far east as Harris County, Texas. In Mexico in the states of Nuevo León, Coahuila, and Chihuahua.

Remarks. The genus name, *Ungnadia*, is in honor of Baron Ungnad, ambassador of Emperor Rudolph II. The species name, *spe-*

ciosa, means showy, with reference to the flowers. Also known under the vernacular names of Monillo, Texas-buckeye, Spanish-buckeye, New Mexican-buckeye, False-buckeye, and Canyon-buckeye. The tree should be grown more for ornament, being very beautiful in the spring. The flowers resemble Redbud or Peach blossoms at a distance. It is also a source of honey. The sweet seeds are poisonous to human beings. Seemingly a few may be eaten with impunity, but a number cause stomach disturbances. The leaves and fruit may also cause some minor poisoning to livestock, but they are seldom browsed except in times of stress. Children in west Texas sometimes use the round seeds for marbles.

Rain-tree

Koelreuteria paniculata Laxm. [D]

Field Identification. A cultivated, deciduous, ornamental tree to 30 ft tall with a rounded crown. Conspicuous by the large panicles of yellow flowers in summer, followed later by the reddish brown, bladdery fruit capsule. Leaves usually pinnate-compound.

Flowers. Borne July–August in wide terminal panicles to 18 in. long, polygamous. Flowers numerous, about ½ in. long, irregular; calyx of 5 unequal lobes; petals 3–4, lanceolate, strongly reflexed, clawed, with 2 upturned appendages at the cordate base; disk crenate above, between petals and stamens; stamens 8 or fewer, filaments long, distinct; ovary superior, usually 3-celled, each cell 2-ovuled; style 3-parted.

Fruit. Capsule 1½–2 in. long, inflated; the 3 loculicidally dehiscent valves with papery walls, ovoid-oblong in shape, narrowed into a mucronate apex. The rounded seeds black.

Leaves. Alternate, to 14 in. long, pinnate, or sometimes bipinnate; leaflets 7–15; shape ovate to oblong-ovate, 1–3¼ in. long; margins coarsely and irregularly crenate-serrate, sometimes incisely lobed or pinnatisect; upper surface dark green and glabrous; lower surface paler and pubescent or glabrous on veins. Winter buds small with 2 outer scales.

Range. Native to China, Korea, and Japan. Often cultivated for ornament.

Remarks. The genus name, *Koelreuteria*, honors Joseph G. Koelreuter (1733–1806), professor of natural history at Karlsruhe. The

species name, *paniculata*, refers to the panicled flowers. Some vernacular names are China-tree, Varnish-tree, and Pride-of-India. It is not to be confused with the China-berry tree (*Melia azedarach*) which bears some of the same vernacular names. Rain-tree was introduced into cultivation in 1763.

BUCKTHORN FAMILY (Rhamnaceae)

Texas Colubrina

Colubrina texensis (Torr. & Gray) Gray [D, E, F]

Field Identification. Thicket-forming shrub rarely over 15 ft, with light gray divaricate twigs.

Flowers. April–May, borne in axillary, subsessile clusters; perfect, tomentose, greenish yellow, less than ⅓ in. across; petals 5, hooded and clawed; calyx 5-lobed, persistent on the fruit, lobes triangular-ovate; stamens 5, inserted below the disk, opposite the petals, filaments filiform; ovary 3-celled, immersed in the disk, styles 3, stigma obtuse.

Fruit. Pedicels recurved, ¼–⅓ in. long, drupes borne at the twig nodes, ovate to subglobose, tomentose at first, later glabrous, dry, crustaceous, brown or black, about ⅓ in. in diameter, style persistent to form a beak, separating into 2–3 nutlets; seeds one in each partition, about 3/16 in. long, rounded on the back, angled on the other 2 surfaces, dark brown, shiny, smooth.

Leaves. Simple, alternate or clustered, grayish green, blades 1/2–1 in. long, ovate, obovate or elliptic, densely hairy at first and glabrous later; 3-nerved, margin denticulate and ciliate; apex rounded, sometimes apiculate; base cuneate, rounded, truncate or subcordate; petioles 1/8–3/8 in. or less, hairy, reddish.

Twigs. Slender, ashy gray, noticeably divergent, scarcely spiniferous, densely white-tomentose at first but glabrous later.

Bark. Gray, smooth, close, cracked into small, short scales later.

Range. Central, western, and southwestern Texas and New Mexico; Mexico in the states of Nuevo León, Coahuila, and Tamaulipas.

Remarks. The genus name, *Colubrina*, is from *coluber* ("a serpent"), perhaps for the twisting, divaricate branches or for the sinuate grooves on the stems of some species. The species name, *texensis*, refers to the state of Texas. A vernacular name is Hogplum. The dark brown or black drupes are persistent.

Bluewood Condalia

Condalia hookeri M. C. Johnst. [D, E, F, G]

Field Identification. Thicket-forming spinescent shrub or tree to 30 ft, with a diameter of 8 in. The branches are rigid and divaricate.

Flowers. Solitary, or 2–4 in axillary clusters, sessile, or on short pedicels about 1/16 in. long; calyx 1/16–1/8 in. broad, glabrous or nearly so; sepals 5, green, spreading, triangular, acute, persistent; disk fleshy, flat, somewhat 5-angled; petals absent; stamens 5, shorter than the sepals, incurved, inserted on the disk margin; ovary superior, 1-celled, or sometimes imperfectly 2–3-celled, styles stout and short, stigma 3-lobed.

Fruit. Ripening at intervals during the summer, drupe black at maturity, shiny, smooth, subglobose, somewhat flattened at apex, 1/4–1/3 in. in diameter, thin-skinned, fleshy, sweet, juice purple; seed solitary, ovoid to globose, flattened, acute at one end and truncate at the other, light brown, crustaceous, about 1/8 in. long.

Leaves. Alternate, or fascicled on short, spinescent branches, obovate to broadly spatulate, margin entire, apex rounded to retuse or truncate and mucronate, base attenuate or cuneate, leathery,

⅓–1½ in. long, ⅓–½ in. wide; light green and lustrous, pubescent at first, glabrous later, paler beneath, midrib prominent, sub-sessile or short-petioled.

Twigs. Divaricate, ending in slender, reddish or gray thorns, green to brown or gray, finely velvety-pubescent at first but glabrous later.

Bark. Smooth, pale gray to brown or reddish on branches and young trunks. Old trunks with narrow, flat ridges, deep furrows, and breaking into small, thin scales.

Wood. Light red, sapwood yellow, close-grained, heavy, hard, dense, specific gravity 1.20.

Range. Dry soil, central, southern, and western Texas. On the Texas coast from Matagorda County to Cameron County, frequent along the lower Rio Grande. In central Texas in greatest abundance on the limestone plateau area and west to the Pecos River. Less common west of the Pecos and north into the Panhandle area of Texas. Also in Mexico in Nuevo León and Tamaulipas.

Remarks. The genus name, *Condalia*, is in honor of Antonio Condal, Spanish physician of the eighteenth century, and the species name, *hookeri*, is for Joseph Dalton Hooker (1817–1911) of England. Some vernacular names are Brazil, Logwood, Purple Haw, Capulin, Capul Negro, and Chaparral. The wood yields a blue dye, and is sometimes used for fuel. The flower pollen serves as bee food, and the black fruit makes good jelly, but it is difficult to gather because of the thorns. Birds eagerly devour the fruit. The bushes often form impenetrable thickets.

A variety has been described as the Edwards Bluewood, *C. hookeri* var. *edwardsiana* (V. L. Cory) M. C. Johnst. It differs from the typical species in its longer and narrower light-colored leaves, which are spatulate instead of obovate. At the type locality the tallest shrubs were about 9 ft high, the average was about 7½ ft. The type locality was 29 airline miles northwest of Rocksprings, Edwards County, Texas, at an altitude of approximately 2,400 ft.

Lote-bush Condalia

Zizyphus obtusifolia (T. & G.) Gray [D, E, F]

Field Identification. Stiff, spiny, much-branched shrub with grayish green grooved twigs.

Flowers. Inconspicuous, in clustered umbels; pedicels ¹⁄₂₅–¹⁄₁₂ in. long, pubescent or villous; corolla small, green, 5-parted; petals 5, hooded and clawed, shorter than the sepals; sepals 5, triangular, acute, soft-hairy; stamens 5, inserted on the edge of the disk, opposite the petals; filaments subulate with anther sacs opening lengthwise; style partly 2-cleft with a basal 2–3-celled ovary immersed in a flattened, obscurely 5-lobed disk.

Fruit. In June, drupe globular, ¹⁄₃–²⁄₅ in. in diameter, black, fleshy, not palatable; stone solitary, hard, with a thin, membranous testa.

Leaves. Alternate, green, thin, firm, glabrous or puberulent, blades ½–1¼ in. long, elliptic, ovate, or narrowly oblong; apex obtuse, acute, retuse or occasionally emarginate; margin entire to coarsely serrate; base narrowed and 3-veined; petioles one-third to one-fourth as long as the blade.

Twigs. Divaricate, grayish green, grooved, glaucous; spines stout, straight or nearly so, green or brown, to 3 in. long.

Bark. Smooth, light or dark gray.

Range. Widespread in central, southern, and western Texas. At altitudes of 5,000 ft in the Chisos Mountains in Brewster County

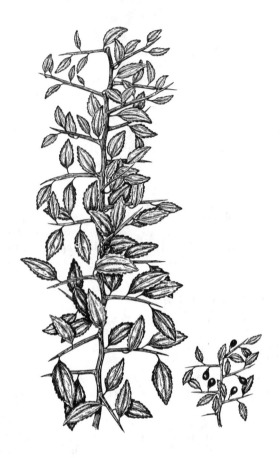

to almost sea level at the mouth of the Rio Grande in Cameron County. On the central Texas limestone plateau. Also in Arizona, New Mexico, and northern Mexico.

Remarks. The genus name, *Zizyphus*, is from an ancient Greek name derived from the Persian *zizafun*. The species name, *obtusifolia*, is for the obtuse-pointed leaves. Other names used at one time are *Z. lycioides* Gray and *Condalia lycioides* (Gray) Weberb. Vernacular names are Texas Buckthorn, Chaparral, Chaparro Prieto, and Abrojo. The mealy drupe is edible but not tasty. It is eaten by gray fox, raccoon, and various birds. The roots are used as a soap substitute and as a treatment for sores and wounds of domestic animals.

Common Jujube

Zizyphus jujuba Lam. [D]

Field Identification. Tree to 50 ft, with a diameter of 10 in. The short trunk supports slender ascending branches formed into a rounded head.

Flowers. Borne March–May in the axils of the leaves, solitary or a few together on glabrous pedicels ¹⁄₁₆–³⁄₁₆ in. long; flowers perfect, ¹⁄₁₆–¹⁄₈ in. across, yellowish green; calyx campanulate, spreading, 5-lobed, lobes ovate-triangular, acute, keeled within; petals 5, hooded, clawed, ¹⁄₂₅–¹⁄₁₂ in. long, much smaller than the sepals and alternating with them; stamens 5, as long as the petals or shorter and opposite to them; ovary 2–4-loculed, style 2-parted.

Fruit. Ripe July–November, slender-pediceled, drupe very variable in size and shape, subglobose to oblong, ½–1 in. long, green at first, turning yellowish, reddish brown or black at maturity, pulp yellow, sweet, shriveling later, acidulous; 1–3-celled; seeds usually 2, deeply furrowed, oblong, reddish brown to gray, apices pointed, about ¾ in. long.

Leaves. Alternate on short thickened spurlike twigs, often somewhat fascicled, ovate to oblong or lanceolate; apex obtuse; base rounded or broadly cuneate, sometimes inequilateral; margin shallowly toothed, some teeth minutely mucronulate; distinctly 3-nerved at base; upper surface dark waxy green and glabrous; lower surface paler and the 3 nerves more conspicuous, glabrous to pubescent, stipules spinescent.

Twigs. Stout, green to gray or black, some nodes thickened, lateral branchlets thickened and leaves often fascicled on them. Spinelike stipules ⅛–¾ in. long, straight or curved.

Bark. Mottled gray or black, smooth on younger branches, on older branches and trunks roughly furrowed and peeling in loose shaggy strips.

Range. Grows on most soils, except very heavy clays or swampy ground. Considered to be a native of Syria. Widely distributed in the warmer parts of Europe, south Asia, Africa, and Australia. Cultivated in North America in Florida, California, and the Gulf Coast states. First introduced into America from Europe by Robert Chisholm in 1837 and planted in Beaufort, North Carolina.

Remarks. The genus name, *Zizyphus*, is from an ancient Greek name derived from the Persian *zizafun*. The species name, *jujuba*, is the French common name, derived from the Arabic. The tree is also known as the Chinese Date. It is popular with the Chinese and as many as 400 varieties have been cultivated by them. The fruit exhibits great variety in shape, size, and color, sometimes becoming as large as a hen egg. It is processed with sugar and honey and is sold in Chinese shops.

In India the wood is used for fuel and small timber, and the leaves for cattle fodder and as food for the Tasar silkworm and lac insect. In Europe it has long been used as a table dessert and dry winter sweetmeat. The Common Jujube has also been used in shelter-belt planting and for wildlife food. *Z. jujuba* var. *inermis* is a thornless variety.

Carolina Buckthorn

Rhamnus caroliniana Walt. [D, E, F]

Field Identification. Shrub or small tree attaining a height of 35 ft, with a diameter of 8 in.

Flowers. May–June, borne solitary or 2–10 in pedunculed umbels, peduncles to ⅖ in. long or often absent, pedicels ⅛–¼ in.; flowers

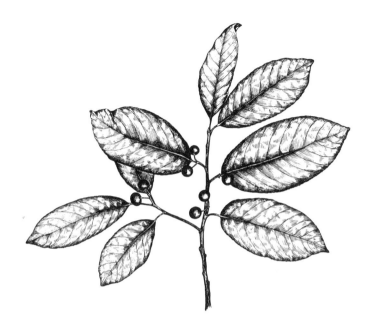

perfect, small, greenish yellow; petals 5, each about ⅟₂₅ in. long or broad, apex broad and notched, base acute, concave; stamens 5, included, anthers and filaments less than ⅟₂₅ in. long; style equaling the calyx-tube, stigma 3-lobed, ovary glabrous and 3-celled; calyx-tube campanulate, about ⅟₁₂ in. long, ⅛ in. wide at apex, the 5 sepals glabrous and triangular, apices acuminate.

Fruit. Drupes August–October, persistent, sweet, spherical, ⅓–⅖ in. in diameter, red at first, at maturity black and lustrous, 3-seeded (occasionally 2–4-seeded); seeds ⅕–¼ in. long, reddish brown, rounded almost equally at apex and base, rounded dorsally, inner side with a triangular ridge from the apex to notch at base.

Leaves. Abundant, scattered along the branches, simple, alternate, deciduous, elliptic to broadly oblong, apex acute or acuminate, base cuneate to acute or rounded, sometimes inequilateral, margin indistinctly serrulate or subentire, rather thin, prominently parallel-veined; upper surface bright green, smooth and lustrous, pubescent to glabrous; lower surface velvety pubescent to only puberulent or glabrous, length of blade 2–6 in., width 1–2 in., turning yellow in the fall; petiole slender, ⅖–⅗ in., widened at base, glabrous or pubescent.

Twigs. Slender, young ones green to reddish, later gray; pubescent at first, glabrous later; sometimes terminating in a cluster of very small folded leaves.

Bark. Gray to brown, sometimes blotched, smoothish, furrows shallow.

Wood. Light brown, sapwood yellow, close-grained, fairly hard, rather weak, weighing 34 lb per cu ft.

Range. Most often in low grounds in eastern, central, and western Texas as far west as the Pecos River, Arkansas, Oklahoma, and Louisiana; eastward to Florida, northward to North Carolina, and west to Missouri.

Remarks. The genus name, *Rhamnus*, is from an ancient Greek word. The species name, *caroliniana*, refers to the state of South Carolina where it grows. Other vernacular names are Yellow Buckthorn, Indian-cherry, Bog-birch, Alder-leaf Buckthorn, and Polecat-tree. The fruit is eaten by several species of birds, especially the catbird. The shrub appears susceptible to the crown rust of oats. The handsome leaves and fruit make the tree a good ornamental possibility. It is apparently adjustable to both moderately acid and alkaline soil types.

LINDEN FAMILY (Tiliaceae)

American Linden

Tilia americana L. [D]

Field Identification. Tree known to attain a height of 130 ft, with a diameter of 4 ft. The branches are usually small and horizontal, or drooping, forming a broad, round-topped head. The root system is wide-spreading, and root sprouts often grow at the base of the trunk.

Flowers. May–June, perfect, borne in loose drooping cymes with pedicels slender and glabrous, 6–15-flowered; peduncle 1½–4 in., slender and glabrous, attached to a large foliaceous bract; bract 2–5 in. long, ¾–1½ in. wide, membranous, glabrous, strongly veined, narrowly oblong, apex rounded or obtuse, base narrowed, sessile or short-stalked; sepals 5, small, ovate, acuminate, pubescent within, puberulent externally, considerably shorter than the

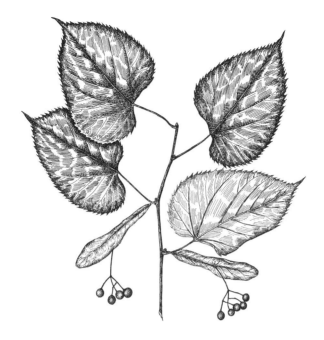

petals; petals 5, yellowish white, lanceolate, crenate, alternate with the sepals, a small scale alternating with each petal; stamens numerous, shorter than the petals; ovary 1, 5-celled, each cell 2-ovuled, ovules anatropous; style simple and tomentose.

Fruit. Drupaceous, dry, persistent, globose to ovoid, apex rounded or pointed, ¼–⅓ in. long, densely brown-tomentose; 1–2-seeded.

Leaves. Simple, alternate, deciduous, broad-ovate, apex acute or acuminate, base commonly unsymmetrical, obliquely cordate or almost truncate, margin coarsely serrate, individual teeth with slender, gland-tipped apices; thick and firm, upper surface dark green and glabrous, lower surface paler green and glabrous or some with axillary tufts of hairs, length of blades 5–6 in., width 3–4 in., prominently yellow-veined; petioles 1½–2 in. long, about one-third the length of the blade.

Twigs. Slender, somewhat divaricate, glabrous, smooth, green to brown, gray later; lenticels numerous, oblong; winter buds dark red, ovoid, about ¼ in. long, mucilaginous; leaf scars half-elliptic, stipule scars conspicuous.

Bark. Light brown to gray, about 1 in. thick on the trunk, the deep furrows separated by narrow, flat-topped, confluent ridges which shed small thin scales.

Wood. Light brown to reddish brown, straight-grained, rather soft, moderately weak in bending and endwise compression, low in shock resistance, works well with hand tools, finishes smoothly, holds glue, paint, and lacquer well, resistant to splitting, holds nails poorly, seasons well but shrinks considerably, low in durability, weighing 28 lb per cu ft.

Range. Rich, moist soil of woods and bottom lands. Northeast Texas, Oklahoma, Arkansas, Missouri, Tennessee, Kentucky, and Georgia; north to Nebraska, Kansas, North Dakota, Minnesota, Illinois, Indiana, Michigan, Pennsylvania, Maine, New Brunswick, Quebec, and Ontario.

Remarks. *Tilia* is the classical Latin name, and the species name, *americana*, refers to its distribution. It has many vernacular names, such as Bast-tree, Lin-tree, Lime-tree, Bee-tree, Blacklime-tree, White Lind, Whitewood, Southern Lind, American Basswood, Yellow Basswood, Whistlewood, Spoonwood, Daddynuts, Monkeynuts, and Wickyup.

The American Linden has been cultivated for ornament since 1752. The tough inner bark was formerly used for mat fiber and rope by the Indians. The flowers are valuable for bee pasture, and young trees furnish wildlife cover. The fruit is known to be eaten by a number of species of birds and rodents. The wood is valuable for paper pulp, woodenware, cheap furniture, plywood, veneers, panels, cooperage, boxes and crates, casks and coffins, handles, shades, blinds, fixtures, appliances, excelsior, and millwork.

Carolina Linden

Tilia caroliniana Mill. [D]

Field Identification. Large tree with an irregular, rounded top.

Flowers. Borne on slender peduncles, pubescent, in 8–15-flowered cymes and subtended by conspicuous papery bracts; bracts linear, elliptic to obovate, cuneate at the base, rounded or acute at apex, somewhat pubescent at first, becoming glabrous later, 4–5 in. long, about ⅘ in. wide, decurrent or almost so to the peduncle base; sepals 5, shorter than petals, ovate, acuminate, ciliate, brown-pubescent on the exterior, white-hairy within; petals 5,

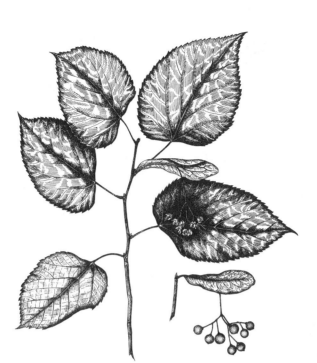

lanceolate, acuminate, somewhat longer than sepals; stamens many, with filaments forked at apex; staminodia about as long as sepals; ovary superior, 5-celled, with a slender style and 5-lobed stigma.

Fruit. Nutlet subglobose to ellipsoid, apiculate, tomentose, or pubescent, rather small, about ⅛ in. in diameter, 1–3-seeded.

Leaves. Alternate, simple, deciduous, blades 2⅓–4½ in. long, 1¾–3½ in. wide, broadly ovate, abruptly acuminate, base truncate or cordate and asymmetrical; margin coarsely dentate with glandular apiculate teeth; upper surface dark green, lustrous and glabrous at maturity, lower surface thinly tomentose with brownish fascicled hairs; leaves tomentose on both sides when young; petioles stout, glabrous or slightly pubescent, 1–1½ in.

Twigs. Slender, reddish brown, pubescent at first, glabrous later.

Bark. Gray, with shallow fissures and flat ridges.

Wood. Light-colored, soft, light, easily worked.

Range. Central and eastern Texas, southwestern Arkansas, and western Louisiana; eastward to Georgia and Florida, and north to North Carolina.

Remarks. The genus name, *Tilia*, is the classical name, and the species name, *caroliniana*, refers to the states of Carolina. Vernacular names are Basswood, Lime-tree, Whitewood, and Bee Basswood. The tree is a rapid grower and is often planted for ornament. The flowers make good honey, and the wood is used with other species for making interior finishing and woodenware. The species has a variety known as *T. caroliniana* var. *rhoophila* Sarg., which occurs in Arkansas, Louisiana, and Texas, west to the Guadalupe River. It is distinguished by pubescent twigs and winter buds, larger leaves, and tomentose clusters of more numerous flowers.

MALLOW FAMILY (Malvaceae)

Shrub-althea

Hibiscus syriacus L. [D, E]

Field Identification. Much-branched shrub or small tree 3–18 ft. Often grown for ornament and developed into a large number of horticultural forms with single and double, variously colored flowers.

Flowers. Showy, perfect, solitary, axillary, on peduncles of variable length; bractlets subtending the calyx usually 5–7, ³⁄₈–³⁄₄ in. long, linear to linear-spatulate; calyx longer or shorter than the bractlets; sepals 5, triangular ovate or lanceolate, about as long as the tube; petals 5, very variable in color in the many horticultural forms, white, pink, lavender, rose, with a crimson or purplish blotch at the base, 1¾–3 in. long, rounded to obovate, margins sometimes undulate; staminal column prominent with numerous anthers below, and apex 5-parted with capitate stigmas; ovary sessile, 5-celled and loculicidally 5-valved.

Fruit. Capsule oblong-ovoid, apex drawn tightly, ³⁄₄–1 in. long, pubescent, more or less dry, larger than the calyx.

Leaves. Alternate, triangular to rhombic-ovate or elliptic to oval, blades 1½–4¾ in. long, margin variously crenate-toothed or notched with rounded or acutish teeth, usually more or less 3-

lobed also; young leaves pubescent, when older becoming glabrous or nearly so; palmately veined with 3 veins more conspicuous; petioles generally shorter than the blades; winter buds
minute. Some forms with variegated leaves are known.

Bark. Gray to brown, somewhat roughened.

Range. Cultivated in gardens and occasionally escaping to roadsides, thickets, and woods. Texas, Oklahoma, Arkansas, and Louisiana; eastward to Florida and northward to Missouri, Ohio, and
Massachusetts. Also in coastal regions of Canada.

Remarks. The genus name, *Hibiscus,* is the ancient name of the
European Marsh-mallow, and the species name, *syriacus,* is for

Syria, where it was once supposed to be native. However, more recent investigations prove it to be originally from China and India. It is also known under the vernacular names of Rose-of-Sharon and Rose-mallow. It was introduced into cultivation about 1600.

CHOCOLATE FAMILY (Sterculiaceae)

Chinese Parasol-tree

Firmiana simplex W. F. Wight [D, E]

Field Identification. Cultivated shrub or tree to 35 ft, with a smooth green bark and a rounded crown.

Flowers. In a pubescent, terminal panicle 4–12 in. long; flowers monoecious, small, greenish yellow; petals absent; calyx petal-like, sepals 5, valvate, colored, linear to narrowly oblong, reflexed, ⅓–⅖ in. long; stamens united in a column, bearing a head of 10–15 sessile anthers; carpels 5, nearly distinct above, each terminating into a peltate stigma, carpels 2¼–4 in. long at maturity.

Fruit. A follicle, stipitate, leathery, carpels veiny, finely pubescent, distinct before maturity and spreading open into 5 leaflike bodies bearing 2–several seeds on their margins; seeds globular, pealike, about ¼ in. or less in diameter, albuminous; carpels rudimentary and free in the staminate flowers. A peculiar feature is the black or brown fluid which covers the fruit and is liberated when the follicle bursts.

Leaves. Alternate, simple, blades 4–12 in. broad and long, cordate to orbicular, palmately 3–5-lobed, lobes entire and acuminate, dull green and glabrous or lightly pubescent above, lower surface glabrous to tomentulose; petiole glabrous or pubescent, usually 5–18 in. long.

Twigs. Stout, smooth, grayish green, bark of trunk also smooth and green.

Range. A native of Japan and China. Cultivated in the United States and escaping to roadsides, woods, and thickets. From South Carolina to Florida and westward to Texas and California. Hardy as far north as Washington.

Remarks. The genus name, *Firmiana*, honors Karl Joseph von Firmian (1718–1782), at one time governor of Lombardy. The species name, *simplex*, refers to the lobed but simple leaves. It is also known as Varnish-tree, Phoenix-tree, and Bottle-tree. It is an excellent tree for lawn and shade and has been cultivated since 1757, being easily grown from seed.

A variety with creamy white, variegated leaves is known as *F. simplex* var. *variegata*. Two other species are cultivated in California.

TAMARISK FAMILY (Tamaricaceae)

French Tamarisk

Tamarix gallica L. [D, E, F, G]

Field Identification. Shrub with contorted branches, or a tree to 30 ft, with a twisted trunk.

Flowers. Borne in summer on the current wood, in white or pink racemes, which are grouped to form terminal panicles of variable length; pedicels about $\frac{1}{50}$ in. long; sepals 5, $\frac{1}{25}-\frac{1}{12}$ in. long, ovate; corolla petals 5, $\frac{1}{25}-\frac{1}{12}$ in. long, oblong, mostly deciduous from the mature fruit; stamens 5, filaments $\frac{1}{12}-\frac{1}{10}$ in., enlarged toward the base and attached to the corners of the 5-angled disc, anthers mucronate, 2-celled; ovary $\frac{1}{25}-\frac{1}{15}$ in. long, set on the disk; styles 3, about $\frac{1}{50}$ in. long, clavate.

Fruit. Capsule very small, $\frac{1}{12}-\frac{1}{8}$ in. long, dehiscing into 3 parts; seeds numerous, minute, tufted with hairs at apex.

Leaves. Foliage sparse, delicate, grayish green, scalelike, alternate, imbricate, $\frac{1}{50}-\frac{1}{8}$ in. long, deltoid to lanceolate, acute to acuminate, entire and scarious, glabrous; bracts $\frac{1}{25}-\frac{1}{15}$ in. long.

Branches. Drooping and graceful, often sweeping the ground, young ones glabrous or glaucous, reddish to gray later.

Wood. Light-colored, close-grained, takes a high polish, often twisted or knotty.

Range. French Tamarisk was introduced to the United States from Europe. It now grows as an escape from cultivation from Texas eastward to Florida, westward to California, and north to Arkansas and South Carolina.

Remarks. The genus name, *Tamarix*, is the ancient name, probably with reference to the Tamaracine people of southern Europe, where the plant grew. The species name, *gallica*, refers to a Gallic tribe, who lived where the plant grew. Other names are Salt-cedar, Manna-bush, Athel, Eshel, Asul, Athul, and Atle. The low-sweeping branches make excellent wildlife cover.

African Tamarisk, *T. africana* Poir., has black to dark purple bark, sessile leaves, and flowers borne in racemes $1\frac{1}{4}-2\frac{3}{4}$ in. long; $\frac{1}{4}-\frac{1}{3}$ in. broad, smaller on green branches of the current year; bracts longer than pedicels. Flowers pentamerous; sepals subentire; the outer 2 slightly keeled and longer than the inner more obtuse ones; petals 5, ovate to broadly trulliform-ovate,

about ¹⁄₁₂–¹⁄₈ in. long in vernal flowers, ¹⁄₈ in. long or more in aestival; staminal filaments inserted on gradually tapering lobes of disk. A native of the European and Mediterranean region. Grown in California, Arizona, Texas, and South Carolina.

Five-stamen Tamarisk, *T. pentandra* Pallas, is a shrub or small tree 10–15 ft high. The branches are long, slender, and plumose, the shoots purplish when young. The largest leaves ¹⁄₁₂–¹⁄₈ in. long, lanceolate, others very small, scalelike, crowded, rather

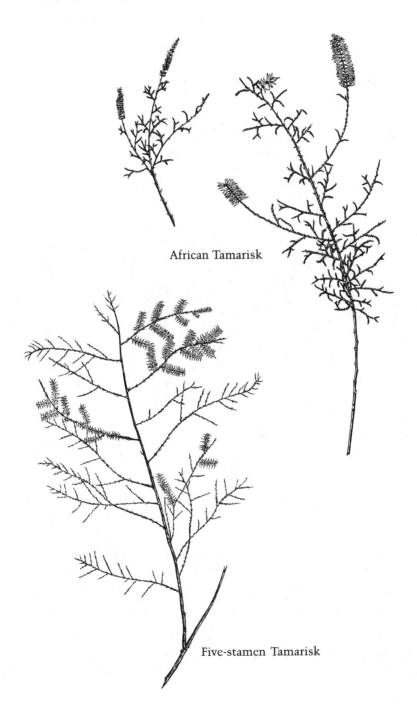

African Tamarisk

Five-stamen Tamarisk

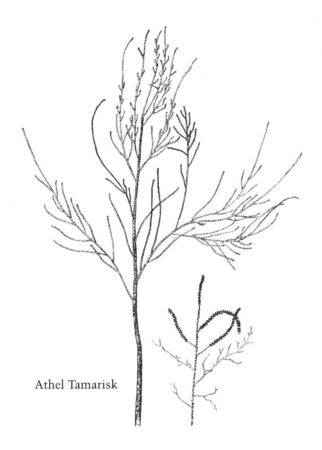

Athel Tamarisk

glaucous. Flowers rosy pink, usually borne August–September, about ⅛ in. wide, in cylindrical racemes 1–2 in. long; the current season's shoots transformed into slender panicles; bearing 5 stamens. A native of southeastern Europe. First cultivated in 1880 and is late flowering. It may be pruned back hard in the winter. Also listed as *T. pallasii*.

Athel Tamarisk, *T. aphylla* Karst., may be either a bush or tree to 25 ft high. The branches are fastigiate, long, slender, cylindrical-jointed. Leaves reduced to a very short sheath minutely glandular-pitted and salt-secreting with a minute point. Flowers borne in July on more or less interrupted spikes, bisexual, nearly sessile, pink in color, about ⅛ in. broad. Also listed under the names of *T. articulata* or *T. orientalis*. A native of India and Africa. Extensively cultivated in coastal Texas, Arizona, and California.

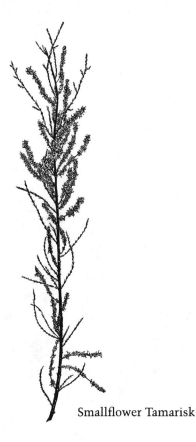

Smallflower Tamarisk

Smallflower Tamarisk, *T. parviflora* DC., has brown to deep purple bark and may be a shrub or small tree 12–18 ft high. Branches slender and dark purple. Leaves sessile, ovate, scalelike with hard points. Flowers in April–May, pale pink in slender racemes about 1 in. long, and ⅛–⅕ in. broad, often on the preceding year's branches; bracts diaphanous, longer than pedicels; sepals eroded-denticulate, the outer 2 trulliform or ovate, acute and keeled, the inner 2 ovate and obtuse; petals usually 4, parabolic or ovate, about 1/12 in. long; stamens 4 or sometimes more, emerging gradually from the disk lobes. A native of southeastern Europe. First cultivated in 1853. Introduced and widely cultivated in the United States.

CACTUS FAMILY (Cactaceae)

Walking-stick Cholla

Opuntia imbricata (Haworth) DC. [F, G]

Field Identification. An arborescent cactus, with a short, woody trunk, and many erect candelabrumlike branches. Attaining a height of 9 ft and trunk diameter of 10 in. Sometimes forming dense thickets.

Flowers. Terminal, 1½–2½ in. long, 2–3 in. broad, petals purple, rounded to obovate, ovary tuberculate, upper areoles with a few bristles.

Fruit. Yellow, dry, 1–1½ in. long, nearly hemispheric, tuberculate-cristate, sometimes falling off and producing new plants from the sprouting tubercles; seeds 1/12–1/6 in. in diameter.

Joints. Cylindric, ¾–1¼ in. in diameter, strongly and prominently tuberculate-crested, tubercles ¾–1 in. long, flattened laterally, very spiny.

Leaves. Terete, ⅓–1 in. long, soon deciduous.

Spines. Stellate-divaricate, 8–30, length ¾–1¼ in., barbed almost entirely, with papery, white to green, brown-tipped sheaths.

Range. Texas, north to Oklahoma and Kansas, south and west through New Mexico. Collected by the author in the Big Bend National Park, Brewster County, Texas. Sometimes in lava-rock soil of foothills.

Remarks. The genus name, *Opuntia*, is from Opus, a town in ancient Greece. The species name, *imbricata*, means "overlapping," with reference to the ridges of the joints. It is also known as Cholla, Tree Cactus, Cane Cactus, Velas de Coyote, Candelabrum Cactus, Devil's Rope, Coyote Prickly Pear, Cardenche, Tuna Juell, Goconoxtie, Estrara, Xoconochtli, Xoconostle, Joconoxtle, Joconostle, Tarajo, Coyonostle, Coyonoxtle, Coyonostli, Tuna Joconctla, and Tuna Huell. The plant covers a wide area, and variable races are known, but they seem to be connected by intermediate forms.

The stems with the tissue removed form a hollow cylinder with a framework of rhombic holes and meshes. Woody skeletons of this sort are made into odd-looking walking canes. The fruit is not known to be eaten by man or animal. Although the spines are sometimes burned off, and the stems fed to cattle, they are not very palatable.

It is reported that before the introduction of coal-tar dyes into Mexico the fruit had an important place in the arts. The fruit was gathered, chopped into small pieces, and boiled, the fiber and seed being filtered out and the extract used to dissolve and set cochineal dye. It is still used this way to a limited extent. Its mordanting property is doubtless due to the high concentration of acids and salts of organic acid present.

Lindheimer Prickly Pear

Opuntia lindheimeri Engelm. [D, E, F, G]

Field Identification. A thicket-forming cactus, heavy-bodied, with a definite cylindrical trunk, erect, or much lower and prostrate. Attaining a height of 3–12 ft.

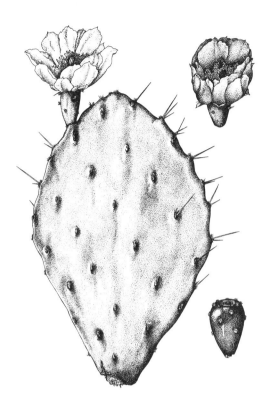

Flowers. April–June, numerous, shallowly bowl-shaped, usually 1 to an areole; sepals and petals numerous, intergrading, hardly distinct, yellow to orange or red, a plant usually producing only 1 shade of flowers, oval to obovate or spatulate, apices rounded or abruptly short-pointed, length ½–2½ in.; stamens numerous, much shorter than the petals; ovary inferior, 1-celled, ovules numerous on thick, fleshy stalks, placentae parietal, withered perianth crowning the ovary and later crowning the fruit; style longer than the stamens, single, thick, stigma lobes short.

Fruit. Ripening July–September, berry very variable in size and shape, clavate to oblong or globose, length ½–2½ in., red to purple, with scattered tufts of glochids; skin thin, rind thick, pulp juicy; seeds very numerous, about ⅛ in. long, flattened, curved, with a thick bony aril on the edge.

Leaves. Very small, ⅛–⅙ in. long, pointed, flattened, early deciduous.

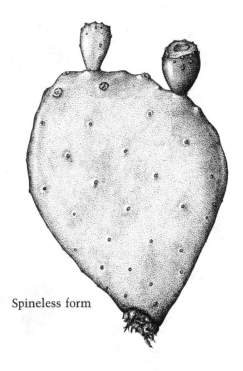

Spineless form

Joints. Green to bluish green, orbicular or obovate, or sometimes asymmetrical, length to 11 in., flat, waxy, succulent; set with areoles 1–2⅓ in. apart, which produce dense tufts of yellow to brown barbed, minute glochids less than ³⁄₁₆ in. long; larger spines 1–6, usually 1–2, one erect or semierect, the others generally smaller and somewhat spreading, color of spines pale yellow to almost white, sometimes brown or black at base; some joints spineless or nearly so. Some forms are known which lack spines.

Range. From coastal southwestern Louisiana westward in drier regions of central Texas (not in east Texas woodlands). The type specimen was collected at New Braunfels, Texas. It is common around San Antonio, Corpus Christi, and Brownsville, Texas. It is not to be confused with *O. engelmannii* of Trans-Pecos Texas.

Remarks. The genus name, *Opuntia*, is the Latinized name for the town Opus in ancient Greece. The species name, *lindheimeri*, is in honor of Ferdinand Lindheimer, a German-born botanist, who collected extensively in Texas in 1836 and 1842.

The plant and its relatives are known under many names in Latin-American countries, such as Nochtli, Culhua, Cancanopa, Pacal, Potzotz, Toat, Pare, Caha, Xantha, and more commonly Nopal. The fruit is known as "tuna."

The Indians and Mexican people formerly used the plant extensively for food. The fruits may be eaten raw or made into a preserve. The joints, when young and tender, are cooked and served with dressing and pepper, and are also made into candy. Syrup is made by boiling the ripe fruit and straining off the seed. The boiled and fermented juice is known as *colonche*. A thick paste made by boiling down the juice is known as *melcocha*. *Queso de tuna* (tuna cheese) is prepared from a pulp of the fruit seed. After evaporation, it is made into small cheeselike pieces. The Indians also believe that a tea made from the fruit will cure ailments caused by gallstones. Commercial alcohol has been made from the sap. The tender young joints are sometimes used as poultices to reduce inflammation. Juice of the joints is boiled with tallow in candlemaking to make the candles hard. The joints are made edible to cattle by burning off the spines. A number of animals and birds feed on the fruit. According to folklore, the coyote brushes the spines off the fruit with his tail before eating it.

The Nopal occupies a prominent place in the history and legend of Mexico. The Nopal and Caracara (Mexican Eagle) are the national emblems of Mexico. About 33 species of *Opuntia* are known in Texas, and about 250 species are found mostly in the southwestern United States, Mexico, and Central and South America.

OLEASTER FAMILY (Eleagnaceae)

Russian-olive

Elaeagnus angustifolius L. [D, E]

Field Identification. Cultivated shrub or small tree to 25 ft, with thorny or thornless branches. Easily recognized by the lanceolate-to-oblong leaves which are conspicuously silvery and brown-dotted beneath.

Flowers. In June, axillary, scattered on the branches in clusters of 1–3, short-pediceled; flowers small, pale yellow or silvery, fragrant, perfect, regular; petals absent; perianth campanulate, 4-

cleft, tube as long as the limb; stamens included, filaments short; style at base included by a tubular disk.

Fruit. Maturing August–October, drupelike, on peduncles about ¼ in.; fruit body ⅜–½ in. long, oval to ellipsoid, apex and base rounded or slightly flattened, yellow to tan, at first densely silvery or brown-scaly, later less so and becoming lustrous; flesh yellow, waxy, mealy, sweet; stone solitary, ellipsoid to oblong, about ⅜ in. long, brown, with darker longitudinal bands.

Leaves. Simple, alternate, blades 2–3½ in. long, ⅜–¾ in. wide, lanceolate to oblong-lanceolate, margin entire, apex acute, base gradually narrowed or cuneate; upper surface bright green with veins obscure except main vein; lower surface densely silvery-scaly, veins more evident; petiole ⅕–½ in., silvery-scaly.

Twigs. Slender, elongate, younger silvery-lepidote, older ones reddish brown, lenticels small and numerous; buds ovoid, ⅛–³⁄₁₆ in. long, silvery-scaly.

Range. Tolerant of considerable amounts of salinity or alkalinity, ascending to an altitude of 5,500 ft. Cultivated in the United States, and occasionally escaping in New Mexico, Arizona, and western Texas. A native of southern Europe and western Asia to the Himalaya Mountains.

Remarks. The genus name, *Elaeagnus*, is from the Greek word *elaia* ("olive") and the Latin *agnus* ("lamb"), probably with reference to the stellate pubescence on the undersides of the leaves. The species name, *angustifolius*, refers to the narrow leaves. Another vernacular name in use is Oleaster. The shrub is used in shelter-belt planting and is ornamental because of the silvery leaves and decorative fruit. It also has some value as a honey plant. The fruit is edible and is also beneficial to wildlife, being eaten by many species of birds. The plant is rarely attacked by insects and is drought resistant.

LOOSESTRIFE FAMILY (Lythraceae)

Common Crapemyrtle

Lagerstroemia indica L. [D, E]

Field Identification. Commonly cultivated shrub or small tree to 35 ft, with a very smooth fluted trunk.

Flowers. In showy, terminal panicles 2½–8 in. long, pedicels and peduncles bracted; corolla 1–1½ in. across; petals 5–7, but usually 6, purple, pink, white, red, lavender, or blue; stamens numerous, elongate, some upcurved; calyx of 5–8 sepals, shorter than the hypanthium; ovary 3–6-celled, style long and curved, stigma capitate.

Fruit. Capsule oval-globose, about ⅓ in. long; seeds with a winged apex.

Leaves. Opposite or alternate, deciduous, obovate-oval, entire, acute or obtuse, broad-cuneate or rounded at base, blades ½–2 in. long, subsessile, glabrous and lustrous above, paler and glabrous or pilose along veins beneath.

Twigs. Pale, glabrous, 4-angled.

Bark. Thin, exfoliating to expose a smooth, often convoluted, pale surface.

Range. A native of India. Cultivated extensively in Texas, Louisiana, Oklahoma, and Arkansas; eastward to Florida, and northward to Virginia. Also cultivated in California.

Remarks. The genus name, *Lagerstroemia*, is in honor of Magnus Lagerstroem (1696–1759), a Swedish friend of Linnaeus, and the species name, *indica*, is for India. Another vernacular name is Ladies' Streamer.

Some of the common color forms of crapemyrtle are Dwarf (*nana*), Dwarf Blue (*lavandula*), Pink, Purple (*purpurea*), Red (*magenta rubra*), and White (*alba*).

POMEGRANATE FAMILY (Punicaceae)

Pomegranate

Punica granatum L. [D, E]

Field Identification. Cultivated, clumped shrub or tree to 25 ft. The branches erect or ascending to form an irregularly shaped crown.

Flowers. In simple, axillary or terminal racemes with 1–5 solitary short-peduncled flowers; flowers to 2 in. across, perfect, perigynous, showy, usually red (occasionally white or pink); calyx tubular to campanulate, later subglobose, persistent; 5–7-lobed; lobes valvate, ascending, fleshy, triangular to lanceolate, apex acute, stiffly persistent in fruit; petals 5–7, inserted on the upper part of the calyx between the lobes, imbricate, wrinkled, ⅝–1 in. long, suborbicular or obovate; stamens numerous, in several series, filaments filiform; style 1, stigma capitate; ovary inferior, embedded in the calyx-tube, comprising several compartments in 2 series, ovules numerous.

Fruit. Berry maturing in September, pendulous, 2–4 in. in diameter, subglobose or depressed, crowned with the persistent calyx; rind thick, leathery, reddish yellow; pulp juicy, pink or red, acidulous; septa membranous, many-celled; seeds numerous, cotyledons convolute and auricled at base.

Leaves. Simple, deciduous, alternate, opposite or clustered, blades ¾–3½ in. long, oval to oblong or elliptic to lanceolate, apex obtuse or acute, base attenuate into a short wing, margin entire, surface bright green; main vein prominent below, impressed above, other veins inconspicuous, glabrous on both surfaces; petiole ⅛–⅓ in., grooved above, green to red; winter buds with 2 pairs of outer scales.

Twigs. Slender; younger ones green to reddish brown, somewhat striate or angular; older ones gray and more terete. Bark on older limbs and trunks gray to brown, smooth at first but eventually breaking into small, thin scales, shallowly reticulate.

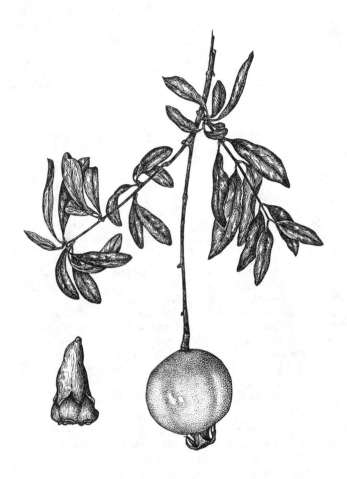

Wood. White to yellowish, hard, close-grained, specific gravity about 0.93.

Range. Old fields, waste places, and abandoned homesites. A native of Arabia, Iran, Bengal, China, and Japan. Hardy in the United States as far north as Washington, D.C., but does best in subtropical southern regions. Escaping cultivation in the Gulf Coast states.

Remarks. The genus name, *Punica*, is from the Latin words for "Punic apple," and the species name, *granatum*, means "many-seeded apple." Known in the countries of Central and South America under the Spanish and Indian names of Granada de

China, Granada Agria, Granado, Granada, Tzapyan, Yaga-zehi, and Yutnudidzi. The wood is sometimes used by engravers as a substitute for Boxwood (*Buxus*).

From the days of Solomon pomegranate has been used for making cooling drinks and sherbets; it is also eaten in its natural state. The astringent rind yields a black or red dye and has been used for tanning morocco leather and for ink. The fruit is sweet in the better varieties, and a spiced wine is made from the juice. The soft seeds are also eaten, sprinkled with sugar or, when dried, as a confection.

GINSENG FAMILY (Araliaceae)

Devil's Walkingstick

Aralia spinosa L. [D]

Field Identification. Spiny, few-branched shrub, or slender, flat-topped tree to 35 ft. Recognized by very large, twice-pinnate leaves which are 3–4 ft long and 2–4 ft wide.

Flowers. July–August the large terminal panicle of flowers is very conspicuous and is divided into smaller umbels of individual flowers. Pedicels light yellow; corolla white, ⅛ in. across; petals 5, ovate, acute; stamens 5, alternate with petals; ovary 5-celled or abortive, styles distinct, sepals triangular.

Fruit. September–October, drupe black, fleshy, juice purple, diameter about ¼ in., flattened, 3–5 angled, style persistent; seed solitary, oblong, rounded at ends, flattened, crustaceous, brownish.

Leaves. Alternate, compound, generally borne at top of trunk, blades 3–4 ft long, 2–4 ft wide, twice-pinnate; pinnae also pinnate with 5–6 pairs of lateral leaflets and a terminal leaflet; leaflets ovate, acute or acuminate, serrate or crenate, cuneate or rounded at base, dark green above, paler beneath, 1–4 in. long, tiny prickles often on midrib, yellow in autumn; petiole 18–20 in. long, clasping the base, prickly; stipules about 1 in. long, acute, ciliate.

Bark. Dark brown, fissures shallow, ridges irregular, armed with orange prickles, inner bark yellow, leaf scars abundant and conspicuous.

Wood. Brown to yellow, weak, soft, light, close-grained.

Range. In rich, moist soil, edges of streams, woods and thickets. East Texas, Oklahoma, Arkansas, and Louisiana; east to Florida; north to New York, Indiana, and Iowa.

Remarks. Origin of the genus name, *Aralia*, is from the French-Canadian *Aralie*, the name appended to the original specimens sent to Tournefort by the Quebec physician Sarrasin. The species name, *spinosa*, refers to the spiny trunk and branches. Vernacular names are Hercules Club, Angelica-tree, Prickly-ash, Prickly-elder, Pick-tree, Pigeon-tree, and Toothache-tree. The seeds are eaten by many birds and the leaves browsed by white-tailed deer. It is reported that the bark, roots, and berries are occasionally used in medicine. Shrub has high ornamental value and is often planted in Europe.

DOGWOOD FAMILY (Cornaceae)

Flowering Dogwood

Cornus florida L. [D]

Field Identification. Shrub or tree to 40 ft, with a straggling, spreading crown.

Flowers. March–June, perfect in terminal dense clusters; corolla tiny, about ⅛ in. wide, greenish white, tubular; petals 4, linear, acute; stamens 4; true flowers subtended by 4 large white or pink, obcordate, emarginate bracts 1¼–2½ in. long; calyx 4-lobed; ovary 2-celled, with a slender style.

Fruit. Drupes clustered, conspicuous, bright red, ovoid, lustrous, ¼–½ in. long; seeds 1–2, channeled, ovoid; calyx and style persistent; fruit ripe September–October, dispersed by birds and mammals.

Leaves. Petioled, simple, opposite, entire, or barely and minutely toothed, blades 3–5 in. long, 1½–2½ in. wide, oval to ovate or elliptic, acute or acuminate at the apex, somewhat cuneate at the base, often unequal at the base, shiny green and somewhat hairy above, much paler and pubescent below, heavily veined; petioles stout, grooved, about ¾ in.

Twigs. Slender, yellowish green to reddish, pubescent to glabrous.

Bark. Grayish brown or black, broken into squarish rough checks.

Wood. Brown or reddish, close-grained, strong, weighing 51 lb per cu ft.

Range. Oklahoma, Arkansas, Texas, and Louisiana; eastward to Florida, northward to Maine, and west to Minnesota and Ontario.

Remarks. The genus name, *Cornus*, is a Latin word for "tough wood," and the species name, *florida*, refers to the showy petal-like bracts. Vernacular names are Arrowwood, Boxwood, Cornelius-tree, False Box, Nature's Mistake, Florida Dogwood, and White Cornel. The wood is used for small woodenware articles, tool handles, wheel hubs, and pulleys. The fruit of dogwood is eaten by at least 28 species of birds and ranks 21 on the list of quail-food plants of the Southeast. It is preferred food for wild turkey, also it is much eaten by squirrels and white-tailed deer. It is reported that Indians made a dye from the roots.

Rough-leaf Dogwood

Cornus drummondii C. A. Meyer [D, E, F]

Field Identification. Irregularly branched shrub or small spreading tree.

Flowers. May–August, perfect, yellowish white, borne in terminal, spreading, long-peduncled cymes 1–3 in. across; peduncles 1–2 in. long, pubescent; individual pedicels ⅛–¾ in. long, branched, glabrous or pubescent; corolla ⅛–³⁄₁₆ in. across, short-tubular; petals 4, spreading, oblong-lanceolate, acute; calyx-teeth 4, minute, much shorter than the hypanthium; stamens 4, exserted, filaments slender, white, longer than the pistil; style sim-

ple, slender, with a terminal somewhat capitate stigma; ovary inferior, 2-celled; annular ring viscid and reddish.

Fruit. Ripening August–October, drupe globular, about ¼ in. in diameter, white, style persistent, flesh thin; 1–2-seeded, seeds subglobose, slightly furrowed.

Leaves. Simple, opposite, deciduous, blades 1–5 in. long, ½–2½ in. broad, conspicuously veined, ovate to lanceolate or oblong to elliptic, apex acute or acuminate, base rounded or cuneate, margin entire, plane surface somewhat undulate; upper surface olive green and rather rough-pubescent above; lower surface paler, pubescent and veins prominent; petiole ⅕–¾ in. long, slender, rough-pubescent, green to reddish.

Twigs. Young ones green and pubescent, older ones reddish brown and glabrous.

Bark. On young branches and trunks rather smooth, pale gray to brown. On old trunks gray with narrow ridges and fissures, scales small.

Wood. Pale brown, with sapwood paler, heavy, hard, strong, durable, close-grained.

Range. Edges of thickets, streams, and fence rows. Central, southern, and eastern Texas, Oklahoma, Arkansas, and Louisiana; east to Alabama and northward to Ontario.

Remarks. The genus name, *Cornus*, is from *cornu* ("a horn"), in reference to the hard wood, and the species name, *drummondii*, is in honor of Thomas Drummond (1780–1835), a Scottish botanical explorer. Vernacular names are Cornel Dogwood, Small-flower Dogwood, and White Cornel. The word *dogwood* comes from the fact that a decoction of the bark of *C. sanguinea* was used in England to wash mangy dogs. Rough-leaf Dogwood was formerly listed by some authorities under the name of *C. asperifolia* Michx., but that name is no longer valid.

Rough-leaf Dogwood is sometimes used in shelter-belt planting in the prairie-plains region. It has been known in cultivation since 1836. The wood is used for small woodenware articles, especially shuttle-blocks and charcoal. The fruit is known to be eaten by at least 40 species of birds, including bobwhite quail, wild turkey, and prairie chicken.

Black Tupelo

Nyssa sylvatica Marsh. [D, E]

Field Identification. Tree to 100 ft, with horizontal branches. Male and female flowers on separate trees, or sometimes together.

Flowers. In axillary clusters April–June; polygamo-dioecious, greenish; staminate flowers in long-peduncled capitate clusters; petals small, thick, ovate or oblong, rounded, erect, early deciduous; calyx 5-lobed, disklike; stamens 5–12, exserted, and inserted on the calyx-disk below; pistillate flowers in slender-peduncled clusters of 2 or more; calyx like that of staminate flowers; bracts small but conspicuous and foliaceous; pistil 1–2-celled, style tubular, stigmas exserted.

Fruit. Ripening September–October, drupelike, 1–3 in a cluster on long peduncles; bluish black, glaucous, about ½ in. long, ovoid, acid, bitter, flesh thin; stone solitary, ovoid to oblong, round or flattened, light brown, indistinctly 10–12-ribbed.

Leaves. Simple, alternate, deciduous, entire, or with a few coarse remote teeth, 2–6 in. long, 1–3 in. wide; apex acute or acuminate; base cuneate or rounded; ovate or obovate to oval; thick, firm, lustrous green above, paler and hairy below; petiole about 1 in. long, villous-pubescent to glabrous.

Bark. Gray to brown or black, sometimes reddish-tinged; deeply fissured and broken into small irregularly shaped blocks.

Wood. Tough, heavy, hard, light brown, grain close and twisted, hard to work, warping easily.

Range. In moist rich soils. Texas, Oklahoma, Arkansas, and Louisiana; east to Florida, north to Maine, and west to Michigan and Wisconsin.

Remarks. The genus name, *Nyssa*, means "water nymph," and the species name, *sylvatica*, refers to the wooded habitat. Vernacular names are Swamp-hornbeam, Yellow Gum, Snag-tree,

Beetle-bung, Hornbeam, Hornpipe, Hornpine, Hornbine, Pepper-
ridge, Bee Gum, and Sour Gum. The wood is used for veneer,
plywood, railroad crossties, boxes, cooperage, pulp, woodenware,
hubs, wharf piles, handles, and planing-mill products. Thirty-two
species of birds eat the fruit. The foliage is browsed by black bear
and white-tailed deer. The flowers serve as bee food.

A variety of Black Tupelo is Swamp Black Tupelo, *N. sylvatica*
var. *biflora* (Walt.) Sarg. It closely resembles the species but has
narrower obtuse leaves and drupes usually in pairs, and the seeds
have ridges and ribs which are more prominent. However, trees
with characters intermediate to the species and the variety are
often found, so the distinctions are not clear cut. Both trees are
desirable for yard planting.

HEATH FAMILY (Ericaceae)

Farkleberry

Vaccinium arboreum Marsh. [D]

Field Identification. Stiff-branched, evergreen shrub, or small crooked tree attaining a height of 30 ft.

Flowers. In axillary racemes, leafy-bracted, perfect; corolla about ½ in. long, bell-shaped, pendent, 5-lobed, white or pinkish; calyx 5-toothed; stamens 10, within the corolla, filaments hairy, anthers slender-tubed; ovary inferior, 5-celled, style filiform with a minute stigma.

Fruit. About ⅓ in. in diameter, globose, black, shiny, sweet, mealy, dry, many-seeded, persistent, long-peduncled, ripening in winter.

Leaves. Alternate, simple, 1–3 in. long, about 1 in. wide, oval to obovate or elliptic, entire or obscurely denticulate, mucronate and acute or rounded at apex, cuneate at base, veiny, leathery, glossy above, duller green and slightly pubescent below, deciduous in the North, persistent in the South; petioles ½₅–³⁄₁₆ in. long.

Twigs. Slender, light brown to dark brown or grayish, divergent, glabrous or puberulous.

Bark. Gray or grayish brown, thin, smooth, ridges narrow and shredding into large plates.

Wood. Brown to reddish brown, close-grained, hard, weighing 48 lb per cu ft.

Range. Eastern Texas, Oklahoma, Arkansas, and Louisiana; east to Florida, northward to Virginia, and west to Missouri.

Remarks. The genus name, *Vaccinium*, is the classical name for an Old World species, and the species name, *arboreum*, refers to the treelike habit, which is unusual for huckleberries. Vernacular names are Whortleberry, Sparkleberry, Tree Huckleberry, Gooseberry, and Winter Huckleberry. The edible fruit is eaten by a number of species of birds. The wood is used for making tool handles, and the bark for tanning leather.

SAPODILLA FAMILY (Sapotaceae)

Woollybucket Bumelia

Bumelia lanuginosa (Michx.) Pers. [D, E]

Field Identification. Shrub or an irregularly shaped tree to 60 ft, with stiff, spinose branchlets.

Flowers. June–July, in small fascicles ¼–1½ in. across, pedicels hairy or subglabrous, ½₁₂–⅗ in. long; corolla white, petals 5, each 3-lobed, middle lobe longest, fragrant, ⅛–⅕ in. long, tube about ½₁₂ in. long; stamens 5, normal and fertile, also 5 sterile stamens (staminodia) which are deltoid-ovate, petaloid, and nearly equaling the corolla-tube; ovary 5-celled, hairy, style 1; calyx 5-lobed, hairy or nearly glabrous, ½₁₂–⅛ in. long, lobes suborbicular or ovate.

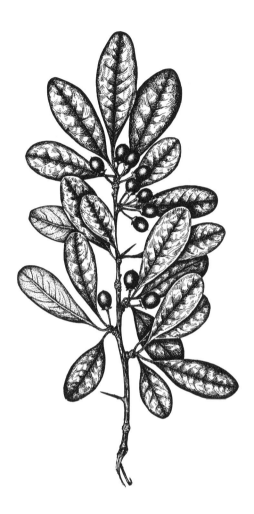

Fruit. Berry September–October, borne on slender, drooping peduncles, subglobose or obovoid, ⅓–1 in. long, lustrous, black, fleshy; seed solitary, large, brown, rounded, scar small and nearly basal, ¼–½ in. long, no endosperm, cotyledons fleshy.

Leaves. Alternate or clustered, often on short lateral spurs, oblong-obovate, elliptic or wedge-shaped, apex rounded or obtuse, base cuneate, margin entire, blade length 1–3 in., width ½–1 in., leathery, shiny green and smooth above, varying from rusty to white or gray-woolly beneath; petioles short, averaging about ½ in. long, tomentose.

Twigs. Gray to reddish brown, zigzag, slender, stiff, spinose, hairy at first with gray, white, or rusty tomentum.

Bark. Dark brown or grayish, fissured and reticulate into narrow ridges with thickened scales.

Wood. Yellow or brown, fairly hard, close-grained, weighing about 40 lb per cu ft.

Range. The species occurs in east Texas, Oklahoma, Arkansas, Louisiana, eastward to Florida, north to Kansas, Missouri, Illinois, and Virginia. In central and west Texas represented by its varieties.

Remarks. The genus name, *Bumelia*, is the ancient Greek name for the European Ash, and the species name, *lanuginosa*, refers to the woolly hairs of the leaf. Vernacular names are Woolly-buckthorn, Woolly Bumelia, Gum Elastic, Gum Bumelia, Chittamwood, False-buckthorn, and Blackhaw. The black fruit is edible, but not tasty, and produces stomach disturbances and dizziness if eaten in quantity (at least this is the experience of the author). Birds are very fond of the fruit; in fact, they get it as soon as it is barely ripe. The wood is used in small quantities for tool handles and cabinetmaking. A gum is freely exuded from wounds on the trunk and branches. The tree has been in cultivation since 1806.

Some botanical authors have split *B. lanuginosa* into a number of varieties and forms according to color, density of hairs on the foliage, and flower parts.

Brazos Bumelia

Bumelia monticola Buckl. [E, F, G]

Field Identification. Spiniferous shrub, or small tree to 25 ft, with an irregular crown.

Flowers. May–June, pedicels ¼–½ in. long, hairy at first, glabrous later, flowers in fascicles; calyx green, hairy, lobes ovate, margin ciliate, shorter than corolla-lobes; corolla short-campanulate, white; lobes 5, broad-ovate, rounded at apex, with a lanceolate appendage on each side at the base; stamens 5, filaments filiform, anthers sagittate; staminodia 5, petaloid, apex obtuse or rounded, margin erose or entire, longer than corolla-lobes; style elongate, simple, stigmatic at apex.

Fruit. August–September, borne in fascicles on spurs ¼–⅓ in. long, black, oblong, obovoid or subglobose, apex rounded or api-

culate; seed hardly over ⅜ in. long, oblong, smooth, obtuse or rounded at apices, straight or somewhat asymmetrical, light brown to white.

Leaves. Deciduous, fascicled on short spurs, blades 1–3 in. long, ⅓–1¼ in. wide, pubescent when young, glabrous at maturity, dark green, lustrous, slightly paler beneath, elliptic to oblong or spatulate, margin entire and barely revolute, apex obtuse, rounded or acute, base gradually narrowed, reticulate-veined; petiole ¼–½ in. long, slightly pubescent but glabrous later.

Twigs. Young twigs zigzag, reddish brown, smooth, the laterals often ending in stout, gray to reddish brown thorns; older twigs gray and smooth.

Bark. Gray, reddish brown beneath, broken into flat, narrow scales and shallow fissures.

Wood. Brown to yellowish, sapwood lighter, hard, moderately strong.

Range. In Texas mostly west of the Brazos River on the Edwards Plateau limestone hills. In Kerr, Kendall, Comal, Real, Uvalde, Palo Verde, Val Verde, Pecos, Brewster, Crockett, Callahan, Coleman, Shackleford, Terrell, and Brown counties. Also in Oklahoma. In Mexico in Coahuila.

Remarks. The genus name, *Bumelia*, is the ancient classical name for the ash tree. The species name, *monticola*, refers to its habitat of hilly or mountainous regions. Vernacular names used are Gum-elastic, Chittamwood, Mountain-gum, and Gum-buckthorn.

Some botanists have listed Brazos Bumelia under the names of *B. texana* Buckl., *B. lanuginosa* var. *texana* Buckl., or *B. riograndis* Lundell.

PERSIMMON FAMILY (Ebenaceae)

Common Persimmon

Diospyros virginiana L. [D, E, F]

Field Identification. Tree generally less than 40 ft, rarely reaching 70–100 ft. Habit of growth variable, usually disposed to an upright or drooping type with rounded or conical crown. Branches spreading or at right angles. Twigs self-pruning or some breaking with heavy fruit to form an irregularly shaped tree.

Flowers. April–June, staminate and pistillate on separate trees; pollen light and powdery, spread by wind and insects; staminate in 2–3-flowered cymes, tubular, ⅓–½ in. long, greenish yellow; stamens usually 16; pistillate solitary, sessile or short-peduncled, about ¾ in. long or less, stamens 8, some stamens abortive and some fertile; ovary 8-celled, styles 4, 2-lobed at apex; corolla fragrant, 4–5-lobed, greenish yellow, thick, lobes recurved.

Fruit. Berry persistent, variable as to season, locality, or individual tree, some early or some late (August–February). The very early or very late fruit generally smaller than fruit which ripens about when the leaves fall, seedless fruit also generally smaller; diame-

ter generally ¾–1½ in., shape variable from subglobose or oblate to short-oblong; calyx thick, lobes ovate and recurved; color when mature yellow to orange or dark red, often with a glaucous bloom, flesh pale and translucent, astringent and puckery to taste when green; when ripe somewhat softer and sweet with a high sugar content; 4–8-seeded, seeds large, oblong, flat, leathery, wrinkled, dark brown, about ½ in. long; some trees seedless.

Leaves. Deciduous, simple, alternate, entire, ovate-oblong to elliptic, apex acute or acuminate, base rounded, cuneate or subcordate, blade length 2–6 in., width 1–3 in., upper surface dark green and lustrous, lower surface paler and pubescent; petiole about 1 in. long or less, glabrous or pubescent.

Bark. Brown to black, fissures deep, ridges broken into rectangular checkered sections.

Wood. Dark brown to black, sapwood lighter, fine-grained, strong, hard.

Range. Thrives on almost any type of soil from sands to shales and mud bottomlands. Generally in the southeastern United

States. Gulf states to Iowa and Connecticut. Seemingly the best zone is from Maryland, Virginia, and Carolinas westward through Missouri and Arkansas. In Texas west to the valley of the Colorado River.

Remarks. The genus name, *Diospyros*, is translated "fruit-of-the-gods," and the species name, *virginiana*, refers to the state of Virginia. Vernacular names are Jove's-fruit, Winter-plum, and Possum-wood. The fruit was known and appreciated by early settlers and explorers, being mentioned in writings of De Soto in 1539, Jan de Laet in 1558, and John Smith in the seventeenth century. The wood of Persimmon is used for handles and shoe lasts, but three-fourths of the supply is made into golf clubs and shuttles. Its hardness, smoothness, and even texture make it particularly desirable for these purposes. The tree is suitable for erosion control on deeper soils because of its deep root system, but this same characteristic makes it difficult to transplant. Also, the rapid spread of a new leaf-wilt disease introduces a factor of caution before extensive plantings are made.

The fruit is eaten by at least 16 species of birds, also by the skunk, raccoon, opossum, gray and fox squirrel, and white-tailed deer. Fallen fruit is also useful in providing some forage for hogs, having a high carbohydrate content. The bark is known to have astringent medicinal properties.

Texas Persimmon

Diospyros texana Scheele [D, E, F]

Field Identification. An intricately branched, smooth-barked shrub or tree up to 40 ft.

Flowers. Dioecious, small, solitary or in few-flowered clusters; corolla urn-shaped, greenish white, pubescent, about ⅓ in. long; lobes 5, spreading, suborbicular, often notched at apex; stamens 16, included, anthers glabrous; ovary sessile, pubescent, 4–8-celled, style united with narrow stigmas; calyx-lobes 5, ovate, obtuse, spreading or reflexed, thickened, pubescent.

Fruit. Depressed-globose, black, apiculate, pulp sweet when mature, astringent when green, about ¾–1 in. long; seeds 3–8, triangular, flattened, hard, shiny, about ⅓ in. long.

Leaves. Persistent, alternate, leathery, entire, oblong or obovate; apex obtuse, retuse, rounded or emarginate, abruptly narrowed at

base, 1–2 in. long, dark green, glabrous above or somewhat pubescent, tomentose below.

Bark. Very smooth, gray, thin layers flaking off.

Wood. Heavy, black, compact, sapwood yellow, takes a high polish.

Range. In Texas and northern Mexico. In central and west Texas usually on rocky hills or the sides of ravines and canyons. Especially abundant in the Texas Edwards Plateau area. When near the coast usually on soils with lime composition because of marine shells. Probably reaching its easternmost limit in Harris County, Texas, near the coast. In Mexico in the states of Nuevo León, Coahuila, and Tamaulipas.

Remarks. The genus name, *Diospyros*, is translated "fruit-of-the-gods," and the species name, *texana*, refers to the state of Texas. Vernacular names are Mexican Persimmon, Black Persimmon,

Chapote, and Chapote Prieto. The fruit is somewhat smaller than that of the Common Persimmon but is likewise sweet and juicy at maturity and is eaten by many birds and mammals. The black juice is used to dye skins in Mexico, and the wood is used for tools and engraving blocks. It was also used in a craft now little practiced—that of ornamenting wooden objects by burning designs into them with an iron.

STORAX FAMILY (Styracaceae)

Two-wing Silver-bell

Halesia diptera Ellis [D]

Field Identification. Shrub or small tree to 30 ft, with diameter 3–12 in. Branches are slender and form a small, rounded crown.

Flowers. March–April, on branches of the previous year with the young leaves, borne in 2–6-flowered axillary fascicles; pedicels slender, hairy, 1½–2 in. long; flowers perfect, corolla white, drooping, broadly campanulate; tube short, about 1 in. long, nearly divided to the base into 4, spreading, oval to obovate lobes, puberulent, calyx-tube obconical, ⅛–⅙ in. long, pubescent; lobes 4, triangular, acuminate; stamens 8 or more, nearly as long as the corolla, filaments hairy; ovary 2- or rarely 4-celled, style slender, elongate, pubescent; bracts obovate, apex rounded or acute, puberulous.

Fruit. Drupe oblong to ellipsoid, dry, flattened, 1–2 in. long, with 2 broad thin wings, the remaining angles sometimes with lesser wings, smooth, beak rather short; stone solitary, about ¾ in. long, ellipsoid, ridged, acuminate at both ends.

Leaves. Buds obtuse, leaves simple, alternate, deciduous, ovate to oval or elliptic to obovate; apex rounded or acute to acuminate, sometimes abruptly so; base rounded or cuneate, margin with remote teeth, blades 3–4 in. long, 2–3 in. wide, upper surface light green and glabrous to pubescent, lower surface paler and soft-pubescent, veins pale and conspicuous; petioles ½–¾ in. long, light green, pubescent, slender.

Twigs. Slender, gray to brown, lustrous; leaf scars cordate, large, raised; buds ovoid, obtuse, hairy; pith chambered.

Bark. Reddish brown to gray, fissures irregular; flakes small, thin, tight.

Wood. Light brown, sapwood lighter, close-grained, light, soft, brittle, of little commercial value.

Range. In sandy, moist soil along streams or in bottomlands. Texas eastward to Florida. Evidently a Gulf Coast plain species, but extending north into Arkansas, Oklahoma, Tennessee, and South Carolina.

Remarks. The genus name, *Halesia*, is in honor of Stephen Hales, an English clergyman (1677–1761). The species name, *diptera*, refers to the 2-winged fruit. Vernacular names are Snowdrop-tree, Snow-bell, and Cowlicks. The tree is not subject to insect damage and, being easily damaged by storms, prefers a sheltered growing site. Gray and fox squirrels sometimes eat the fruit. Silver-bell flowers are attractive but unfortunately the tree is generally irregular in shape. It has been cultivated since 1758 and is occasionally grown in Europe.

ASH FAMILY (Oleaceae)

White Fringe-tree

Chionanthus virginicus L. [D]

Field Identification. Usually a shrub with crooked branches, but sometimes a tree to 35 ft, with a narrow, oblong crown.

Flowers. March–June, perfect or polygamous, in delicate drooping panicles 4–6 in. long; pedicels pubescent; bracts of panicles sessile, oval-oblong, leaflike; calyx small, 4-lobed, persistent, lobes ovate-lanceolate and acute, green, glabrous; petals 4–6, linear, acute, about 1 in. long, white with purple spots near the base, barely united at base, longer than the tube, fragrant; stamens 2; filaments short, adnate to corolla-tube; anthers 2, ovate, light yellow, subsessile; ovary ovoid, 2-celled; style short, thick, 2-lobed; staminate flowers sometimes with sterile pistils.

Fruit. August–October, drupe borne in loose clusters; bracts leaflike, oval or short-oblong, some 2 inches long; drupe bluish black, glaucous, globose-oblong, ½–¾ in. long, pulp thin, 1-celled, 1–3-seeded; seeds about ⅓ in. long, ovoid, brown, somewhat reticulate. Plants 5–8 years old begin to produce seed.

Leaves. Simple, opposite, deciduous, oval to oblong or obovate-lanceolate; apex obtuse, acute or acuminate; base wedge-shaped; margin entire or wavy; 4–8 in. long, 1–4 in. wide, dark green and glabrous above, paler below with hairs on veins; petioles ½–1 in. long, puberulent.

Twigs. Stout, pubescent, light brown to orange, later gray.

Bark. Brown to gray, thin, close, appressed, broken into small thin scales.

Wood. Light brown, sapwood lighter, hard, heavy, close-grained, weighing about 39 lb per cu ft.

Range. Oklahoma, Arkansas, Texas, and Louisiana; eastward to Florida and northward to Pennsylvania and New Jersey.

Remarks. The genus name, *Chionanthus*, is a combination of two Greek words meaning "snow flower," and the species name, *virginicus*, refers to the state of Virginia. Vernacular names are Flowering Ash, Old Man's Beard, Grandfather-graybeard, Snow-flower-tree, Sunflower-tree, Poison Ash, White-fringe, Shavings, and Graybeard-tree. The bark has medicinal uses as a diuretic and fever remedy. The tree is cultivated to some extent for the fragile

panicles of flowers in spring and for the dark green foliage. It has
been cultivated since 1736. The staminate plants display the attractive delicate, drooping flowers but bear no fruit. The leaves are
persistent in winter in the Gulf Coast area, but farther north fall
after turning bright yellow.

Downy Forestiera

Forestiera pubescens Nutt. [D]

Field Identification. Sometimes a small tree to 15 ft, and 5 in. in
diameter, but usually only a straggling, irregularly shaped shrub.

Flowers. Polygamo-dioecious, appearing before the leaves in
spring from branches of the preceding year; clusters lateral, from
bracts which are obovate, ¹⁄₁₂–¹⁄₈ in. long, ciliate, densely pubescent; staminate fascicles greenish; sepals 4–6, small, early-deciduous; petals absent; stamens 2–5; pistillate clusters on slender

pedicels of short spurs; ovary 2-celled, 2 ovules in each cell, style slender, stigma capitate or somewhat 2-lobed.

Fruit. June–October, drupes pediceled, clustered, bluish black, glaucous, ellipsoid, ¼–⅓ in. long, fleshy, 1-seeded; stone oblong to ellipsoid, ribbed.

Leaves. Simple, opposite, deciduous, ½–1¾ in. long, varying from elliptic to oblong or oval, margin obscurely serrulate, apex obtuse or rounded, base cuneate or rounded; dull green and glabrous or slightly pubescent above; lower surface densely soft-pubescent; petioles short, yellowish green, pubescent.

Twigs. Green to yellowish and pubescent when young, older ones light to dark gray and glabrous.

Range. Mostly in rich, moist soil along streams. New Mexico, Texas, and Oklahoma; eastward to Florida.

Remarks. The genus name, *Forestiera*, honors the French physician and naturalist Charles Le Forestier, and the species name, *pubescens*, refers to the soft-hairy leaves. Also known under the vernacular names of Devil's-elbow, Chaparral, Spring-herald, Spring-goldenglow, and Tanglewood. The shrub has no particular economic value but has been recommended for erosion control and wildlife cover. It has been cultivated since 1900. About 20 species of *Forestiera* are known, these being distributed in North America, the West Indies, and Central to South America. The various species are propagated by cuttings and seeds, and some are rooted by layering.

New Mexico Forestiera

Forestiera pubescens Nutt. var. *glabrifolia* Shinners [D, E, F, G]

Field Identification. Erect, spreading shrubs or small trees to 12 ft, often clumped at the base and with semispinescent branches.

Flowers. March–May before the leaves in the axils of the last year's leaves; flowers small, polygamo-dioecious, crowded, the dense, sessile clusters subtended by 4 small bracts; petals absent; stamens 2–4, anthers oblong and yellow; ovary superior, ovate, 2-celled, with 2 pendulous ovules in each cell; style slender, stigma somewhat 2-lobed; pistillate flowers with 2–4 sterile stamens.

Fruit. Ripening June–September, drupe ⅕–⅓ in. long, bluish black, ovoid to ellipsoid, obtuse, 1-celled and 1-seeded; seeds bony, germinating 40–70 percent.

Leaves. Simple, opposite, deciduous, spatulate-oblong to ovate-oblong, apex obtuse or short acuminate, base cuneate, margin minutely serrulate or sometimes entire toward the base, length ½–1¾ in., width ¼–¾ in., surfaces glabrous above and below, grayish green, membranous; petioles ⅛–¼ in. long, glabrous; smaller leaves sometimes fascicled at the base of the older ones.

Twigs. Stiff, lateral ones often shortened, gray to whitened, smooth, glabrous.

Range. New Mexico Forestiera is found on hillsides or mesas, or in moist valleys, at altitudes of 3,000–7,000 ft, from the northern parts of Trans-Pecos Texas to New Mexico, Arizona, Colorado, Utah, and westward into California.

Remarks. The genus name, *Forestiera*, honors Charles Le Forestier (d. *circa* 1820), a French naturalist and physician, and the variety name, *glabrifolia*, refers to the smooth foliage. It is also known as Desert Olive and Palo Blanco. The Hopi Indians are said to have made digging sticks of the branches.

New Mexico Forestiera is also listed in the literature as *F. neomexicana* Gray. *F. neomexicana* var. *arizonica* Gray is not accepted. Instead, the listed characters of *arizonica* appear to make it a synonym of *F. pubescens*.

Texas Forestiera

Forestiera acuminata Poir. [D]

Field Identification. Straggling shrub or tree to 30 ft, growing in swampy ground.

Flowers. Dioecious or polygamous; staminate in dense green fascicles subtended by yellow bracts; calyx ring narrow, slightly lobed; petals none; stamens 4; filaments long, slender, erect; anthers oblong, yellow; ovary in staminate flowers abortive; pistillate flowers in short panicles, ¾–1¼ in. long; ovary ovoid with a slender style and 2-lobed stigma, stamens usually abortive or absent.

Fruit. Drupe ovoid-oblong, purplish, apex acute, tipped with style remnants, base rounded, fleshy, dry, about 1 in. long, young fruit somewhat falcate; seed usually solitary, ridged, compressed, light brown, about ⅓ in. long, one side often flatter than the other.

Leaves. Simple, opposite, deciduous, elliptical or oblong-ovate, acuminate at apex, cuneate at base, remotely serrulate above the middle, 2–4½ in. long, 1–2 in. wide, glabrous and yellowish green above, paler with occasional hairs on veins beneath; petioles slender, ¼–½ in., slightly winged by leaf bases.

Twigs. Light brown, glabrous, slender, warty, with numerous lenticels, sometimes rooting on contact with the mud.

Bark. Dark brown, thin, close, slightly ridged.

Wood. Yellowish brown, close-grained, light, weak, soft, weighing about 39 lb per cu ft.

Range. In swamps or bottom lands, Oklahoma, Arkansas, Texas, and Louisiana; eastward to Florida and northward to Tennessee, Indiana, Illinois, and Missouri.

Remarks. The genus name, *Forestiera*, is in honor of the French physician and botanist Charles Le Forestier, and the species name, *acuminata*, refers to the acuminate leaves. Another vernacular name is Swamp Privet. It has no particular economic use, except that the fruit is considered to be a good wild duck food.

Japanese Privet

Ligustrum japonicum Thunb. [D, E]

Field Identification. A much cultivated evergreen, or deciduous in cold climates, becoming a bushy shrub or small tree to 18 ft. Sometimes escaping cultivation. Bark rather smooth and gray. Sometimes confused with the *L. lucidum* Ait., but the latter has larger leaves ovate-lanceolate in shape, with an acute or acuminate apex, and not as glossy as in *L. japonicum* Thunb.

Flowers. Borne July–September, bisexual. Panicles terminal, to 4½ in. long. Corolla funnelform, the tube usually somewhat longer than the calyx; the 4 corolla lobes spreading; calyx campanulate, obscurely 4-toothed; stamens 2, slightly longer than the lobes, attached to the corolla tube; ovary 2-celled, with 2 ovules in each cell, or sometimes 1-seeded by abortion.

Fruit. A drupelike berry, black, oblong or sometimes falcate.

Leaves. Opposite; 2–4 in. long; shape roundish-ovate to ovate-oblong; base rounded or broadly cuneate; margin entire; apices acute to obtuse; texture coriaceous; color dark green and glossy;

with 4–5 pairs of lateral veins, the veins rather obscure beneath; midrib and margin sometimes reddish. Petiole ¼–½ in. long.

Twigs. Slender, gray to brown, minutely puberulous at first, but glabrous later and lenticellate.

Range. A native of Japan and Korea. Introduced into cultivation in 1845. A handsome, much cultivated, evergreen shrub or tree. Sometimes pruned for hedges or for rounded poodle forms.

Remarks. The genus name, *Ligustrum*, is an ancient Latin name, and the species name, *japonicum*, is for its place of origin. Vernacular names are Privet-berry and Prim. The fruit is greedily eaten by the cedar waxwing and other birds.

A variety known as the Round-leaf Japanese Privet, *L. japonicum* var. *rotundifolium* Bl. (*L. japonicum* var. *coriaceum* Lav., *L. coriaceum* Carr.), is described as a compact shrub to 6 ft, with stiff short branches and leaves crowded; shape broad-ovate or suborbicular; length 1¼–2½ in.; margin obtuse or emarginate; surface dark green and lustrous, often curved; panicle dense, 2–4 in. long; flowers sessile; fruit subglobose, about ⅕ in. in diameter. Introduced into cultivation in about 1860.

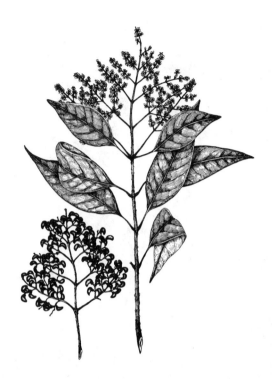

Glossy Privet

Ligustrum lucidum Ait. [D, E]

Field Identification. A cultivated, evergreen, erect, large shrub or tree to 30 ft tall. The branches spreading and lenticellate. Trunk rather smooth and pale to dark gray or blotched gray or whitish.

Flowers. Borne July–August in terminal panicles 4–9 in. long, almost as wide. Flowers white, perfect, sessile or subsessile. Corolla salverform, with a rather short tube about as long as the calyx; lobes 4, spreading, about as long as the tube; calyx campanulate and obscurely 4-toothed; stamens 2, about as long as the corolla-lobes; style cylindric, not exceeding the stamens; ovary 2-celled, cells 2-ovuled.

Fruit. A berrylike drupe, oblong, blue-black, about ⅜ in. long.

Leaves. Opposite, 3¼–5 in. long; shape ovate-lanceolate; apices acuminate to acute; margin entire; base usually broad-cuneate; venation with lateral veins usually 6–8 pairs which are distinct on both sides; veinlets often impressed; surface glabrous; winter buds ovoid, with about 2 outer scales. Petioles ⅓–¾ in. long.

Twigs. Slender, light to dark gray.

Range. Native to China, Korea, and Japan. Commonly planted in warm regions. Often planted for ornament in the Gulf Coast cities. Common in Houston, Texas. Introduced into cultivation in 1794.

Remarks. The genus name, *Ligustrum*, is the ancient Latin name. The species name, *lucidum*, refers to a shiny leaf surface. However, this has caused some confusion of names in the nursery trade, because the Japanese Privet, *L. japonicum* Thunb., has a much more glossy leaf surface than *L. lucidum* Ait. Both *L. lucidum* and *L. japonicum* yield a white wax, an exudation of the branches, caused by an insect, Pe-lah; therefore, it is cultivated in China. A number of varieties and horticultural clones have been named.

Chinese Privet

Ligustrum sinense Lour. [D, E]

Field Identification. Shrub or small tree to 20 ft, and 5 in. in trunk diameter. Trunks often clumped and inclined, branches slender and spreading.

Flowers. Inflorescence March–May, fragrant, perfect; borne in panicles which are terminal, narrow, elongate, 2–6 in. long and ½–3 in. wide; corolla white, tubular, limb about ⅜ in. across, 4-lobed, lobes spreading, oblong or ovate, acute; stamens 2, filaments adnate to the corolla-tube, exserted, longer than the prominent corolla-lobes; pistil shorter than the stamens, stigma spatulate, flattened; calyx campanulate, about 1/12 in. long, glabrous, shallowly 4-lobed, lobes acute; pedicels 1/16–⅛ in. long, pubescent.

Fruit. Drupe bluish black, subglobose to oval or obovoid, seeds 1–2.

Leaves. Opposite, oval to elliptic, apex rounded to obtuse or slightly notched, base cuneate or rounded, margin entire, length 1–2 in., width ½–1 in., main vein apparent but others obscure; upper surface dark green and semilustrous, glabrous or slightly pubescent along the main vein; lower surface paler, glabrous or slightly pubescent on the main vein; petiole ⅛–½ in., pubescent.

Twigs. Slender, spreading, gray to brown, pubescent; older branches and trunk smooth, glabrous, and various shades of gray to brown, lenticels pale and scattered.

Range. A native of southeast Asia. Grown for ornament in Texas, Oklahoma, Arkansas, Louisiana, and elsewhere throughout the North Temperate Zone, sometimes escaping cultivation.

Remarks. The genus name, *Ligustrum*, is the ancient classical name, and the species name, *sinense*, refers to its Chinese origin. It is a handsome plant, much cultivated for hedges and screens in the South. A number of varieties have been listed.

Quihoui Privet

Ligustrum quihoui Carr. [D]

Field Identification. Shrub cultivated, slender, erect or spreading, to 10 ft.

Flowers. April–June, heavy-scented, borne in narrow racemes 2–8 in. long and ½–1 in. wide, lateral branches of inflorescence ¼–½ in. long, rather densely flowered from the axils of smaller leaves below, usually leafless above; calyx sessile or nearly so, puberulent, shallowly 4-toothed; corolla white, tubular, about ⅛ in. long, the tube as long as the 4 lobes of the limb or longer, lobes ovate, acute to obtuse; stamens 2, much exserted, anthers short-oblong, about 1/16 in. long; pistil much shorter than the stamens, included or slightly exserted, simple, erect, stigma slightly capitate.

Fruit. Ripening September–November, bluish black, slightly glaucous, 3/16–¼ in. long, subglobose or slightly flattened; seeds

1–2, about ³⁄₁₆ in. long, short-oblong to oval; when 2-seeded the outer surfaces are rounded and sculptured and the inner faces plane.

Leaves. Opposite, simple, partly folded, ²⁄₃–1½ in. long, ³⁄₁₆–¼ in. wide, linear to narrowly oblong or elliptic, margin entire; apex obtuse, sometimes slightly notched, base gradually narrowed, upper surface dark green and glabrous; lower surface paler and duller green, glabrous or barely puberulent on the midrib; leaves sessile or short-petiolate, glabrous or puberulent.

Twigs. Younger ones green and finely pubescent, older ones gray or pale brown and glabrous; bark gray, smooth, and with numerous pale lenticels.

Range. A native of China, cultivated in the Gulf Coast states, sometimes escaping.

Remarks. The genus name, *Ligustrum*, is the ancient classical name. The species name, *quihoui*, honors Antoine Quihou, a French botanist who worked in the late nineteenth century. The plant has been cultivated since 1862. It is an attractive shrub with erect or spreading stems and late-flowering habit and grows well in the Houston area.

Berlandier Ash

Fraxinus berlandieriana A. DC. [D]

Field Identification. Small round-topped tree of western distribution, seldom seen east of the Colorado River except in cultivation. Rarely over 30 ft.

Flowers. Dioecious, greenish, staminate and pistillate flowers on different trees; calyx of staminate flower obscurely 4-lobed; stamens 2, filaments short, anthers linear-oblong and opening laterally; calyx of pistillate flower campanulate, deeply cleft; ovary with a slender style and stigmas 2-lobed.

Fruit. Ripening in May. Samara spatulate to oblong-obovate, 1–1½ in. long, about ¼ in. wide; wing acute or acuminate at apex, decurrent down the seed body almost to the base, set in a deeply lobed calyx; samaras sometimes 3-winged.

Leaves. Deciduous, opposite, odd-pinnate, slender, petioled, 3–10 in. long; leaflets 3–5, petiolulate, elliptic, lanceolate or obovate, acuminate to acute at apex, cuneate or rounded at base, entire or

remotely serrate, thickish, dark green and glabrous above, glabrous or a few axillary hairs beneath, 3–4 in. long, ½–1½ in.
wide, petiolule of terminal leaflet longer than those of lateral leaflets. Leaflets fewer, smaller, more coarsely toothed, and more
widely separated than those of White Ash or Green Ash.

Twigs. Green, reddish or gray, with scattered lenticels, leaf scars
small, raised, oval.

Bark. Gray or reddish, fissures shallow and ridges narrow.

Wood. Light brown, sapwood lighter, close-grained, light, soft.

Range. Moist canyons and stream banks. Central Texas to Trans-
Pecos Texas; southward in Mexico in Coahuila, Durango, and
Veracruz.

Remarks. The genus name, *Fraxinus*, is the ancient Latin name,
and the species name, *berlandieriana*, is in honor of the Swiss
botanist Jean Louis Berlandier (1805–1851), who collected extensively in Mexico and Texas. Local names for the tree are Plumero,
Fresno, and Mexican Ash. The wood has no particular commercial importance, but the tree is widely planted as an ornamental
in western and southwestern Texas and Mexico.

Carolina Ash

Fraxinus caroliniana Mill. [D]

Field Identification. Tree of deep swamps, with small branches and rounded open head, to 40 ft.

Flowers. Dioecious, appearing in fasciculate panicles before the leaves, yellowish green; no petals; staminate panicles dense; staminate calyx minute; stamens 2–4, with linear-oblong, apiculate anthers opening longitudinally; pistillate flowers in slender clusters about 2 in. long; pistillate calyx campanulate, deeply cleft, persistent; ovary globose, elongated into a forked style.

Fruit. Samara oblong-obovate to elliptic, yellowish brown, flattened, thin, smooth, 1–3 in. long, ½–¾ in. broad; seed elliptic, flattened, surrounded by the broad wing; wing pinnately veined, midvein impressed, apex acute, rounded, or emarginate.

Leaves. Deciduous, opposite, odd-pinnately compound of 5–9 (usually 7) leaflets, 7–12 in. long, petiole elongate; leaflets long-petiolulate, the blades 2–6 in. long, ½–3 in. broad, oblong-ovate, thick, acute, or acuminate at apex, rounded or cuneate at base, serrate or sometimes entire on margin; dark green, lustrous and glabrous above; paler and glabrous or pubescent beneath.

Twigs. Slender, terete, green, pubescent at first, later brown to gray and glabrous.

Bark. Gray, often blotched, thin, smoothish, with small scales.

Wood. Yellowish white, close-grained, soft, weak, weighing 22 lb per cu ft, not important commercially.

Range. Swamplands, eastern Texas, Arkansas, and Louisiana; eastward to Florida and northward to Washington, D.C., Virginia, and Missouri.

Remarks. The genus name, *Fraxinus*, is the ancient Latin name, and the species name, *caroliniana*, refers to the states of Carolina. Vernacular names are Poppy Ash, Pop Ash, and Water Ash.

Green Ash

Fraxinus pennsylvanica var. *subintegerrima* (Vahl) Fern. [D, E]

Field Identification. Spreading, round-topped tree attaining a height of 70 ft or more.

Flowers. Dioecious, borne in spring in slender-pediceled, terminal, glabrous panicles; no petals; staminate with a campanulate, obscurely toothed calyx; stamens 2, composed of short, terete filaments and linear-oblong, greenish purple anthers; calyx of pistillate flowers deeply cleft; ovary 2–3-celled, style elongate, with 2 green stigmatic lobes.

Fruit. Samaras in panicles; samaras flat, 1–2 in. long, ¼–⅓ in. wide, winged; wing decurrent down the side of seed body often past the middle, spatulate or oblanceolate; end of wing square, notched, rounded or acute; seed usually 1-celled, or rarely 2–3-celled.

Leaves. Deciduous, opposite, odd-pinnately compound, 8–12 in. long, rachis glabrous; leaflets 5–9 (usually 7) ovate to oblong-lanceolate, acute or acuminate at apex, cuneate at base, entire or irregularly serrate on margin, lustrous green on both sides or somewhat paler beneath; glabrous above, usually glabrous below or with scant pubescence on veins, 2–6 in. long, 1–2 in. wide.

Twigs. Gray, glabrous, terete; lenticels pale.

Bark. Brown, tight, ridges flattened, furrows shallow, scales thin and appressed.

Wood. Light brown, sapwood lighter, coarse-grained, heavy, hard, strong, weighing 44 lb per cu ft.

Range. Texas, New Mexico, Oklahoma, Arkansas, and Louisiana; eastward to Florida, northward to Nova Scotia, and west to Manitoba, Montana, Wyoming, Colorado, and Kansas.

Remarks. The genus name, *Fraxinus*, is the ancient name of ash tree. The variety name, *subintegerrima*, means spaced between, with reference to the somewhat remote teeth of the leaf margin. Vernacular names are Water Ash, River Ash, Red Ash, Swamp Ash. The wood is not as desirable as that of White Ash but is used for the same purposes, such as tool handles, furniture, interior finishing, cooperage, and wagons. A number of birds eat the seeds, and the foliage is browsed by white-tailed deer and cottontail.

Texas Ash

Fraxinus texensis (Gray) Sarg. [D, E, F]

Field Identification. Tree to 50 ft, 2–3 ft in diameter, with a short trunk and contorted branches.

Flowers. With the leaves in March, in large glabrous panicles, buds with ovate, rounded, brown to orange-colored scales, from the axils of last year's leaves; staminate and pistillate panicles separate; staminate with petals absent and a minute 4-lobed calyx; stamens 2, filaments short, anthers linear-oblong and apiculate, purplish; pistillate calyx with 4 deep, acute lobes; ovary attenuate into a slender style.

Fruit. Samara borne in compact panicles 2–3¾ in. long on slender pedicels ⅛–¼ in. long, fruit ½–1 in. long, ³⁄₁₆–¼ in. wide, body rounded; wing terminal on the seed body or extending only slightly on the sides, apex rounded or notched (rarely with more than 1 wing).

Leaves. Odd-pinnately compound, 5–8 in. long; leaflets 5 (more rarely 7); petiolules ¼–1½ in. long, slender, yellowish green; blades elliptic to oblong or ovate to obovate, apex acute, base broadly cuneate or rounded, margins obscurely serrate or entire toward the base, length 1–3 in., width ¾–2 in.; upper surface olive green to dark green and glabrous; lower surface paler and often somewhat glaucous and glabrous, or with a few white hairs on the main vein.

Twigs. Numerous, stout, terete, green to reddish brown or gray, younger slightly puberulous, older glabrous, smooth; lenticels scattered, oblong, pale; leaf scars large, raised, with conspicuous fibrovascular bundles; buds acute, ovate, apex rounded or truncate, brown to orange, densely hairy.

Bark. Gray to brown or black, ½–¾ in. thick, furrows deep, the wide ridges confluent to give a netlike appearance.

Wood. Light brown, sapwood paler, strong, hard, heavy.

Range. From the Arbuckle Mountains of Oklahoma southward over the limestone Edwards Plateau of Texas. In Texas in Dallas, Tarrant, Travis, Bandera, Kerr, Edwards, and Palo Pinto counties. Collected by the author between Utopia and Tarpley, Texas.

Remarks. The genus name, *Fraxinus*, is the ancient Latin name, and the species name, *texensis*, refers to the state of Texas where it occurs. It is also known as Mountain Ash because of its growth on limestone hills. The wood is used for fuel or flooring, but is hardly abundant enough to be of commercial importance. It is a handsome tree and should be more extensively grown for ornament. It was first cultivated in 1901. Texas Ash is closely related to White Ash, *F. americana*, and some botanists consider it as only a variety of the latter.

White Ash

Fraxinus americana L. [D, E]

Field Identification. Tree attaining a height of 100 ft and a diameter of 3 ft. Records show that some trees have reached a height of

175 ft and a diameter of 5 to 6 ft, but such trees are no longer to be found. The general shape is rather narrow and rounded.

Flowers. Borne April–May, dioecious, with or before the leaves in staminate and pistillate panicles; staminate clusters short and dense; individual flowers minute, green to red, glabrous; no petals; calyx campanulate, 4-lobed; stamens 2–3, filaments short, anthers oblong-ovate and reddish; pistillate clusters about 2 in. long, slender, calyx deeply lobed; style split into 2 spreading, reddish purple stigmas.

Fruit. Ripening August–September. Samaras in dense clusters often 6–8 in. long; seed body terete; wing slightly extending down the body of the seed, but usually not at all, oblong or spatulate; often notched at the end, thin, smooth, flat, yellow to brown, 1–2½ in. long, about ¼ in. wide.

Leaves. Simple, opposite, deciduous, odd-pinnately compound, 8–13 in. long, leaflets 5–9, usually 7, ovate-lanceolate, acuminate or acute, rounded or cuneate at base, entire or crenulate-serrate on margin, dark lustrous green above, paler and whitish and glabrous or pubescent beneath, 3–5 in. long, 1½–3 in. wide; petiole glabrous.

Twigs. Green to brown or gray, stout, smooth with pale lenticels.

Bark. Light gray to dark brown, ridges narrow and separated by deep fissures into interlacing patterns.

Wood. Brown, sapwood lighter, close-grained, strong, hard, stiff, heavy, tough, weighing 41 lb per cu ft, seasons well, takes a good polish, moderately durable, shock resistant.

Range. Typical White Ash is distributed in Oklahoma, Arkansas, Texas, and Louisiana; eastward to Florida, northward to Nova Scotia, and west to Ontario, Minnesota, Michigan, and Nebraska.

Remarks. The genus name, *Fraxinus*, is the ancient Latin name, and the meaning of the species name, *americana*, is obvious. Also known as Small-seed White Ash, Cane Ash, Biltmore Ash, and Biltmore White Ash. It has been known in cultivation since 1724. It is an important timber tree and is widely planted as an ornamental. It is estimated that 45 percent of all ash lumber used is from the White Ash. The center of production is now the lower Mississippi valley. No differentiation is made in the lumber trade as to the species of ash; however, the term "white ash" generally designates top quality ash. Ash wood is used for tanks, silos, toys, musical instruments, cabinets, refrigerators, millwork, sash, doors, frames, vehicle parts, farm utensils, woodenware, butter tubs, veneer, fuel, railroad cross ties, sporting goods, furniture, cooperage, handles, ships, boats, railroad cars, and frame parts of airplanes. It usually grows in association with other hardwoods in well-drained soils on slopes. It is valuable in small tracts for woodland management. Although sometimes used, it is not as valuable for shelter-belt planting as Green Ash. The fruit is known to be eaten by a number of birds, including the purple finch and pine grosbeak, and the foliage is browsed by rabbit, porcupine, and white-tailed deer.

DOGBANE FAMILY (Apocynaceae)

Common Oleander

Nerium oleander L. [D, E]

Field Identification. Cultivated, clumped shrub to 18 ft, 3–8 in. in diameter at the base.

Flowers. Odorless, blooming during summer in compound, terminal cymes; flowers variously colored, and often double; corolla-tube funnelform, dilated into a narrow-campanulate throat with crownlike appendages 3–5-toothed; limb salverform, 1½–3 in. across, 5-lobed; lobes convolute in the bud, obliquely apiculate, twisted to the right; stamens 5, alternating with corolla-lobes,

filaments partly adnate to corolla-tube; anthers with 2 basal tails, apex long-attenuate, hairy, 2-celled; styles united, slender, stigma simple, ovary superior and 2-carpellate; calyx of 5 persistent sepals, imbricate in the bud, lanceolate, acuminate, ⅙–¼ in. long.

Fruit. The 2 ovaries forming follicles, erect or nearly so, 4–8 in. long, seeds twisted.

Leaves. Numerous, opposite, or in whorls of 3–4, linear to elliptic, margin entire and often whitened, revolute, apex and base acute or acuminate, firm and leathery, many-nerved; dark green and glabrous with a conspicuous yellowish green main vein above; paler beneath with numerous, delicate, almost parallel lateral veins.

Twigs. Erect or arching, young ones green, older ones light brown to gray; lenticels numerous, oval.

Range. Cultivated in gardens in Texas and Louisiana, sometimes escaping cultivation. A native of Asia and widely distributed from the Mediterranean region to Japan. Cultivated throughout the tropics and subtropics.

Remarks. The genus name, *Nerium*, is from the Greek *neros* ("moist"), referring to places the wild plants grow. The species name, *oleander*, is from the Latin, meaning "olivelike," referring to the leaves. The flowers are poisonous if eaten by human beings, and the leaves have been known to kill cattle. They also contain a small amount of rubber. Oleander has been used for rat poison in Europe for many centuries. The symptoms of poisoning in human beings are abdominal pain, dilation of the pupil, vomiting, vertigo, insensibility, convulsive movements, small and slow pulse, and in fatal cases epileptiform convulsions with coma ending in death. The erratic pulsation of the heart where death has not followed has been pronounced, the pulse for 5 days remaining as low as 40 beats per minute. An infusion made from 4 ounces of the root is affirmed to have taken life. The active principle of the plant is a glycoside, oleandrin, which hydrolyzes into a gitoxigenin.

VERBENA FAMILY (Verbenaceae)

Lilac Chaste-tree

Vitex agnus-castus L. [D, E]

Field Identification. Cultivated, aromatic tree to 30 ft, often with many trunks from base. Branches slender and spreading outward to form a wide, broad-topped crown.

Flowers. May–September, panicled spikes conspicuous, terminal, dense, puberulent to pulverulent, 4–12 in. long, ½–1¼ in. wide; flowers sessile or very short pediceled; corolla blue to purplish, ¼–⅓ in. long, funnelform; tube slightly curved, densely white-pubescent above the calyx; limb ⅕–¼ in. broad, slightly oblique, ciliate, white hairs at the limb sinuses, somewhat 2-lipped, 5-lobed, upper 2 lobes and lateral 2 lobes ovate and obtuse, lower lobe largest, obtuse to rounded; stamens 4, exserted, 2 sometimes longer than the others but not always, anthers with nearly parallel, arched or spreading sacs; stigma exserted, slender, 2-cleft; ovary 4-celled and 4-ovuled; calyx campanulate, ¹⁄₁₂–⅛ in. long, densely white-puberulent, irregularly and shallowly 5-toothed, teeth triangular and acute; bractlets and bracteoles linear-setaceous, ¹⁄₂₅–⅙ in. long.

Fruit. Small, globular, brown to black, ⅛–⅙ in. long, the persistent calyx membranous; stone 4-celled, no endosperm.

Leaves. Internodes 1¼–4 in. long, leaves decussate-opposite, deciduous, digitately compound of 3–9 (mostly 5–7) leaflets, (blades) 1¼–5 in., central one usually largest, linear to linear-elliptic or lanceolate, apex attenuate-acuminate; base gradually narrowed into a semiwing and channeled, sessile in the smaller leaves; margin entire or plane surface undulate-repand, texture thin; upper surface dull green and glabrous or minutely pulverulent; lower surface paler or almost whitened, puberulent, veins reticulate under magnification; petioles ½–3 in. long, densely grayish or reddish brown, puberulent to pulverulent or cinereous, resinous-granular.

Twigs. Slender, elongate, quadrangular, green to reddish brown or gray, grayish puberulent and pulverulent, pith stout.

Bark. Smooth, light to dark gray on young branches, on old trunks gray with broad ridges and shallow fissures.

Range. Dry, sunny situations, in various types of soils. From China and India, widely cultivated in Europe and Asia. In the

United States cultivated from Texas eastward to Florida and
northward to North Carolina. Sometimes escaping cultivation.

Remarks. The genus name, *Vitex*, is the ancient Latin name. The
species name, *agnus-castus*, is from *agnus* ("lamb") and *castus*
("pure, holy, or chaste"). Vernacular names are Monk's Pepper-
tree, Wild Pepper, Indian Spice, Abraham's Balm, Hemp-tree,
Sage-tree, Wild Lavender, Common Chaste-tree, True Chaste-tree,
Tree of Chastity, Chaste Lamb-tree.

The seeds of the Chaste-tree are reported to be sedative. In Brazil a perfume is made from the flowers, and the aromatic leaves are used to spice food.

TRUMPET-CREEPER FAMILY
(Bignoniaceae)

Southern Catalpa

Catalpa bignonioides Walt. [D, E, F]

Field Identification. Tree to 60 ft and 2–4 ft in diameter. Trunk short, crown broad and rounded, branches stout and brittle.

Flowers. May–July, borne in large, erect, broad-pyramidal panicles up to 10 in. long; irregular, perfect, showy and attractive; calyx deeply 2-lipped, about ½ in. long, glabrous, purplish, lips broad-concave, abruptly pointed; corolla white, bell-shaped, tube expanded into throat, 1½–2 in. long, about 1½ in. wide, channeled and keeled on lower side; limb oblique, 2-lipped, upper lip 2-lobed, lower lip 3-lobed, lobes crisped; interior of corolla with 2

rows of yellow and purple spots; fertile stamens 2 (rarely, 4), but some sterile and rudimentary; filaments filiform with spreading linear-oblong anthers; ovary sessile, 2-celled; style filiform with 2 exserted stigmas.

Fruit. Ripening in October, capsule beanlike, linear, cylindrical, woody, 8–18 in. long, ⅜–½ in. wide, thin-walled, pointed, tardily dehiscent into 2 valves; seeds numerous, flat, about 1 in. long and ¼ in. wide, apices winged and fringed with white hairs.

Leaves. Simple, opposite or whorled, deciduous, ovate, apex abruptly acuminate or acute, base subcordate or truncate, entire, sometimes lobed, blades 5–12 in. long, upper surface glabrous and light green, lower surface paler and pubescent, strong-scented; petioles stout, terete, shorter than the blade, 5–6 in. long, pubescent.

Twigs. Stout, brittle, greenish purple to grayish brown, lustrous; lenticels large and pale; leaf scars suborbicular, bundle scars about 10; buds large, subglobose; pith large, white.

Bark. Thin, light brown to gray, divided into narrow scales.

Wood. Grayish brown to lavender-tinged, sapwood lighter, coarse and straight-grained, no characteristic odor or taste, very durable, weighs about 28 lbs per cu ft, shrinks little, weak in endwise compression, soft, moderately high in shock resistance, weak in bending.

Range. Thought to be native from Florida and Georgia, westward into Louisiana. Doubtful whether native in Texas, Oklahoma, and Arkansas, though planted for many years and escaping cultivation in those states and elsewhere.

Remarks. The genus name, *Catalpa*, is the American Indian name, and the species name, *bignonioides*, refers to its flowers resembling the Bignonia-vine. Abbé Jean Paul Bignon was the court librarian to Louis XV. Vernacular names for the tree are Candle-tree, Cigar-tree, Smoking-bean, Bean-tree, Catawba, Indian-bean, and Indian-cigar. The wood of Southern Catalpa is used for posts, poles, rails, crossties, interior finish, and cabinet work.

Desert-willow

Chilopsis linearis (Cav.) Sweet [D, E, F, G]

Field Identification. Shrub or slender tree to 30 ft, with trunks usually leaning.

Flowers. Mostly May–June, but blooming sporadically after rains in other months, showy, perfect, in short panicles 2–4 in. long; corolla funnelform-campanulate, slightly oblique, 1–1½ in. long, 5-lobate, lobes suborbicular and undulate on the margins, disposed in 2 lips; lower lip 3-lobed, dark pink or purple with the central lobe longest; upper lip 2-lobed and pink, throat white, yellow, or streaked purple (corolla variable in color shades from white or purple); 4 stamens, 2 long and 2 short, included, adnate to the wall of the corolla within; filaments filiform, glabrous; anthers oblong, cells divergent at maturity; a solitary staminodium, shorter than the stamens, which is also included; pistil simple, usually longer than the stamens; ovary 2-celled, glabrous, lobes flattened, ovate, rounded; ovules numerous; calyx splitting into 2 lips, lips about ¼ in. long, ovate, concave, acute, thin, papery, pubescent or glabrous.

Fruit. Capsule borne on stout peduncles ½–1 in. long, linear, 4–12 in. long, about ¼ in. thick, subterete, striate, 2-valved, apiculate at the apex, persistent; seeds numerous, compressed, oblong, about ⅓ in. long, in 2 ranks, extended into wings with long fimbriate white hairs.

Leaves. Deciduous, opposite or alternate, linear to lanceolate, entire, thin, 3-nerved, 4–12 in. long, average length 3–5 in., ¼–⅓ in. wide, attenuate long-pointed at the ends, pubescent or glabrous, rather pale green on both sides, sometimes viscid-sticky; petiole short or none, almost winged by the leaf base.

Twigs. Slender, green the first year, somewhat pubescent later, gray to reddish brown and glabrous.

Bark. Smooth and brown on young trunks, dark brown to black later and breaking into broad ridges with small scales, fissures irregular and rather deep.

Wood. Dark brown with lighter streaks, coarse-grained, soft, weak, rather durable in contact with the soil, specific gravity 0.59.

Range. The species, *linearis*, and its varieties grow along arid desert washes or dry arroyos from Texas north into New Mexico, west to Arizona and California, south into the Mexican states of Nuevo León, Tamaulipas, Zacatecas, Chihuahua, Sonora, Durango, and Baja California.

Remarks. The genus name, *Chilopsis*, is from the Greek words *cheilos* ("lip") and *opsis* ("likeness"), with reference to the corolla lips. The species name, *linearis*, refers to the narrow leaves. Also known under the vernacular names of Flowering-willow, Willow-leaf-catalpa, and Flor de Mimbre. These names arise from the fact that the flowers resemble those of the catalpa tree and the leaves are willowlike in appearance.

The wood is used for fence posts and fuel, and baskets are woven from the twigs. It is reported that in Mexico a decoction of the flowers is used for coughs and bronchial disturbances. The flowers also make good honey. The foliage is unpalatable to livestock and is eaten only under stress. Various birds consume the winged seeds, which average about 75,000 per lb. Only about half the seeds are viable, and according to United States Forest Service data only about 4,000 usable plants can be obtained from a pound of seed. The tree grows readily from cuttings and is being planted extensively for ornament.

MADDER FAMILY (Rubiaceae)

Common Button-bush

Cephalanthus occidentalis L. [D, E, F, G]

Field Identification. Shrub or small tree to 18 ft, growing in low areas, often swollen at the base.

Flowers. June–September. Borne on peduncles 1–3 in. long, white, sessile, clustered in globular heads 1–1½ in. in diameter;

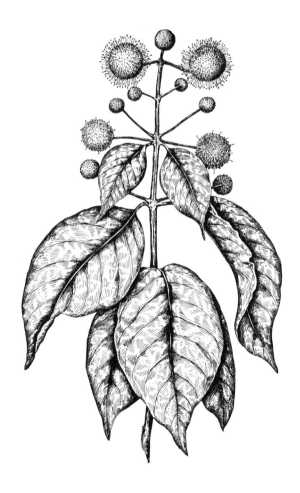

corolla ¼–½ in. long, tubular with 4 short, ovate, spreading lobes; stamens 4, inserted in corolla-throat, anthers oblong; style slender, exserted; stigma capitate; ovary 2-celled; calyx-tube obpyramidal with 4–5 rounded sepals.

Fruit. September–October. Round cluster of reddish brown nutlets; nutlets dry, obpyramidal, ¼–⅓ in. long.

Leaves. Opposite, or in whorls of 3, simple, deciduous, short-petioled, ovate or lanceolate-oblong, acuminate or acute at apex, rounded or narrow at base, entire; blades 2–8 in. long, 1–3 in. wide, dark green and glabrous above or somewhat hairy beneath; petioles glabrous, stout, ½–¾ in. long; stipules small, triangular.

Twigs. Dark reddish brown, lustrous, glaucous when young; lenticels pale and elongate.

Bark. Thin, smooth, gray to brown, later with flattened ridges and deep fissures.

Range. New Mexico, Oklahoma, Texas, Arkansas, and Louisiana; eastward to Florida, and throughout North America from southern Canada to the West Indies, also in eastern Asia.

Remarks. The Greek genus name, *Cephalanthus*, means "head-flower," and the species name, *occidentalis*, means "western." Vernacular names for the shrub are Spanish Pincushion, River-brush, Swampwood, Button-willow, Crane-willow, Little-snow-ball, Pinball, Box, Button-wood, Pond-dogwood, Uvero, and Crouper-brush. It is frequently cultivated as an ornamental shrub and provides good bee food. According to stomach records the nutlet is eaten by at least 25 species of birds, mostly water birds. The wood is of no economic value.

HONEYSUCKLE FAMILY (Caprifoliaceae)

American Elder

Sambucus canadensis L. [D, E]

Field Identification. Stoloniferous shrub with many stems from the base, or under favorable conditions a tree to 30 ft. Stems thinly woody with a large white pith.

Flowers. Borne May–July in conspicuous, large, terminal, convex or flattened cymes, sometimes as much as 10 in. across. Peduncles and pedicels striate, green at first, reddish later. Corolla

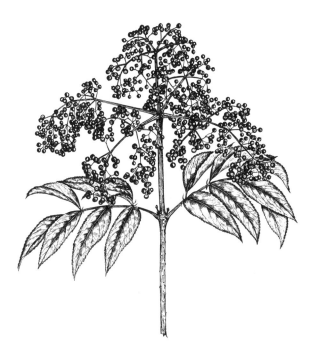

white, ⅕–¼ in. wide, tube short and expanding into 5 lobes; lobes ovate to oblong, rounded, about ⅛ in. long; calyx minute, 5-lobed; stamens 5, exserted, inserted at the base of the corolla; filaments slender, white, about ⅛ in. long, anthers oblong, yellow; style short, depressed, 3-parted; ovary inferior, 4-celled and 1-seeded.

Fruit. Drupe berrylike, deep purple or black, subglobose, ⅙–¼ in. in diameter, bittersweet, 4-celled, seed roughened.

Leaves. Deciduous, opposite, 4–12 in. long, odd-pinnately compound of 5–11 (usually 5–7) leaflets; rachis glabrous or pubescent; leaflets elliptic to lanceolate or ovate to oval, apex acute or acuminate, base rounded or broadly cuneate, margin sharply serrate, blades 2–6 in. long, width 1–2 in.; petiolules ⅛–¼ in. long, pubescent; upper surface lustrous, bright green and glabrous; lower surface paler, barely or copiously pubescent.

Stems. Smooth to angular or grooved, green to red when young, older stems reddish, yellowish or gray, bark sometimes with warty protuberances, nodes sometimes enlarged; external woody layer thin, pith large and white.

Range. In rich moist soil, along streams, low places, fence rows. In Oklahoma, Arkansas, Texas, and Louisiana; eastward to Florida and Georgia, northward to Nova Scotia, and westward to Kansas and Manitoba.

Remarks. The genus name, *Sambucus*, is the classical Latin name, and the species name, *canadensis*, refers to Canada, where the plant grows at its most northern limit. It is also known under the local names of Elder-berry, Common Elder, Sweet Elder, Pie Elder, and Elder-blow. The various parts of the plant have been used for food or medicine in domestic practice. The fruit is made into pies, wines, and jellies. The flowers are used to flavor candies and jellies, and the Indians made a drink by soaking them in water. The dried leaves have been used as an insecticide, and the bark in preparing a black dye. The stems, with the pith removed, were formerly used as drains in tapping maple sugar, and children make whistles, flutes, and popguns from them. The plant has considerable value as a wildlife food, being eaten by about 45 species of birds, especially the gallinaceous birds, such as the quail, pheasant, and prairie chicken. It is also browsed by white-tailed deer and is considered highly palatable to livestock; however, its use by livestock should be investigated further. The writer has noted that in some localities it is browsed, but in other localities the cattle refuse to touch it even under stress conditions.

Mexican Elder

Sambucus mexicana Presl. [G]

Field Identification. Shrub or half-evergreen tree to 30 ft, with a diameter of 6–18 in. Trunk often much thickened at the base.

Flowers. Mostly April–June, but sometimes at other seasons after rains; cymes flat or depressed, occasionally somewhat rounded, 4–8 in. broad, the axis seldom continuous; calyx minutely 5-sepaled; corolla yellowish white, ⅛–⅙ in. broad, tube short; petals 5, rotate, equal, distinct; stamens 5, adnate to the corolla-base, filaments short, anthers opening, extrorsely by clefts; stigmas 3, styles short, ovary 3-celled, ovule solitary in each cavity and pendulous.

Fruit. Berrylike drupe about ¼ in. in diameter, ovoid to sub-globose, black, more rarely slightly glaucous, when glaucous having a bluish appearance; seeds elongate and somewhat flattened, usually 1–3 in a drupe.

Leaves. Opposite, odd-pinnately compound of 3–5 leaflets (more rarely 7), the lower ones rarely 3-parted, rachis densely pubescent; leaflets elliptic to narrowly oblong or ovate, occasionally somewhat obovate, apex short-acuminate, margins finely serrate, mostly less than 3 in. long, pale green, thick and leathery, rather variable in hairiness on the surfaces, some plants almost glabrous, others with varying degrees of pubescence to densely so at the other extreme.

Twigs. Slender, green to reddish brown, when young striate, when older less so, pithy.

Bark. Gray, thickened, on older trunks furrowed and scaly.

Wood. Brownish, soft, coarse-grained, specific gravity about 0.46.

Range. Along low places, ditches, and streams, at altitudes of 1,000–4,000 ft in the desert or desert grassland. In Texas and New Mexico, west to southern California; also in Mexico.

Remarks. The genus name, *Sambucus*, is the classical Latin name, and the species name, *mexicana*, refers to Mexico. It is known in the Latin American countries under the names of Saúco, Azumiatl, Cubemba, Cumdumba, Xumetl, Uttzirza, Bixhumi, Yutnucate, Shiilsh, and Coyopa. The fruit is also of considerable value for wildlife, being eaten by at least a dozen species of birds. The leaves are browsed by mule deer and have some value as livestock browse in winter. Dyes from the stems are used for coloring baskets. The fruit makes excellent wines and pies and is often dried by the Indians and stored for future use.

Rusty Blackhaw Viburnum

Viburnum rufidulum Raf. [D, E, F]

Field Identification. An irregularly branched shrub or tree to 40 ft, with opposite, finely serrate, shiny leaves.

Flowers. In flat cymes 2–6 in. across with 3–4 stout rays and minute subulate bracts and bractlets; corolla small, ¼–⅓ in. in diameter, regular; petals 5, rounded orbicular or oblong, white; stamens 5, attached to the corolla, exserted, anthers oblong and introrse; pistil with style absent and stigmas 1–3, sessile on the ovary, ovary 3-celled, only 1 cell maturing.

Fruit. Ripe July–October, in drooping clusters, drupes ⅓–½ in. long, oblong to obovoid, bluish black, glaucous; seed solitary, flattened, oval to ovate, ridged toward one end.

Leaves. Simple, opposite, deciduous, or half-evergreen southward, dark green, leathery, shiny above, paler below with red hairs on veins, margin finely serrate, elliptic to obovate or oval, apex rounded to acute or obtuse, base cuneate or rounded, 1½–4 in. long, 1–2½ in. broad, petiole grooved, wing-margined, clothed with red hairs, length ½–¾ in.

Bark. Rather rough, ridges narrow and rounded, fissures narrow, breaking into dark reddish brown or black squarish plates.

Twigs. Young ones gray with reddish hairs, older ones reddish brown, more glabrous.

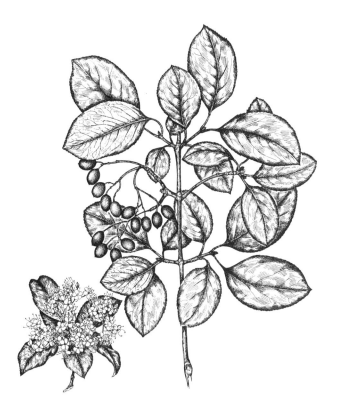

Wood. Fine-grained, hard, heavy, strong, with a disagreeable odor.

Range. In river-bottom lands or dry uplands. Oklahoma, Arkansas, Texas, and Louisiana; eastward to Florida, northward to Virginia, and west to Kansas.

Remarks. The genus name, *Viburnum*, is the classical name of the Wayfaring-tree, *V. lantana* L., of Eurasia, which is often cultivated. The species name, *rufidulum*, refers to the rufous-red hairs on young parts. This character prompted the use of the name *V. rufotomentosum* Small at one time. Some vernacular names are Rusty Nanny-berry, Southern Nanny-berry, Blackhaw, Southern Blackhaw. The tree is worthy of cultivation because of the lustrous leaves, cymes of white flowers in April, and bluish black fruit in October. The wood is of no particular value.

Blackhaw Viburnum

Viburnum prunifolium L. [D]

Field Identification. Shrub or small tree to 28 ft, with a diameter of 10 in., the stiff spreading branches forming an irregular crown.

Flowers. April–June, with the leaves or slightly before, cymes sessile or nearly so, compound, round-topped, white, 3–4-rayed, 2–4 in. wide; individual flowers ⅙–¼ in. wide; calyx 5-toothed; corolla-tube short, deeply 5-lobed, rotate and spreading, lobes suborbicular; stamens 5, filaments slender, exserted, inserted on the corolla-tube; anthers oblong, introrse; style absent; stigmas 3, minute and sessile; ovary 3-celled, 1 ovule usually maturing.

Fruit. August–October, drupe ⅓–½ in. long, ellipsoid to subglobose, bluish black, glaucous or only slightly so, flesh thin and dry but sweet; seed solitary, flat, oval or elliptic, or one side slightly convex, anatropous, embryo small, albumen fleshy.

Leaves. Simple, opposite, deciduous, 1–2¾ in. long, oval to ovate or obovate, or oblong to elliptic; apex acute to obtuse or rounded;

base obtuse to rounded, margin finely serrulate; upper surface dull green (not lustrous), smooth, lower surface paler, membranaceous but later subcoriaceous; petiole green to red, slender, ¼–¾ in. long, not winged or only slightly so; buds slender, short-pointed, with small reddish fascicled hairs and whitish crystals, scales involute.

Twigs. Slender, rigid, green to reddish or brown, some with short lateral spurs.

Bark. Gray to brown with narrow rounded ridges broken into short sections.

Wood. Reddish brown, hard, weighs 52 lb per cu ft, of no commercial importance.

Range. Thickets, roadsides, borders of woods, and along streams. Oklahoma, Arkansas, Texas, and Louisiana; east to Florida, north to Connecticut, and west to Michigan and Kansas.

Remarks. The genus name, *Viburnum*, was the Latin name applied to the Wayfaring-tree but is of uncertain origin. The species name, *prunifolium*, means "plum-leaved." It also is known under the vernacular names of Sheep-berry, Nanny-berry, Sweet-haw, Sweet-sloe, Stag-bush, and Arrowwood. The plant has been cultivated for ornament since 1727. The fruit is sweet and edible and is known to be eaten by 12 species of birds, including bobwhite quail, and also by the gray fox and white-tailed deer.

Possum-haw Viburnum

Viburnum nudum L. [D]

Field Identification. Irregularly branched shrub or small tree, rarely over 20 ft.

Flowers. April–June, white, perfect, borne in flat or round-topped cymes 2–4½ in. across, primary peduncles ½–1 in. long, often with ovate, acute bracts; pedicels ¼–⅓ in. long; corolla about 3/16 in. broad, 5-lobed; lobes spreading or reflexed, broad-ovate to rounded, apex obtuse to rounded; stamens 5, exserted about ⅛ in. beyond the corolla; filaments white, filiform, with short-oblong anthers; pistil short, included at anthesis; calyx about 1/16 in. long, greenish, short-tubular, lobes short-ovate, obtuse or acute.

Fruit. Mature in autumn, in cymes 2–4½ in. across, pink at first but glaucous-blue later, about ¼ in. in diameter, subglobose to short-oblong or somewhat flattened, wrinkling early, fleshy; seed black, compressed, rounded, rugose, ridged down the middle, apices with abrupt points; fruiting peduncles with rusty brown scales, finely grooved, ½–1 in. long, rebranched into short pedicels about ¼ in. long.

Leaves. Opposite, leathery, shiny, variable in size, shape, and scurfiness, oblong to elliptic or oval, blades 2–5 in. long, 1–2 in. broad, margin entire or obscurely serrulate; apex acute, obtuse, acuminate, rounded or abruptly pointed; base rounded or cuneate into a narrow wing on petiole; olive green to dark green and lustrous above, lower surface paler and with rusty brown scales; petioles slender, somewhat winged, pubescent and brown-scaly, about ½ in. long; buds usually acuminate, ½–¾ in. long, with reddish brown scales.

Bark. Gray to brown, rather smooth.

Twigs. Young ones gray to reddish brown or green, lustrous, finely grooved, rusty brown, scaly; older twigs glabrous.

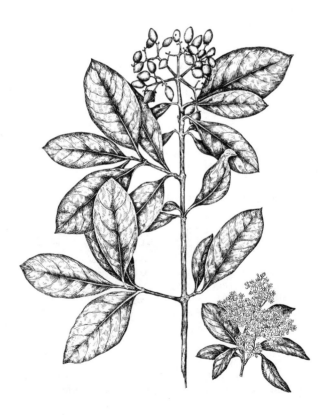

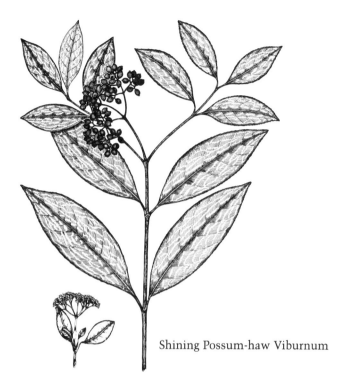

Shining Possum-haw Viburnum

Range. In sandy, acid swamps, usually in pinelands. East Texas, Louisiana, Oklahoma, and Arkansas; eastward to Florida and north to Tennessee and Kentucky.

Remarks. Viburnum is the classical name of a Eurasian tree, and the species name, *nudum*, refers to the rather naked stems with remote leaves. Vernacular names in use are Withe-rod, Smooth Withe-rod, Naked Withe-rod, Bilberry, Nanny-berry, and Swamp-haw Viburnum. The sweet but unpalatable fruit is consumed by a number of species of birds, including the bobwhite quail.

Shining Possum-haw Viburnum, *V. nitidum* Ait., is hardly different from *V. nudum* L., but the leaves may vary to somewhat narrower, acuminate, shiny, and less coriaceous or they may be smaller. It also grows in low wet grounds and appears to have about the same distribution. However, these characteristics are not constant and some authors use the names of *V. nudum* var. *angustifolium* T. & G. or *V. cassinoides* var. *nitidum* (Ait.) McAtee.

DIAGRAMS

Inflorescence

  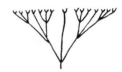

Head   Corymb   Compound umbel   Spadix

Leaf Apices

Acuminate   Acute   Obtuse   Truncate   Retuse

Leaf Margins

Entire   Serrate   Dentate   Crenate   Undulate   Sinua

Leaf Forms

Linear   Lanceolate   Oblong   Elliptical   Ovate

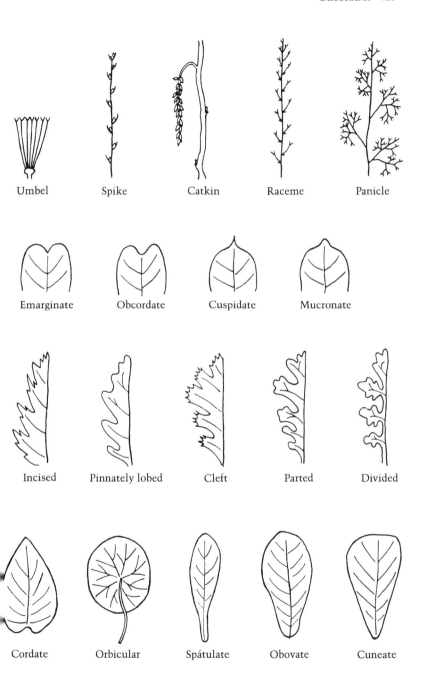

Umbel Spike Catkin Raceme Panicle

Emarginate Obcordate Cuspidate Mucronate

Incised Pinnately lobed Cleft Parted Divided

Cordate Orbicular Spátulate Obovate Cuneate

Flower Parts

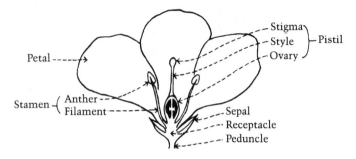

GLOSSARY

A- (prefix). Without, lacking.

Abaxial. On the dorsal side, away from the axis.

Aberrant. Not normal, atypical.

Abortive. Imperfectly developed.

Abruptly acuminate. Suddenly pointed from a rounded or truncate apex.

Abruptly pinnate. A pinnate leaf ending with a pair of leaflets; even-pinnate.

Acaulescent. Without a stem aboveground.

Accrescent. Increasing in size with age.

Accumbent. Lying against and face to face.

Acerose. Needlelike.

Achene. A small, dry, hard, one-seeded, indehiscent fruit.

Acicular. Bristlelike.

Acidulous. Slightly acid or bitter.

Acorn. The fruit of oaks.

Acotyledonous. Without cotyledons.

Acrid. Bitter or sharp tasting, usually referring to the fruit or sap.

Acropetal. Borne in succession toward the apex, as in certain inflorescences.

Acuminate. Referring to an acute apex whose sides are concave.

Acute. Terminating with a sharp angle.

Adherent. Referring to two dissimilar parts or organs which touch but are not fused.

Adnate. Grown together; organically united.

Adventive. A recent, perhaps temporary, introduction, not as yet naturalized, or barely so.

Aerenchyma. Spongy respiratory tissue in stems of many aquatic plants, characterized by large intercellular spaces.

Aerial. Parts above the ground or water.

Aggregate. Referring to a type of fruit with a cluster of ripened coherent ovaries.

Alkaloid. An organic base produced in some plants, sometimes with medicinal or poisonous properties.

Allergic. Subject to irritation by foreign substances.

Alpine. At high elevations; above the tree line.

Alternate. Placed singly at different levels on the axis.

Alternation of generations. Alternate sexual and asexual generations.

Alveola. Surface cavity of carpel or seed.

Ament. A catkin or scaly-bracted, often pendulous, spike of naked or reduced flowers.

Amplexicaul. Clasping the stem.

Ampliate. Expanded or enlarged.

Anastomosing. Netted; said of leaf blades with cross veins forming a network.

Anatropous. Referring to an ovule's position when the micropyle is close to the point of funiculus attachment.

Androecium. Stamens, in the collective sense.

Androgynous. Bearing staminate and pistillate flowers in the same inflorescence.

Androphore. Supporting stalk of a group of stamens.

Angulate. Angled.

Annulus. A ring-shaped part or organ.

Anterior. Away from the axis; the front; toward a subtending leaf or bract.

Anther. The polleniferous part of a stamen.

Anther cells. The actual chambers or locules of an anther.

Anther sac. Pollen sac of an anther.

Antheriferous. Having anthers.

Anthesis. Time of expansion of a flower; pollination time.

Anthocarp. A fruit condition in which at least a portion of the perianth is united with the ovary wall itself.

Antrorse. Directed upward.

Apetalous. Lacking petals.

Apex. The top or termination of a part or organ.

Apiculate. Ending in a short pointed tip.

Apomixis. Reproduction without sexual union.

Appendages. Various subsidiary or secondary outgrowths.

Appressed. Closely and flatly pressed against.

Approximate. Adjacent or close.

Aquatic. Growing in water.

Arachnoid. Bearing weak, tangled, cobwebby hairs.

Arboreal. Referring to trees, treelike.

Arborescent. Like trees in size and growth habit.

Arcuate. Somewhat curved.

Arenicolous. Sand loving.

Areole, areola (pl. *areolae*). An open space or island formed by anastomosing veins in a foliar organ; spine-bearing area of cactus.

Aril. An appendage or complete additional covering of the seed, arising as an outgrowth from hilum or funicle.

Aristate. With a stiff, bristlelike appendage.

Articulated. Jointed and cleanly separating to leave a scar.

Ascending. Growing upward, but not erect.

Asexual. Without sex, reproduction without sexual union, such as by cuttings, buds, bulbs, etc.

Assurgent. Ascending.

Asymmetric. Not symmetrical; with no plane of symmetry.

Atypical. Not typical.

Attenuate. Slenderly tapering.

Auricle. Earlike attachment, such as at the base of some leaves or petals.

Auriculate. Furnished with auricles.

Autophytic. Having chlorophyll, self-sustaining.

Axial. Referring to the axis.

Axil. The upper angle formed by a leaf with the stem, or veins with other veins.

Axile. Situated on the axis.

Axillary. Situated in an axil.

Axis. The center line of any organ; the main stem.

Baccate. Berrylike; bearing berries.

Banner. Upper or posterior petal of a papilionaceous flower.

Barb. A bristlelike hooked hair or projection.

Bark. External tissues of woody plants, especially the dead corky layer external to the cortex or bast in trees.

Basal. At or near the base.

Beak. A narrow pointed outgrowth of a fruit, a petal, etc.

Berry. A fruit in which the ovary becomes a fleshy or pulpy mass enclosing one or more seeds, as is seen in the tomato.

Bi- (prefix). Two or two-parted.

Bifid. Cleft into two lobes.

Biglandular. With two glands.

Bilabiate. Two-lipped, as in some irregular corollas.

Bipinnate. Twice pinnate.

Bisexual. Having both sex organs in the same flower.

Biternate. Twice ternate.

Blade. The expanded portion of a leaf.

Brackish. Partially saline.

Bract. A more or less modified leaf subtending a flower or belonging to a cluster of flowers.

Bracteole. A small bract or bractlet.

Bractlet. The bract of a pedicel.

Bud. The rudimentary state of a shoot; an unexpanded flower.

Bud scales. Modified leaves protecting a bud, often dry, resinous or viscid.

Caducous. Falling early.

Caliche. A hard calcareous soil.

Callose. Bearing a callus.

Callus. A thickened or hardened protuberance or region.

Calyculus. Usually in the Compositae, referring to the short outer sepallike phyllaries of an involucre.

Calyx. The outer perianth whorl of the flower.

Campanulate. Bell-shaped.

Canaliculate. Having one or a few prominent longitudinal grooves.

Cancellate. With cross hatching or latticed ridges.

Canescent. Hoary with a gray pubescence.

Capillary. Hairlike.

Capitate. In a head, or headlike.

Capsule. A dry dehiscent fruit composed of more than one carpel.

Carina. A dorsal ridge or keel.

Carpel. A simple pistil, or one member of a compound pistil; the ovule-bearing portion of a flower, believed to be of foliar origin.

Cartilaginous. Firm or tough tissue, suggestive of animal cartilage.

Caruncle. A seed protuberance; a small hard aril.

Catkin. A delicate, scaly bracted, usually pendulous, spike of flowers; an ament.

Caudate. Long-attenuate; taillike.

Caudex. Enlarged basal part of stems, or combined root and stem.

Caulescent. Having an evident stem, as contrasted to acaulescent.

Cauline. Borne on the stem.

Centrifugal inflorescence. Flowers developing from the center outward; a determinate type, such as a cyme.

Centripetal inflorescence. Flowers developing from the outer edge toward the center; an indeterminate type, such as a corymb.

Cespitose, caespitose. In tufts.

Chaff. A small scale, as is found on the receptacle of many Compositae.

Chaparral. A type of low scrub, commonly with dense twiggy, thorny habit and evergreen leaves.

Chartaceous. Like old parchment; papery.

Ciliate. Bearing marginal hairs.

Ciliolate. Bearing short marginal hairs.

Cinereous. Ashy gray.

Circinate. Referring to a leaf that is coiled from the tip toward the base, the lower surface outermost.

Cirrhus. A tendril.

Clambering. Leaning on other plants or objects, not self-supporting.

Clasping. Enveloping the stem partially or wholly at the base, as leaf bases, bracts, stipules, etc.

Clavate. Club-shaped.

Claw. Narrowed petiolelike base of a petal or sepal.

Cleft. Incised or cut nearly or quite to the middle.

Cleistogamous. Said of flowers that are self-fertilized without expanding; modified or reduced flowers.

Climber. Plant seeking support by twining or by tendrils.

Coalescent. Grown together, as in similar parts.

Coat. Covering of a seed.

Coherent. Having similar parts in close contact but not fused.

Column. A body formed by the union of parts, such as a union of stamens to form the staminal column in Malvaceae.

Coma. A hair tuft, usually at the apex of seeds.

Commisure. A line of coherence, such as where two carpels are joined.

Compound leaf. A leaf with the blade divided into two or more leaflets.

Compressed. Flattened.

Concavo-convex. Convex on one side and concave on the other.

Concolorous. The same in color.

Conduplicate. Folded lengthwise.

Cone. An inflorescence of flowers or fruit with overlapping scales.

Confluent. Gradually passing into each other.

Congested. Crowded, as flowers in a dense inflorescence.

Conic. Cone-shaped.

Coniferous. Cone-bearing.

Connate. Said of similar parts which are united, at least at the base.

Connective. Extension of the filament of a stamen connecting the anther lobes.

Connivent. Arched inward so that the tips meet.

Consimilar. Alike.

Constricted. Narrowed between wider portions.

Contiguous. Adjacent or adjoining similar or dissimilar parts, not fused.

Contorted. Twisted.

Contracted. Narrowed or shortened.

Convergent. Tending toward a single point, as with leaf veins approaching each other.

Convolute. Rolled together, as with petals in buds of certain plants.

Copious. Abundant, plentiful.

Cordate. Heart-shaped, as in some leaves.

Coriaceous. Leathery in texture.

Corneous. Horny, as in margins of some leaves.
Corniculate. Hornlike in appearance.
Cornute. Spurred or horned.
Corolla. The inner perianth whorl of a flower.
Corona. A crownlike structure on the corolla and the stamens.
Coroniform. Crown-shaped, applied to the pappus of certain Compositae.
Corrugate. Strongly wrinkled.
Corymb. A flat-topped or convex open flower cluster, with its marginal flowers opening first.
Costa. A thickened vein or midrib.
Cotyledon. Plant embryo leaf, usually rich in stored food.
Creeping. Referred to a trailing shoot which strikes root along most of its length.
Crenate. Dentate with the teeth much rounded.
Crenulate. The diminutive of crenate.
Crest. A crown or elevated ridge, often entirely or partly of hair.
Crispate. Crisped or crumpled.
Cross-pollination. Transfer of pollen from flower to flower.
Crown. Usually referring to the branches and foliage of a tree; or thickened bases of stems.
Cruciform. Shaped like a cross.
Crustaceous. Dry and brittle.
Cucullate. Hood-shaped.
Cuneate. Wedge-shaped.
Cupulate. Cup-shaped, as the involucre of an acorn.
Cuspidate. Having a sharp rigid point.
Cyathium. A specialized form of inflorescence of some of the Euphorbias.
Cylindric. Elongate and circular in cross section.
Cylindroid. Like a cylinder but elliptic in cross section.
Cymbiform. Boat-shaped.
Cyme. A usually broad and flattish inflorescence with its central or terminal flowers blooming earliest.
Cymose. Cymelike.
Cymule. A small cyme.

Deciduous. Not persistent, not evergreen.
Declined. Turned downward or outward, as in some stamens.
Decompound. Several times divided, as in repeatedly compound leaves and inflorescences.
Decumbent. Reclining, but ascending at the apices.
Decurrent. Extensions downward, as of some petioles or leaves along the stem.
Decurved. Curved downward.

Decussate. Leaves opposite, with each pair at a right angle to the pair above or below.

Deflexed. Bent downward.

Dehiscent. Opening regularly by valves.

Deltoid. Triangular.

Dentate. Toothed, specifically when teeth have sharp points and spreading bases.

Denticulate. Minutely toothed.

Denudate. Becoming bare.

Depressed. Flattened from above.

Dermatitis. Irritation or inflammation of the skin.

Determinate. Having fixed limits, as in an inflorescential axis ending with a bud; also referring to a cymose, or centrifugal, inflorescence.

Diadelphous. With stamens in two groups.

Dichotomous. Forked in pairs.

Didymous. Twice, two-lobed, in pairs.

Didynamous. With four stamens in two pairs of differing length.

Diffuse. Spreading.

Digitate. Said of a compound leaf in which all the leaflets arise from one point.

Dilated. Expanded or enlarged.

Dimidiate. Reduced to one-half, often by abortion.

Dimorphic. Having two forms.

Dioecious. Unisexual, with the two kinds of flowers on separate plants.

Diploid. Having the somatic number of chromosomes; twice as many as in the germ cells after reduction.

Disarticulate. Breaking at a joint.

Disc, disk. Outgrowth of the receptacle or hypanthium within the perianth, often composed of fused nectaries; central portion of the head in Compositae.

Disciform. Disk-shaped.

Discoid. Referring to a rayless head of flowers, as in some Compositae.

Discolored. Usually of two colors, as in leaf surfaces.

Dissected. Deeply cut or divided into many narrow segments, as in some leaves.

Distal. The apex of an organ, the part most distant from the axis.

Distended. Swollen.

Distichous. In two vertical ranks.

Distinct. Separate, not united.

Diurnal. Opening during the day.

Divaricate. Widely spreading.

Divergent. Spreading apart.

Divided. Lobed to near the base.

Division. Segment of a parted or divided leaf.

Dorsal. Upon or relating to the back or outer surface of an organ.

Dorsifixed. Attached to the dorsal side.

Drupe. A fleshy or pulpy fruit in which the inner portion is hard and stony, enclosing the seed.

Drupelet. A small drupe.

E- (prefix). Without or lacking a structure or organ.

Echinate. Prickly.

Ecology. Science dealing with plants in relation to their environment.

Eglandular. Without glands.

Ellipsoid. Referring to the geometric figure obtained by rotating an ellipse on its longer axis.

Elliptic. Of the form of an ellipse.

Elongate. Lengthened, drawn out.

Emarginate. Referring to a notch, usually of a leaf apex.

Embryo. A young plant, still enclosed in the seed.

Endemic. Known only in a limited geographical area.

Endocarp. Inner layer of the pericarp of the ovary or fruit.

Endosperm. Part of the seed outside the embryo; the albumen or stored food.

Ensiform. Sword-shaped.

Entire. Without toothing or divisions.

Ephemeral. Lasting for only a short period.

Epidermis. The superficial layer of cells.

Epigaeous, epigeous. Growing on the ground, or close to the ground.

Epigynous. Attached to or borne on the pistil, as in some stamens or petals.

Erose. Irregularly toothed.

Estipulate. Exstipulate.

Exalbuminous. Without albumen or endosperm, the embryo filling the seed instead.

Excavated. Referring to some pitted or channeled seeds.

Excurrent. Prolongation of nerves into awns or mucros of a leaf or fruit body; also the prolongation of the main stem or axis of a plant in certain conifers.

Excurved. Curved outward.

Exfoliating. Referring to bark separating into strips or flakes.

Exocarp. The outer layer of pericarp.

Exogenous. Growth by increase of tissue beneath the expanding bark; the cambium region in dicotyledonous woody plants; as opposed to endogenous growth by internal multiplication of tissues in monocotyledonous plants.

Expanded. Spreading, opened to the greatest extent.

Explanate. Flattened out.

Exserted. Projecting beyond an envelope, as stamens from a corolla.

Exstipulate. Lacking stipules.

Extra-axillary. Being near the axil but not truly axillary, as in some flowers.

Extrafloral. Outside the flower, as extrafloral nectaries.

Extrorse. Directed outward.

Exudate. An excretion of wax, gum, sap, etc.

Faceted. Usually applied to seeds with several plane surfaces.

Facial. On the plane surface or face rather than the margin.

Falcate. Sickle- or scythe-shaped.

Farinose. Covered with mealy or floury particles.

Fascicle. A close bundle or cluster.

Fastigiate. Having closely set erect branches.

Faveolate. Honeycombed.

Feather-veined. With secondary veins branching from the main vein.

Fertile. Applied to flowers with pistils capable of producing seeds, or to stamens with functional pollen.

Fetid. Malodorous.

Fibrilla. A very small fringe.

Fibrillose. Having fine fibers, as the leaf margins of some Yuccas.

Fibrous. Bearing a resemblance to fibers, or possessing fibers, as in fibrous roots.

Filament. The part of a stamen which supports the anther.

Filamentose. Having threadlike structures; threadlike.

Filiferous. Bearing threads.

Filiform. Thread-shaped.

Fimbriate. Fringed, frayed at the ends or on the margin.

Flabellate. Fan-shaped.

Flaccid. Lax, limp, flabby.

Flexuose, flexuous. Zigzag, or bent in an alternating manner.

Floccose. Clothed with tufts of soft woolly hairs.

Flora. Referring to flowers.

Floret. A small flower, as in the disk flowers of Compositae.

Floriferous. Having flowers, usually abundantly.

Floristic. Referring to the aggregate aspects of the vegetation, as to species, abundance, and distribution in a geographical sense.

Fluted. Regularly marked by alternating ridges and groovelike depressions.

Foliaceous. Leaflike in texture and appearance.

Foliate. Referring to leaves as opposed to leaflets.

Foliolate. Referring to the leaflets in a compound leaf, such as bifoliolate or trifoliolate.

Follicle. A dry fruit opening along the single suture, the product of a simple pistil.

Fruit. Seed-bearing part of a plant.

Frutescent. Shrubby.

Fugacious. Referring to early-deciduous parts, such as petals or sepals of certain plants.

Fulvous. Tawny, dull yellow.

Functional. Able to produce normally.

Funiculus. The stalk attaching ovule to ovary wall or placenta.

Funnelform. Shaped like a funnel.

Fuscous. Dark brownish gray.

Fusiform. Spindle-shaped.

Gamopetalous. Referring to the petals being more or less united.

Gamosepalous. Referring to the sepals being more or less united.

Geminate. In pairs, twins.

Gene. A unit of inheritance which occupies a fixed place on a chromosome.

Geniculate. Bent like a knee joint.

Gibbous. Swollen or inflated on one side.

Glabrate. Somewhat glabrous or becoming glabrous.

Glabrous. Smooth; pubescence or hairs absent.

Gland. A secreting protuberance or appendage.

Glandular. Bearing glands, or of the nature of a gland.

Glaucous. Covered with a white, waxy bloom.

Globose. Globular, spherical.

Glochid. A hair or minute prickle, often with retrorse or hooklike projections, as in some cacti.

Glomerate. In a headlike or crowded inflorescence.

Glomerule. A small headlike inflorescence.

Glutinous. Gluelike, sticky.

Graduated. Rows or series of bracts, or phyllaries, of different size, as on the involucre of some Compositae.

Granules. Small particles on the surface of a plant, such as resinous granules, wax granules, etc.

Gynoecium, gynecium. The total female element of a flower.

Gynophore. The stalk of a pistil.

Habitat. The environment of a plant.

Halophyte. A plant tolerant of saline conditions.

Haploid. Possessing half of the diploid number of chromosomes, as in the germ cells after the reduction division.

Hastate. Halberd-shaped; sagittate, but with the basal lobes more or less at right angles.

Head. A spherical or flat-topped inflorescence of sessile or nearly sessile flowers borne on a common receptacle.

Heartwood. The oldest wood, inclosing the pith; the hard central, often deeply colored, portion of a tree trunk.

Hermaphrodite. Bisexual.

Heterogamous. Having two or more kinds of flowers with respect to the distribution of sex organs.

Heteromorphic. Unlike in form or size, as sometimes the length of stamens or pistils on different plants of the same species.

Heterostylous. Having styles of different length or character.

Hexamerous. With the parts in sixes.

Hilum. The scar of a seed, marking the point of attachment.

Hip. Fruit in *Rosa*, composed of swollen hypanthium bearing achenes within.

Hirsute. Covered with rather coarse or stiff hairs.

Hirsutulous. Finely or minutely hirsute.

Hispid. Beset with rigid or bristly hairs or with bristles.

Hispidulous. Minutely hispid.

Hoary. Densely grayish white pubescent.

Homochromous. Of uniform color.

Homogeneous. Of the same kind, uniform.

Homomorphic. Of uniform size and shape.

Hood. A concave organ, usually referring to certain petals.

Hyaline. Very thin and translucent.

Hybrid. Product of genetically dissimilar parents.

Hybridization. The production of a hybrid.

Hydrophilous. Referring to a tendency to grow in water.

Hydrophyte. An aquatic plant.

Hypanthium. Upward or outward extension of receptacle derived from fused basal portions of perianth and androecium.

Hypogynous. Inserted beneath the gynoecium, but free from it.

Imbricate. Overlapping.

Immersed. Submerged.

Imparipinnate. Pinnate with a single terminal leaflet; odd-pinnate.

Imperfect. Diclinous; lacking functional stamens or pistils.

Implicate. Twisted together or interwoven.

Impressed. Lying below the general surface; as, impressed veins.

Incanous. Hoary with whitish pubescence.

Incised. Cut sharply, irregularly, and more or less deeply.

Included. Not protruding, not exserted.

Incomplete. Descriptive of flowers in which one or more perianth whorls are wanting.

Incurved. Curved inward.

Indehiscent. Not opening.

Indeterminate. Applied to inflorescences in which the flowers open progressively from the base upward.

Indigenous. Native to an area.

Indument. A covering of hairs or wool.

Induplicate. Having the edges folded together.

Indurate. Hardened.

Inequilateral. Asymmetrical.

Inferior. Usually referring to an ovary being adnate to and appearing as if below the calyx.

Infertile. Not fertile or viable.

Inflated. Bladderlike.

Inflexed. Bent inward.

Inflorescence. A flower cluster; the disposition of flowers.

Inframedial. Below the middle, but not at the base.

Infrastaminal. Below the stamens.

Inodorous. Lacking odor.

Inserted. Attached to or growing out of.

Inter- (prefix). Between.

Intercostal. Between the ribs, veins, or nerves.

Internode. That portion of stem lying between two successive nodes.

Interrupted. Referring to an inflorescence with sterile intervals, mostly of varying length, between the flowers.

Intricate. Densely tangled, as in some branches.

Introflexion. State of being inflexed.

Introrse. Turned inward; facing the axis.

Intrusion. Protruding or projecting inward.

Inverted. Reversed, opposite to the normal direction.

Investing. Enclosing or surrounding.

Involucel. A secondary involucre, subtending a secondary division of an inflorescence as in Umbelliferae.

Involucral. Belonging to an involucre.

Involucre. One or more series of bracts, surrounding a flower cluster or a single flower.

Involute. With edges rolled inward.

Irregular. Said of flowers that are not bilaterally symmetrical.

Joint. A node; a unit of a segmented stem as in *Opuntia.*

Keel. The united pair of petals in a papilionaceous flower; a central or dorsal ridge.

Laciniate. Cut into lobes separated by deep, narrow, irregular incisions.

Lanate, lanuginose. Covered with matted hairs or wool.

Lanceolate. Shaped like a lance head.

Lanulose. Short-woolly.

Leaf. The usually thin and expanded organ borne laterally on the stem; in a strict sense inclusive of the blade, petiole, and stipules; but in common practice referred to the blade only.

Leaflet. A single division of a compound leaf.

Legume. A dry fruit, the product of a simple unicarpellate pistil, usually dehiscing along 2 lines of suture.

Lenticels. Corky growths on young bark.

Lenticular. Having the shape of a double convex lens.

Lepidote. Covered with minute scales or scurf.

Liana. A climbing woody plant.

Ligneous. Woody.

Ligulate. Tongue-shaped.

Ligule. Usually referring to an expanded ray flower in the Compositae.

Limb. The ultimate or uppermost extension of a gamopetalous corolla or calyx; distinct from the tube or throat.

Linear. Long and narrow.

Lingulate. Tongue-shaped.

Lip. One of the (usually two) divisions of an unequally divided corolla or calyx.

Littoral. Growing near the sea.

Lobe. Any segment or division of an organ.

Lobed. Divided into lobes, or having lobes.

Lobulate. With small lobes.

Locule. A compartment of an anther, ovary, or fruit.

Loculicidal. Longitudinally dehiscent dorsally, midway between the septa.

Loment. A fruit of the Leguminosae usually constricted between the seeds, the one-seeded indehiscent portions breaking loose.

Longitudinal. Lengthwise.

Lunate. Crescent-shaped.

Lyrate. Lyre-shaped, or a pinnatifid form with the terminal lobe usually longest.

Marcescent. Persistent after withering.

Marginal. On or pertaining to the margin of a plane organ.

Mealy. Farinose or floury.

Medial, median. Referring to or at the middle.

Membranaceous, membranous. Thin, rather soft, and more or less translucent.

Meniscoid. Concavo-convex, like a watch crystal.

Mericarp. A one-seeded indehiscent carpel of a fruit whose carpels separate at maturity.

-Merous (suffix). Referring to the number of parts; as 4-merous.

Mesophyte. Plant requiring a moderate amount of water.

Microphyllous. Small-leaved.

Midnerve. The central vein or rib.

Midrib. The main rib of a leaf.

Monadelphous. Union of all stamens by their filaments.

Moniliform. Necklacelike.

Monochasial. Applied to a cymose inflorescence with one main axis.

Monochromatic. Of one color.

Monoecious. With stamens and pistils in separate flowers, but on the same plant.

Monopodial. Applied to a stem having a single continuous axis.

Montane. Growing in the mountains.

Mottled. Spotted or blotched.

Mucilaginous. Sticky and moist.

Mucro. A short and small abrupt tip.

Mucronate. Tipped with a mucro.

Mucronulate. Diminutive of mucronate.

Multicipital. With several or numerous stems from a single caudex or taproot.

Multifoliolate. Referring to a compound leaf with numerous leaflets.

Multiple fruit. One that results from the aggregation of ripened ovaries into one mass.

Muricate. With surfaces bearing hard sharp tubercles.

Muriculate. Diminutive of muricate.

Naked. Lacking a customary part or organ; flowers without a perianth, a receptacle without chaff, a stem without leaves, etc.

Nectariferous. Producing nectar.

Nectary. A gland, or an organ containing the gland, which secretes nectar.

Nerve. An unbranched vein.

Neuter. Referring to flowers lacking stamens or pistils; or in some flowers of the Compositae having an ovary but lacking style or stigmas.

Nigrescent. Turning black.

Nocturnal. Night blooming.

Nodding. Arching downward.

Node. The joint of a twig; usually a point bearing a leaf or leaflike structure.

Nut. A hard, indehiscent, one-celled and one-seeded fruit.

Ob- (prefix). Inversely, upside down, as an obovate leaf (inversely ovate), etc.

Obcordate. Inverted heart-shaped.

Oblanceolate. Lanceolate with the broadest part toward the apex.

Oblique. Slanting; with unequal sides.

Oblong. Longer than broad and with nearly parallel sides.

Obovate. Inverted ovate.

Obovoid. Appearing as an inverted egg.

Obsolete. Not evident; very rudimentary; vestigial.

Obtuse. Blunt.

Ochroleucous. Yellowish white.

Ocrea. A tubular sheath formed by the union of a pair of stipules.

Odd-pinnate. A pinnate leaf with a single terminal leaflet.

Opposite. Opposed to each other, such as two opposite leaves at a node.

Orbicular. Circular.

Organ. A part of a plant with a definite function, as a leaf, stamen, etc.

Oval. Broadly elliptical.

Ovary. The part of the pistil that contains the ovules, or seeds after fertilization.

Ovate. Egg-shaped, with the broader end closer to the stem.

Ovoid. Referring to a solid object of ovate or oval outline.

Ovulate. Bearing ovules; referring to the number of ovules.

Ovule. The body which after fertilization becomes the seed.

Palea. A chaffy bract on the receptacle of Compositae.

Pallid. Pale or light colored.

Palmate. Said of a leaf radiately lobed or divided.

Palmatifid. Palmately cleft or lobed.

Palmatisect. Palmately divided.

Palustrine. Growing in wet ground.

Panicle. A branched raceme.

Pannose. Feltlike, covered with closely interwoven hairs.

Papilionaceous. Descriptive of the flowers of certain legumes having a standard, wings, and keel petals; resembling a sweet pea.

Papilla. A small soft protuberance on leaf surfaces, etc.

Papillate. Bearing papillae.

Pappus. Modified calyx of certain Compositae, often elaborate in the fruit, consisting of hairs, bristles, awns, or scales.

Parcifrond. A long leafy usually sterile shoot of a floricane, arising from below the ordinary floral branches.

Parietal. Attached to the wall within the ovary.

Parted. Cleft nearly to the base.

Parthenogenetic. Asexual development of an egg, without fertilization by a male sex cell.

Parti-colored. Variegated.

Pectinate. With narrow, toothlike divisions.

Pedate. Palmate, with the lateral lobes or divisions again divided.

Pedicel. The stalk of a single flower in a cluster.

Pedicellate. Borne on a pedicel.

Peduncle. Primary flower stalk supporting either a cluster or a solitary flower.

Pedunculate. Borne on a peduncle.

Pellucid. Transparent or nearly so.

Peltate. Referring to a leaf blade in which the petiole is attached to the lower surface, instead of on the margin as in the garden nasturtium.

Pendent. Hanging or drooping.

Pendulous. More or less hanging.

Pentagonal. Five-angled.

Pentamerous. Of five parts, as a flower with five petals.

Perennial. Usually living more than two years.

Perfect. Referring to a flower having both pistil and stamens.

Perfoliate. A sessile leaf whose base passes around the stem.

Perforate. Pierced with holes; dotted with translucent openings which resemble holes.

Perianth. The floral envelope, usually consisting of distinct calyx and corolla.

Pericarp. The outer wall of an ovary after fertilization, hence of the fruit.

Perigynous. Referring to petals and stamens whose bases surround the pistil, or pistils, and are borne on the margin of the hypanthium, as in some Rosaceae.

Persistent. Said of leaves that are evergreen, and of flower parts and fruits that remain attached to the plant for protracted lengths of time.

Petal. The unit of the corolla.

Petaloid. Resembling a petal.

Petiole. The stalk of a leaf.

Petiolar. Relating to or borne on the petiole, as a petiolar gland.

Petiolate. Having a petiole.

Petiolulate. Having a petiolule.

Petiolule. The footstalk of a leaflet.

Phyllary. One of the bracts of the involucre in Compositae.

Pilose. Hairy, especially with long soft hairs.

Pinnae. The primary divisions of a pinnate leaf.

Pinnate. Descriptive of compound leaves with the leaflets arranged on opposite sides along a common rachis.

Pinnatifid. Pinnately cleft, the clefts not extending to the midrib.

Pinnatilobate. Pinnately lobed.

Pinnatisect. Pinnately divided, the clefts extending to the midrib.

Pinnule. A leaflet or ultimate segment of a pinnately decompound leaf.

Pistil. The seed-bearing organ of the flower, consisting of ovary, stigma, and style.

Pistillate. Provided with pistils, but lacking functional stamens.

Pith. The central tissue of a (usually exogenous) stem, composed of thin-walled cells.

Placenta. The structure in an ovary to which the ovules are attached.

Plano-convex. Flat on one side, convex on the other.

Pleiochasium. A compound cyme with more than two branches at each division.

Plicate. Folded into plaits.

Plumose. Having fine hairs on each side like the plume of a feather.

Pluriseriate. In many series.

Pod. Any dry and dehiscent fruit.

Pollen. The male germ cells, contained in the anther.

Pollen sac. Pollen-bearing chamber of the anther.

Pollination. Deposition of pollen upon the stigma.

Polygamo-dioecious. Essentially dioecious, but with some flowers of other sex or perfect flowers on same individual.

Polygamous. With both perfect and unisexual flowers on the same individual plant or on different individuals of the same species.

Polygonal. With several sides or angles.

Polymorphic. With a number of forms, as, a very variable species.

Polyploid. With chromosome number in the somatic nuclei greater than the diploid number, sometimes accompanied by increased size and vigor of the plant.

Pome. A kind of a fleshy fruit of which the apple is the typical form.

Pore. A small opening, as found in certain anthers or fruits.

Porrect. Reaching or extending perpendicular to the surface, as with spines of some cacti.

Posterior. Toward the rear, behind, toward the axis.

Prickle. A rigid, straight or hooked, outgrowth of the bark or epidermal tissue.

Procumbent. Lying on the ground.
Prominent. Higher than the adjacent surface, as in prominent veins.
Prophyllum. A bracteole.
Prostrate. Flat on the ground.
Proximal. Near the base or axis, the opposite of distal.
Pruinose. Covered with a white bloom or powdery wax.
Puberulent. Very slightly pubescent.
Pubescence. A covering of short hairs.
Pubescent. Covered with hairs, especially if short, soft, and downlike.
Pulverulent. Powdered, appearing as if covered by minute grains of dust.
Punctate. Dotted with depressions or translucent internal glands or colored spots.
Pungent. Sharply and stiffly pointed; bitter or hot to the taste.
Pyriform. Pear-shaped.

Quadrangular. Four-angled.
Quadrate. Square.

Raceme. A single indeterminate inflorescence of pediceled flowers upon a common more or less elongated axis.
Racemose. Resembling a raceme; in racemes.
Rachis. The axis of a compound leaf or of an inflorescence.
Radial. Developing around a central axis.
Raphe. In anatropous ovules, the ridge formed by the fusion of a portion of the funicle to the ovule coat; ridge often persistent and prominent in seeds.
Ray. Usually referring to the more or less strap-shaped flowers in the head of Compositae.
Receptacle. The expanded portion of the axis that bears the floral organs.
Reclining. Bending or curving toward the ground.
Recurved. Curved downward or backward.
Reduced. Not normally or fully developed in size.
Reflexed. Abruptly bent or turned downward.
Regular. Uniform in shape or distribution of parts; radically symmetrical.
Remote. Referring to leaves or flowers which are distant or scattered on the stem.
Reniform. Kidney-shaped.
Repand. Having a somewhat undulating margin.
Repent. Prostrate, with the creeping stems rooting at the nodes.
Reticulate. Forming a network.

Retrorse. Turned downward or backward.

Retuse. Rounded and shallowly notched at the apex.

Revolute. Rolled or turned downward or toward the under surface.

Rhizome. A prostrate stem under the ground, rooting at the nodes and bearing buds on nodes.

Rhombic. With equal sides forming oblique angles.

Rib. A primary vein.

Rigid. Stiff.

Rosette. A cluster of basal leaves appearing radially arranged.

Rostrate. With a beaklike point.

Rotate. Wheel-shaped, usually referring to a flattened, short-tubed, sympetalous corolla.

Rotund. Rounded in shape.

Rudiment. A vestige, a much reduced organ, often nonfunctional.

Rufous. Reddish brown.

Rugose. Wrinkled.

Runcinate. Sharply incised pinnately, the incisions retrorse.

Runner. A stolon.

Sagittate. Shaped like an arrowhead.

Salient. Conspicuously projecting, as salient teeth or prominent ribs.

Salverform. Referring to a sympetalous corolla, with the limb at right angles to the tube.

Samara. An indehiscent winged fruit as in the maples and elms.

Scaberulous. Minutely scabrous.

Scabrous. Rough to the touch.

Scale. A leaf much reduced in size, or an epidermal outgrowth.

Scandent. Climbing.

Scape. A flower-bearing stem rising from the ground, the leaves either basal or scattered on the scape and reduced to bracts.

Scarious. Thin and dry.

Schizocarp. Referring to a septicidally dehiscent fruit with one-seeded carpels.

Sclerotic. Hardened, stony.

Scurf. Small scales, usually borne on a leaf surface or on stems.

Secondary. The second division, as in branches or leaf veins.

Secund. One-sided.

Seed. A ripened ovule.

Segment. Part of a compound leaf or other organ, especially if the parts are alike.

Self-pollination. Pollination within the flower.

Semi- (prefix). Approximately half; partly or nearly.

Sepal. A unit of the calyx.

Septicidal. Splitting or dehiscing through the partitions.

Septum (pl. *septa*). A partition or crosswall.

Seriate. Arranged in rows or whorls.

Sericeous. Bearing straight silky hairs.

Serrate. Having sharp teeth pointing forward.

Serrulate. Serrate with small fine teeth.

Sessile. Without stalk of any kind.

Seta (pl. *setae*). A bristle.

Sheath. A tubular structure, such as a leaf base enclosing the stem.

Shoot. A young branch.

Shrub. A woody plant with a number of stems from the base, usually smaller than a tree.

Silicle. A silique broader than long.

Silique. A long capsular fruit typical of the Cruciferae, the two valves separating at maturity.

Silky. Covered with close-pressed soft and straight hairs.

Simple. In one piece or unit, not compound.

Sinuate. Deeply or strongly wavy.

Sinus. The cleft or recess between two lobes.

Solitary. Alone, single.

Somatic. Referring to the body, or to all cells except the germ cells.

Spatulate. Gradually narrowed downward from a rounded summit.

Spherical. Round.

Spike. A racemose inflorescence with the flowers sessile or nearly so.

Spine. Modification of a stipule, petiole, or branch to form a hard, woody, sharp-pointed structure.

Spinescent. Ending in a spine.

Spiniferous. Bearing spines.

Spinulose. With small spines.

Spur. A tubular or saclike projection of the corolla or calyx, sometimes nectar bearing; a short, compact twig with little or no internodal development.

Squamella. A small scale, usually as in the pappus of some Compositae.

Squamose. Bearing scales.

Squamulose. Diminutive of squamose.

Stamen. The pollen-bearing organ, usually two or more in each flower.

Staminal column. A column or tube formed by the coalescence of the filaments of the stamens.

Staminate. Bearing stamens but lacking pistils.

Staminodium (pl. *staminodia*). A sterile stamen, often reduced or otherwise modified.

Standard. Usually referring to the upper or posterior petal of a papilionaceous corolla; a banner.

Stellate. Having the shape of a star; starlike.

Stem. Main axis of the plant.

Sterile. Unproductive.

Stigma. That part of the pistil which receives the pollen.

Stigmatic. Relating to the stigma.

Stipe. A stalklike support of a pistil or of a carpel.

Stipel. The stipule of a leaflet in compound leaves.

Stipitate. Having a stipe.

Stipulate. Having stipules.

Stipule. An appendage at the base of a petiole or on each side of its insertion.

Stolon. A branch or shoot given off at the summit of a root.

Stoma. A minute orifice in the epidermis of a leaf.

Stone. The hard endocarp of a drupe.

Striate. With fine grooves, ridges, or lines.

Strict. Erect and straight.

Strigillose. Diminutive of strigose.

Strigose. Bearing hairs which are usually stiff, straight, and appressed.

Strobile. An inflorescence or cone with imbricate bracts or scales.

Style. Upward extension of the ovary terminating with the stigma.

Sub- (prefix). Under, below, less than.

Subshrub. Perennial plant with lower portions of stems woody and persistent.

Subtend. Adjacent to an organ, under or supporting; referring to a bract or scale below a flower.

Subulate. Awl-shaped.

Succulent. Juicy.

Sucker. A stem originating from the roots or lower stem.

Suffrutescent. Slightly shrubby or woody at the base.

Suffruticose. Referring to a slightly shrubby plant; especially applied to low subshrubs.

Sulcate. Grooved or furrowed.

Superior. Above or over; applied to an ovary when free from and positioned above the perianth.

Supra- (prefix). Above.

Suture. Line of dehiscence; a groove denoting a natural union.

Symmetric. Divisible into equal and like parts; referring to a regular flower having the same number of parts in whorl or series.

Sympetalous. Petals more or less united.

Sympodial. Development by simultaneous branching rather than by only a main continuous axis.

Taproot. The main or primary root.

Taxonomy. The science of classification.

Tendril. Usually a slender organ for climbing, formed by modification of leaf, branch, inflorescence, etc.

Terete. Circular in transverse section.

Terminal. At the end, summit, or apex.

Ternate. Divided into three parts.

Testa. The outer seed coat.

Tetragonal. Four-angled.

Tetrahedral. Four-sided.

Theca. Anther sac.

Thorn. A sharp-pointed modified branch.

Throat. The orifice of a sympetalous or gamopetalous corolla.

Thyrse. A shortened panicle with the main axis indeterminate and the lateral flower clusters cymose; loosely, a compact panicle.

Tomentellous. Diminutive of tomentose.

Tomentose. Densely hairy with matted wool.

Tomentulose. Slightly pubescent with matted wool.

Toothed. Having teeth; serrate.

Tortuous. Zigzag or bent in various directions.

Torulose. Cylindrical and constricted at intervals.

Torus. The receptacle, or thickened terminal axis, of a flower head, especially in the Compositae.

Toxic. Poisonous.

Trailing. Growing prostrate but not rooting at the nodes.

Translucent. Transmitting light but not transparent.

Transpiration. Passage of water vapor outward, mostly through the stomata.

Transverse. A section taken at right angles to the longitudinal axis.

Tri- (prefix). In three parts, as trilobate (3-lobed); trifid (3-cleft).

Trichome. A hair arising from an epidermal cell.

Trichotomous. Three-branched or forked.

Truncate. Ending abruptly, as if cut off transversely.

Trunk. The main stem or axis of a tree below the branches.

Tube. A hollow cylindric organ, such as the lower part of a sympetalous calyx or corolla, the upper part usually expanding into a limb.

Tuber. A thickened underground stem usually for food storage and bearing buds.

Tubercle. A small tuberlike body.

Tumid. Inflated or swollen.
Turbinate. Top-shaped.
Turgid. Swollen.
Twining. Climbing by means of the main stem or branches winding around an object.

Ultimate. The last or final part in a train of progression, as the ultimate division of an organ.
Umbel. An inflorescence with numerous pedicels springing from the end of the peduncle, as with the ribs of an umbrella.
Umbilicate. Depressed in the center.
Umbo. A central raised area or hump.
Uncinate. Scythe-shaped, sometimes referring to hooked hairs or prickles.
Undershrub. A low plant generally woody only near the base.
Undulate. With a wavy surface or margin.
Unequally pinnate. Pinnate with an odd terminal leaflet.
Uni- (prefix). Solitary or one only; such as unifoliate (with one leaflet) or unilocular (with one cell).
Unilateral. One-sided.
Uniseriate. In one series, or in one row or circle.
Unisexual. Of one sex, either staminate or pistillate only.
Urceolate. Pitcher-shaped, usually with a flaring mouth and constricted neck.
Utricle. An achenelike fruit, but with a thin, loose outer seed covering.

Vallecula (pl. *valleculae*). A channel or groove between the ridges on various organs, such as on stems or fruits.
Valve. One of the pieces into which a capsule splits.
Vascular. Referring to the conductive tissue in the stems or leaves.
Vascular bundle. A bundle or group of vascular tubes or ducts.
Vegetative. Nonreproductive, as contrasted to floral.
Veins. Ramifications or threads of fibrovascular tissue in a leaf, or other flat organ.
Velutinous. Covered with dense velvety hairs.
Venation. A system of veins.
Venose. Veiny.
Ventral. Belonging to the anterior or inner face of an organ; the opposite of dorsal.
Ventricose. Asymmetrically swollen.
Vernation. Arrangement of leaves in a bud.
Verrucose. Covered with wartlike excrescences.

Versatile. Swinging free, usually referring to an anther attached above its base to a filament.

Verticil (adj. *verticillate*). A whorl of more than two similar parts at a node; leaves, stems, etc.

Verticillate. Disposed in a whorl.

Vesicle (adj. *vesicular*). A small inflated or bladderlike structure.

Vespertine. Opening in the evening.

Vestigial. A rudimentary, usually nonfunctioning, or underdeveloped organ.

Villosulous. Diminutive of villous.

Villous, villose. Bearing long soft hairs.

Virgate. Straight and wandlike.

Viscid. Glutinous or sticky.

Viviparous. Precocious development, such as the germination of seeds or buds while still attached to the parent plant.

Whorl. Cyclic arrangement of like parts.

Wing. Any membranous or thin expansion bordering or surrounding an organ.

Woolly. Clothed with long and tortuous or matted hairs.

Xeric. Characterized by aridity.

Xerophilous. Drought resistant.

Xerophyte. A desert plant or plant growing under xeric conditions.

INDEX